Standards of Value

Founded in 1807, John Wiley & Sons is the oldest independent publishing company in the United States. With offices in North America, Europe, Australia, and Asia, Wiley is globally committed to developing and marketing print and electronic products and services for our customers' professional and personal knowledge and understanding.

The Wiley Finance series contains books written specifically for finance and investment professionals as well as sophisticated individual investors and their financial advisors. Book topics range from portfolio management to e-commerce, risk management, financial engineering, valuation, and financial instrument analysis, as well as much more.

For a list of available titles, visit our Web site at www.WileyFinance.com.

Standards of Value

Theory and Applications

Second Edition

JAY E. FISHMAN,
SHANNON P. PRATT,
WILLIAM J. MORRISON

WILEY

Published by John Wiley & Sons, Inc., Hoboken, New Jersey.
First edition of Standards of Value: Theory and Applications published in 2006 by
John Wiley & Sons, Inc.
Published simultaneously in Canada.

For general information on our other products and services or for technical support, please contact
our Customer Care Department within the United States at (800) 762-2974, outside the United
States at (317) 572-3993 or fax (317) 572-4002.

Wiley also publishes its books in a variety of electronic formats. Some content that appears in print
may not be available in electronic books. For more information about Wiley products, visit our web
site at www.wiley.com.

Library of Congress Cataloging-in-Publication Data

Fishman, Jay E.
  Standards of value : theory and applications / Jay E. Fishman, Shannon P. Pratt, William J.
Morrison.—Second edition.
       page cm.—(Wiley finance series)
  Includes index.
    ISBN 978-1-118-13853-3 (cloth); ISBN 978-1-118-22540-0 (ebk);
ISBN 978-1-118-26351-8 (ebk); ISBN 978-1-118-23891-2 (ebk)
    1. Valuation.   2. Fair value—Accounting.   I. Pratt, Shannon P.
II. Morrison, William J.   III. Title.
    HF5681.V3F57 2013
    657'.73--dc23
                                                    2012049070

10 9 8 7 6 5 4 3 2 1

Jay E. Fishman
To Marjan: Altijd.
To our triple trouble: Micha, Justin, and Seth.

Bill Morrison
To my wife, Margaret, the love of my life.
To my children, Christina and William, my pride and joy.

Shannon Pratt
To my wife, Millie, and to our four children and ten grandchildren.

Contents

CHAPTER 2
Fair Market Value in Estate and Gift Tax   35

CHAPTER 3
Fair Value in Shareholder Dissent and Oppression   89

Gilbert E. Matthews and Michelle Patterson

Foreword

The authors of this very useful book have again asked me to write the Foreword. I'll start this with the ending in the Foreword I wrote in the first edition. "Shannon, Jay, and Bill, thank you for putting the time into this. It's a welcome enhancement to our profession's body of knowledge."

Since the first edition was published in 2006, I can't tell you how many times I have referred to it. It is a very valuable and easy-to-navigate resource. It's incredible that these three authors have put so much time into keeping us all up to date in the practice areas of tax, divorce, dissenting rights and shareholder oppression, and fair value for financial reporting. These four areas make up four of the six chapters.

Right up front, it is important to note that this book is not just about the definitions of the various standards of value. The real value of this important resource is that the authors have taken an enormous amount of time to explain the history, evolution, and application of standards of value in different venues. Also, for state-specific valuations, such as marital dissolution and shareholder dissent and oppression, they have looked at all the states and provide definitions, nuances, applications, supporting regulations, statutes, and case law.

They have also added a new chapter, "Standards of Value for Partnership and Limited Liability Company Buyouts." This chapter discusses general partnerships, limited partnerships, limited liability partnerships, and limited liability companies. These types of business entities are often misunderstood by valuation analysts, often to the detriment of their clients and their advisors. Nowhere else have I ever seen these types of entities discussed in such detail. Furthermore, they present individual states' definitions of value under partnership statutes and relevant court cases.

The proper definition of the standard of value sets the criteria upon which valuation analysts rely. Among many factors, it dictates whether you use a hypothetical buyer and seller, a market-participant buyer and seller, value to a single person, or a willing or unwilling buyer and seller. It also sets the stage for consideration of the various levels of value and whether discounts and/or premiums apply. My experience with standards of value in various dispute settings makes me realize how different the value can be if the analyst uses the wrong standard of value. It can also make your work indefensible, regardless of whatever good valuation work you perform.

This book, with its well-known group of authors, helps clarify an area that many analysts think is simple and straightforward. It is anything but that. This is a complex area with differing interpretations, particularly when dealing with multiple definitions within each state. Even the universally defined standard of value—"fair market value"—has some interpretation problems. Sure, it's a willing buyer and seller, a hypothetical buyer and seller, with no compulsion and both with reasonable knowledge of the relevant facts. However, who are the hypothetical buyer and seller? Is it the most likely buyer and seller? Some courts say no. Is it the average buyer and seller? If so, how do you average people? Is it a standalone value, a strategic buyer or a financial buyer? These are tough questions concerning a standard of value that many analysts choose to ignore. This book breaks down the walls of uncertainty and does much to help answer many of these difficult questions.

The authors connect the dots by introducing five standards of value: fair market value, investment value, intrinsic value, fair value (state actions), and fair value (financial reporting). They put these into service line applications for valuations in tax, marital dissolution, dissenting rights and shareholder oppression, and financial reporting. The various standards of value are then connected to the service line applications through the premise-of-value concepts of "value in exchange" and "value to the holder."

Again, one of the best parts of the book is the obvious attention to detail concerning the standards of value and their definition, by state, for marital dissolution and dissenters' rights and shareholder oppression. There are charts showing each state and the important cases that set the criteria for valuation in these two areas. These charts will be extremely helpful to valuation analysts who practice in multiple states, as well as a good refresher for those whose practices are more local or regional.

In Chapter 5, "Standards of Value in Divorce," the authors present clear, concise charts titled "Continuum of Value." For example, one of these charts links the premise of value to the standard of value and segments it into enterprise and personal goodwill, with references to relevant case law and the important underlying assumptions. Discounts and premiums and the effect of buy–sell agreements are also presented and explained.

Gil Matthews and Michelle Patterson have substantially rewritten Chapter 3, "Fair Value in Shareholder Dissent and Oppression," which now also includes a section that discusses shareholder dissent in Delaware. The exhibits include, on a state-by-state basis, the applicability of the market exception for appraisals, the availability of the buyout remedy in oppression, statutory language regarding valuation techniques, and summaries of significant court decisions regarding discounts.

The chapter on "Fair Value for Financial Reporting," Chapter 6, has benefited immeasurably by the changes that have occurred since 2007 as well as the rewriting by Neil Beaton.

All of the chapters include the history and development of the standard of value and concise summaries of relevant case law and applicable regulations, statutes, and standards. Again, readers may think this is a simple subject. However, as the authors have so eloquently presented here, it is quite complex. These authors have done their homework and compiled the state-by-state research to help valuation analysts better understand the many nuances within each state. I'll end as I began. Shannon, Jay, and Bill, thank you for putting the time into this. It's a welcome enhancement to our profession's body of knowledge.

James R. Hitchner, CPA/ABV/CFF, ASA
Managing Director, Financial Valuation Advisors
President, The Financial Consulting Group
CEO, Valuation Products and Services
Editor in Chief, *Financial Valuation and Litigation Expert*

Preface

We have all heard the expression, "Value lies in the eyes of the beholder" (a play on words from the expression, "Beauty lies in the eyes of the beholder"). We cannot imagine a sense in which this could be more true than in the value of a business or an interest in a business. *Value* has no meaning until it is defined. In the nomenclature of business valuation, these different definitions of value are called *standards of value*.

In some contexts, the standard of value is mandated by statute or regulations. For example, *fair market value* is the statutory standard of value for all federal gift, estate, and income taxes. *Fair value* is the mandated standard of value for financial reporting that is subject to regulation by the Securities and Exchange Commission. The expression *fair value* is also used as the standard of value in almost every state's statutes for dissenting and oppressed stockholder actions, but the definitions are very different from the definition of fair value for federally regulated financial reporting purposes and differ somewhat from state to state.

Even when the standard of value is statutorily defined, it leaves much room for interpretation in case law. Very few state statutes dealing with property settlements for divorce address *any* definition of a standard of value. Therefore, in the context of valuations for divorce, virtually *all* the guidance as to the accepted standard of value is found in the case law, which varies greatly from state to state and even in different jurisdictions within some states.

It comes as a surprise to many people that the same identical shares of stock can have different values in different contexts. For example, one of the authors valued shares in a dissenting stockholder suit and was later retained to value the same shares for the estate when a stockholder died. For the estate tax valuation, the value was considerably less because of minority and marketability discounts, which were not mandated under the standard of value applicable in the dissenting stockholder action.

Standards of value that apply in certain circumstances may also be mandated in company articles of incorporation, articles of partnership, buy–sell agreements, arbitration agreements, and other documents. It is essential that attorneys and others drafting these documents have a clear understanding of the standards of value specified in the document and that they convey this understanding to their clients. How many times have we been confronted with language such as "the fair market value of the shares" and when the triggering event occurred found the shareholder shocked to find that the language did not mean a proportionate share of the total company value, but much less after discounts for minority interest and lack of marketability?

When embarking on a business or intangible asset appraisal assignment, the first thing one needs to know is the definition of value. Yet this is the first full book to comprehensively address this important issue. We address standards of value in several contexts:

- Gift, estate, and income taxes
- Dissenting and oppressed stockholder actions
- Buyout of owners of partnerships, limited partnerships, and limited liability companies
- Marital dissolution proceedings
- Fair value for financial reporting

This book lists each of the major federal statutes and regulations and relevant statutes of all states and territories so that the valuation report can cite the specific authority, and the attorney or valuation analyst can go to the full text of the relevant authority in case of a need to know more.

We have analyzed hundreds of court cases interpreting the various statutes and regulations. From these we have extracted the points that we believe to be most representative of the respective jurisdiction's view on interpretation of various issues and included selected quotations from the case opinions. These range from a sentence to several paragraphs, and collectively include several hundred court case citations. They reveal the many different nuances of interpretation of the standards of value in different jurisdictions.

If there is a "case of first impression" on an issue (an issue that has not been tried before in that jurisdiction), courts sometimes look to precedent from other jurisdictions that have similar statutes.

We do not express opinions (except for our perception of consensus among the business appraisal community) on what the interpretations of the appropriate standards of value *should be*. Instead, we merely report what the interpretations are as we understand them. We try hard to point out commonalities and differences of interpretation among jurisdictions and, sometimes, within the same jurisdiction.

Business valuations are extremely case specific. Frequently, what may seem like a contradiction from one case to another can be explained by different facts and circumstances. Therefore, it is dangerous to draw broad generalizations from specific case opinions. A study of case precedents, however, is important to provide the attorney or the analyst some conception of the court's thinking on certain issues.

Use of the research compiled in this book as a starting point for understanding the relevant standard of value for a certain type of case in a certain jurisdiction will save attorneys and appraisers a great deal of time. We hope that it will also provide insight into the perspectives of the various courts on interpretation of various issues related to standards of value. Since the nature of the subject material contained in this book is evolving, the authors will attempt to monitor changes in theory, statute, and case law. The reader is invited to forward any questions, concerns, and comments to the authors as they arise.

Jay E. Fishman
Financial Research Associates
Bala Cynwyd, Pennsylvania
jfishman@finresearch.com

Shannon P. Pratt
Shannon Pratt Valuations, Inc.
Portland, Oregon
shannon@shannonpratt.com

William J. Morrison
WithumSmith+Brown, PC
Paramus, New Jersey
wmorrison@withum.com

Acknowledgments

This book has been written by three active business valuation practitioners who each have at least 25 years of experience in the business valuation profession. However, this book would not have been possible were it not for the unstinting efforts of many others. First and foremost are Noah J. Gordon, of Shannon Pratt Valuations, and Christina Giorgio and Ernest Stalzer, CPA/ABV/CFF, MBA, CDFA, both of WithumSmith+Brown, who performed a significant amount of work on this book. Ottaviana De Ruvo and Holden Warriner, also both of WithumSmith+Brown, provided research services.

This book has benefited immensely from review by many individuals with a high level of knowledge and experience in business valuation. The following people reviewed most or all of the entire manuscript, and the book reflects their tremendous efforts and legion of constructive suggestions:

Stephen J. Bravo, CPA/ABV, ASA, CBA, CFP, PFS
Apogee Business Valuations, Inc.
Framingham, Massachusetts

James R. Hitchner, CPA/ABV, ASA
The Financial Valuation Group
Atlanta, Georgia

Kenneth J. Pia, Jr., CPA/ABV, ASA, MCBA
Meyers Harrison & Pia, LLC

Ronald Seigneur, CPA/ABV/CFF, ASA, CVA, CGMA
Seigneur, Gustafson, Knight, LLP
Lakewood, Colorado

Gary R. Trugman, CPA/ABV, MCBA, ASA, MVS
Trugman Valuation Associates
Plantation, Florida
New Haven, Connecticut

In addition, this book covers a number of specific topics and covers areas where business valuation and law intersect. The following people reviewed certain chapters and provided significant constructive suggestions:

Chapter 1 Common Standards and Premises of Value

Frank A. Louis, Esq.
Louis and Judge, PC
Toms River, New Jersey

Gilbert E. Matthews, CFA
Sutter Securities
San Francisco, California

Michelle Patterson, Esq.
Consultant to Sutter Securities
San Francisco, California

Chapter 2 Fair Market Value in Estate and Gift Tax

Roger J. Grabowski, ASA
Duff & Phelps, LLC
Chicago, Illinois

Frank A. Louis, Esq.
Louis and Judge, PC
Toms River, New Jersey

Chapter 3 Fair Value in Shareholder Dissent and Oppression

Kyle S. Garcia, CPA/ABV, ASA, CFA
Financial Research Associates
Edison, New Jersey

Roger J. Grabowski, FASA
Duff & Phelps, LLC
Chicago, Illinois

Lawrence A. Hamermesh, Esq.
Ruby R. Vale Professor of Corporate and Business Law
Widener University School of Law
Wilmington, Delaware

Mark Lee, CFA, ASA
EisnerAmper
New York, New York

Peter G. Verniero, Esq.
Former Justice, New Jersey Supreme Court
Sills Cummis & Gross, PC
Newark, New Jersey

Michael L. Wachter
William B. and Mary Barb Johnson Professor of Law and Economics
University of Pennsylvania Law School
Philadelphia, Pennsylvania

Chapter 4 Standards of Value for Partnership and Limited Liability Company Buyouts
Peter G. Verniero, Esq.
Former Justice, New Jersey Supreme Court
Sills Cummis & Gross, PC
Newark, New Jersey

Chapter 5 Standards of Value in Divorce
Kyle S. Garcia, CPA/ABV, ASA, CFA
Financial Research Associates
Edison, New Jersey

John Johnson, CPA/ABV, CBA, CFF, DABFA
BST Valuation and Litigation Advisors, LLC
Albany, New York

John A. Kornfeld, Esq.
Aronson Mayefsky & Sloan, LLP
New York, New York

Frank A. Louis, Esq.
Louis and Judge, PC
Toms River, New Jersey

Adam John Wolff, Esq.
Kasowitz Benson Torres & Friedman LLP
New York, New York

Judge Thomas Zampino, JSC (Ret.)
Snyder & Sarno LLC
Roseland, New Jersey

Chapter 6 Fair Value in Financial Reporting
Kyle S. Garcia, CPA/ABV, ASA, CFA
Financial Research Associates
Edison, New Jersey

John Johnson, CPA/ABV, CBA, CFF, DABFA
BST Valuation & Litigation Advisors, LLC
Albany, New York

For permission to reprint material from his works, we thank Michael Mard of the Financial Valuation Group for the information on subsequent events. We greatly appreciate the enthusiastic cooperation of the professionals at John Wiley & Sons: John DeRemigis, executive editor, and Judy Howarth, associate editor. We would also like to thank Gil Matthews and Michelle Patterson for substantially rewriting Chapter 3, Noah J. Gordon for coauthoring our new Chapter 4, and Neil Beaton for significantly rewriting Chapter 6.

We also would like to thank our colleagues and families for the support they gave us over the time this book was written.

Jay E. Fishman
Bala Cynwyd, Pennsylvania

Shannon P. Pratt
Portland, Oregon

William J. Morrison
Paramus, New Jersey

About the Authors

Jay E. Fishman, FASA, is a managing director of Financial Research Associates, a regional business valuation and forensic accounting firm with offices in Bala Cynwyd, Pennsylvania, New York City, and Edison, New Jersey. He has been actively engaged in the appraisal profession since 1974 and specializes in the valuations of business enterprises and their intangible assets. Mr. Fishman has coauthored several books, including the highly acclaimed *Guide to Business Valuations* (with Shannon Pratt and Jim Hitchner), and written numerous articles on business valuations as well as qualifying as an expert witness and providing testimony in 12 states and federal courts. He has taught courses on business valuation to the Internal Revenue Service, the National Judicial College, and the American Institute of Certified Public Accountants (AICPA) in the United States and internationally, in the People's Republic of China, on behalf of the World Bank in St. Petersburg, Russia, and in Moscow, Russia.

He holds bachelor's and master's degrees from Temple University as well as an MBA from LaSalle University. Mr. Fishman is a fellow and life member of the American Society of Appraisers, a former chairman of its Business Valuation Committee, former editor of the *Business Valuation Review*, chair of ASA's Government Relations Committee, a fellow of the Royal Institution of Chartered Surveyors, an accredited senior member of the Institute of Business Appraisers, Inc., a former member of the Appraisal Standards Board of the Appraisal Foundation, and chair of its Appraisal Practice Board. He was also a member of the Internal Revenue Service's Advisory Council.

Shannon P. Pratt, CFA, ARM, ABAR, FASA, MCBA, CM&AA, has a reputation for knowledge and experience in the field of business valuation that is unparalleled. He is the best-known authority in the field of business valuation and has written numerous books that articulate many of the concepts used in modern business valuation around the world.

Dr. Pratt is chairman and chief executive officer of Shannon Pratt Valuations, Inc., a business valuation firm headquartered in Portland, Oregon; publisher emeritus for Business Valuation Resources, LLC; and a member of the board of directors of Paulson Capital Corporation, an investment banking firm specializing in small-firm IPOs and secondary offerings.

Over the past 40 years, Dr. Pratt has performed valuation engagements for mergers and acquisitions, employee stock ownership plans, fairness opinions, gift and estate taxes, incentive stock options, buy–sell agreements, corporate and partnership dissolutions, dissenting stockholder actions, damages, marital dissolutions, and many other business valuation purposes. He has testified in a wide variety of federal and state courts across the country and frequently participates in arbitration and mediation proceedings.

Dr. Pratt holds an undergraduate degree in business administration from the University of Washington and a doctorate in business administration, majoring in finance, from Indiana University. He is a fellow of the American Society of Appraisers, a master certified business appraiser, a chartered financial analyst, a master certified business counselor, and is certified in mergers and acquisitions.

Dr. Pratt's professional recognitions include being designated a life member of the Business Valuation Committee of the American Society of Appraisers, a life member of the American Society of Appraisers, past chairman and a life member of the ESOP Association Advisory Committee on Valuation, a life member of the Institute of Business Appraisers, the Magna Cum Laude in Business Appraisal award from the National Association of Certified Valuation Analysts, and the distinguished service award of the Portland Society of Financial Analysts. He recently completed two three-year terms as trustee-at-large of the Appraisal Foundation. Dr. Pratt is the author of *The Market Approach to Valuing Businesses, 2nd edition; Business Valuation Body of Knowledge: Exam Review and Professional Reference, 2nd edition; and Business Valuation Discounts and Premiums, 2nd edition;* coauthor with Roger Grabowski of *Cost of Capital: Estimation and Application, 4th edition; Cost of Capital: Workbook and Technical Supplement, 4th edition;* and *Cost of Capital in Litigation;* coauthor with the Honorable David Laro of *Business Valuation and Federal Taxes: Procedure, Law and Perspective, 2nd edition,* all published by John Wiley & Sons; and *The Lawyer's Business Valuation Handbook, 2nd edition,* published by the American Bar Association. He is author of *Valuing a Business: The Analysis and Appraisal of Closely Held Companies, 5th edition,* and coauthor of *Valuing Small Businesses and Professional Practices, 3rd edition,* both published by McGraw-Hill. He is also coauthor of *Guide to Business Valuations, 22nd edition,* published by Practitioners Publishing Company.

He is publisher emeritus of a monthly newsletter, *Shannon Pratt's Business Valuation Update* (primarily for the professional appraisal community). Dr. Pratt develops and teaches business valuation courses for the American Society of Appraisers, the AICPA, and the National Association of Valuators and Analysts (NACVA), and frequently speaks on business valuation at national legal, professional, and trade association meetings. He also developed and often teaches a full-day seminar on business valuation for judges and lawyers.

William J. Morrison, CPA/ABV, is a partner in the Paramus, New Jersey, office of WithumSmith+Brown, PC, and has over 25 years experience as a valuation analyst. He is a CPA in New Jersey and is accredited in business valuation and forensics by the AICPA. He is the partner in charge of the firm's Litigation, Valuation and Insolvency Group.

He founded and was president of the forensic accounting firm, Morrison & Company (merged with WithumSmith+Brown in December 2010). He is a CPA licensed in New Jersey with over 30 years experience as an investigator, forensic accountant, and business valuator. He has also served as a special agent for the Federal Bureau of Investigation (FBI), an internal auditor, and a CPA. Mr. Morrison has been qualified as an expert for the Supreme Court, Superior Court, and Federal Court of New Jersey, and has been appointed as an expert for the federal and state courts in New Jersey in over a thousand matters as a forensic accountant, valuation expert, and mediator. He has provided expert witness services in complex civil and criminal matters involving stockholder oppression, high-net-worth divorces, economic damage claims, and federal, criminal, and tax matters, among others.

He has lectured to organizations such as the New Jersey Institute of Continuing Legal Education, American Society of Appraisers, NACVA, and New Jersey Society of Certified Public Accountants (NJSCPA).

A graduate of Boston College with a bachelor of arts degree in history, he also earned his master's degree in business administration from Fairleigh Dickinson University. He is a member of the AICPA, NJSCPA, and the Society of the Former Agents of the Federal Bureau of Investigation.

Gilbert E. Matthews, CFA, co-author of Chapter 3, "Fair Value in Shareholder Dissent and Oppression," is chairman and a senior managing director of Sutter Securities, an investment banking firm headquartered in San Francisco. He has more than 50 years of experience in investment banking, having worked with a wide variety of clients in mergers, acquisitions, and divestitures, friendly and unfriendly tender offers, public and private offerings of securities, recapitalizations, bankruptcy and other financial restructurings, and international transactions. Mr. Matthews has provided expert testimony in more than 20 states with respect to valuation, investment banking practice, and other matters.

Prior to joining Sutter in 1995, Mr. Matthews was with Bear Stearns in New York, where he had been a senior managing director and a general partner of its predecessor partnership. He was in the Corporate Finance Department from 1967 through 1995 and a security analyst from 1960 through 1967. From 1970 through 1995, he was chairman of Bear Stearns' Valuation Committee, which was responsible for all opinions and valuations issued by the firm.

Mr. Matthews received an AB from Harvard and an MBA from Columbia. He has spoken on fairness opinions, valuations, and related matters before numerous professional groups. In addition, he has written several book chapters and articles on fairness opinions, corporate valuations, and litigation relating to valuations and appraisals. He is on the editorial boards of *Business Valuation Review*, published by the American Society of Appraisers, and *Business Valuation Update*, published by Business Valuation Resources, and is a member of the Fairness Opinions Working Group of the International Valuation Standards Council.

Michelle Patterson, JD, PhD, co-author of Chapter 3, "Fair Value in Shareholder Dissent and Oppression," is a lawyer and retired professor. She received her JD from UCLA in 1982, her PhD from Yale in 1975, and her AB from the University of Chicago in 1965. Having been a professor for many years at Brandeis University and the University of California, Santa Barbara, she attended law school at UCLA and practiced litigation with a national corporate law firm. Dr. Patterson subsequently moved to San Francisco, taught law and other courses at San Francisco State, was the director of Pre-Law Advising, and did professional jury analysis with a litigation support company. Since 2001, she has been a consultant to Sutter Securities, where she has assisted in litigation matters and financial advisory services. Dr. Patterson has served on various editorial boards and published numerous articles, some with Gil Matthews in the areas of business finance and corporate law.

Noah J. Gordon, Esq., author of Chapter 4, "Standards of Value for Partnership and Limited Liability Company Buyouts," is legal counsel for Shannon Pratt Valuations, Inc., where he is regularly involved with business valuations. He regularly contributes to business valuation publications and has served as a contributing author and editor of several legal treatises and publications. He has recently contributed to *Guide to Business Valuations* (2013), *The Lawyer's Business Valuation Handbook, 2nd edition* (2010), *Business Valuation Discounts and Premiums, 2nd edition* (2009), *Valuing a Business: The Analysis and Appraisal of Closely Held Companies, 5th edition* (2008), *Cost of Capital: Applications and Examples, 4th edition* (2010), and *The Market Approach to Valuing a Business, 2nd edition* (2005). He served as associate editor of *Shannon Pratt's Business Valuation Update*, *Economic*

Outlook Update, and *BV Q&A Update* for Business Valuation Resources, and he also was an executive editor with Wolters Kluwer/Aspen Publishers and a managing editor with Prentice Hall in those publishers' legal publications divisions. He also maintains a freelance editorial business. Mr. Gordon is admitted to the bars of Oregon, New York, New Jersey (resigned), the District of Columbia (resigned), and the United States Supreme Court. He holds a BA from Haverford College, and a JD from the Benjamin N. Cardozo School of Law.

Neil J. Beaton, CPA/ABV/CFF, CFA, ASA, co-author of Chapter 6, "Fair Value in Financial Reporting," is a managing director at Alvarez & Marsal Valuation Services, LLC. He has over 25 years of experience analyzing and valuing both closely held and publicly traded companies. Neil has appeared as an expert witness in numerous courts across the country and internationally, was an instructor for the AICPA's business valuation courses, and speaks nationally on business valuation topics with a special emphasis on early-stage and high-technology companies. He has authored or coauthored a number of books and articles throughout his career. In addition, Neil has served on the AICPA's Merger & Acquisitions Disputes Task Force and the AICPA ABV Exam Committee, and is currently co-chair of the AICPA's Cheap Stock Task Force. He has served on the AICPA's National Accreditation Commission and Business Valuation Committees and the FASB's Valuation Resource Group. Neil has a BA in economics from Stanford University and a MBA in finance from National University. In addition to his formal education, Neil is a CPA, accredited in business valuation, a chartered financial analyst, and accredited senior appraiser in business valuation by the American Society of Appraisers.

Introduction

PURPOSE

From a practical point of view, the appraisal process can be viewed as no more than answering a question: "What is the value?" Before this question can be answered, however, a definition of value is required. Defining the term *value* begins with identifying the *standard of value*, that is, the type of value being sought. Each standard of value contains numerous assumptions that represent the underpinnings of the type of value being utilized in a specific engagement.

Even when a standard of value is specified, there is no guarantee that all would agree on the underlying assumptions of that standard. As James C. Bonbright wrote in his pioneering book, *Valuation of Property*:

> When one reads the conventional value definitions critically, one finds, in the first place, that they themselves contain serious ambiguities, and in the second place, that they invoke concepts of value acceptable only for certain purposes and quite unacceptable for other purposes.[1]

It has been our observation that Bonbright's 1937 quote still applies today. This book is an attempt to address some of the ambiguities inherent in the application of common standards of value. It has been written by valuation practitioners who deal with these issues on a daily basis. Since we are not attorneys, the book is not written to provide legal advice but rather to discuss the interaction between valuation theory and its judicial and regulatory application.

In this book, we address the standard of value as applied in four distinct contexts: estate and gift taxation, shareholder dissent and oppression,

---

[1] James C. Bonbright, *Valuation of Property* (Charlottesville, VA: Michie, 1937), at 11.

divorce, and financial reporting. We have written this book for judges, lawyers, CPAs and appraisers, in the hopes of fostering a better understanding of the theory and application of the standard of value in the judicial and regulatory areas in which they are applied. We hope to provide a framework of appraisal theory as to the standards of value and the underlying premises of value generally applied in these four contexts.[2] With this analysis, we discuss the resulting methodologies and applications that flow from these standards.

This book is not designed to explain specific valuation techniques and methodologies. For instance, we address the applicability of shareholder-level discounts for lack of control and marketability, but we do not discuss how to calculate them. Our hope is that this book will help practitioners understand some of the intricacies of performing services in these venues so they will ask appropriate questions and seek relevant guidance. We also hope that the book will help appraisal users to understand why the practitioners are asking such questions. Finally, we hope this book will contribute to a continuing dialogue on these issues.

Our chapter on fair value in financial reporting addresses aspects of valuation and auditing under the pronouncements of the Financial Accounting Standards Board (FASB), the Securities and Exchange Commission (SEC), and the Public Company Accounting Oversight Board (PCAOB). Valuations for estate and gift tax, shareholder dissent and oppression, and divorce matters are presented within their respective judicial frameworks, whether the federal courts for estate and gift tax cases or the state courts for shareholder dissent and oppression cases and the family law courts for the valuation and distribution of property upon divorce.

The breadth of our research deals with standards of value as they relate to judicial and regulatory matters, and we have found that valuation literature, legal scholarship, economics, and case law are all evolving. We have attempted to look at the development of these concepts as they have emerged over time as well as how they differ among the states.

Generally, the judicial decisions appear to endorse certain valuation methodologies that are designed to address the specific fact pattern of a case. It is our observation that in many cases, the courts seem to look at valuation from the perspective of equity to the parties rather than adhering strictly to any one specific standard of value and properly following valuation theory, especially in the context of family law.

---

[2] Premises of value represent the general concepts of property under which the standards of value fall. As we will explain, the premises of value can be as important as the standard of value.

In preparing this book, we have utilized a variety of resources in the fields of appraisal and law. In order to find state-specific language and case law applicable to our analysis, we have reviewed the annotated statutes of the 50 states and the District of Columbia in shareholder dissent and oppression and in property distribution in divorce. We have also reviewed law journals to seek legal perspective and identify the most important precedent-setting cases. In addition, we have reviewed articles in various publications to identify the major issues for the valuation professional. Finally, and most important, we have reviewed the cases themselves for perspective on the reasoning behind appraisal-related decisions.

As stated previously, we are not lawyers, and therefore in our review of case law, statutes, and varying legal analysis we are approaching the issues from a valuation professional's perspective. We look to present the language used in the application of law and financial standards pertaining to business valuations and the specific assumptions that most practitioners make when that language is used.

We are not providing an opinion in any chapter as to the appropriate treatment of the standard of value. Our analysis represents a survey of how the standard of value is being treated across the United States in varying contexts. For instance, in divorce, we have attempted to discern how each state addresses the standard of value as it applies to businesses and business interests. We offer no opinion as to what is the correct standard. Instead, we survey and report the standards of value we see being applied in the different states.

Every Appraisal Is Unique

In preparing an appraisal on a judicial matter, whether for a valuation for a federal jurisdiction in an estate or gift tax matter or for a state court matter pertaining to stockholders or divorcing spouses, the practitioner must be sensitive to the facts and circumstances of the case at hand. The practitioner must realize that the interpretation of the standard of value previously used in court cases may not apply across all cases. The specific fact pattern of a reported case might distinguish it from the case at hand.

The practitioner must also be aware that in prior case law, the terminology used and the ultimate outcome of the valuation may not be in sync. Additionally, jurisdictional differences may exist, and the way a certain standard of value is used in one jurisdiction may differ from its use in other state and federal jurisdictions.[3]

---

[3] David Laro and Shannon P. Pratt, *Business Valuation and Federal Taxes* (Hoboken, NJ: John Wiley & Sons, 2011), at 5.

Fair Value versus Fair Market Value

The two most widely used standards of value are *fair market value* and *fair value*. Before we discuss the definitions of these terms in valuation and law, we can look at their application on a purely linguistic level.

In plain language, fair value is a much broader concept than fair market value. Webster's thesaurus gives these synonyms for the word *fair*: *just, forthright, impartial, plain, upright, candid, sincere, straightforward, honest, lawful, clean, legitimate, honorable, temperate, reasonable, civil, uncorrupted, equitable, fair-minded*.[4] Without the *market* modifier, fair value can be seen as a broad concept of a "value" that is "fair." Accordingly, the term *fair* gives a court wide latitude in reaching a judgment. The fair value of an asset could be its market value, its intrinsic value, or an investment value. Similarly, it could be a value in exchange, or a value to the holder; it could represent a liquidation value or a going-concern value.

The term *fair market value* is more limiting, by its use of the word *market*. Whether *market* applies to *fair* (as in *fair market*) or *value* (as in *market value*), we are limited to finding the value an asset would have in exchange, that is, on a market in the context of a real or hypothetical sale. Fair market value is the cornerstone for all other judicial concepts of value. Following a brief overview of common standards and premises of value in Chapter 1, we move first to a discussion of fair market value, as it sets the benchmark from which other standards of value are viewed.

Later, when we apply definitions set forth by the Internal Revenue Service (IRS), or the American Bar Association (ABA), or the FASB, or any other professional or regulatory body providing guidance, we arrive at a set of assumptions that determine the scope of the valuation. As we will see, fair value is indeed subject to wider interpretation from a judicial perspective than fair market value. Fair market value is well-defined and established in legal, tax, and accounting settings, and fair value is defined in terms of financial reporting. However, there is no universal definition of fair value in the context of dissent and oppression cases. Perhaps the most relevant definition was laid out in the landmark 1950 shareholder dissent case, *Tri-Continental Corp. v. Battye*,[5] where the court expressed the basic concept of fair value under the dissent statute as being "that the stockholder is entitled to be paid for that which has been taken from him, viz., his proportionate interest in a going concern."[6]

---

[4] *Webster's New World Dictionary and Thesaurus* (New York: Simon & Schuster Macmillan, 1996), at 222.

[5] 74 A.2d 71.

[6] *Id.* , at 3.

Interestingly, the definition of fair value in *Black's Law Dictionary* says "See fair market value." Under the definition of fair market value, there is an example of a bankruptcy case.[7] In that case, the term *fair value* is used, as opposed to *fair market value*, as if the terms were interchangeable. This circular referencing makes the concepts of fair value and fair market value difficult to separate in a broad legal context; however, as we show through a review of case law, statutes, and commentary, the two concepts are regularly viewed as different.

We will explain how fair value differs from fair market value in its application in shareholder dissent and oppression. In divorce matters, we will look at a continuum over which businesses are valued and see how, under certain circumstances in certain jurisdictions, fair value is closely related to fair market value and, under others, it is not.

Historical Perspective

Today, the term *fair market value* is used often in the statutory context. For example, New Jersey's statutes use the term in 125 different sections of the code, from library material (§ 2A:43A-1) to farmland (§ 4:1C-31) to hazardous substances (§ 58:10-23.11b). The term *fair value* is much less pervasive. Today, it is used mainly for financial reporting, shareholder oppression and dissent, and sometimes divorce matters. The historical development of fair market value, fair value, and the standard of value in divorce are briefly summarized next.

1800 to 1850 In searching case law, we begin to see references to standards of value in the early nineteenth century; however, the standards of value are not necessarily defined as such. One of the earliest references to fair market value is in a tariff case from 1832.[8] The term was set forth without further definition.

1850 to 1900 In the late nineteenth century, the emergence of the railroads allowed an expansion of commerce to a national scale and aided the development of national, multishareholder corporations. As tax law developed and business organizations progressed, there came a need for judicial and legislative involvement in corporate law. Majority rule emerged in corporations when the courts recognized the operational necessity of

---

[7] Bryan A. Garner, *Black's Law Dictionary*, 8th ed. (St. Paul, MN: Thompson West, 2004), at 1587.

[8] *United States v. Fourteen Packages of Pins*, 1832 U.S. Dist. LEXIS 5.

abandoning unanimous consent for corporate decisions. The courts began to look for a manner by which to value property for taxation and to find equitable solutions to the disagreements of shareholders that naturally grew out of this evolution.

The earliest references to fair value were found in cases involving contractual agreements between individuals regarding the ownership of stock, property, or other assets.[9] Like fair market value, the concept of fair value that emerged from these events remained undefined.

1900 to 1950 At the beginning of the twentieth century, the courts, the states, and other regulatory and advisory organizations began dealing more commonly with litigation involving business valuations. In the 1920s, the Commissioners for Uniform State Laws began developing a model code for businesses, but the Model Business Corporation Act of the ABA gained popularity and began to influence state legislatures in the codification of dissenters' rights in their statutes. In 1933, the Illinois Business Corporation Act became the model statute for shareholder oppression, and in the early 1940s, California instituted a statutory buyout provision where a corporation could elect to buyout a shareholder who claimed to be oppressed, rather than going through dissolution litigation. In 1950, the landmark case *Tri-Continental Corp. v. Battye* introduced the concept that fair value should compensate a shareholder for that which had been taken.

In the 1920s, the definition of fair market value began to emerge through various case decisions. The concepts of *willing buyer, willing seller, known and knowable,* and the effect of compulsion on fair market value were discussed and established as elements to consider in determining fair market value. The first discount was applied for lack of control of a corporation at the behest of the IRS in *Cravens v. Welch,*[10] a California Tax Court case. A shareholder was looking to deduct taxable losses on the minority shares of a corporation, and while the shareholder desired to set a higher initial value of his shares, the IRS looked to lessen that value by applying a discount. Later, the application of the minority discount (though benefiting the IRS in this case) would be applied commonly in estate and gift tax matters to the benefit of the shareholder.

---

[9] *Montgomery v. Rose,* Court of Virginia, Special Court of Appeals 1855 Va. LEXIS 65; 1 Patton & H. (5 January 1855); *The United States Rolling Stock Company v. The Atlantic and Great Western Railroad Company,* Court of Ohio, 34 Ohio St. 450 (December 1878).

[10] 10 F. Supp. 94 (D.C. Cal. 1935).

1950 to 1980   Businesses began to change in the latter half of the twentieth century. The most valuable assets of a business were often no longer tangible assets, such as real property and equipment, but were intangible assets, such as patents, trademarks, trade names, and goodwill. Because of this, valuation theory itself had to evolve to cope with new sorts of assets, which required complex valuations. The need for judicial valuations grew because of the disputes that arose over the value of intangible assets.

In family law, equitable distribution and the concept of community property emerged in the 1970s and, along with the emergence of intangible value, created a new need for business valuations in the judicial context of divorce. In estate and gift tax matters, the definition of fair market value was codified and explained in Treasury Regulations as well as by IRS Revenue Rulings.

In stockholder matters, the states more broadly adopted dissent and oppression statutes. By the 1970s, the states widely implemented the fair value buyout provision in dissolution statutes. Previously, the resolution to shareholder oppression was generally achieved by dissolving the existing corporation. Because of the availability of the fair value buyout, oppressed shareholders were now better able to recover their investment upon filing suit as oppressed shareholders.

1980 to the Present   Despite codification, in the past three decades, the Tax Court continues to deal with fair market value issues, including shareholder-level discounts, trapped in capital gains, and subsequent events. The family courts have struggled with the treatment of goodwill, the application of shareholder-level discounts, and the weight accorded buy–sell agreements.

Some of the most significant developments have occurred in shareholder oppression and dissent in the past 30 years. The courts had previously been hesitant to dissolve a company unless extremely harsh conduct was recognized, but with the institution of the fair value buyout in many states, the courts in those states became more inclined to allow the minority shareholder to be compensated with a payment for the value of his or her stock. In the late 1970s, tests for oppression emerged in the form of cases establishing that a shareholder may be awarded his or her fair value if there is a breach of fiduciary duty, unfair or unreasonably burdensome conduct by the majority, or a breach of the minority shareholder's reasonable expectations. In 1983, the Delaware decision *Weinberger v. UOP, Inc.*[11] established the notion that customary and current valuation techniques may be used in determining fair value in shareholder dissent cases instead of the rigid guidelines previously applied. Several iterations of the Revised Model Business

---

[11] 457 A.2d 701 (Del. 1983).

Corporation Act (RMBCA) published by the ABA and the Principles of Corporate Governance set forth by the American Law Institute (ALI) set suggested guidelines for determining fair value in these situations, and the states increasingly adopted these guidelines over this time period.

CHAPTER PREVIEW

Chapter 1: Common Standards and Premises of Value

Chapter 1 gives a general overview of the concepts of value, cost, and price. We introduce the standards of value generally, their application, and their basic underlying assumptions. In addition, we introduce the premises of value that underlie the assumptions of the standards of value.

Chapter 2: Fair Market Value in Estate and Gift Tax

Chapter 2 deals with fair market value in estate and gift tax valuations. In this chapter, we discuss the history and development of fair market value as well as its definition. We deconstruct the definition of fair market value in detail and discuss the implications of the definition on valuation in federal estate and gift tax matters.

In the federal tax arena, fair market value is an established standard with a generally uniform interpretation. The most common definition of fair market value comes from the estate and gift tax definition in Treasury Regulation 20.2031-1:

> The fair market value is the price at which the property would change hands between a willing buyer and a willing seller, neither being under any compulsion to buy or to sell and both having reasonable knowledge of relevant facts.[12]

By this definition, assets are valued using a premise of value in exchange[13] under the fair market value standard. While there are many issues that must be decided in each case under the fair market value standard, practitioners can generally rely on the assumption that the property to be valued is that which the shareholder or the shareholder's estate holds, whether it

---

[12] *Gift Tax Regulation* 25.2512-1 defines the term similarly.

[13] As used within this book, value in exchange presumes some sort of hypothetical transaction where the ownership interest in a business or business interest is exchanged for cash or a cash equivalent.

is a minority or a majority share of a given asset. We surveyed court cases dealing with fair market value, focusing on those concerned with what constitutes a marketplace, shareholder-level discounts, and the effect of events subsequent to the valuation date.

Through case law, IRS rulings, and valuation literature there is an established body of law and theory that frames the issues dealt with on an ongoing basis by the federal Tax Court. We review a sample of the major federal Tax Court cases to provide clarity on the legal framework applicable to business appraisal. We also explain the elements of fair market value so that later we can show the characteristics that distinguish other valuation standards, such as fair value, from this well-known benchmark.

Chapter 3: Fair Value in Shareholder Dissent and Oppression

Chapter 3 discusses fair value in dissenting and oppressed shareholder matters. Because modern corporations function under a system of majority rule, minority shareholders are vulnerable to exclusion or abuse by those with a controlling interest. As a special protection, minority shareholders are granted limited rights in dissent and oppression statutes as a check against majority rule. However, there remains ambiguity in the statutory language, which lends itself to varying interpretations of exactly what the shareholder will receive as compensation in those cases.

Shareholders are generally entitled to the fair value of their shares when they dissent from particular actions defined by statute or petition for the dissolution of a corporation because of the alleged abuse at the hands of majority shareholders. Some have argued that the term *fair value* is used in statutes to distinguish it from fair market value and the assumptions one would make when determining fair market value. In its theory and application, fair value is a broader standard.

In this chapter, we summarize the history and development of both shareholder dissent and oppression as well as the development of fair value as a standard of value in these matters. We look at the guidance provided by law associations and landmark cases in each state in an attempt to classify them in terms of their interpretation of various elements of fair value.

Although dissent and oppression are addressed under separate statutes, cases in both areas reference each other in their common use of the term *fair value*. Most states define the term only in their dissent statutes. The model corporate business statutes set forth by the ABA's RMBCA and the ALI's Principles of Corporate Governance also provide guidance as to procedural requirements of both oppression and dissent, as well as in setting guidelines for the determination of fair value.

One major issue addressed in the determination of fair value in these matters is the application of shareholder-level discounts. The trend over the past 25 years, as guided by the ABA and the ALI and precedential case law, has generally been, in the absence of special circumstances, to not apply these discounts. Many courts (and much of the modern commentary and scholarship) direct that the minority shareholder's value be determined as a pro rata share of the equity value of a corporation, without the application of shareholder-level discounts for lack of control and lack of marketability.

Depending on state law and the facts and circumstances of a case, discounts may or may not be applied.

As discussed in Chapter 3, the ABA and the ALI definitions of fair value have suggested clarification with regard to the application of shareholder-level discounts. In 1999, the ABA followed the 1992 ALI in recommending that discounts not be applied. The state legislatures and courts have established their own definitions, with or without reference to these suggested guidelines. However, we have seen statutes and case law moving toward the 1992 ALI and 1999 ABA definitions described previously.

Chapter 3 presents an extensive review of statutes, case law, and commentary on fair value analyses performed pursuant to dissent and oppression cases to achieve a better understanding of the rights of minority shareholders and the valuation process that leads to the ultimate determination of what that shareholder will receive. The chapter includes a chart showing how the market exception (which limits appraisals for publicly traded companies) is applied in various states, and a chart summarizing court cases regarding discounts.

We have also created a chart on the dissent and oppression standards of value in the 50 states and the District of Columbia, which is in Appendix B. In this chart, each state's statutory standard of value is listed, with any definition of that term, the valuation date, the availability of oppression as a trigger for dissolution, whether an election to buy out in lieu of dissolution is permitted by statute, and recent precedential case law governing the application of discounts. Using this chart, we have grouped the states through an evaluation of case law in order to establish common themes among states that treat fair value similarly.

Chapter 4: Standards of Value for Partnership and Limited Liability Company Buyouts

Chapter 4 is a new chapter. This chapter addresses the buyout of the partner in a partnership (including limited liability partnerships (LLPs)) and limited partnerships as well as for members of limited liability companies (LLCs). It grows out of our research into the buyout of a dissenting or oppressed minority corporate shareholder presented in Chapter 3. These are different entities from corporations and, as such, we have put them into a separate chapter.

Corporate stockholders do not have the right to be bought out of their ownership interest unless the court finds that the minority is dissenting from a specified action by the majority or that the minority shareholder is being oppressed by the majority shareholders.

In partnerships, limited partnerships, and limited liability corporations, there is often a buyout provision that provides for the purchase of the stock of a disassociating or deceased owner without the need for a finding of dissent or oppression.

The National Conference of Commissioners on Uniform State Laws (NCCUSL) has established model laws for each of these types of entities. Most states have used some of these model laws as the basis for their own statutes. For instance, § 701, "Purchase of disassociated partner's interest," in the Revised Uniform Partnership Act (RUPA) bides to the purchase of a disassociated partner's interest in the following manner:

(a) If a partner is disassociated from a partnership without resulting in a dissolution and winding up of the partnership business under Section 801, the partnership shall cause the dissociated partner's interest in the partnership to be purchased for a buyout price determined pursuant to subsection (b).
(b) The buyout price of a dissociated partner's interest is the amount that would have been distributable to the dissociating partner under Section 807(b) if, on the date of dissociation, the assets of the partnership were sold at a price equal to the greater of the liquidation value or the value based on a sale of the entire business as a going concern without the dissociated partner and the partnership were wound up as of that date. Interest must be paid from the date of dissociation to the date of payment.
(c) Damages for wrongful dissociation under Section 602(b), and all other amounts owing, whether or not presently due, from the dissociated partner to the partnership, must be offset against the buyout price. Interest must be paid from the date the amount owed becomes due to the date of payment.

While this does not include the term *fair value*, comments to the section describe the definition in which minority discounts are not taken, but marketability discounts are considered. The standard of value set forth in many of the limited partnership and LLC statutes is described as fair value.

This chapter also presents the emerging body of case law for each of these entities, which typically follows the standard of value that is used in dissent and oppression matters for corporations.

Chapter 5: Standards of Value in Divorce

Chapter 5 addresses the premises and standards of value used when valuing a business in divorce. In this chapter, we review the history and development of the concepts of marital and separate property as well as the manner in which the concepts of equitable distribution and community property have developed. We then clarify the standards of value that the states apply consciously or by implication through the decisions of their courts.

In matrimonial valuations, there is no one consistent business valuation trend across the nation. States, and even different jurisdictions within the states, treat various issues such as goodwill, shareholder-level discounts, and buy–sell agreements very differently. In reviewing these issues, we have found that there is a continuum over which the standards of value fall, ranging from the most stringent interpretation of the value in exchange to the broadest view of the value of property to its owner (holder). Based on their treatment of goodwill, shareholder-level discounts, and the weight accorded buy–sell agreements, we have attempted to classify states as to where they fall on that continuum.

Other than as a matter of public policy and legislative intent, we find no consistent pattern as to why the states diverge in their application of standard of value. The bodies of law in the 50 states and the District of Columbia have developed independently, and these laws are continually evolving. Recently, some states have had cases of first impression dealing with the standards by which businesses are valued, and in these cases the courts have performed an analysis of nationwide case law to guide their decisions. There does not, however, appear to be an overwhelming demand in divorce to centralize the standards of value across the states as the ABA and the ALI have done in dissent and oppression matters.

Through our survey of precedential case law, annotated statutes, as well as legal and valuation publications, we have attempted to group states based on their treatment of goodwill, shareholder-level discounts, and the weight accorded buy–sell agreements in order to understand the standard of value generally applied in each state. We have grouped states according to the premise of value and the standards of value either stated in their statutes or stated or implied in their case law. With this analysis, we hope to provide appraisers and appraisal users with some insight as to the standard of value used in a particular jurisdiction.

The basic elements of this continuum involve two general premises of value:[14] value in exchange and value to the holder; and three standards of value: fair market value, fair value, and investment value. We use these two

---

[14] General premises, to be distinguished from operational premises like liquidation value and value as a going concern. This will be discussed in further detail in Chapter 1.

premises and three standards of value to create a chart that groups the precedential cases of each state as follows:

Value in Exchange	Value to the Holder
Fair Market Value	Fair Value / Investment Value

Basically, we analyze each state's position on this continuum through its treatment of goodwill, shareholder-level discounts, and the weight afforded buy–sell agreements.

Chapter 6: Fair Value in Financial Reporting

Chapter 6 addresses fair value in financial accounting. In this chapter, we discuss the current standards for the reporting of assets and liabilities for corporations as established by the FASB. Further, we discuss the history and development of the concept of fair value in financial reporting and how changes in the nature of businesses led to the publication of FASB's Accounting Standards Codification (ASC) 820 Fair Value Measurements (formerly SFAS 157).

As we looked at the ALI and ABA guidelines for fair value in oppression and dissent, we look at the guidelines laid out by the pronouncements of the FASB and regulations from the SEC to better define and understand fair value in the financial reporting context.

Within this analysis, we address the hierarchy of fair value techniques and the preference for using established market prices over present value measurements in determining fair value. We discuss the mechanisms in the ASC/SFAS guidelines governing the treatment of intangible assets, including goodwill. We also compare fair value in financial reporting to fair value in shareholder dissent and oppression, investment value, and fair market value. We arrive at the emerging trends in financial accounting, including expansion of fair value measurement guidelines, consistency in the application of valuation techniques, and new practices in the auditing of fair value measurements.

HOW STANDARD OF VALUE CAN AFFECT THE ULTIMATE CONCLUSION OF VALUE

The standard of value underlies the theoretical and practical applications of valuation and defines for the appraiser the type of value being sought.[15] In some circumstances, the applicable standard of value is fairly clear. In tax

---

[15] Shannon P. Pratt and Alina Niculita, *Valuing a Business: The Analysis and Appraisal of Closely Held Companies*, 5th ed. (New York: McGraw-Hill, 2008), at 41.

cases, fair market value is applied in accordance with the definition set forth in the Treasury Regulations and the guidance of IRS Revenue Rulings and Tax Court cases. There may still be controversies, such as the size of discounts allowed or the inclusion of events subsequent to the valuation date, but essentially the definition stands and provides relatively unambiguous guidance in a valuation assignment.

In other applications, however, the standard of value is not necessarily as clear. While the statutory application of fair value is nearly ubiquitous among the 50 states and the District of Columbia in dissenters' rights and oppression cases, the term is rarely meaningfully defined by those statutes. Over the past century, the courts, law associations, and state legislatures have weighed in on the appropriate definition of fair value to clarify its application.

Even less clear, in divorce, the standard of value is rarely explicitly established by case law and even less frequently by statute. For most states, we have to sort through various elements of a business's value and valuation issues such as the application of discounts in order to determine how a given state's courts determine the applicable standard.

The value of a business is the present worth of the future benefits of ownership, at a given point in time.[16] However, values can change for the same asset as premises and standards of value change. As will be discussed in this book, the application of a particular standard of value has a substantial effect on the valuation conclusion.

To better illustrate this concept, we will demonstrate through a hypothetical example how value could be viewed using different standards as applied to different purposes. We will use, as an example, an accounting practice owned in equal share by three accountants.

For the estate tax valuation upon the death of one of the owners, the business interest in this closely held entity would be valued using fair market value. Accordingly, the one-third interest would be valued in exchange. Since the one-third interest lacks control and marketability, shareholder-level discounts would be considered.

Alternatively, should two of the shareholders oppress the third, the wronged party could allege oppression and the remaining shareholders could choose to exercise their buyout option rather than risk an expensive and drawn-out court proceeding that could result in a judicially mandated dissolution and possibly even the awarding of damages to the wronged shareholder. Under the fair value buyout remedy in his or her state's dissolution statute, the shareholder could be paid the fair value of his or her interest. In this case, the majority of states (as prescribed by the guidelines

---

[16] *Id.*, at 56.

set by the ABA and the ALI) would value the company as a whole—the enterprise—and take a pro rata share of that value based on percentage ownership. Generally, no shareholder-level discounts would be applied, as the courts attempt to compensate the shareholder for that which had been taken from him or her.

Upon divorce, a whole range of values could arise based on the differing premises and standards of value. Depending on the statutes and case law in a given state, the value might be determined at fair market value, fair value, or investment value. Accordingly, for divorce purposes, shareholder-level discounts might be considered, considerable weight may be accorded buy–sell agreements, or none of these considerations may apply.

While the concept of fair value for financial reporting purposes has been around for a long time, it has recently received a great deal of visibility. It should not be confused with fair value for dissent and oppression matters, nor is it the same as fair market value. As the standard used in valuations for financial reporting purposes on a company's financial statements, fair value strives to reflect the value of a company's assets on its balance sheet on an economic basis, rather than the traditional cost basis. Based on a hierarchical system of valuation, the values expressed are the company's assets and liabilities that would exchange hands in an orderly transaction between market participants. While seemingly straightforward, fair value in this context has myriad nuances that the practitioner will need to address.

As can be seen, each of these situations could result in significantly different dollar amounts for the same ownership interest. This example illustrates the importance of understanding the premises and standards of value in a particular venue and for a particular purpose, and it is our hope that this book will contribute to continuing professional dialogue surrounding these issues.

CHAPTER 1

Common Standards and Premises of Value

COMMON STANDARDS AND PREMISES

In this chapter, we provide a brief introduction to the standards of value that we discuss and analyze throughout this book. The premises and standards discussed in this chapter will be discussed in more detail in the upcoming chapters.

We begin by analyzing the meaning of value itself and why it is necessary to understand the elements of each standard of value. We also introduce two fundamental premises of value: *value in exchange* and *value to the holder*. Then we briefly address how these premises of value impact the standard of value and the assumptions that underlie any given standard of value.

Price, Value, and Cost

Oscar Wilde wrote:

> What is a cynic? A man who knows the price of everything and the value of nothing.[1]

Wilde's quote illuminates the relationship between price and value as social concepts, highlighting clearly that the words are not interchangeable. Although not interchangeable, in various reference works, *price*, *value*, and *cost* are all defined with reference to one another.

Price, for example, is defined by *Webster's New World Dictionary* as "the amount of money, etc., asked or paid for something; cost. 2. Value or

---

[1] Oscar Wilde, *Lady Windermere's Fan*, Act 3 (1893).

worth. 3. The cost, as in life, labor, etc. of obtaining some benefit."[2] *Black's Law Dictionary* defines price as "the amount of money or other consideration asked for or given in exchange for something else. The cost at which something is bought or sold."[3]

Webster's defines cost as "the amount of money, etc. asked or paid for a thing; price"[4]; *Black's* defines it as "expense; price. The sum or equivalent expended, paid, or charged for something."[5]

While price and cost are transactional concepts, value is a less concrete concept, not necessarily requiring the arrival at a set price between parties in a transaction. Value, in fact, represents a more general concept of worth that may not be easily represented by a transactional price or cost. Value exists in a sale, in an ongoing business, and in liquidation. The main question (and the primary focus of this book) is: By what standard should value be judged? Price certainly can sometimes represent value—one arrived at in an arm's-length transaction. Cost sometimes can as well, insofar as it is the amount of money or compensation required to produce or purchase a product or service.

In his classic work, *Valuation of Property*, James C. Bonbright writes:

> The contrast between "value" and "cost" as fundamental concepts is that the former term refers to the advantage that is expected to result from the ownership of a given object of wealth (or to the market price that this advantage will command), whereas the latter term refers to the sacrifice involved in acquiring this object. This distinction is clear in our minds when we ask whether anything or any desirable human achievement "is worth what it costs". . . . Cost, then, is the price that must be paid for value.[6]

Cost can take the form of an outlay of resources or forgoing other opportunities, the so-called opportunity cost. While cost may be incurred in acquiring value, value does not necessarily equate to cost.

Webster's has 13 definitions for value, ranging from "a fair or proper equivalent in money commodities, etc., for something sold or exchanged;

---

[2] *Webster's New World Dictionary of the American Language* (New York: Macmillan, 1996), at 487.

[3] Bryan A. Garner, *Black's Law Dictionary*, 8th ed. (St. Paul, MN: Thompson West, 2004), at 1266.

[4] *Webster's New World Dictionary*, at 136.

[5] Garner, *Black's Law Dictionary*, at 371.

[6] James C. Bonbright, *Valuation of Property* (Charlottesville, VA: Michie Company, 1937), at 19.

fair price" to "that which is desirable or worthy of a scheme for its own sake; a thing or quality having intrinsic worth."[7]*Black's* contains two pages of definitions for value, beginning with its primary general definition: "(1) the significance, desirability, or utility of something." The second definition is "(2) the monetary worth or price of something; the amount of goods, services, or money that something will command in an exchange."[8]

The interrelationship between the terms *price, cost,* and *value* and the ambiguities associated with them necessitates clear, internally consistent definitions of these terms.

Defining a Standard of Value

In 1989, the College of Fellows of the American Society of Appraisers published an opinion in which it recognized:

> . . . the necessity to identify and define the applicable standard of value as a critical part of any appraisal report or appraisal engagement. It (*identifying and defining the applicable standard of value*) also recognizes that there legitimately can be different definitions of the same appraisal term and different contexts based either on widely accepted usage or legal definitions through statutes, regulations, case law and/or legally binding documents.[9]

With regard to business valuation, the College of Fellows asserts that "every appraisal report or engagement should identify the applicable standard of value."[10] In addition, the Uniform Standards of Professional Appraisal Practice mandate identification of the standard of value in every appraisal.[11]

Whereas stating a standard of value in an appraisal engagement seems like a straightforward concept, different standards may have different meanings in different contexts. Therefore, defining *value* and adhering to the assumptions inherent in a particular standard of value, especially in connection with a valuation for tax, judicial, or regulatory purposes, often is no easy task.

---

[7] *Webster's New World Dictionary*, at 1609.

[8] Interestingly, these two ideas represent the two premises of value that will be discussed later in this chapter, the first representing a value to the holder premise, the second representing a value in exchange premise.

[9] *Valuation*, Vol. 34, No. 2 (June 1989), "Defining Standards of Value." Opinion of the College of Fellows.

[10] *Id.* at 4.

[11] *Uniform Standards of Professional Appraisal Practice*, 2012-2013, Standards Rule 2-2 a(v), "state the type and definition of value and cite the source of the definition."

Bonbright perhaps sets the issue up best when he writes:

> At first thought one might suppose the problem with defining value is a fairly simple one—or at all events, that it might be settled once and for all by consensus of those experts who were called upon to pass judgment on property values.[12]

He continues:

> When one reads the conventional value definitions critically, one finds, in the first place, that they themselves contain serious ambiguities, and in the second place, that they invoke concepts of value acceptable only for certain purposes and quite unacceptable for other purposes.[13]

Bonbright further suggests:

> [T]he problem of defining value, for the many practical purposes for which the term is used, is an exceedingly difficult one, deserving quite as much attention as does the technique in proof.[14]

The standard of value is a definition of the type of value being sought. The premise of value is an assumption as to the actual or hypothetical set of circumstances applicable to the subject valuation. Later in this chapter, we introduce the standards and premises of value that are critical to understanding valuation in the judicial and regulatory context.

Premises of Value

Throughout this book, we discuss two fundamental premises of value: value in exchange and value to the holder. The premise chosen establishes the "value to whom?"

> ▪ *Value in exchange.* Value in exchange is the value of the business or business interest changing hands, in a real or a hypothetical sale. Accordingly, discounts, including those for lack of control and lack of marketability, are considered in order to estimate the value of the property in exchange for cash or cash equivalent. The fair market value standard

---

[12] Bonbright, *Valuation of Property*, at 11.
[13] *Id.*, at 11.
[14] *Id.*, at 11–12.

and, to some extent, the fair value standard fall under the value in exchange premise.

■ *Value to the holder.* The value to the holder premise represents the value of a property that is not being sold but, instead, is being maintained in its present form by its present owner. The property does not necessarily have to be marketable in order to be valuable. We discuss later, however, that the value to the holder may be more or less than the value in exchange. The standard of investment value falls under the premise of value to the holder, as does, in certain cases, fair value.

These two premises represent the theoretical underpinnings of each standard of value. In other words, they represent the framework under which all other assumptions follow.

COMMON STANDARDS OF VALUE

In many situations, the choice of the appropriate standard of value is often dictated by circumstance, objective, contract, operation of law, or other factors. For instance, What is being valued? Does the property change hands? Who are the buyer and seller?

In many instances, the choice of the standard of value may be clear, but the meaning of that standard of value is less clear. To the valuation professional, the application of a specific standard of value has significant implications regarding the assumptions, methodologies, and techniques that should be used in a valuation.

In a judicial context, the standard of value is generally set by regulations (as in estate or gift tax), by statute (as in dissent and oppression), by case law (as either stated or implied by divorce cases in most states), or some combination of the above. In financial reporting, the standard is set by the Statements of Financial Accounting Standards. Next, we introduce some common standards of value.

Accordingly, it is essential that the practitioner have a clear understanding of what the appropriate standard of value should be for the given circumstance. This includes seeking clarification from legal counsel, preferably in writing.

Fair Market Value

Fair market value is perhaps the best-known standard of value and is commonly applied in judicial and regulatory matters. Fair market value applies to virtually all federal and state tax matters, including estate, gift, inheritance, income, and ad valorem taxes, as well as many other valuation situations.[15]

The Treasury Regulations give the most common valuation definition of fair market value:

> The fair market value is the price at which the property would change hands between a willing buyer and a willing seller, neither being under any compulsion to buy or to sell and both having reasonable knowledge of relevant facts.[16]

Black's Law Dictionary defines fair market value as "the price that a seller is willing to accept and a buyer is willing to pay on the open market and in an arm's length transaction; the point at which supply and demand intersect."[17]

The willing buyer and willing seller are presumed to deal at arm's length; they are independent third parties, not specific individuals, and therefore the price arrived at will not be influenced by any special motivations or synergies of a specific buyer. Fair market value implies a market on which the buyer and seller transact and assumes current economic conditions as of the date of the valuation.[18]

Under fair market value, discounts may be applied to shares of a closely held company if they lack control over the corporation or lack marketability. Additionally, the property is being valued assuming a sale, regardless of whether the property actually will be sold.

Estate and gift tax cases applying fair market value provide the most frequent interpretation of the definition and application of its principles. Using these principles, fair market value has been applied in other areas. In this book, when used in other contexts, the terms of fair market value are discussed only when they depart from the interpretation in estate and gift tax matters.

Fair market value is the espoused standard of value used in a number of states for valuations in connection with divorce. Generally, only assets that can be sold are considered under a fair market value standard. In these cases, only the elements of a company's assets, including certain types of goodwill that are salable, will be included in the valuation. In addition, discounts for lack of control or lack of marketability are usually considered.

---

[15] Shannon P. Pratt and Alina Niculita, *Valuing a Business: The Analysis and Appraisal of Closely Held Companies*, 5th ed. (New York: McGraw-Hill, 2008), at 41.

[16] Treasury Regulation § 20.2031-1.

[17] Garner, *Black's Law Dictionary*, at 1587.

[18] Pratt and Niculita, *Valuing a Business*, at 42.

Fair Value

Fair value may be the applicable standard of value in a number of different situations, including financial reporting, appraisals for dissenting shareholders, buyouts of oppressed shareholders, fairness opinions, and divorce.

The definition of fair value depends on its context. For financial reporting, fair value is defined in relevant accounting literature and is closely akin to, but not the same as, fair market value. The definition of fair value from the Financial Accounting Standards Board for financial reporting purposes is:

> The price that would be received to sell an asset or paid to transfer a liability in an orderly transaction between market participants at the measurement date.[19]

This definition is similar to the one used in estate and gift tax regulations, but it does not require that buyers and sellers be as well informed as in fair market value for estate and gift tax; it is also an *exit value*. While the parties are required to be uncompelled under the Treasury Regulations, fair value for financial reporting purposes prohibits only a forced or liquidation sale.[20] Commentators have been clear that *fair value* for financial reporting purposes is not identical to *fair market value* as used for estate and gift tax purposes. For example, blockage discounts are not considered in fair value for financial reporting purposes while they are typically considered under fair market value.

In judicial appraisals, fair value is a legally mandated standard that applies to specific transactions and is commonly used in matters involving dissenters, shareholder oppression, and litigation challenging the fairness of transactions. Until recently, there was no clear consensus on the definition of fair value in judicial valuations, but prevailing precedents have suggested that use of the term *fair value* distinguishes it from *fair market value* and the assumptions that underlie its application. While not clearly defined until the last 20 years or so, the most recent applications have established that the fair value of the shares, absent special circumstances, is their pro rata share of enterprise value. Two prominent commentators on Delaware law define fair value as the pro rata share of "the present value of the corporation's existing assets [plus] the present value of the reinvestment opportunities available to and anticipated by the firm."[21]

---

[19] FASB Accounting Standards Codification (ASC) Topic 820 (formerly SFAS 157).

[20] David Laro and Shannon P. Pratt, *Business Valuation and Federal Taxes* (Hoboken, NJ: John Wiley & Sons, 2011), at 14.

[21] Lawrence A. Hamermesh and Michael L. Wachter, "Rationalizing Appraisal Standards in Compulsory Buyouts," 50 B.C.L. Rev. 1021 (2009).

Investment Value

Investment value, in the nomenclature of business valuation, means the value of an asset, business, or business *interest to a specific or prospective owner.* Accordingly, this type of value considers the owner's (or prospective owner's) knowledge, abilities, expectation of risks and earning potential, and other factors.[22] Investment value often considers synergies available to a specific purchaser.

For example, for some companies, investment value may reflect the added value to that company of vertical or horizontal integration. For a manufacturer, it may reflect the added value of a distributor in order to control the channel of distribution of the manufacturer's particular products. For other companies, it may reflect the added value of acquiring a competitor in order to achieve the cost savings of combined operations and possibly eliminate some price competition.

For an individual, investment value considers value to the owner and often includes a person's reputation, unique skills, and other attributes.

For these reasons, reflecting the added value of the combination of the company's or individual's unique attributes with the subject property, investment value may result in a higher value than fair market value, which reflects the value to a hypothetical investor and may not reflect the added value to an owner or unique purchaser.

Investment value crops up primarily in the context of marital dissolutions, whether the court calls it by that name or not. It is not uncommon to have a family law court's opinion refer to a standard of value by name, but upon reading the text of the opinion, one may find that the court considered some aspects of what the business appraisal community would view as a different standard of value, often investment value. In this context, investment value usually considers the value of property, not to a hypothetical buyer or seller, but to its current owner. From a business valuation perspective, when a divorce court uses investment value in this manner, the particular buyer is the current owner, and the application of value to that particular buyer translates to an investment value. Hence, *investment value* is often used synonymously with *value to the holder.*

Fair market value is impersonal, but investment value reflects the unique situation of a particular person or company. For example, whereas Revenue Ruling 93-12 did away with family attribution in fair market value, a minority holder who is part of a family control group may not necessarily be accorded a minority discount under the standard of investment value.

---

[22] *Id.*, at 16–17.

Investment value can be measured, for example, as the discounted net cash flow that a particular investor would expect a company to earn, in the way that particular investor would operate it. For a potential corporate acquirer, for example, investment value could be measured as the standalone value of the subject company plus any revenue increases or cost savings that the buyer would expect to achieve as a result of the synergies between the companies.

Investment value considers value from these perspectives of the potential sellers and buyers:[23]

- The economic needs and abilities of the parties to the transaction
- The parties' risk aversion or tolerance
- Motivation of the parties
- Business strategies and business plans
- Synergies and relationships
- Strengths and weaknesses of the target business
- Form of organization of target business

Intrinsic Value

Intrinsic value is the value considered to be inherent in the property itself. *Intrinsic value* is defined by *Webster's Dictionary* as "being desirable or desired for its own sake without regard to anything else";[24] and by *Black's Law Dictionary* as "the inherent value of a thing, without any special features that might alter its market value. The intrinsic value of a silver coin, for instance, is the value of the silver within it."[25]

Intrinsic value is not the legal standard of value in any federal or state statute. Nevertheless, the phrase *intrinsic value* is found in many judicial opinions regarding business valuation, particularly in family law cases and dissenting stockholder or oppressed stockholder cases. Because it connotes the inherent value of a thing, the term *intrinsic value* has often been used synonymously with the term *investment value*.

The concept of intrinsic value arises out of the literature and practice of security analysis. In fact, the most widely sold book ever on security analysis, *Graham and Dodd's Security Analysis*, has an entire chapter on intrinsic value.[26] Graham and Dodd define intrinsic value as *"the value which*

---

[23] *Id.*, at 16.

[24] *Webster's Third New International Dictionary* (Springfield, MA: G&C Merriam Company, 1966).

[25] Garner, *Black's Law Dictionary*, at 1587.

[26] Sidney Cottle, Roger Murray, and Frank Block, *Graham and Dodd's Security Analysis*, 5th ed. (New York: McGraw-Hill, 1988).

is justified by assets, earnings, dividends, definite prospects, and the factor of management" (emphasis original).[27]

According to Graham and Dodd, these four factors are the major components of intrinsic value of a going concern:

1. Level of normal earning power and profitability in the employment of assets as distinguished from the reported earnings, which may be, and frequently are, distorted by transient influences.
2. Dividends actually paid or the capacity to pay such dividends currently and in the future.
3. A realistic expectation about the trend line growth of earning power.
4. Stability and predictability of these quantitative and qualitative projections of the future economic value of the enterprise.

In general, investment practitioners now concede the existence of an intrinsic value that differs from market price. Otherwise, the merit of substantial expenditures by both Wall Street and investment management organizations for the development of value estimates on broad lists of common stocks would be highly questionable.[28]

In other words, when a security analyst says something like "XYZ stock is selling at $30 per share, but on the basis of its fundamentals, it is worth $40 per share," the $40 value is that analyst's estimate of the stock's intrinsic value, but the trading price on that date is $30 per share. If the analyst is right, the stock price may make it to $40 per share, in which case the intrinsic value would equal the fair market value.

Graham and Dodd say that "perhaps a more descriptive title for this estimated value is central value. . . . [I]ntrinsic value is in essence the central tendency in price."[29]

However, as mentioned, the term *intrinsic value* has not been restricted to securities analysis. It has been used in connection with valuations for other purposes. Here is a representative example from a divorce case.

While using the language of "intrinsic worth," the court applied a standard of value more closely associated with fair value, as treated in dissenting and oppressed stockholder matters.

Intrinsic value and investment value may seem like similar concepts, but they differ in that intrinsic value represents a judgment of value based on the perceived characteristics adhering to an investment itself, while investment

---

[27] *Id.,* at 41.

[28] *Id.,* at 43.

[29] *Id.*

value is more reliant on characteristics adhering to a particular purchaser or owner.[30]

> The value of an item of marital property is its intrinsic worth to the parties; the worth to the husband and wife, the value to the marital partnership that the court is dissolving.[31]

Below is another representative example from a dissenting stockholder case:

> In *Robbins v. Beatty*, 246 Iowa 80, 91, 67 N.W.2d 12, 18, we define "real value" as the "intrinsic value, determined from a consideration of every relevant factor bearing on the question of value," including "the rate of dividends paid, the security afforded that dividends will be regularly paid, possibility that dividends will be increased or diminished, the size of the accumulated surplus applicable to payment of dividends, record of the corporation, its prospects for the future, selling price of stocks of like character, value of its assets, book values, market conditions, and reputation of the corporation. It is unwise to attempt to state every factor that may bear on value of stock in a particular case."[32]

As can be seen, courts may use the term *intrinsic value* rather liberally. Because of this, if practitioners are requested to determine the intrinsic value of a company or a fractional interest in a company, they should seek further definition or clarification of what type of value is being sought.[33]

Book Value

We do not go into depth about book value, as it is not viewed as a standard of value in the way standards of value are discussed in this book. *Book value* is an accounting term and refers to an asset's historical cost reduced by any allowances for unrealized losses or depreciation, impairment, and amortization. Essentially, for a company, book value is the value of owner's equity on a balance sheet, that is, assets less liabilities.[34] Practitioners often will see

---

[30] Pratt and Niculita, *Valuing a Business*, at 44.

[31] *Howell v. Howell*, 31 Va. App. 332, 523 S.E.2d 514 (2000).

[32] *Robbins v. Beatty*, 246 Iowa 80, 91, 67 N.W.2d 12, 18.

[33] Jay E. Fishman, Shannon P. Pratt, J. Clifford Griffith and James R. Hitchner, *PPC's Guide to Business Valuation* (Fort Worth, TX: Thompson PPC, 2011), at 201.15.

[34] Pratt, *Valuing a Business*, at 350.

"book value," or some slight modification to book value, in shareholder agreements, where a transfer of stock is based on historical audited financial statements. Sometimes a modification would include replacing adjusted book value of real estate with market value. Here, again, this is not the same as a fair market value on a going-concern premise of value.

COMMON OPERATIONAL PREMISES UNDERLYING THE STANDARD OF VALUE

While value in exchange and value to the holder are general premises under which the standards of value fall, other operational premises further refine the assumptions that should be made under a given standard of value. For instance, in finding fair market value (a standard falling under a value in exchange premise), typically the valuation professional is looking to establish a value of a company either as a going concern or, when appropriate, upon liquidation.

These operational premises impact the amount that will be paid upon the exchange of a business. For example, most businesses are valued under the premise that they will continue operating as going concerns and managed to maximize shareholder value. However, when valuing a controlling interest, there are times when the amount realized upon the liquidation of the assets and extinguishment of all liabilities is more appropriate. Either could be higher, depending on the nature of a business and the composition of its balance sheet. An accounting practice might have a high going concern value but a low liquidation value. A golf driving range, however, might be worth more if the land could be zoned for property development and sold in liquidation.

Going Concern

Most judicial valuations look to determine the value of a company as a going concern. *Black's Law Dictionary* defines *going concern value* as: "the value of a commercial enterprise's assets or of the enterprise itself as an active business with future earning power as opposed to the liquidation value of the business or of the assets."[35]

In judicial valuations, it is often assumed that a company will continue functioning as it had been during and after the valuation. The circumstances of a business may be different because of the event necessitating or triggering the valuation, such as the death of a shareholder or key person, or

---

[35] Garner, *Black's Law Dictionary*, at 1587.

the departure of a dissenting or oppressed shareholder. In other cases, the business may continue as usual, as in the case of a valuation upon divorce.

Liquidation Value

Black's Law Dictionary defines *liquidation value* as "the value of a business or of an asset when it is sold in liquidation, as opposed to being sold in the ordinary course of business."[36] This definition broadly encompasses the idea of liquidation value, that is, that assets and liabilities are valued individually. However, there may be additional refinements to the assumptions under liquidation value, mostly dealing with the time and circumstances surrounding the disposal of the assets and extinguishment of liabilities. Methodologically, liquidation value not only considers the proceeds from selling the assets of a business but also may take into consideration any associated expenses.[37]

The liquidation value of a business is most relevant in the case of an unrestricted 100% control interest.[38] There are different levels of liquidation. In the valuation of machinery and equipment, these levels are fairly well developed; there is orderly liquidation, liquidation value in place, and liquidation in a forced sale. As discussed, each level deals with the time and circumstances surrounding the disposition of the machinery and equipment. Pratt has attempted to apply these definitions to valuing a business:[39]

- *Value as an orderly disposition.* A value in exchange on a piecemeal basis; a value in exchange that contemplates the price at which the assets of a business will be sold with normal exposure to their appropriate secondary markets.
- *Value as a forced liquidation.* A value in exchange that contemplates the price at which assets will be sold on a piecemeal basis, but instead of normal exposure to the market, these assets will have less-than-normal exposure.
- *Value as an assemblage of assets.* A value in exchange, consisting of the value of the assets in place, but not in their current use in the production of income and not as a going-concern business enterprise.

---

[36] *Id.*

[37] Fishman, Pratt, Griffith and Hitchner, *PPC's Guide to Business Valuation*, at 201.12.

[38] Michael Bolotsky, "Valuation of Common Equity Securities When Asset Liquidation Is an Alternative," in *Financial Valuation: Businesses and Business Interests*, James H. Zukin, ed. (New York: Warren Gorham & Lamont, 1990), at 10-3.

[39] Pratt and Nicalita, *Valuing a Business*, at 47–48.

Fair Value in Alternative Contexts

In this book, we discuss fair value in the context of judicial valuations in oppression, dissent, and divorce and in the regulatory context of financial reporting. Although we do not go into further detail in this book, other contexts for fair value deserve mention.

Fair value is a central element in most fairness opinions because it is the "minimum level of financial fairness."[40] A *fairness opinion* is generally prepared by a knowledgeable financial advisor in the form of a letter to state whether the financial terms of a proposed transaction are fair, from a financial point of view, to investors. Fairness opinions are advisable in a variety of situations, including acquisitions, recapitalizations, share buybacks, sales of assets, and related-party transactions.[41]

Another alternative context in which the fair value standard is applied is when the Delaware courts are evaluating "entire fairness" in transactions with conflicted parties. The Delaware courts generally utilize the same standard of fair value in these cases as is used in determining fair value in a dissenting shareholder action.[42]

The term *fair value* is also frequently used in the securities and futures markets. While it is not generally defined in this context, there are some specific definitions. Capital Markets Risk Advisors explains fair value as referring to "the price at which a single unit of an instrument would trade between disinterested parties in an arm's-length transaction. Fair value does not generally take into account control premiums or discounts for large or illiquid positions."[43]

Standard & Poor's Advisor Insight gives this explanation for its use of what it calls "fair value" (this description is closer to the definition of intrinsic value, as we discussed earlier): "helps determine if the stock is a good buy based on S&P's proprietary quantitative model and our analysis of what the stock is currently worth."[44] These assessments, however, are all outside the scope of our studies for the purposes of this book, as we are primarily

---

[40] M. Mark Lee and Gilbert E. Matthews, "Fairness Opinions," in *The Handbook of Advanced Business Valuation*, Robert Reilly and Robert Schweihs, eds. (New York: McGraw-Hill, 2000), at 311.

[41] *Id.*

[42] Hamermesh and Wachter, "Rationalizing Appraisal Standards," at 1030; *In re Southern Peru Copper Corp. S'holder Deriv. Litig.* 30 A.3d 60, 117 (Del. Ch. 2001), *aff'd; Americas Mining Corp. v. Theriault,_A.3d_*(Del. 2012), 2012 Del. LEXIS 459.

[43] Capital Market Risk Advisors, www.cmra.com/html/body_glossary.html.

[44] S&P Advisor Insight Glossary, www.advisorinsight.com/pub/cust_serv/glossary.html.

concerned with the tax, judicial, and regulatory treatment of standards of value, rather than their use in the financial markets.

Fair Market Value in Alternative Contexts

In this book, we are looking at fair market value solely in the context of a business valuation. One of the most common applications of fair market value is in the valuation of real property. However, in the valuation of real property, it is referred to as *market value*. The 2012-2013 *Uniform Standards of Professional Appraisal Practice* defines market value as:

> A type of value, stated as an opinion, that presumes the transfer of a property (i.e., a right of ownership or a bundle of such rights), as of a certain date, under specific conditions set forth in the definition of the term identified by the appraiser as applicable in an appraisal.[45]

Fair market value in real estate is generally expressed in terms of the highest and best use for the property, as established by the Tax Court in the early twentieth century as may be seen in the Tax Court case *Kaplan v. United States*.[46] In this case, the owners of a parcel of property in Arizona were assessed a tax deficiency based on their acquisition of that property as payment for services rendered. While the taxpayers' assessor valued the property at $54,000, the tax commissioner valued the property at $120,000 based on what he considered to be comparable sales in the area. The court acknowledged that the land should be assessed at its highest and most profitable use, given sufficient exposure to the market and the various other requirements of fair market value. In this case, however, the majority of the property was unimproved desert land located in the floodplain of a nearby river. Only a small proportion of the property had the potential for development, and therefore the land could not be valued as comparable to land with the potential for development.

It should be noted that in prior versions of this definition, the phrases *the most probable price* and *the highest price for property* have been used. Interestingly, the term *highest price*, used by real property appraisers in the United States, is also used in Canadian business and property valuations.[47]

---

[45] http://commerce.appraisalfoundation.org/html/2012%20USPAP/DEFINITIONS.htm.

[46] 279 F. Supp. 709; 1967 U.S. Dist. LEXIS 10787; 68-1 U.S. Tax Cas. (CCH) P9113; 21 A.F.T.R.2d (RIA) 331.

[47] "Market Value—The highest price in terms of money, which the property will bring to a willing seller if exposed for sale on the open market allowing a reasonable

In the United States, the concept of highest and best use may stretch into business valuations when determining whether to apply a value to the holder or value in exchange concept, or in determining whether to consider strategic purchasers. However, as mentioned, there are hundreds of different statutes that use fair market value, and most of them are beyond the scope of our analysis.

Standards of Value in the International Context

Just as the nature of business has changed within the United States in the past 150 years, the need for valuation guidelines has transcended national borders. Just as each state treats the standard of value differently across different areas of valuation, each country involved in business internationally may have its own independent standards and definitions of value.

In an attempt to resolve differences in definition, the International Valuation Standards Board (IVSB), a nongovernmental organization of the United Nations, has established guideline definitions. For example, *market value* is defined as:

> The estimated amount for which an asset should exchange on the valuation date between a willing buyer and a willing seller in an arm's-length transaction after proper marketing wherein the parties had each acted knowledgeably, prudently, and without compulsion.[48]

It defines *investment value* as:

> The value of an asset to the owner or a prospective owner for individual investment or operational objectives. This is an entity-specific *basis of value.* Although the value of an asset to the owner may be the same as the amount that could be realized from its sale to another party, this *basis of value* reflects the benefits received by an entity from holding the asset and, therefore, does not necessarily involve a hypothetical exchange. *Investment value* reflects the circumstances and financial objectives of the entity for which the

---

time to find a willing purchaser, buying with the knowledge of all the uses to which it is adapted and for which it is legally capable of being used, and with neither party acting under necessity, compulsion or peculiar and special circumstances." (www.coldwellbanker.ca/genglossary.html).

[48] *International Valuation Standards, 2011* (London: International Valuation Standards Council, 2011), at 20.

valuation is being produced. It is often used for measuring investment performance. Differences between the *investment value* of an asset and its *market value* provide the motivation for buyers or sellers to enter the marketplace.[49]

Similarly, the recent Toronto Valuation Accord[50] has attempted to bring nations together in terms of accounting policy and definitions, and the Royal Institute of Chartered Surveyors, a group out of the United Kingdom, has attempted to resolve the differences in the U.K.'s standards and the International Valuation Standards established by the IVSB.

A broader discussion of International Valuation Standards is available in Appendix A, where we have compiled further information and definitions regarding international standards of value.

SUMMARY

This chapter provides a brief introduction to the premises and standards that we will address throughout the book. In the chapters to come, we address the origins of the standards of value in varying contexts and the judicial and regulatory decisions that provide insight into the underlying assumptions inherent in them. We will further discuss the standards in each context and issues surrounding their application.

---

[49] *Id.*, at 23.

[50] The Toronto Valuation Accord is comprised of organizations and representatives of the valuation profession. These organizations take steps to coordinate efforts to work jointly with legislative and regulatory bodies, standards-setting groups, and other professions to aid in expediting the simplification and convergence of financial reporting standards. For more information, see the Financial Accounting Standards Board Letter of Comment Number 47. www.fasb.org/cs/BlobServer?blobkey=id& blobwhere=1175818471205&blobheader=application%2Fpdf&blobcol=urldata& blobtable=MungoBlobs>

CHAPTER 2

Fair Market Value in Estate and Gift Tax

INTRODUCTION

In this chapter, we review the history and development of fair market value and address the elements comprising this standard of value, which is cited more frequently than any other standard of value. In fact, one court remarked:

> Disputes over valuation fill our dockets, and for good reason. We approximate that 243 sections of the Code require fair market value estimates in order to assess tax liability, and that 15 million tax returns are filed each year on which taxpayers report an event involving a valuation-related issue.[1]

Fair market value is a theoretical construct commonly used in judicial valuations. It is the most widely utilized standard of value, as it applies to all federal and many state tax matters, including estate taxes, gift taxes, income taxes, and ad valorem taxes, as well as in certain states for marital dissolution cases and in a few states for shareholder oppression and dissent. In this chapter, our focus is on fair market value as it applies in federal estate, income, and gift tax matters because of the well-developed body of rulings, regulations, expert opinion, and case law regarding each element of this standard of value for those purposes. More specifically, we look at various court rulings that have addressed the theoretical underpinnings of fair market value.

In later chapters of this book, we discuss other standards of value that arise in judicial valuations. These standards, particularly fair value, may best be understood by comparison to the elements of fair market value and the

---

[1] *Auker v. Commissioner*, T.C. Memo. 1998-185.

assumptions that follow. Many of the assumptions in those standards are derived from an understanding of fair market value.

Hundreds of sources define fair market value in various ways and provide guidelines for its application.[2] Although the term is almost ubiquitous in valuation, there is often little consistency in the underlying assumptions and its application. Recently one commentator noted:

> Critics of the term "fair market value" correctly point out that its application is highly uncertain, sometimes with little connection with objective reality.[3]

These sentiments are not particularly new. In the 1930s, Bonbright commented:

> On the whole, . . . however, the courts have preferred to keep the statutory language, fair market value, while not taking its implications too seriously.[4]

Later in this chapter, we discuss the hypothetical nature of fair market value and its similarities and differences with actual real-world transactions.

Common Definitions of Fair Market Value

Fair market value is probably the most pervasive standard of value that exists. Its popularity stems from its longevity and the considerable amount of attention paid to its theoretical underpinnings.

Although Congress has never defined fair market value,[5] Estate Tax Regulation Section 20.2031-1 defines the term in this way:

> The fair market value is the price at which the property would change hands between a willing buyer and a willing seller, neither being under any compulsion to buy or to sell and both having reasonable knowledge of relevant facts.[6]

---

[2] ASA College of Fellows Opinions, "The Opinion of the College on Defining Standards of Value," 347 *Valuation*, No. 2 (June 1989), at 6.

[3] John A. Bogdanski, *Federal Tax Valuation* (New York: Warren, Gorham & Lamont, 2002), at 1–25.

[4] James C. Bonbright, *Valuation of Property* (Charlottesville, VA: Michie Company, 1937), at 983.

[5] *Bank One v. Commissioner*, 120 T.C. 174; 2003 U.S. Tax Ct. LEXIS 13; 120 T.C. No. 11.

[6] IRS Treasury Regulations, Estate Tax Regulation § 20.2031-1. IRS Treasury Regulations, Gift Tax Regulations 25.2512-1, define the term similarly.

These regulations go on to explain that fair market value should not be determined by virtue of a forced sale, nor should it be determined in a market other than that where it is most commonly transacted. This definition clearly places fair market value under a value-in-exchange premise. Therefore, the price in question is the asset's value in a real or hypothetical exchange rather than its value in its current state to the current owner.

The *International Glossary of Business Valuation Terms* defines fair market value similarly, going into slightly more detail:

> The price, expressed in terms of cash equivalents, at which property would change hands between a hypothetical willing and able buyer and a hypothetical willing and able seller, acting at arm's length in an open and unrestricted market, when neither is under compulsion to buy or sell and when both have reasonable knowledge of the relevant facts.[7]

Although this definition is somewhat different from the one in *Estate Tax Regulations*, it expresses many of the same underlying assumptions. Willing buyers and sellers are assumed to be able, and transactions are assumed to take place at arm's length.

Interestingly, later in this chapter we will see that British and Canadian courts include the term *highest price* in their definition of fair market value for business and real property valuation. Thus, in Britain and Canada, unlike in the United States, potential synergies[8] can be reflected in fair market value. In the United States, there continues to be an ongoing debate between analysts as to whether potential synergies should be included in a valuation[9].

History of Fair Market Value

While most practitioners are familiar with the definition of fair market value as it appears in the Internal Revenue Service's (IRSs) Revenue Ruling 59-60, the term *fair market value* has its roots in the early nineteenth century. One of the earliest mentions of fair market value is from a case involving a false

---

[7] Jay E. Fishman, Shannon P. Pratt, J. Clifford Griffith, and James R. Hitchner, *Guide to Business Valuations* (Fort Worth, TX: Thomson Reuters, February 2012), at 2–35. This is the definition recommended by a task force comprised of members of the AICPA, ASA, IBA, NACVA, and CICBV and adopted by their respective organizations.

[8] Synergies were considered in the fair market value cases *BTR Dunlop Holdings Inc., et al. v. Commissioner*, TC Memo 1999-377.

[9] Late in this chapter, we will discuss the issue of potential synergies as they relate to the application of fair market value in the United States.

invoice on 14 packages of pins shipped from England to the United States, discussed next.

United States v. Fourteen Packages of Pins

In the 1832 case of the *United States v. Fourteen Packages of Pins*,[10] a case dealing with tariffs, the court questioned a discrepancy in invoices prepared on two different dates in two different cities prior to the shipment. The earlier invoice, printed as a regular bill of sale between the buyers and sellers in London, showed a higher price than the later invoice printed in Liverpool, the city from which the pins were shipped.

Because of the discrepancy, the United States looked to prove that the second invoice was created only for the purpose of defrauding the ad valorem tax on the shipment. The judge instructed the jury in this way:

> All the evidence which has been given of prices, or market value, or fair market value, or current value, or true value, or actual value, is to bring you to the same conclusion, to a satisfactory answer to the question you are trying, to wit, is the valuation of these goods in this invoice a "false valuation," which is the offence described in the act of congress of 1830, on which this information is founded? Were these goods really worth more in the London market? Were the buying and selling prices higher in that market than those charged in this invoice, at the time when this invoice was made up? However the phrases may vary in the different acts of congress, current value, actual value, or market value, the inquiry with you always is the same; does this invoice contain a true valuation of these pins, or a false one? The phraseology of the laws is important on this issue, only as it may assist you in answering and deciding the question whether these pins, or similar pins, were bought and sold in the London market, in June, 1830, at these prices? Or is the valuation false and untrue, and the prices not those at which such pins were bought and sold at that time and place? *You are not to take a sale under particular circumstances which may have depressed or raised the price, but the fair and just price of buying and selling in the market.*[11][emphasis added].

The jury found in favor of the United States.

---

[10] *United States v. Fourteen Packages of Pins*, 25 F. (at 1182, 1185 (D.C. PA, 1832)
[11] *Id.*

Although *United States v. Fourteen Packages of Pins* introduced the term and the principle of an *uncompelled fair and just price*, other elements of fair market value evolved along with tax law in the United States. To put this evolution into context, we provide a short background on the institution of federal taxes from the late eighteenth to the early twentieth century and look at the development and purpose of various taxes that were instituted (and in some cases repealed) during this period.

In the late eighteenth and early nineteenth century, the states experimented with various taxes to raise revenue, including tariffs, property taxes, and progressive income taxes. By the Civil War, most states had instituted a property tax that covered not only real estate and fixtures but also intangible personal property, such as cash, credits, notes, stocks, bonds, and mortgages. The government also relied considerably on tariffs to raise revenues. During the Civil War, the need to bring in revenue to fund wartime expenditures led the Republican Congress to increase tariffs and excise taxes. This led to the creation of the Office of the Commissioner of Internal Revenue.[12]

In a further attempt to raise money to fund Civil War expenditures, in 1862 the federal government instituted an income tax. The first income tax imposed a basic rate of 3% on incomes above a personal exemption of $800. Subsequently, the tax was modified to impose a 5% tax on incomes between $600 and $5,000 and 10% on incomes over that level. In 1865, the income tax produced 21% of federal tax revenues. After the war, however, more affluent citizens lobbied Congress to discontinue the tax. In 1872, the tax was allowed to expire, but high tariffs and certain taxes on alcohol, tobacco, and luxury items remained in place from the Civil War tax system.[13]

When the Democrats took control of Congress in the 1890s, they attempted to again raise an income tax affecting mainly the wealthiest families. However, because of the direct nature of the tax and the fact that the federal government had failed to allocate the tax across states according to population, the tax was ruled unconstitutional in the 1895 Supreme Court decision *Pollock v. Farmers' Loan and Trust Co.*[14]

In 1888, the idea of taxing an estate for an intergenerational wealth transfer was raised by economist Richard T. Ely, who believed that each person should start equally in the race of life. The nation's wealthiest citizens viewed the tax as less threatening than an income tax, and some supported the idealism embodied by the tax. This led the Republican leadership to

---

[12] W. Elliot Brownlee, *Federal Taxation in America: A Short History*, 2nd ed. (Washington, DC: Woodrow Wilson Center Press, 2004), Chapter 1.

[13] *Id.*

[14] 157 U.S. 429; 15 S. Ct. 673; 39 L. Ed. 759; 1895 U.S. LEXIS 2215; 3 A.F.T.R. (P-H) 2557.

institute the tax in 1898, when funds were needed for intervention in the Boxer Rebellion among other conflicts. The tax was repealed in 1902.[15]

Over the following years, support for taxation grew. In 1913, the Underwood-Simmons Tariff Act reestablished the income tax and established a "normal" rate of 1% on nearly all personal and corporate income with a personal exemption of $3,000. After several years of income tax, about 2% of American households paid taxes.[16] The Sixteenth Amendment to the Constitution allows Congress to levy taxes without apportioning among the several states and without regard to any census or enumeration.[17] The amendment was ratified on February 3, 1913.

In *Bank One Corporation v. Commissioner*,[18] Judge David Laro traces the modern history of fair market value and the establishment of the IRS. A summary based on the material presented in Judge Laro's decision follows.

Fair market value's modern history begins with the implementation of the modern income tax with the Revenue Act of 1918.[19] This act provides that, for purposes of determining gain or loss on the exchange of property, the value of any property received equals the cash value of its fair market value.

Over time, various judicial tribunals defined the term by articulating certain elements that should be addressed in a determination of fair market value. The Revenue Act of 1918 created an Advisory Tax Board, whose function was to advise on the interpretation or administration of income, war profits, or excess profits tax.[20] While this board was in existence for only a short time, in 1919, it recommended that fair market value should be the "fair value that both a buyer and a seller, who are acting freely and not under compulsion and who are reasonably knowledgeable about all material facts, would agree to in a market of potential buyers at a fair and reasonable price."[21]

Soon after, the Board of Tax Appeals, the predecessor of the current Tax Court, was formed by the Revenue Act of 1924.[22] In a 1925 decision, this board described the buyer and seller as "willing" in a fair market value

---

[15] Brownlee, *Federal Taxation in America*.

[16] *Id.*

[17] Amendment Sixteen, Constitution of the United States.

[18] 120 T.C. No. 11.

[19] Chapter 18, 40 Stat.1057,§ 202(b), 40 Stat. 1060.

[20] *Williamsport Wire Rope Co. v. United States*, 277 U.S. 551 (1928), Footnote 7.

[21] T.B.R. 57, 1 C.B. 40 (1919).

[22] *Williamsport Wire Rope Co. v. United States*.

context.[23] In the same decision, the board advised on subsequent events, stating that the fair market value must be determined without regard to any event that occurs after the date of valuation.

Two years later, the Board of Tax Appeals adopted the Advisory Tax Board's opinion on the willingness of the buyer and seller under no compulsion.[24] The Board of Tax Appeals soon after adopted the concept that the buyer or seller in question was not a particular person, but a hypothetical person mindful of all the relevant facts.[25]

In the 1930s, the concept of the "highest and best use" for the subject of the valuation was recognized as a requirement for fair market value of real property, when the court held that two adjacent pieces of land should be valued at the same per square foot, regardless of the fact that one was being used in its highest and best use while the other was not.[26] While the term *highest and best use* is generally used in real property valuations, it is not explicitly used in U.S. business valuations but rather covered under the assumption that the business should be operated to maximize its shareholders' wealth. As will be discussed, Canada and Britain utilize the concept of highest and best use in business valuations.

The next section decomposes the definition of fair market value and discusses some of the issues that have arisen in interpreting it. We also highlight several important cases and IRS Revenue Rulings that have enhanced our understanding of fair market value. Further, we discuss the implications of each element of the definition and their effects on the appraisal process. Throughout the chapter, we look at these elements through the prism provided by various tax cases that have addressed this issue.

ELEMENTS OF FAIR MARKET VALUE

We begin by looking at the elements of value applicable in fair market value, the basic assumptions that the elements provide, and one court's view of how elements of value affect the ultimate valuation. We then decompose the definition and define its constituent parts:

- Price at which a property would change hands
- The willing buyer
- The willing seller
- Neither being under any compulsion

---

[23] *Hewes v. Commissioner*, 2 B.T.A. 1279, 1282 (1925).

[24] *Hudson River Woolen Mills v. Commissioner*, 9 B.T.A. 862, 868 (1927).

[25] *Natl. Water Main Cleaning Co. v. Commissioner*, 16 B.T.A. 223 (1929).

[26] *St. Joseph Stock Yards Co. v. United States*, 298 U.S. 38, 60 (1936).

- Both having reasonable knowledge of the relevant facts
- Valuation date and use of subsequent events

Price at Which a Property Would Change Hands

Premise of Value Determining fair market value requires the establishment of the premise of value to understand exactly how the business should be valued. The general premise driving the theoretical underpinnings of fair market value is that fair market value is a value in exchange. This value in exchange is estimated whether the property is offered for sale or not; it is presumed to be for sale in a hypothetical transaction at a point where there is a meeting of the minds between a willing buyer and willing seller. As such, fair market value presumes the property is exchanged for cash or cash equivalents in a hypothetical sale consummated between a willing buyer and willing seller. Simply stated, when the property is sold, the seller gets cash and the buyer gets the property.

How will the property be sold? The valuation of an ongoing business is usually conducted under the premise that the business will continue as a going concern. The *going concern* premise provides the framework that drives the other assumptions in the appraisal process. In other situations, a business may be valued under a *liquidation* premise. It may be liquidated and broken up for the value of its underlying assets.

The value in exchange presumption is different from the premise of value concerning the operational characteristics of the enterprise (i.e., going concern or liquidation). As it applies to the enterprise, the premise of value is the value of the business in a hypothetical sale either operating as a going concern or, when appropriate, in liquidation. Those are two different concepts: Value in exchange deals with the base from which the property is valued, whereas consideration of the enterprise as a going concern or in liquidation deals with operational characteristics of the business rather than the ideological framework of the valuation.

Under the value-in-exchange premise, a business can be viewed as a going concern or in liquidation, a determination that can depend on a number of factors, including the nature and condition of the company and the prerogatives of control inherent in the interest being valued. A company may be worth more in liquidation than as a going concern. In making such an assessment, the practitioner may consider the likelihood of liquidation (and the rights of the shareholder to liquidate). Such was the issue in *Estate of Watts v. Commissioner*.[27]

---

[27] 823 F.2d 483; 1987 U.S. App. LEXIS 10281; 87-2 U.S. Tax Cas. (CCH) P13,726; 60 A.F.T.R.2d (RIA) 6117.

ESTATE OF WATTS V. COMMISSIONER

Martha Watts owned a 15% interest in a lumber company, subject to a shareholders' agreement that provided guidelines for death of a partner, dissolution, and disposition of the partnership interests. Upon her death, her interest in the lumber company was valued by the estate's expert at $2,550,000. Upon audit, the commissioner valued her partnership interest at $20,006,000, based on the fair market value of the corporation's underlying assets upon liquidation rather than the value of the company as a going concern.

In the Tax Court case, the estate argued that the interest should be valued as a going concern. The commissioner looked to value the partnership interest in liquidation. The Tax Court sided with the estate on the grounds that there was no intention of the remaining partners to liquidate the corporation, and valued the shares at $2,550,000.

The commissioner appealed the Tax Court's decision based on the intention of the partners. The Court of Appeals agreed that the Tax Court erred in its judgment when it based the valuation on the intention of the partners, but did not reverse the decision to value the partnership as a going concern.

The Court of Appeals noted that as a minority shareholder, the estate's shares did not come with the rights to liquidate the company. Therefore, regardless of the intentions of the other partners, the estate's shares should be valued on a going-concern basis.

This case has been distinguished from cases where partnership agreements have differing requirements upon the death or departure of a partner, including less clear guidance on the continuation of the corporate form at the shareholder's death.[28] As we have discussed, the particular facts and circumstances of a given case may have substantial effects on the final outcome.

Price versus Value: Cash or Cash Equivalent   The definition of fair market value begins with finding the price at which a property would change hands in a transaction. *Black's Law Dictionary* defines *price* as "The amount of money or other consideration asked for or given in exchange for something else; the cost at which something is bought or sold";[29] *value* is

---

[28] *Estate of McFarland v. Commissioner*, T.C. Memo 1996-424.

[29] Bryan A. Garner, *Black's Law Dictionary*, 9th ed. (St. Paul, MN: Thompson West, 2009), at 1308.

defined as "1: the significance, desirability, or utility of something to the general public. 2: The monetary worth or price of something; the amount of goods, services, or money that something will command in an exchange."[30]

Although these definitions use the terms *price* and *value* interchangeably, they are not always viewed to mean the same things. As discussed in Chapter 1, there can be a significant difference between price and value. The important issue is that the first element of the definition of fair market value establishes that the premise of value is a value in exchange. As we have indicated, value is determined in a hypothetical transaction regardless of whether the asset is expected to be sold. Moreover, the term *price* requires a single-point estimate, not a range of value. As will be discussed, value is determined at the single point where the expectations of the buyer and the expectations of the seller meet. The point estimate is viewed in terms of cash or cash equivalent. The concept of *cash and cash equivalency* is a critical component of this standard of value. The fact that the definition of fair market value refers to price generally indicates that value should be expressed in terms of money or money's equivalent, that is, cash today or the present value of future consideration.

This is an important distinction in that many real-world transactions take place in stock for stock deals that may be either more or less valuable than a cash transaction.[31] By receiving stock, the seller is subject to more risk because of the lack of immediate liquidity of the stock. Therefore, while there may be, over time, an upside to this form of payment should the stock appreciate, there is also the possibility that the stock will decline in value. This risk does not occur in an all-cash transaction, nor are the potential gains available with stock available with cash. The fair market value construct does not allow the kind of flexibility seen in real-world transactions, as all of these considerations are impounded in a single-point estimate.

Willing Buyer

Marketplace   The value at any particular time is the result of supply and demand, and is always that which is necessary to create a market for the existing supply.[32]

---

[30] *Id.*, at 1587.

[31] Reiner H. Kraakman and Bernard S. Black, "Delaware's Takeover Law: The Uncertain Search for Hidden Value," 96 *Northwestern University Law Review* (Winter 2002), at 521.

[32] John Stewart Mill, *Principles of Political Economy*, 7th ed., William J. Ashley, ed. (London: Longmans, Green &Co., 1909), Book III, Chapter III.

By definition, fair market value will be the price a hypothetical willing buyer and a hypothetical willing seller will arrive at after successfully negotiating a sale of the property or asset in question.[33] This theoretical meeting of the minds needs to occur in some kind of marketplace. As stated by a 1923 case in the Third Circuit, *Walter v. Duffy*,[34] the existence of a market suggests the existence of both supply and demand for a property. Offers to sell without buyers to buy are not evidence of fair market value, and neither are offers to buy without anyone willing to sell.

A marketplace should not be made up only of sellers, nor can it be made up only of buyers. While the buyer is viewed as willing, this buyer will buy only for a rational economic amount. Similarly, sellers will sell only for a rational economic amount. A market will be created only when the rational economic analysis of value intersects between buyers and sellers.

The most probable market for a business may not be easily identifiable. Minority shares in closely held corporations are usually not readily marketable. In the case of various closely held businesses or business interests, there may be no readily apparent market or probable buyers or sellers. The courts typically look for evidence of what a willing buyer and seller would agree on if they indeed existed. The court in *Alvary v. United States*,[35] for example, suggested that there is a difference between value and liquidity, and a lack of readily accessible buyers does not mean that they do not exist. The risks of a private corporation may be higher due to the lack of liquidity, but in turn there may be a higher potential for reward. A willing buyer of a private corporation will look to analyze the same information that a willing buyer of a public corporation would, comparing its risks and returns to other potential uses for that investment.

Individual Buyer or Pool of Buyers   On the surface, in a strict fair market value interpretation, a marketplace of hypothetical buyers and sellers will bid and eventually reach an agreeable price. The marketplace, however, may be made up of a variety of different types of buyers.[36] There might be entrepreneurs looking to continue the business on their own. There might be financial buyers who see the business as a good investment. There may also be synergistic buyers who see a conjunctive value with other acquisitions or owned assets.

---

[33] John Bogdanski, *Federal Tax Valuation*, at 2.02[2][a].

[34] 287 F.41, 45 (3d Cir. 1923).

[35] 302 F.2d 790, 794 (2nd Cir. 1962).

[36] Roger J. Grabowski, "Identifying Pool of Willing Buyers May Introduce Synergy to Fair Market Value," Shannon Pratt's Business Valuation Update, 7 *Business Valuation Resources*, No. 4 (April 2001).

As discussed earlier, the Estate Tax Regulations require that the value of the property be measured in the market where it would most likely be sold. When assessing the price that a hypothetical willing buyer would pay, the practitioner seeks to identify that marketplace. By definition, buyers are presumed to have reasonable and relevant knowledge of the facts. This reasonable knowledge will include an understanding of prior transactions and identification of other shareholders. There may be an instance in which only a specific pool of buyers make up the usual marketplace for a certain block of stock. The practitioner should carefully analyze the marketplace so as to identify who would constitute the most likely pool or pools of potential buyers.

The issue of marketplace was addressed in the *Estate of Newhouse v. Commissioner*,[37] where the valuation involved a block of common stock in a large media conglomerate.

ESTATE OF NEWHOUSE V. COMMISSIONER

In this case, the decedent had owned all of the Class A voting stock and Class B nonvoting stock in a giant media corporation involving numerous divisions and locations involved in the publication of over 50 magazines and newspapers in 22 markets. Other family members held the preferred shares in the company.

The estate had the shares appraised by Chemical Bank and arrived at a total value of $247,076,000. The commissioner valued the shares at $1,323,400,000. The commissioner determined that the estate valuation performed by Chemical Bank was deficient by $609,519,855 in taxes.

The taxpayers argued that the only potential buyers for the stock would be other large media businesses. These potential buyers could not engage in the transaction, however, because they would violate antitrust laws. In addition, no other buyers would purchase the business without eliminating the preferred stock, which would be an expensive and prohibitively difficult process that would lower the value of the company to an outside purchaser.

The court sided with the taxpayer in considering that the market would be made up of a specific potential pool of buyers rather than nonspecific hypothetical buyers.

---

[37] 94 T.C. 193(1990).

Later, in *Estate of Mueller v. Commissioner*,[38] the court identified a characteristic of the market by stating: "We assume that the potential buyers of the shares would bid up the price of the shares until the person who values the shares most highly . . . wins the bidding." However, the court also stated that it need not identify a particular potential buyer or class of buyers, as the concern in determining fair market value should be the hypothetical buyer. This suggests that regardless of who the bidders are, the highest price a bidder is willing to pay may be higher than what the market would bring. Indeed, many valuation practitioners believe that fair market value would be best expressed by the amount the second-highest bidder would pay.

Alternatively, according to *Estate of Winkler v. Commissioner*,[39] the willing buyer does not and, indeed, should not necessarily belong to a particular group of individuals. This case addressed the situation when the block of stock in question is 10% of the voting shares of a corporation, where one family held 50% of the company and another family held 40%. These shares could be considered a swing vote, and the court decided that the willing buyer should not be identified as a member of either family, but, instead, the stock should be viewed as an independent unit and valued as if an independent third party were the potential buyer.

Even in a hypothetical transaction, the court may be sensitive to the real owners and the particular facts and circumstances of a given case. This may influence the final determination of value more than the requirements of any stated standard. The court's view of who constitutes a willing buyer appears to be greatly influenced by the facts and circumstances of each individual case.

Synergistic Buyers When a controlling block of shares is the subject of valuation, a willing buyer with reasonable and relevant knowledge of the marketplace will understand that there may be synergistic buyers bidding for the business. These synergistic buyers may give up a portion of the synergistic value to the sellers in order to outbid other buyers.[40] It should also be pointed out that certain synergies are inherent in most acquisitions, as there most likely will be certain cost savings. It is not all synergies that are at issue, but those synergies typically not available to the typical willing buyer.

---

[38] *Estate of Mueller v. Commissioner*, T.C. Memo. No 1992-284 at 1415, 63 T.C.M. 3027-17.

[39] T.C. Memo 1989-231; 1989 Tax Ct. Memo LEXIS 231; 57 T.C.M. (CCH) 373; T.C.M. (RIA) 8923.

[40] Grabowski, "Identifying Pool of Willing Buyers."

Some believe that there is an interrelationship between the synergistic value to a seller and the highest and best use to a buyer. The 1936 case of *St. Joseph Stock Yards Co. v. United States*[41] introduced the concept of the highest and best use in real estate valuations. Interestingly, the term *highest price* is used as part of fair market value in Canadian business valuations. The Canadian definition of fair market value is:

> The highest price, expressed in terms of cash equivalents, at which property would change hands between a hypothetical willing and able buyer and a hypothetical willing and able seller, acting at arm's length in an open and unrestricted market, when neither is under compulsion to buy or sell and when both have reasonable knowledge of the relevant facts.[42]

British and Canadian courts view fair market value as the highest price that could be achieved upon sale, as there may be consideration of a purchaser willing to include the value of synergies in their offer. Courts in the United States generally look to consider synergistic buyers in the context of investment value.[43] However, many courts have looked to determine the highest bid price that could be achieved by willing buyers. Both U.S. and Canadian practitioners acknowledge that if, in addition to ordinary purchasers, several special-interest purchasers are involved in the bidding, the market itself will eventually exclude the ordinary purchasers as the new equilibrium price would reflect the synergistic value.[44]

In Canada, if a willing and able strategic buyer can be identified, a strategic purpose premium may be added to the standalone fair market value to reflect the additional amount a strategic purchaser would pay, although that premium would be difficult to quantify. However, cases in both Canada and Great Britain do not allow a hypothetical strategic purchaser.[45] Instead, in order to apply a strategic premium, there must be evidence that an actual purchaser exists, has made an offer, is able to pay that price, and that these facts were known publicly.[46]

---

[41] *St. Joseph Stock Yards Co. v. United States*, 298 U.S. 38, 60 (1936).

[42] www.bvappraisers.org/glossary/glossary.pdf.

[43] Ian Campbell, *Canada Valuation Service* (Scarborough, ON: Carswell, October 2004), at 4–28.

[44] Shannon P. Pratt, *The Market Approach to Valuing Businesses* (Hoboken, NJ: John Wiley & Sons, 2001), at 142.

[45] Richard M. Wise, "The Effect of Special Interest Purchasers on Fair Market Value in Canada," *Business Valuation Review* (December 2003).

[46] *Dominion Metal & Refining Works, Ltd. v. The Queen*, 86 D.T.C. 6311 (Trial Division).

Although Canada has the "highest price" requirement, a premium is not necessarily required to reflect the highest price. A single strategic purchaser will not have to pay far above the fair market value to outbid regular market purchasers. If there were others willing to compete with the strategic purchaser at the higher price, a new market would be created where the equilibrium price will reflect any strategic premiums.[47]

In *Mueller v. Commissioner*,[48] the court looked to an expert analysis to determine the fair market value of a family corporation that was in the midst of a sale at the time of the decedent's death. The court received three separate valuations, one of which represented a range of values over which the fair market value could fall. All of these valuations considered a discount from the executed purchase price (due to uncertainty of sale and illiquidity) a few months after the decedent's death. One expert asserted that the willing buyer would be looking to obtain the low-end price and the willing seller would be looking to obtain the high-end price, and then averaged the two to find the fair market value. The court did not accept the midpoint in the range, but instead considered an auction-based environment, where the willing buyers will outbid each other until a maximum bid price is reached. The court ultimately accepted the high-end value.

The case of *BTR Dunlop Holdings, Inc. v. Commissioner*[49] addressed the issue of whether synergistic buyers should be considered as a factor in determining fair market value.

BTR DUNLOP HOLDINGS, INC. V. COMMISSIONER

In this case, BTR Dunlap, a wholly owned U.S. subsidiary of an international corporation, purchased Schlegel Corporation, a European company with various subsidiaries involved in the production of automobile and building products. The main issue in this case was the value of Schlegel UK, a British subsidiary of Schlegel with plants throughout England. Whereas the petitioner's (BTR Dunlap) experts attempted to value the entity on a standalone basis, the respondent (Commissioner) looked to value it as a synergistic acquisition.

(*continued*)

---

[47] Richard Wise, "The Effect of Special Interest Purchasers of Fair Market Value in Canada," 22 *Business Valuation Review, Quarterly Journal of the Business Valuation Committee of the American Society of Appraisers*, No. 4 (December 2003).

[48] T.C. Memo 1992-284; 1992 Tax Ct. Memo LEXIS 310; 63 T.C.M. (CCH) 3027.

[49] T.C. Memo 1999-377; 1999 Tax Ct. Memo LEXIS 432; 78 T.C.M. (CCH) 797.

Several experts were retained to value Schlegel UK and Schlegel GMBH at the date of purchase for tax purposes. While the petitioner (BTR Dunlap Holdings, the holding company for the now-merged shares of BTR Dunlap and Schlegel Corporation) asserted values of $21,846,000 and $9,400,000 for Schlegel UK and Schlegel GMBH respectively, the IRS came up with values of $49,069,000 and $13,246,000 respectively. The experts retained in the case came up with a range of values, using both market and income approaches, and allowed the impact of synergies to varying degrees.

The respondent's expert used a *capital asset pricing model (CAPM)* formula with a beta of .84 for Schlegel UK. He viewed the company as part of a strategic purchase to come to the $49,069,000 figure. The other valuation experts came to lower values, excluding the impact of synergies, or claiming that these synergies were minimal. The court's decision reflected that property should be valued at its highest and best use and the fact that synergistic purchasers available at the time of the company's sale provided sufficient evidence that synergies should be reflected in the valuation.

One of the petitioner's experts who excluded synergies from his calculation was asked whether he would sell the business for his figure. He replied that the business would be worth more to him and therefore he would not sell it at that figure. The court rejected the notion that the standalone price would be that which a willing buyer and a willing seller would agree on.

While not agreeing with the respondent expert's specific price, the court did agree that synergies must be accounted for in the ultimate valuation. To find the appropriate capitalization rate, the court adjusted the beta from the respondent's valuation upward to 1.18 and excluded the small-company risk premium and company-specific risk premium one of the petitioner's experts had applied. In the final determination, the court adjusted the valuations to arrive at a 20% capitalization rate, which included consideration of potential synergistic purchasers.

Valuation practitioners do not have the luxury of knowing whether the buyer with the highest synergistic value will prevail. Typically, no buyer is going to offer more than the market clearing price, and there may be several buyers willing to pay that price.[50] In a fair market value context, by

---

[50] Roger J. Grabowski, "Identifying Pool of Willing Buyers."

assuming reasonable knowledge and ability to negotiate at arm's length, it is likely that if synergistic buyers are available, they will bid to reach the highest price available for a business.

Roger Grabowski has pointed out:

> The first step in estimating fair market value should be assessing the make-up of the likely pool of hypothetical willing buyers. In this author's experience, the pool differs in cases where one is valuing a minority interest in a closely held entity versus cases where one is valuing controlling interests or entire closely-held companies.[51]

Knowledge of the marketplace for willing minority buyers typically includes the identities of the other shareholders and the blocks of stocks owned by those shareholders. When valuing controlling interests in closely held businesses, the valuation consultant should study the market of potential buyers, including entrepreneurs or financial buyers on the one hand or a pool of potentially synergistic or strategic buyers on the other hand.[52]

Unfortunately, there is no conclusive guidance on whether potential synergies are applicable in every determination of fair market value. Whether synergies are a relevant consideration will depend on the facts and circumstances of the case.

Valuation of Different Classes of Stock An interesting issue arises when valuing different types of stock held by one person. Nonvoting shares are generally less valuable than those with voting power and are generally valued at a discount when valued as standalone shares. However, when held in conjunction with control voting shares of a corporation, are they any less valuable to a potential willing buyer? The question is, would the buyer purchase one block of stock (both voting and nonvoting) at one price, or would the stock be considered as two blocks because of the two types of shares within? *The Estate of Curry v. United States*[53] addressed this issue.

---

[51] Roger J. Grabowski, "Fair Market Value and the Pool of Willing Buyers." Unpublished paper.

[52] *Id.*

[53] 7 06 F.2d 1424; 1983 U.S. App. LEXIS 28894; 83-1 U.S. Tax Cas. (CCH) P13, 518; 51 A.F.T.R.2d (RIA) 1232. This case was heard in the United States Federal District Court, in front of a jury.

ESTATE OF CURRY V. UNITED STATES

In this case, the estate held both voting and nonvoting shares of a privately held corporation. Initially, the jury accepted the estate's valuation, as it valued the two types of shares separately, with a nonvoting share discount for one block and a control premium for the other. The court had not informed the jury of the government's instructions, that the value of the nonvoting stock should be determined at the same level as the voting stock.

Upon review, the Court of Appeals concluded that the trial court had erred in rejecting the government's instruction that the stock should be viewed as a whole, as that is how it exists in the estate—as a block of shares having voting control over the corporation. The court suggested that the trial court arbitrarily disaggregated the shares under one possible subsequent transaction scenario.

The court quoted a previous Ninth Circuit decision that said, "There is nothing in the statutes or in the case law that suggests that valuation of the gross estate should take into account that the assets will come to rest in several hands rather than one."[54]

In addition, if fair market value assumes that a willing buyer will seek to maximize his advantage, he would purchase the whole block, rather than a portion thereof; otherwise the nonvoting shares would be at a significant disadvantage. Conversely, a willing seller would seek to sell the whole block in order to maximize the value of his shares.[55]

Estate of Simplot v. Commissioner[56] is another example of a case dealing with the valuation of different classes of stock.

ESTATE OF SIMPLOT V. COMMISSIONER

In *Estate of Simplot v. Commissioner,* Class A voting shares and Class B nonvoting shares were initially valued differently in an estate

---

[54] *Ahmanson Foundation v. United States,* 674 F.2d 761 (9th Cir. 1981).

[55] 706 F.2d 1424; 1983 U.S. App. LEXIS 28894; 83-1 U.S. Tax Cas. (CCH) P13,518; 51 A.F.T.R.2d (RIA) 1232.

[56] 249 F.3d 1191; 2001 U.S. App. LEXIS 9220.

valuation. The decedent, Richard Simplot, held 23.55% of the Class A voting shares and 2.79% of Class B nonvoting shares.

The estate obtained a valuation by Morgan Stanley that valued both Class A and B shares at $2,650 per share. The commissioner of Internal Revenue valued Class A shares with a premium as control shares and came to a value of $801,994 per share, and valued Class B shares at $3,585 per share. A deficiency of $17,662,886 was assessed with penalties of $7,057,554.

Upon petition, the Tax Court reasoned that the voting shares were substantially more valuable because a hypothetical buyer would be able to play a role in the company as an owner of voting shares. Additionally, the shares held by the decedent represented the largest single block of shares.

The court valued Class A shares at $331,595.70, subject to a 35% lack of marketability discount, arriving at a value of $215,539 per share, and valued Class B shares at $3,417 per share. The Tax Court determined a deficiency of $2,162,052 and removed the penalties.

The Ninth Circuit Court of Appeals reversed the Tax Court's judgment, citing that the Tax Court had valued all Class A shares as a whole and took a pro rata value rather than valuing the minority share held by the estate. In addition, upon liquidation, the Class A shareholders would be no better off than Class B shareholders, and the dividends paid were the same. Therefore, there would be no economic advantage of holding a minority share of voting stock leading to the application of a premium. The judgment of the Tax Court was reversed and remanded for judgment in favor of the estate.

This holding should not be confused with the treatment of discounts addressed in Revenue Ruling 93-12 (family attribution). This Revenue Ruling addresses the situation where the holder owns a noncontrolling share of stock, but the family as a whole owns a control share (either before or after the decedent's shares are acquired). This ruling instructs that the gifted or bequeathed shares should *not* be valued as a family unit, but should be valued in their form as held by the estate. Revenue Ruling 93-12 also specifically refers to a corporation with a single class of stock, and therefore is not in conflict with either case just described.[57] The ruling refers to the particular buyer or seller, while the "one-block" concept may be applied to any willing seller owning both classes of stock.

---

[57] IRS Revenue Ruling 93-12.

Willing Seller

Like the willing buyer, the willing seller considers certain information before deciding to engage in a transaction, including liquidity, alternative uses for the investment, future cash flows, and risk.[58] A willing seller is one who can be convinced to sell for the right price, for a variety of reasons, including gaining liquidity or desiring the ability to invest in a higher-yielding investment. The hypothetical buyer evaluates the same economic and financial conditions as the seller. Therefore, when a hypothetical seller chooses not to sell, theoretically, he or she willingly buys the asset by retaining the interest with the asset's existing opportunity costs and associated liquidity (or illiquidity). The owner prefers owning the property to the alternative of selling it.

The Tax Court has been critical of those who view fair market value from only the perspective of the buyer. Both the buyers' and the sellers' perspectives should be considered. In the case of *Mandelbaum v. Commissioner*,[59] the court addressed one expert's overreliance on a willing buyer while ignoring the need for a willing seller.

MANDELBAUM V. COMMISSIONER

In a family-owned retail conglomerate, Big M, Inc., the court sought to devise a fair market value for the purposes of a gift tax over a period of five years. The respondent's (IRS's) expert asserted a 30% marketability discount was appropriate, relying on three "restricted stock" studies, the notion that the shareholders' agreements do not seriously affect marketability, and the fact that the risk associated with holding Big M stock is neutralized by the size of the company and the stable gross profits.

The petitioner's (taxpayer's) expert, however, contended that a 75% marketability discount applies to the value for the first four years in question while a 70% discount applies for the last. This expert concluded that Big M's stock was virtually illiquid and assumed that an investor would have to wait 10 to 20 years for the investment to become liquid. The expert relied on the facts that members of the Mandelbaum family have always owned Big M, the family had no plans to seek outside investors, Big M's senior management was far from retirement, and the gifts at issue did not affect management.

---

[58] Z. Christopher Mercer, *Quantifying Marketability Discounts* (Memphis, TN: Peabody, 1997), at 178.
[59] T.C. Memo 1995-255; 1995 Tax Ct. Memo LEXIS 256; 69 T.C.M. (CCH) 2852.

The court rejected both experts' valuations and looked to determine the marketability discount independently. In its view, the respondent's expert did not put enough weight on the fact that there was a shareholder agreement in place that would restrict value. The petitioner's expert placed too much weight on the willing buyer's expectations in terms of rate of return and the restrictive nature of the shareholder agreement, and misidentified the willing buyers by interviewing the types of investors who would require a higher rate of return. In providing an above-average marketability discount, the petitioner's expert ignored the perspective of a hypothetical willing seller.

In the court's own review, it used the petitioner's expert's determination of the average marketability discount and reviewed the factors in Exhibit 2.1 to come to its conclusion on the size of the applicable marketability discount (which coincidentally equaled the respondent's conclusion).

Reviewing these factors and the conclusions that followed, the court found that because of the facts and circumstances of the case, a below-average discount was required. It applied a 30% discount.

EXHIBIT 2.1 Factors and Adjusted Benchmark Percentages in *Mandelbaum*

Factor	Conclusion
Studies of private versus public sales of the stock	Benchmark for the marketability discounts should be set between 35% and 45%
Financial statement analysis	Below-average discount
Company's dividend policy	Below-average discount
Nature of the company, its history, its position in the industry, and its economic outlook	Below-average discount
Company's management	Below-average discount
Amount of control in transferred shares	Average discount
Restrictions on transferability of stock	Above-average discount
Holding period for stock	Neutral
Company's redemption policy	Below-average discount
Costs associated with making a public offering	Above-average discount
Court's final conclusion:	**30% Marketability discount**

This case points out that consideration of a willing buyer is not enough. A willing buyer seeking stock in Big M would likely demand a large discount on its value based on the family nature of the company and the agreements in place. However, if shareholders of Big M were willing to sell, that might lead to a substantially different value.

Another example of having to consider the willing seller is the recent case of *Giustina v. Commissioner.*[60]

GIUSTINA V. COMMISSIONER

This case dealt with the fair market value of a 41.128% limited partnership interest in a partnership running forestry operations. The issue in this estate tax case was the weight accorded the discounted cash flow method as compared to the net asset value method in determining the value of this minority interest. Although operating as a going concern, the partnership owned a substantial amount of timberlands. As would be expected in this type of business, the discounted cash flow method produced a value substantially below the net asset value method. The power to sell the partnership's timber and other property resided with the general partners while the interest in question was a limited partnership interest and, therefore, had no ability to cause a sale of the assets. The court noted, however, that a general partner could be removed by the concurrence of limited partners owning two-thirds of the interests in the partnership.

Referencing the *Estate of Davis*,[61] the *Giustina* court indicated that the willing buyer and willing seller would be hypothetical, rather than specific, individuals and that these hypothetical participants would be presumed to be dedicated to achieving the maximum economic advantage. Accordingly, the court noted that, although the limited partner did not have the power to solely cause the removal of a general partner, under the theory that a willing buyer would seek the maximum economic benefit from the asset, either the owner of the 41.128% block could, in essence, join with other limited partners to replace the two general partners with two partners who would sell the assets, or the vote of two-thirds of the limited partners could cause the dissolution of the partnership.

---

[60] *Giustina v. Commissioner*, T.C. Memo 11-141.

[61] *Davis v. Commissioner.* 1998 U.S. Tax Ct. LEXIS 35, Daily Tax Report (BNA) No. 126, at K-17 (T.C. June 30, 1998).

> This rationale was used to estimate the probability of a sale of the assets, which, as the court conceded, was uncertain but not improbable. Accordingly, the court assigned a 25% weight to the net asset value method. Further, the court presumed that a discount for lack of control was impounded in the 25% weight assigned to the net asset value. It also presumed that the 40% discount applied to the real property valuation was to reflect the delays in selling the land. No discount for lack of marketability to the results from the net asset value method was warranted.

Earlier we briefly discussed the *family attribution* principle in Revenue Ruling 93-12. This issue is best understood from the point of view of the willing seller. In the case of *Bright v. United States*,[62] the government attempted to add a control premium to non-controlling shares of the decedent's wife because the husband owned the balance of the shares that would add up to a controlling value when combined with the wife's shares. The government claimed that the husband would not be willing to sell his 27.5% of the shares unless it was part of the 55% control block combined with the decedent's shares. The court cited several cases where this type of family attribution was rejected, ultimately rejecting the government's argument and affirming the district court's ruling that the interest to be valued was only the 27.5% common stock interest. This brings us back to the fact that a seller is a hypothetical willing seller, selling in a hypothetical market, rather than a specific individual selling in a specific market. The question was not the value the estate would accept if it held 27.5% of shares that could potentially be sold as part of a 55% control block, as the government contended, but instead the value that a willing seller would accept for 27.5% of a property's shares.

A similar issue was discussed in the case of *Propstra v. United States*.[63] In this case, the Court of Appeals addressed issues of the willing seller and control as well as of the effect of subsequent events on claims against property.

---

[62] 658 F.2d 999; 1981 U.S. App. LEXIS 17205; 81-2 U.S. Tax Cas. (CCH) P13,436; 48 A.F.T.R.2d (RIA) 6159; 48 A.F.T.R.2d (RIA) 6292.
[63] 680 F.2d 1248; 1982 U.S. App. LEXIS 17696; 82-2 U.S. Tax Cas. (CCH) P13,475; 50 A.F.T.R.2d (RIA) 6153.

PROPSTRA V. UNITED STATES

At the death of Arthur Price, his estate was comprised mainly of property shared by him and his wife, the executrix of the estate. John Propstra was the estate's personal representative. Upon Price's death and the valuation of his estate for tax purposes, his wife made two adjustments: One was a 15% lack of marketability discount for an undivided one-half interest in parcels of real estate and another an adjustment for liens against the property for penalties and assessments by the Salt River Valley Water Users' Association that remained unsettled.

On the first issue of the discount for partial ownership, the government argued that the estate must prove that the property was likely to be sold as a partial interest in a parcel of real estate rather than as an undivided interest by the estate. The court found that there was no reason to see a hypothetical seller as necessarily belonging to the estate and that indeed the property to be valued at fair market value and by its definition was the one-half interest. The court found this situation analogous to that in *Bright v. United States*.[64]

On the second issue of the lien, at the time of the initial tax payment, Mrs. Price was looking to settle the claims with the Salt River Valley Water Users' Association. At that time, however, the association's bylaws did not allow the settlement claims for less than the full amount due, and the tax deduction was based on this understanding. After the decedent's death and the payment of the estate taxes, the association amended its bylaws and settled the claims against the property owned by the Prices for less than the full amount owed. The government looked to recoup the taxes that the estate had deducted because of the full lien on the property at the time of death.

The Court of Appeals found that at the time of death, there was no anticipation that the association would settle the claim due to its bylaws at the time, regardless of Mrs. Price's hope that the claim would be settled. It ruled that, as a matter of law, "when claims are for sums certain and are legally enforceable as of the date of death, post-death events are not relevant in computing the permissible deduction."

---

[64] 658 F.2d 999; 1981 U.S. App. LEXIS 17205; 81-2 U.S. Tax Cas. (CCH) P13,436; 48 A.F.T.R.2d (RIA) 6159; 48 A.F.T.R.2d (RIA) 6292.

No Compulsion to Buy or Sell

In the real world, the parties involved in a transaction may be compelled to buy or sell based on involvement in bankruptcy or insolvency, a need for immediate liquidity, the need of an immediate sale for charitable purposes, or a variety of factors.[65] This is another reason that a sale price in and of itself is not necessarily evidence of fair market value. In a fair market value transaction, the buyer and seller have equal negotiating power. The buyer is looking for the lowest price at which to buy, and a seller is looking for the highest price to sell.[66] There will be competition in the marketplace from other bidders willing to offer a higher price or from other sellers willing to sell for less. The fact that there is no compulsion to sell also suggests that the company be valued with ample exposure to an appropriate market, rather than in a forced liquidation.[67]

In the 1923 Tax Court case *Walter v. Duffy*,[68] the court addressed the value of stock in what was judged to be a forced liquidation.

WALTER V. DUFFY

Emeline C. Blanchard owned 1,890 shares of Prudential Life Insurance stock. The government looked to assess and tax the increase in value of the stock based on the value of a sale in 1915, where 1,881.41 shares were transferred for $455 per share.

Unaware of the cost of Blanchard's initial purchase, the IRS based the incremental increase on the difference between $455 per share and a sale at $262.50 per share that had occurred two years prior to this transfer.

However, the individual who had sold the shares for the $262.50 price testified that he had sold the shares solely to achieve necessary liquidity to satisfy several loan debts. This was evidence that the seller was compelled to seek a quick sale to satisfy creditors. Had he not been so compelled, the stock would have had greater exposure to the market and he likely could have held out for a higher figure.

The court held that the $262.50 value could not have been a fair market price and a reassessment was ordered by virtue of a new trial.

---

[65] Bogdanski, *Federal Tax Valuation*, at 2.01[2][b].

[66] Jay Fishman and Bonnie O'Rourke, "Value: More Than a Superficial Understanding Is Required," 15 *Journal of the American Academy of Matrimonial Lawyers*, No. 2 (1998).

[67] *Id.*

[68] 287 F.41, 45 (3d Cir. 1923).

There may be many types of compulsion. Financial pressure might cause a buyer or seller to act more quickly, thereby causing insufficient exposure to the marketplace. In the case of *Troxel Manufacturing Co. v. Commissioner*,[69] the sale of the property was seen to be made in haste, as the seller was in urgent need of cash and had to sacrifice a particular property at a price less than its supposed real value. The court in that case decided that the sale was not an arm's-length transaction and that the price reached was not representative of fair market value. However, the desire for cash in lieu of property may be viewed by some as a preference rather than compulsion, as represented by the dissenting opinion in *McGuire v. Commissioner*,[70] where a dissenting judge states that a seller is not necessarily unwilling if the decision to sell is a matter of wanting cash over property.

Importance of Restrictive Agreements   Transactions in a hypothetical market may not be subject to the restrictions that may exist on an open market. That does not mean, however, that these restrictions cannot or should not be considered in a fair market value transaction. Instead, buyers are often assumed to account for these restrictions in assessing the value of the business interest because they themselves will be subject to these restrictions after purchase.[71]

Internal Revenue Code (IRC) § 2703(b)[72] sets forth four general considerations in determining the applicability of a buy–sell agreement to fair market value.

1. The agreement must be a bona-fide business arrangement.
2. It must not be a device to transfer property to family members for less than full and adequate consideration.
3. The agreement must be entered into pursuant to an arm's-length transaction.
4. It must also be binding both before and after the holder's death.[73]

The courts generally have respected restrictions on transfers in determining fair market value, often applying discounts for lack of marketability. In some divorce cases, great weight is afforded restrictive agreements in determining value as long as that agreement is kept current and is used

---

[69] 1 B.T.A. 653,655 (1925).

[70] 44 T.C. 801,813 (1965).

[71] Campbell, *Canada Valuation Service*, at 4–32.

[72] U.S. Code Title 26, Section 2703(b).

[73] Stephen C. Gara and Craig J. Langstraat, "Property Valuation for Transfer Taxes," 12 *Akron Tax Journal*, Vol. 125(1996), at 139.

regularly in the course of business; other cases have found these agreements to have no true influence on value as they have never been used. The Tax Court was confronted with the issue of a restrictive agreement in the *Estate of Lauder v. Commissioner*.[74]

ESTATE OF LAUDER V. COMMISSIONER

Estate of Lauder v. Commissioner addressed the valuation of shares in the decedent's estate based on the applicability of a restrictive agreement that afforded the corporation the right of first refusal in the purchase of a departed shareholder's shares at book value.

The terms of the agreement were executed upon Lauder's death. The initial Tax Court's review (*Estate of Lauder v. Commissioner*, T.C. Memo. 1992-736) decided that the agreement was not determinative of fair market value, but instead a device by which shareholders could transfer their shares to their family for less than adequate consideration (thereby violating the requirement of IRC section 2703(b)). The court held that the shareholders' agreement was not controlling for the valuation of the decedent's stock at his death because it did not reflect fair market value at the time it was executed.

In the subsequent case to value the shares (*Estate of Lauder v. Commissioner*, T.C. Memo. 1994-527) the court reviewed the valuations provided by various experts and ultimately adopted a valuation method proposed by Lehman Brothers, because their analysis emphasized that "the price/earnings ratios of comparable companies within the industry, provides the most objective and reliable basis for determining the fair market value of the stock in question."

The court valued the company using a 12.2 multiple of price to earnings and applied a 40% discount due to illiquidity to arrive at the fair market value of the stock.

Another significant case, *Estate of Joyce Hall v. Commissioner*,[75] may be distinguished from Lauder in its consideration that the fair market value of a corporation is affected by certain restrictions in the shareholder agreements. In this case, the agreements were *not* found to be in place simply for the purpose of an intergenerational wealth transfer.

---

[74]T.C. Memo 1994-527; 1994 Tax Ct. Memo LEXIS 535; 68 T.C.M. (CCH) 985.
[75]92 T.C. 312; 1989 U.S. Tax Ct. LEXIS 24; 92 T.C. No. 19.

ESTATE OF JOYCE HALL V. COMMISSIONER

In this case, the company in question, Hallmark, was intentionally kept private by the decedent and his family. There were three classes of stock:Class A preferred stock, Class B common voting stock, and Class C common nonvoting stock. The estate included shares of both B and C common stock. All classes of stock were subject to restrictions.

Subject to a 1963 indenture, these shares were required to be offered to a "permitted transferee," that is, Hallmark, members of the Hall family or their estates, and trusts set up for their benefits. Only after this exercise could the stock be sold to an outsider. Additionally, the indenture provided that Class B shares could be purchased at their adjusted book value, with the possibility of a payment plan for cash and installments. Should the shares be purchased by an outside holder, the interest would still be subject to the same restrictions on any subsequent transfer. The same sale restrictions were in place for the Class C common shares.

In 1981, Hall entered into an option agreement with Hallmark to purchase his shares not subject to other buy–sell provisions. Upon Hall's death, Hallmark's directors voted to exercise that option and purchase those shares at the adjusted book value as of December 31, 1981.

The adjusted book value was computed annually by virtue of a formula provided by the 1963 indenture. At the valuation date, Hallmark computed the adjusted book value at $1.98157 per Class B common share and $1.87835 per Class C common share.

The commissioner argued that the adjusted book value could not be the fair market value because of the possibility of "permitted transferees" buying the stock at a higher price. The court did not allow this contention because, unlike Lauder, there was no evidence that even a permitted buyer would pay more than the adjusted book value, and in addition, this contention suggested the relevant buyer for the purposes of valuation was a specific class of buyer, a concept that ignored the requirement of a hypothetical willing buyer.

The court decided: "Agreements and restrictions not invalid on their face cannot be disregarded on such tenuous evidence of coincidence. . . . After weighing the respective opinions of the parties' experts, we cannot conclude that the fair market value is more than the adjusted book value of the stock."

Alternatively, the value set by a restrictive agreement was ignored in *Estate of Obering v. Commissioner.*[76] In this matter, the agreement gave the first option to the corporation and the other shareholders to purchase the stock at a set price, but allowed sale to the public should the corporation or the shareholders not elect to make the purchase. Because the agreement did not completely exclude a third party from purchasing the stock, the court precluded its representation of fair market value.

In addition to the requirements set forth by IRC section 2703(b),[77] buy–sell agreements are scrutinized for their reasonableness, whether they are periodically reviewed, and whether the price arrived at is representative of an arm's-length transaction. This is especially important when the shares of a company are held by family members, where often buy–sell agreements are viewed as testamentary devices that transfer shares at artificially low values. The courts will likely also look at the events and circumstances surrounding the execution of the agreement in determining whether it is a valid agreement. These events might include relationship of the parties, the purpose of the agreement, and the source of the agreement price.[78]

Reasonable Knowledge of Relevant Facts

Known and Knowable   Fair market value requires that both the willing buyer and the willing seller be reasonably informed of the relevant facts affecting the property in question. This information is generally referred to as that which was "known or knowable" at the valuation date. As discussed earlier, in determining fair market value, a reasonable degree of knowledge is assumed. A valuation at fair market value should include information that is known by any party to the transaction as well as any information that may not be apparent at the valuation date but would have been knowable at that time by the parties involved.[79]

The Fifth Circuit Court of Appeals case *United States v. Simmons*[80] demonstrates that value may exist, even if it is unknown at the valuation date. In this case, after the decedent's death, the estate hired an accountant to investigate the decedent's tax filings. After discovering evidence of

---

[76] 48 T.C.M. (CCH) 733 (1984).

[77] U.S. Code Title 26, § 2701.

[78] Stephen C. Gara and Craig J. Longstraat, "Property Valuation for Transfer Taxes," at 12 Akron Tax J 139.

[79] Bogdanski, *Federal Tax Valuation*, at 2.01[3][a].

[80] 346 F.2d 213; 1965 U.S. App. LEXIS 5425; 65-2 U.S. Tax Cas. (CCH) P12,321; 15 A.F.T.R.2d (RIA) 1430.

a deficiency payment made in error, the estate filed a claim for a refund. In the meantime, when the estate filed its estate tax returns, it assessed the claim at no value because there was no certainty that it would ever have any value. Eventually, the claim did settle for $41,187. In a trial to determine whether the $41,187 should be included in the estate, the jury found that the claim had no value at the decedent's death. The Court of Appeals did not agree. The court reasoned that even if the fact that the claim had value was unknown, the estate suspected that value existed because it retained professionals to investigate the decedent's tax records. Consequently, the Court of Appeals ruled that, although the estate may not have known that value existed, value (even if not in the full amount of the settlement) did indeed exist at the time of death.

Reasonable knowledge (as intended by the definition of fair market value) does not require that a buyer have all information and be totally informed, as some previous revenue procedures have suggested.[81] Additionally, Revenue Ruling 78-367 suggests that sellers will overemphasize the favorable facts and buyers will attempt to elicit all the negative information pertaining to a sale. These are two extreme views. In the real world, the requirement of perfect knowledge is likely to be unachievable. In determining fair market value, only reasonable knowledge of the relevant facts should be assumed. Therefore, cases addressing this point have insisted only on reasonable knowledge of the relevant facts.[82] As one commentator noted:

> Reasonable knowledge is a level of awareness that usually falls somewhere between perfect knowledge and complete ignorance—even if the actual owner of the property is at one extreme or the other.[83]

Estate of Tully v. United States[84] held that knowable information that may not be known by the owner can affect the determination of value. In this case, the decedent was not aware that company officials had been illegally rigging bids for contracts with the company's biggest customer. This information came to light four years after the valuation date. The court viewed the bid rigging as a knowable event (although unknown) that could affect value at the valuation date. The court reasoned that information was available at the valuation date that could have led to the discovery of this wrongdoing, particularly, that the gross profits of the business were so high compared to industry standards that careful inspection of the records could

---

[81] IRS Revenue Procedure 66-49.
[82] Bogdanski, *Federal Tax Valuation*, at 2.01[3][a].
[83] *Id.*, at 2.01[3][a], 2–47.
[84] 41 A.F.T.R.2d 1477 (Ct. Cl. Tr. Div. 1978) (not officially reported), at 1490.

have led to the discovery of this impropriety. Therefore, in determining the company's value, the court discounted the value by 30% due to the information that could have been discovered on the valuation date with proper investigation.[85]

Postvaluation-Date Information and Subsequent Events Since valuation is as of a particular point in time, practitioners are required to reach their conclusions based on information that is known or knowable (or reasonably foreseeable) at the valuation date. Typically, in a retrospective valuation, postvaluation-date information may be available. Subsequent events that were foreseeable at the valuation date may be considered in a valuation. However, if an event was completely unforeseen at the date of valuation, it is generally not considered. Although the practitioner might want this data to have been available at the valuation date, the possibility of occurrence is not the same as a recognizable probability, and it is important for the practitioner to use judgment in determining that information was truly knowable as of that time. A court may go to great lengths to determine what was known or knowable at the valuation date regarding information or factors affecting value.

The Tax Court's decision in the case *Couzens v. Commissioner*[86] described the ability to include subsequent events if indeed they were reasonably foreseeable at the date of valuation. The court stated:

> Serious objection was urged by [the government] to the admission in evidence of data as to events which occurred after [the valuation period]. It was urged that such facts were necessarily unknown on that date and hence could not be considered. . . . [I]t is true that value . . . is not to be judged by subsequent events. There is, however, substantial importance of the reasonable expectations entertained on that date. *Subsequent events may serve to establish that the expectations were entertained and also that such expectations were reasonable and intelligent.* Our consideration of them has been confined to this purpose. [Emphasis added]

The issue of what was known or knowable as applied to the financial results of the company and its publicly traded counterparts is one that practitioners often encounter. What happens when the valuation date is a few weeks or months prior to the formal issuance of certain financial information? This issue was recently addressed in *Gallgher Estate v. Commissioner*.[87]

---

[85] The court also applied a discount for lack of control for unrelated reasons.

[86] *Couzens v. Commissioner*, 11 B.T.A. 1040; 1928 B.T.A. LEXIS 3663.

[87] *Gallagher Estate v. Commissioner*, T.C. Memo 2011-148.

In *Gallagher*, the issue was which financial statements for the company and its publicly traded counterparts should have been used. The date of death was July 5, 2004. The appraiser hired, on behalf of the IRS, used internally generated financial statements for the period of June 27, 2004, and financial information for the guideline public companies for the quarter ended June 30, 2004. The Estate's appraiser used the latest (at July 5, 2004) issued internally generated financial statements as of May 30, 2004, and data for the guideline public companies as of the closest quarter, or March 28, 2004, under the assumption that the participants in the hypothetical transaction would not have known of the latest financial statements.

The Tax Court agreed with the IRS expert that the June 2004 financial statements should have been used in valuing the decedent's units. The court opined that, although the June financial information was not publicly available as of the valuation date, the "hypothetical actors"[88] could make inquiries of both the subject and guideline public companies and elicit non-publicly available information as to the end-of-June conditions. Further, the court indicated that the June 2004 financial information accurately depicts the market conditions on the valuation date and that there were no intervening events between the valuation date and the June financial statements that would cause them to be incorrect.

This is another example of a court going beyond what was technically known or knowable to reach an equitable conclusion.

Other cases in the Tax Court have dealt with unexpected windfalls after the valuation date. In the case of *Ridgely v. United States*, the decedent owned a 368-acre farm valued at $372 per acre.[89] Around the time of death, the family tried to sell 40 acres of the farm to a local school board for $3,000 per acre. The family reduced the sale price to $2,000 and finally to $1,000. The school board declined to purchase the land because the location was not desirable. The decedent died in January 1962. In February of that year, General Foods began a search for land for a new Jell-O plant. In May 1962, General Foods purchased 112 acres of land for $2,700 per acre. While the IRS claimed that the entire tract was worth $2,700 per acre, the court did not consider the General Foods transaction as an indicator of value, as no one could have foreseen the purchase at the time of death.

As mentioned previously, in the *Estate of Tully*, the court allowed the use of postvaluation-date information some four years after the valuation date to determine what was knowable at the valuation date.[90] The courts have generally acknowledged that evidence of value at the valuation date

---

[88] The Court's characterization, at 15.

[89] 20 A.F.T.R.2d 5946 (1967).

[90] 41 A.F.T.R.2d 1477 (Ct. Cl. Tr. Div. 1978) (not officially reported), at 1490.

may be considered, while events affecting value after the valuation date, which were not reasonably foreseeable, are generally not considered.[91] An example of this is the case of *Estate of Jung v. Commissioner*, where the price of a postvaluation-date sale was used to value the company.[92]

ESTATE OF JUNG V. COMMISSIONER

In the case of *Estate of Jung v. Commissioner*, a postvaluation-date sale was used to demonstrate that the business was undervalued in the initial estate valuation. The case involved 20.74% of shares outstanding in Jung Corp., an integrated manufacturer and distributor of elastics.

The court looked to determine the fair market value of the decedent's interest at the date of death. The business was valued at the date of death in 1984 at $33 million, and a 35% discount for lack of marketability was to be applied to the decedent's pro-rata share. Two years later, in 1986, a majority of shares were sold to an outside company and the remainder was liquidated. The ultimate value of the company's equity appeared to have been over $60 million.

The court's opinion made clear that the sale of the company was not foreseeable at the valuation date; however, the court was persuaded by the IRS argument that the sale soon after the valuation was evidence that the value was understated at the valuation date, rather than an event that affected value.

Similarly, in *Estate of Scanlan v. Commissioner*,[93] prior to the decedent's death, shares were gifted to six family members and appraised at $34.84 per share. The date-of-death value was $35.20. Both figures included a 35% marketability discount derived by comparison with publicly traded companies. After the decedent's death, the company received an offer of $75.15 per share, and family members exercised their right to have the company buy out any other shareholders at that price. The IRS considered this information and valued the stock at $72.15 per share and applied a 4% minority discount. The family argued that the offers were for the entire company, not

---

[91] Although, as illustrated by *Tully*, *Gallagher*, and *Couszens*, consideration of post-valuation date events are a function of particular facts and circumstances and, in some cases, the courts have gone to great lengths to indicate they were foreseeable and sometimes used even when it is acknowledged they were not foreseeable.

[92] 101 T.C. 412; 1993 U.S. Tax Ct. LEXIS 69; 101 T.C. No. 28.

[93] T.C. Memo. 1996-331 (7/24/96).

the estate's minority share. As it was so near the valuation date, the court allowed the offer to be considered, but then applied a 30% combined minority and marketability discount and arrived at a value of $50.21 per share.

The same issue was addressed in *Estate of Cidulka v. Commissioner*,[94] where a sale of a commercial billboard corporation four years after the date of death was utilized to establish fair market value. The court acknowledged that four years may be considered too remote to have bearing on the valuation of the stock at the earlier date, but the multiplier for the later sale was similar to that of the sales of comparable companies around the valuation date, and therefore the evidence of the later sale was applicable to the valuation at the valuation date. As will be seen in the next chapter, in some venues this principle has been extended to the determination of fair value in dissenting shareholder actions.

Generally, the courts are careful to note whether later events have changed the value of the property. The distinction between a subsequent event affecting value as contrasted with the event providing evidence of value may be best illustrated by an example set forth in the case of *First National Bank v. United States*.[95] The court stated:

> For instance, if the proposition advanced is that a farm had a Fair Market Value of $800,000 on March 13, the fact that oil was unexpectedly discovered on June 13 (causing the Fair Market Value of the property to skyrocket) makes the proposition advanced no more or less likely. However, the fact that someone under no compulsion to buy and with knowledge of the relevant facts bought the property on June 13 for $1,000,000 is relevant, for it makes the proposition advanced (i.e., that the Fair Market Value on March 13 was $800,000) less likely.[96]

As can be seen, the use of postvaluation-date information dealing both with events that affect value (known or knowable) and with those that provide evidence of value (subsequent transactions) depends on the facts and circumstances of each particular case. Indeed, a plethora of cases have addressed this issue. Exhibit 2.2 presents a compendium of cases compiled by Michael Mard of the Financial Valuation Group dealing with subsequent events in estate and gift tax cases. The cases on this list span from 1929 to 2005, and the chart references the key considerations of each decision.

---

[94]T.C. Memo 1996-149; 1996 Tax Ct. Memo LEXIS 157; 71 T.C.M. (CCH) 2555.
[95]763 F.2d 891; 1985 U.S. App. LEXIS 19780; 85-2 U.S. Tax Cas. (CCH) P13,620; 56 A.F.T.R.2d (RIA) 6492; 18 Fed. R. Evid. Serv. (Callaghan) 290.
[96]*Id.*

EXHIBIT 2.2 Compendium of Cases

DATE	JURISDICTION	REFERS TO CASE(S)	REFERENCE TO USE OF SUBSEQUENT INFORMATION
1929	United States Supreme Court	*ITHACA TRUST CO. v. U.S.* (279 U.S. 151 (1929))	The value of the thing to be taxed must be estimated as of the time when the act is done. Like all values, as the word is used by the law, it depends largely on more or less certain prophecies of the future, and the value is no less real at that time if later the prophecy turns out false than when it comes true.
1956	United States Court of Appeals, Eighth Circuit	*FITTS' Estate v. Commissioner,* 237 F 2d 729 (8th Cir. 1956)	It was determined in this case that actual sales made in reasonable amounts in arm's-length transactions, in the normal course of business, within a reasonable time frame after or before the date of value, are the best criteria of market value.
1964	United States Court of Appeals, Seventh Circuit	*Chester D. TRIPP v.* Commissioner (No. 14560 (1964))	In this case, the court chose to use the purchase price of an antique jewelry collection (given to charity two and one-half years after date of purchase) to establish value because it found "no substantial evidence that any situation arose or development occurred in the interim which increased the value of the collection."
1972	United States Tax Court	*Estate of David SMITH* (57 TCM 650)	The dissenting Tax Court judge stated that more weight should be given to the actual sales of a sculptor's art both before and after his death as uncontested evidence of value.
1975	United States Supreme Court	*LOWE v. Commissioner* (4236 U.S. 827 (1975))	Sales after the valuation date "may be used to corroborate the ultimate determination of value."
1983	United States Tax Court	*Estate of JEPHSO v.. Commissioner* (81 TCM 999)	The Tax Court ruled that ". . . subsequent events may be considered for the limited purpose of substantiating reasonable expectations."

(continued)

EXHIBIT 2.2 (*continued*)

DATE	JURISDICTION	REFERS TO CASE(S)	REFERENCE TO USE OF SUBSEQUENT INFORMATION
1987	United States Tax Court	*Estate of Saul R. GILFORD* (88 TCM 38)	In this case the price of decedent's stock was determined by the price it was sold for in a merger six months after the date of death.
1987	United States Tax Court	*Estate of Euil S. SPRUILL* (88 TCM 1197)	In this case, the court considered the actual selling price of real estate that was sold 14 months after the date of death to determine value.
1989	United States Tax Court	*Estate of Ruben RODRIGUEZ* (56 TCM 1033)	Evidence showed that the business lost customers and suffered a sharp decline in profits after the death of the decedent. The court upheld the reduction in value due to loss of key employee.
1989	United States Claims Court	*KRAPF, Jr. v. U.S.* (89-2 USTC par. 9448 (U.S. Claims Court 1989))	In this case, the court made two exceptions to the general rule that valuations must be made without reference to events that occur after the valuation date by stating, "First, post-gift date can be used in valuation when there has been no material change of circumstances or conditions in the cooperation between the valuation date . . . and the subsequent information). Second, the post-gift evidence is indicative of gift value when the subsequent information could have been foreseen on the valuation date."
1989	United States Court of Appeals, District of Columbia Circuit	*Charles S. FOLTZ v. U.S. News & World* RztReport Report (98-7151 U.S.App. (D.C. Jan. 13, 1989))	The court noted: "The approach to be used is not retrospective, but prospective. One must look at the situation as of the time that each employee separated from the company. Therefore, the appropriate inquiry is whether the company was properly valued during the class period, not whether former employees become eligible for a greater share of benefits upon the contingency of a subsequent sale."

EXHIBIT 2.2 *(continued)*

DATE	JURISDICTION	REFERS TO CASE(S)	REFERENCE TO USE OF SUBSEQUENT INFORMATION
1992	United States Tax Court	*Estate of Bessie I. MUELLER* (63 TCM (CCH) 3027)	In this case subsequent events, which occurred 67 days after date of death, were admissible by the Tax Court and allowed to set the value of the shares of stock in question at the date of death on the premise that merger negotiations were initiated prior to the date of death.
1992	United States District Court, M.D. Pennsylvania	*GETTYSBURG National Bank v. U.S.* (1992 WL 472022 (M.D. Pa.))	This case deals with a suit brought to recognize a sale price lower than the appraised value submitted in the estate tax return. The court allowed the use of a real estate sales price that occurred 16 months after the date of death to determine value at the date of death.
1993	United States Tax Court	*Estate of JUNG v. Commissioner* (101 TCM 412 (1993))	A common argument as evidenced by this case is that a subsequent sale does not affect the value on an earlier valuation date; rather it is evidence to that value.
1993	United States District Court, S.D. Florida	*RUBENSTEIN v. U.S.* (826 F. Supp. 448 (S.D. Florida 1993))	This court allowed a pending settlement of a claim made subsequent to the valuation date to be considered in the determination of value, even though a lawsuit had yet to be filed at the date of death.
1994	United States Tax Court	*Estate of Robert C. SCULL v. Commissioner* (67 TCM (CCH) 2953)	The Tax Court ruled that actual selling price at an art auction held 10 1/2 months after the date of death of Scull was the best evidence of the fair market value of works of art in the estate.
1994	United States Tax Court	*SALTZMAN v. Commissioner* (TCM 1544, 1559)	The Tax Court ruled: "The test to consider a later sale is not whether the sale is forseeable, but is rather whether or not later events have materially changed the value of the property."

(continued)

71

EXHIBIT 2.2 (*continued*)

DATE	JURISDICTION	REFERS TO CASE(S)	REFERENCE TO USE OF SUBSEQUENT INFORMATION
1994	United States District Court, E.D. Virginia, Norfolk Division	*Estate of Virginia C. ANDREWS v. U.S.* (850 F. Supp. 1279)	The court ruled that events occurring subsequent to death permit consideration of evidence of actual price received after date of death so long as sale occurred within reasonable time after death and no intervening events drastically changed the value of the asset.
1995	United States Tax Court	*Estate of Dominick A. NECASTRO* (68 TCM 227)	The Tax Court did not allow a reduction in the value of property based on the possibility that contamination might have existed at the valuation date. However, nearly four years after the valuation date, postmortem information was obtained and admitted, which resulted in a revised valuation.
1995	United States Federal District Court, Seventh Circuit	*The FIRST NATIONAL BANK OF KENOSHA v. U.S.* (763 F.2d 891)	In this case, the estate had been approached 15 months after the valuation date about a purchase of the property. The court allowed the postmortem event into evidence, thus impacting the jury's determination of value.
1995	United States Tax Court	*Estate of Max SHLENSKY* (36 TCM 629)	In this case, subsequent events that occurred 15 months after the date of death were admissible by the Tax Court and allowed the value of the real property in question to be set at the date of death on the premise that the facts and circumstances that gave rise to the transaction had not materially changed during the subsequent period.
1995	United States Federal District Court, Fifth Circuit	*U.S. v. G. SIMMONS* (346 F.2d 213)	This case dealing with an income tax refund stated that the amount of the refund was not agreed on until five years after the valuation date. The court held that reasonable knowledge of the facts would have revealed the refund claim had value and, as such, the court allowed the value to be set by the subsequent event.

EXHIBIT 2.2 (*continued*)

DATE	JURISDICTION	REFERS TO CASE(S)	REFERENCE TO USE OF SUBSEQUENT INFORMATION
1996	United States Tax Court	*Estate of Joseph CIDULKA v. Commissioner* (TCM 1996-149 (Mar. 26, 1996))	The Tax Court relied primarily on a sale of the company, structured as an asset sale, to the company's competitor four years following the valuation date. Not only was the sale removed four years in time, but it involved a high level of investment value as opposed to fair market value. The price might could also have been influenced by the structure of the transaction as an asset sale, while the estate owned stock.
1996	United States Tax Court	*Estate of Arthur G. SCANLAN v. Commissioner* (TCM 1996-331 (July 25, 1996))	Decedent died in July 1991. The court relied on an offer to buy the entire company in March 1993 (resulting in a sale consummated in January 1994) and discounted the sale price by 30% to account for both a marketability and minority discount, as well as the change in the setting from the date of the decedent's death.
1997	United States Tax Court	*Nathan and Geraldine MORTON v. Commissioner* (TCM 1997-166 (April 1, 1997))	The Tax Court stated, "Subsequent events or conditions which affect the value of the property can be taken into account only if they are reasonably foreseeable on the valuation date . . . Subsequent events which merely provide evidence of the value of the property on the valuation date can be taken into account regardless of whether they are foreseeable on the valuation date."
1998	United States Tax Court	*Estate of Emanual TROMPETER v. Commissioner* (TCM 1998-35)	The court revealed that it disagreed with the estate and believed that certain postmortem events, although they do not set the market value of the stock, would have an impact on the value.

(*continued*)

EXHIBIT 2.2 (*continued*)

DATE	JURISDICTION	REFERS TO CASE(S)	REFERENCE TO USE OF SUBSEQUENT INFORMATION
1998	United States Tax Court	*Estate of Milton FELDMAR* (56 TCM 1998)	The court rejected both IRS arguments that no key man discount was in order and that the company could use the $2 million life insurance policy settlement to replace him (key man) without loss to the company.
2001	United States Court of Appeals, Sixth Circuit	*GROSS v. Commissioner* (2001 F. App. 0405P (6th Cir.))	The IRS expert utilized pre- and postvaluation date transactions to determine an appropriate lack of marketability discount. The Tax Court found that reliance on such figures was appropriate because they demonstrated more accurately than the flawed earlier studies what willing buyers and willing sellers were actually doing at the time of valuation.
2001	United States Court of Appeals, Tenth Circuit	*Estate of Evelyn M. McMORRIS* (99-9031 U.S. App. (10th Cir. Mar. 20, 2001))	The Appeals Court ruled that the estate tax deduction for the decedent's income tax liabilities should not be reduced by the amount of an unexpected income tax refund that the estate received after the date of death (i.e., after the valuation date).
2001	United States Court of Appeals, Eleventh Circuit	*Estate of O'NEAL v. U.S.* (00-11663 U.S. App. (11th Cir. July 26, 2001))	The Appeals Court ruled that the deduction (for claims against the estate) must be valued as of the date of Mrs. O'Neal's death. All events that have occurred after her death that may alter the value of the estate must be disregarded.
2005	United States Tax Court	*Estate of Helen NOBLE* (TCM 2005-2)	The court found subsequent sale of shares to be determinant of fair market value.

The list should be viewed as informational and not an endorsement of the treatment of the subsequent event. The practitioner should be well advised to use this list as a starting point for the inquiry as it is not to be considered as definitive.

The cases listed in the exhibit provide evidence that courts do consider events occurring after the valuation date. Actual factors considered by the court range from later sales of the asset in question to later sales of comparable companies.

In any case where a transaction occurred after the valuation date and was substantially different from the estimate of value at the valuation date, the analyst would be well advised to attempt to reconcile the two values. This reconciliation could include changes in market conditions, control versus minority status, or a variety of other factors.

Notional Market   As previously noted, judicial valuations make up only a small percentage of price determinations. In the market, every day, supply and demand dictate price in the thousands of transactions that take place, and these transactions largely influence the judicial valuations that follow.[97] Judicial valuations do not, however, take place in a vacuum, and the court generally uses wide discretion, regardless of the stated standard of value to achieve what it perceives as an equitable result.[98]

In the case of *Andrews v. Commissioner*,[99] the court acknowledged that in reality there was a likelihood in the closely held corporation at hand that the stock would be sold to identifiable parties. However, cases like *Bright v. United States*[100] have clarified that while not completely independent of real-world factors, fair market value must be determined with respect to that which a hypothetical willing buyer and seller (who are assumed to exist) would pay for the property rather than that which an actual or specific buyer would pay.

As we have discussed, fair market value transactions do not necessarily take place on the open market. The *notional market* is a concept that is used mainly in Britain and Canada to distinguish a hypothetical market for the determination of fair market value from a real one where transactions are actually consummated. The requirements of fair market value may not always reflect what would happen in the open market, nor is it usually

---

[97] James C. Bonbright, "The Problem of Judicial Valuations," 27 *Columbia Law Review* (May 1927), at 497.

[98] *Id.*, at 503.

[99] 79 T.C. 938; 1982 U.S. Tax Ct. LEXIS 12; 79 T.C. No. 58.

[100] 658 F.2d 999; 1981 U.S. App. LEXIS 17205; 81-2 U.S. Tax Cas. (CCH) P13,436; 48 A.F.T.R.2d (RIA) 6159; 48 A.F.T.R.2d (RIA) 6292.

possible for a completely hypothetical sale to stand on its own without any real-world forces.

The notional market looks to identify a sale price without an actual sale.[101] This may occur in the context of an estate or gift tax filing, divorce, the appraisal remedy, commercial litigation, or a variety of other valuations that do not involve actual sales of property.[102] Although a British and Canadian concept, the notional market represents many of the underlying assumptions of fair market value in the United States.[103]

In an open market transaction, the buyers and sellers are identifiable and negotiations between them eventually will lead to an agreed-upon price. In a notional market, the buyer and the seller are not any one person or entity in particular; therefore, the pool of potential buyers is larger. In the notional market, buyers and sellers are assumed to be at arm's length and willing, even though in reality they may not be.[104]

In addition, while on the open market the buyer and seller may pursue the information necessary to make an informed sale, on a notional market there is an assumption that both buyer and seller have reasonable knowledge of relevant information. In United Kingdom and Canadian fair market value cases, full knowledge is assumed. In the United States, only reasonable knowledge is required.[105] In the open market, due to earnouts, contingency payments, and similar deal structures, there are occasions when the final price is not known at the date of sale. In the notional market, these types of payments must be estimated at the valuation date.

Exhibit 2.3, prepared by Jay E. Fishman and Bonnie O'Rourke, compares the elements of a notional market with those of an open market.

The notional market assumes: an arm's-length transaction; economic rather than sentimental value; equally informed and uncompelled parties; equal financial strength and bargaining ability; a consistent market; and a free, open, and unrestricted market environment.[106] The real world does not always work in these terms, and that is why often there are discrepancies between fair market value and open market price, due to a lack of information, compulsion, or other factors. An example of this is the 1962 Tax Court decision, *Dees v. Commissioner*.[107]

---

[101] William B. Barker, "A Comparative Approach to Income Tax Law in the United Kingdom and the United States," 46 *Catholic University Law Review* (Fall 1996), at 40.

[102] Campbell, *Canada Valuation Service*, at 4–20.

[103] Fishman and O'Rourke, "Value," at 321.

[104] Campbell, *Canada Valuation Service*, at 4–20.

[105] *Id.*

[106] Fishman and O'Rourke, "Value."

[107] T.C. Memo. No. 1962-153 at 919,21 T.C.M. 845, aff'd 332 F.2d 725 (3d Cir. 1963).

EXHIBIT 2.3   Notional versus Open Market Transactions

Notional Market	Open Market
Arm's length	Some transactions include non–arm's-length parties
Economic value	May include sentimental value
Equally informed	One party may not be as informed as the other
Equally uncompelled	One party may be more "compelled" to transact than the other
Consistent market	Marketplace could include booms and panics
Free, open, unrestricted	Restrictions a possibility
Equal financial strength	One party may be financially stronger
Equal bargaining ability	One party may be in a better bargaining position

Source: Jay E. Fishman and Bonnie O'Rourke, "Value: More Than a Superficial Understanding Is Required," 15 *Journal of the American Academy of Matrimonial Lawyers* (1998), at 322.

DEES V. COMMISSIONER

In this case, W.W. Dees acquired shares of an insurance company that he and two other colleagues had set up in the 1950s. They had also established an underwriting company that owned the majority of the insurance company's common stock. To raise money to fund this venture, however, the holding company sold its shares to the public. The tax commissioner determined that Dees's tax payments on his personal income tax return for 1953 and 1954 were deficient; the primary valuation issue was determining the fair market value of certain shares.

The Tax Court decided that the difference between Dees's cost ($1.25 for 5,000 shares, $1.00 for 5,000 shares, and 3,800 shares free as a bonus) and the fair market value of the stock should be taxable as compensation. The court then intended to determine the fair market value of those shares at the applicable dates.

Upon the first sales to the public, the stock sold at $16.00 (or $20.00 per share in subscription contract sales payable over three years), with $12.80 per share remittance to the insurance company. The tax commissioner looked to collect a deficiency on the taxable portion of the shares purchased at a price far less than the public sales price. According to the commissioner, for two separate blocks of shares purchased on different dates, Dees should pay tax on the difference between the purchase price he paid and the value of the stock at which it was sold to the public. *(continued)*

The insurance company had been using salespeople to aggressively market their stock. A salesperson might solicit potential buyers up to 15 times to purchase shares of the corporation. Nearly all the shares owned by individuals outside the company were owned in 25-, 50-, or 100-share blocks.

In determining the fair market value of the shares, the court decided that although the public was paying $16.00 and $20.00 per share around the valuation dates, the shares should be valued at $5.00 and $5.50 respectively.

At the time of the original purchase, during the formative stage of the company, the book value of the shares was approximately $3.00. At the subsequent purchase, the shares were worth little more.

Individuals purchasing the stock from the salespeople were not provided with relevant financial information about the company, and therefore the court viewed the purchasers as uninformed, with the price paid being representative of their ignorance and gullibility as well as the company's aggressive (but not illegal) sales techniques rather than reasonable knowledge of the relevant facts about the corporation's operation.

This case not only relates directly to the level of information that should be known and knowable in establishing fair market value, but it also shows the difference between open market prices and the assumptions necessary to arrive at fair market value. As was discussed in Chapter 1, there are times when the intrinsic value of a stock is different from its trading price. This is the essence of security analysis in the public market. However, in this case it is apparent that the higher price paid by the public was the result of sales tactics and not a difference due to the intrinsic value of the stock.

While attempting to adhere to the strict guidelines of the willing seller and the willing buyer construct, it may be impossible to ignore the circumstances of real individuals acting out of varying motivations. As one commentator noted:

> Though black-letter law may hold that the willing buyer and seller are hypothetical parties, rather than real ones, the circumstances of actual buyers, sellers, and owners are often important in the determining fair market value. Case law on assemblage values, corporate liquidation arguments, charitable donee conduct, and other valuation issues reveal that real parties' individual

needs and desires sometimes play a significant role in the valuation analysis.[108]

Ideally, the desired market for a determination of fair market value may be akin to the notional market as discussed earlier, but real-world issues are likely to affect any valuation. The notional concept does not preclude the practitioner from investigating all available market information but may place constraints on its use—for example, the use of transactions involving synergies not available to all buyers.

The incorporation of actual market data into a valuation can be a good indicator of how a company will fare on the market, whether in the open market or in determining fair market value. This can be seen in the Tax Court's willingness to place weight on the guideline public company method despite seemingly broad criteria for what constitutes meaningful comparison.

Earlier we discussed *Estate of Joyce Hall v. Commissioner*[109] in terms of restrictive agreements, but the court also comments on the use of guideline public companies. The decedent owned shares in Hallmark, the greeting card company. American Greetings was acknowledged as the other leading firm in the greeting cards industry, and the only publicly traded greeting card company that compared to Hallmark. The commissioner's expert based his valuation of the decedent's shares on a comparison with American Greetings. He claimed that American Greetings was the only public company with a similar capital structure and product mix. Alternatively, the taxpayer's expert, not wanting to rely on one guideline public company as the sole basis for comparison, chose a variety of publicly traded companies, such as AT Cross, Coca-Cola, and Lenox, Inc., which he considered comparable to Hallmark based on certain similarities but not in the same industry. The expert believed that these public companies had business and financial characteristics similar to Hallmark, in that they were leaders in their industries producing brand-name consumer goods. The court ultimately applied the taxpayer's expert's logic, finding one company too narrow a comparison for the determination of fair market value under the notion that "the good fortune of one company in an industry may be at the expense of its direct competitors."[110] In this case, the court allowed broad criteria in choosing guideline public companies for comparison purposes with Hallmark.

However, such broad criteria (shared economic influences or use of public companies with dominant market share and brand name recognition) are

---

[108] John Bogdanski, *Federal Tax Valuation*, at 2.01[2][c], 2–45.

[109] 92 T.C. 312; 1989 U.S. Tax Ct. LEXIS 24; 92 T.C. No. 19.

[110] 92 T.C. 312; 1989 U.S. Tax Ct. LEXIS 24; 92 T.C. No. 19 at 340.

not always accepted. In some circumstances, the court may consider the subject company unique. For example, in the case of *Righter v. United States*,[111] which involved the valuation of a game company, the court decided that diversified publicly traded toy and game companies were not sufficiently useful as guideline companies when compared to a company producing only two types of games appealing to specific age groups.

This is contrasted with the court's decision in the *Estate of Joyce Hall v. Commissioner*. Similarly, in the *Estate of Gallo v. Commissioner*,[112] in valuing a wine company, the court accepted the estate's expert's use of guideline public companies representing a variety of brewing, distilling, and food processing companies subject to similar market forces.

Righter is an older case that demonstrates a restrictive view of what constitutes a guideline public company. As has been seen in more recent cases, the court has often used the broader concept of shared economic influences as a criterion of what constitutes a usable guideline public company.

Finally, after selecting the appropriate guideline companies, care must also be used in determining the guideline level of value(i.e., marketable shares should not be compared directly with nonmarketable shares and minority shares cannot be directly compared with majority or control shares without proper adjustments).

Common Discounts

Discounts for Lack of Control   All else being equal, shares with decision-making power in a corporation are usually considered more valuable than shares that lack these prerogatives. However, majority ownership is not necessarily a guarantee of increased value. The statutes of each state have some influence over the degree of control a particular block of stock possesses. Some states require supermajority votes to authorize actions such as mergers, sales, or liquidations. The articles of incorporation or bylaws of a company may require similar supermajority approval. Any ownership position of a corporation that is less than 100% comes with disadvantages. The business decisions made by a shareholder without 100% ownership may be the subject of contention with minority shareholders through dissent or oppression statutes. In a state with supermajority requirements, control shares are often worth more if the block of shares are at or exceed the supermajority threshold. Conversely, if ownership of a minority share prevents the controlling shareholder from achieving the supermajority threshold, it may not

---

[111] 439 F.2d 1244 (1971).
[112] T.C. Memo 1985-363.

be discounted as heavily as a smaller block of shares as it has the ability to block a corporate action.

There are inherent risks in making an investment that does not come with control. These include the chance that:

- Poor decisions by the majority could lead to losses for the company.
- A change in direction will take place that the minority shareholder does not support.
- The majority shareholders could victimize the minority shareholders in any number of ways, including cancellation of dividends, freeze-outs, squeeze-outs, or other actions that are unfair to the minority shareholders.

These risks will be discussed further in Chapter 3 of this book, but the bottom line is that minority shares are typically worth less than controlling shares. However, it is worth noting that in some circumstances, the aggregate minority could exceed the value of the enterprise.

The first case we have found in which a minority discount was judicially recognized was the 1935 tax case *Cravens v. Welch*.[113] In this case, the taxpayer was looking to deduct the losses from the value of his minority interest shares in a close corporation from his income. The shareholder determined that the value of the stock at the applicable date was $2.25 per share, which was the pro-rata share of the enterprise value. The IRS, however, claimed that the value was $1.21 per share because a minority interest was being valued. The court held in favor of the IRS and the minority discount, in all likelihood to support the conclusion of the government witness.[114] Whereas in this instance the minority discount was beneficial to the IRS, the concept of the minority discount has remained and has since become a mechanism by which a shareholder can reduce the taxable value of his or her minority shares.

In the case of *Sol Koffler v. Commissioner*,[115] the court discussed the lack of control discount when comparing minority shares of a private company to their publicly traded equivalent. The court stated:

Almost any available block of publicly-traded stock sold in day-to-day transactions, whether over the counter or on one of the exchanges, is a minority interest which could not determine dividend

---

[113] 10 F. Supp. 94 (D.C. Cal. 1935).

[114] Edwin T. Hood, John J. Mylan, and Timothy P. O'Sullivan, "Valuation of Closely Held Business Interests," 65 *University of Missouri at Kansas City Law Review*, No. 399 (Spring 1997).

[115] T.C. Memo 1978-159.

or other company policy. But the important consideration is that there is a day-to-day market for such stock, and in the absence of some unusual circumstance a purchaser can convert his investment to cash at any time. He would have no such assurance with respect to the minority block of ALW stock.

Another court described the adjustment as reflecting "the minority shareholder's inability to compel liquidation and thereby realize a pro rata share of the corporation's net asset value."[116] That distinction leads to the necessity of discounting minority shares for their lack of control and similarly, if more cash flow can be extracted from the company, adding a premium to control shares when compared with the shares of guideline public companies.

Discounts for Lack of Marketability   The fair market value of a private business or business interest may suffer due to a lack of marketability. While a minority discount adjusts for lack of control over an entity, a marketability discount compensates for the inability to convert the interest immediately into cash.[117]

The *International Glossary of Business Valuation Terms* defines marketability as "the ability to quickly convert property to cash at minimal cost."[118] The owner of a publicly traded security may execute a trade and liquidate the asset within three business days. The sale of minority shares in a privately held company may take time and expense in identifying likely and able buyers and negotiating a transaction. In this notional market, the inability to liquidate one's position immediately requires consideration of a discount for lack of marketability.

However, the issue of applying a discount for lack of marketability for a controlling interest is unsettled. Some Tax Court decisions reference such a discount, and others argue no such discount is required as enterprises are not typically sold through the public exchanges. The authors believe that discounts for lack of marketability for controlling interests are applicable in some circumstances. Those circumstances are fact sensitive.

After addressing the marketability of the company as a whole, applicable shareholder-level discounts may need to be applied. Because public minority stock can be sold relatively quickly and easily (many times on a public exchange, such as the New York Stock Exchange, where there are

---

[116] *Estate of Thomas A. Fleming, et al. v. Commissioner*, T.C. Memo 1997-484 (October 27, 1997).

[117] Gara and Langstraat, "Property Valuation for Transfer Taxes," at 154.

[118] *Guide to Business Valuations* at 2–40.

potentially thousands of buyers), minority shares of a private company suffer by comparison. The universe of buyers for private minority stock is typically much smaller. Restricted stock studies have revealed the significant differential in value between freely tradable shares and those that are restricted from trading on an open market for a certain time period.[119]

Investors prefer liquidity to illiquidity. A liquid asset may be sold quickly for a variety of reasons: lack of confidence in management, a belief that value will decrease, or the possibility of a need for cash. With an illiquid asset, it may be difficult or expensive to obtain cash, so investors may be forced to hold the asset even if value is declining or management policies are poor.[120]

As discussed earlier, the court in *Mandelbaum v. Commissioner*[121] addressed the applicability of the marketability discount on minority shares of private company stock gifted over the course of several years. In quantifying the discount, the court reviewed the factors shown previously in Exhibit 2.1 and adjusted benchmark percentages for lack of marketability based on the results.

Blockage Discounts   A blockage discount may be appropriate when a block of public stock is so large in relation to its total trading volume that it could not be offered for sale without depressing the market. Essentially, a discount is needed because the market would be flooded by the sale and supply would outweigh demand.[122] The discount may be calculated based on the estimated amount of time it would take to sell the entire quantity in smaller lots. This may be applicable to large blocks of public shares[123] or holdings of other types of assets like an art collection, that if sold en masse could have a depressing effect on the marketplace.[124] In the public marketplace there is a debate as to whether a specific block of stock should be discounted for blockage or, when appropriate, afforded a premium for control.

Estate of O'Keeffe v. Commissioner[125] was a case valuing artwork rather than stock, but for demonstration purposes it clearly illustrates why a discount for blockage may be appropriate. The court looked at

---

[119] David J. Laro and Shannon P. Pratt, *Business Valuation and Federal Taxes*, 2nd ed.(2011), at 283–290. John Wiley.

[120] Laro and Pratt, *Business Valuation and Taxes*, at 285.

[121] T.C. Memo 1995-255; 1995 Tax Ct. Memo LEXIS 256; 69 T.C.M. (CCH) 2852.

[122] Gara and Langstraat, "Property Valuation for Transfer Taxes," at 158.

[123] *Estate of Friedberg v. Commissioner*, 63 T.C.M. (CCH) 3080, 3081-82 (1992).

[124] *Estate of O'Keeffe v. Commissioner*, 63 T.C.M. (CCH) at 2704.

[125] *Id.*

the individual market values of each piece of a large art collection and concluded that, if all the artwork entered the market at the same time, it would depress the marketplace. Therefore, the value of the collection as a whole was less than the aggregate total of each individual piece of art. The court divided the collection into two groups and allowed the application of a 25% discount for the more salable group and a 75% discount for the less salable group.

Key-Person Discounts   While the hypothetical natures of buyers and sellers are generally relied upon in a determination of fair market value, in certain circumstances it is important to consider the actual position of a particular individual, sometimes the position that a decedent held within a company and the effect of his or her death.

Key-person discounts reflect the reliance of a company on a particular individual. This could be for a variety of reasons, including thin management, a wealth of personal relationships that benefit a business, knowledge and experience in the marketplace, or any other factors that, absent key-person life insurance, might make any individual very difficult to replace. It has been suggested that the magnitude of this discount may be quantified by identifying the cash flows with and without the continued presence of the key person. Several identifiable factors may influence the application of a key-person discount, including:[126]

- Services rendered by the key person
- Extent of the corporation's dependence on that person
- If the key person is still active, the likelihood of his or her loss
- Depth and quality of other management personnel
- Availability of adequate replacement
- Key person's compensation and probable compensation for a replacement
- Value of irreplaceable factors and skills lost
- Risks associated with operation under new management personnel
- Lost debt capacity

There are also potential offsets to the loss of a key person. These are:

- Life or disability insurance proceeds payable to the company that are not specifically designated for other purposes, such as repurchase of a decedent's stock

---

[126] Steven Bolten and Yan Wang, "Key Person Discounts," *Business Valuation: Discounts and Premiums* (Hoboken, NJ: John Wiley & Sons, 2003), at 3.

■ Amount of compensation saved if the replacement's probable compensation is lower than that of the key person
■ Covenants not to compete
■ Depth in middle management

The Tax Court case *Estate of Feldmar v. Commissioner*[127] addressed the implications of a key man for the value of a company's stock. A company selling nontraditional insurance products had been founded by the decedent and relied on his unique marketing skills. The court recognized that the value of the corporation would be less without that individual than it would be with the continued presence of that individual, and a reasonable investor would require a discount to make up for the loss of the key person in buying the company. The respondent claimed that the life insurance policy made up for the loss of the key person. The court, however, viewed the policy as a nonoperating asset. The respondent also claimed that management could be replaced by the salary that was now available due to the decedent's death, but the court found the current management of the company incapable of carrying on without the key individual. Ultimately, the court discounted the value of the corporation by 25% to account for the loss of the key person.

Other cases have addressed this issue as well, including the previously mentioned *Sol Koffler v. Commissioner*, in which the court applied a 15% thin management discount.

Trapped-in Capital Gains Discounts   In a case where a company holds assets that have appreciated substantially over time, there may be capital gain that will eventually trigger a capital gains tax upon sale. Recently the courts have allowed for discounts that adjust for the need to pay eventual taxes. The main argument against the trapped-in capital gains discount is that the asset is not necessarily going to be sold. However, the repeal of the General Utilities Doctrine (the general rule was that a corporation recognized no gain or loss on the distribution of appreciated property to its shareholders[128]) brought renewed attention to this issue. One of the more recent cases on the subject is *Eisenberg v. Commissioner*.[129]

---

[127] *Estate of Feldmar v. Commissioner*, T.C. Memo 1988-429, 56 T.C.M. (CCH) 118 (1988).

[128] Pillsbury Winthrop Shaw and Pittman, LLP, "Tax Page" (http://pmstax.com/acq-basic/genUtil.shtml).

[129] 155 F.3d 50 (2d Cir. 1998).

EISENBERG V. COMMISSIONER

The case of *Eisenberg v. Commissioner* illustrates the necessity of considering trapped-in capital gains. In gifting her shares of stock to her son and two grandchildren over the course of three years, the appellant reduced the value of the shares for gift tax purposes to account for the trapped-in capital gains tax she would have incurred had the corporation been liquidated or sold. She later received notice of a tax deficiency, solely on the grounds of the reduction of value to account for the trapped-in capital gains.

The Tax Court decided that precedent dictated that no discount for trapped-in capital gains was permitted when there was no evidence to suggest that liquidation or sale was likely to occur. Additionally, the court found that no hypothetical willing buyer would purchase the corporation with a view toward liquidation or sale, and, therefore, the trapped-in capital gains would be a nonissue.

On appeal, the appellant (Mrs. Eisenberg) argued that no willing buyer would purchase the stock without taking the trapped-in capital gains into account. The Second Circuit Court of Appeals found the appellant's argument more compelling, stating: "The issue is not what a hypothetical willing buyer plans to do with the property, but what considerations affect the fair market value of the property he considers buying."[130]

Therefore, the court concluded that the valuation should take those potential taxes into account when determining value.

In its decision, the court also looked to a recent decision addressing similar issues, *Davis v. Commissioner*,[131] which examined whether the corporation's built-in capital gains tax should be accounted for in the valuation of stock. Both experts in that case recommended that the built-in capital gains tax be taken into account, regardless of whether liquidation or sale of the corporation or its assets was contemplated.

---

[130] *Id.*, at 25.

[131] 1998 U.S. Tax Ct. LEXIS 35, Daily Tax Report (BNA) No. 126, at K-17 (T.C. June 30, 1998).

SUMMARY

This chapter has addressed the history and development of fair market value and its well-established definition. Fair market value is a legal construct related to tax, regulatory, and judicial issues, especially federal estate and gift taxes. Its use and associated assumptions grew as federal taxation became more widespread. We have analyzed court cases that have shaped the definition of fair market value and seen that largely, although certain overarching guidelines apply, the facts and circumstances of each case have often influenced the outcome of a fair market value assessment. The standard of fair market value is often applied in contexts other than tax, for example, in marital dissolutions.

To better guide the application of fair market value, the IRS has established regulations and revenue rulings (the best-known of which is Revenue Ruling 59-60) with which valuations should comply. The Estate and Gift Tax Regulations establish the general requirements of fair market value, all of which are applied as hypothetical constructs:

- The price at which a property would change hands
- A willing buyer
- A willing seller
- Neither being under any compulsion
- Both having reasonable knowledge of the relevant facts
- Specific value as of a specific valuation date
- Applicability of subsequent events

Within these general hypothetical considerations, specific issues develop, including the natures of the buyer and seller and the marketplace created:

- Synergistic buyers
- Valuing individual classes of stock together or separately
- Applicability of restrictive agreements
- Subsequent events and postvaluation-date information
- Applicability of entity- and shareholder-level discounts

In determining fair market value, the courts consistently value the stock that is in the hands of the shareholder, whether for purposes of estate, gift, or income tax. The ultimate value represents a value in exchange and lack of control and lack of marketability discounts are commonly applied, as are control premiums (if appropriate and depending on the cash flow used). However, the courts have not been fully consistent across jurisdictions in their treatment of the issues discussed. Circumstances and practical considerations may make each case unique, and therefore each judge or jury decides on a specific fact pattern.

The fair market value standard forms the basis of understanding the fair value standard in dissent and oppression. Furthermore, the concepts applied in fair market value are used in many states for value in divorce. Therefore, Chapter 3, "Fair Value in Shareholder Dissent and Oppression," and Chapter 5 , "Standards of Value in Divorce," build on the concepts discussed in this chapter.

Fair Value in Shareholder Dissent and Oppression

Gilbert E. Matthews and Michelle Patterson

FAIR VALUE AS THE STANDARD OF VALUE IN DISSENT, OPPRESSION, AND ENTIRE FAIRNESS CASES

State courts employ *fair value* as the predominant standard to determine the value of minority shares in both appraisal (also known as dissent)[1] and oppression cases. When the courts determine the minority's share price in an appraisal or order the buy out of an oppressed minority shareholder, the price of the award or buyout is critical for both parties and sets the "fair value" of the minority's shares.[2] Although appraisal and oppression statutes in most states expressly or effectively stipulate that the minority's shares are to be valued at "fair value," there remains considerable confusion about what "fair value" means. To understand fair value as a standard of measurement, it must be considered in contrast to the standards of value called *fair market value* and *third-party sale value*, as will be discussed in this Chapter.

The authors thank Michael A. Graham, Ph.D., for his assistance in editing this chapter.

[1] Since shareholders who *dissent* from a transaction are entitled to *appraisal* of their shares, the terms *dissenters' rights* and *appraisal rights* are interchangeable.

[2] Douglas K. Moll, "Shareholder Oppression and 'Fair Value': Of Discounts, Dates, and Dastardly Deeds in the Close Corporation," 54 *Duke L. J.* 293, 310 (2004). In this chapter, we extensively cite Professor Moll's expert writings in the area of oppression and fair value. For a fuller discussion of these standards, see the section below entitled "Fair Value as Defined by Various Authorities and Statutes."

Both appraisal and oppression cases are governed by state law. That state law includes corporate law statutes, the judicial interpretations of those statutes, and the courts' holdings under their equitable authority, even when the state lacks corresponding statutes.[3] Although fair value is now the state-mandated or accepted standard for judicial appraisal and oppression valuations in almost all states, there are differing interpretations of its meaning and measurement that have evolved through legislative changes and judicial interpretation.

The model statutes proposed by the American Bar Association (ABA) and the American Law Institute (ALI), together with Delaware appraisal law, have greatly influenced a majority of state statutes. The ABA and the ALI have developed definitions of fair value that are set forth in the ABA's *Revised Model Business Corporation Act* (RMBCA)[4] and the ALI's *Principles of Corporate Governance*.[5] Although statutes and legal organizations have contributed to the development of the fair value standard, the Delaware courts' decisions are central to its definition.

Delaware's appraisal statute explicitly mandates fair value as the measure of value, and the Delaware Supreme Court clarified its meaning in *Tri-Continental v. Battye*[6] in 1950. *Fair value* was defined as the value that had been taken from the dissenting shareholder:

> The basic concept of value under the appraisal statute is that the stockholder is entitled to be paid for that which has been taken from him, *viz.*, his proportionate interest in a going concern. By value of the stockholder's proportionate interest in the corporate enterprise is meant the true or intrinsic value of his stock which has been taken by the merger. In determining what figure represents this true or intrinsic value, the appraiser and the courts must take into consideration all factors and elements which reasonably might enter into fixing the value.[7]

This concept of value has since been cited in numerous appraisal and oppression cases as the basic standard. In recent years, most (but not all)

---

[3] *Id.*

[4] The ABA's Model Business Corporation Act is a model code designed for use by state legislatures in revising and updating their corporation statutes. It was initially published by the ABA in 1950, and revised in 1971, 1984, and 1999. There were amendments with respect to appraisals in 1969 and 1978.

[5] "The American Law Institute . . . drafts, discusses, revises, and publishes Restatements of the Law, model statutes, and principles of law." www.ali.org/index. cfm?fuseaction=about.overview.

[6] *Tri-Continental v. Battye*, 74 A.2d 71 (Del. 1950).

[7] *Tri-Continental*, 74 A.2d 71, 72.

jurisdictions have accepted the position that *what has been taken from the shareholder* is a *pro rata share* of the value of the company as a whole.

It is helpful to understand the different legal actions of appraisal, oppression, and breach fiduciary duty in which fair value is used as the standard of valuation. The appraisal action is a "limited legislative remedy which is intended to provide minority shareholders who dissent from a merger asserting the inadequacy of the [consideration], with an independent judicial determination of the fair value of their shares."[8] Dissenting minority shareholders may petition for appraisal under a state statute, commonly known as *appraisal* or *dissenters'* rights. Shareholders customarily have appraisal rights when they are involuntarily cashed out in a merger or consolidation, but some states also permit dissenters to seek appraisal in other circumstances, such as a sale of assets, recapitalization, stock-for-stock mergers, amendments to articles of incorporation, or other major changes to the nature of their investment. In an appraisal action, the exclusive remedy is cash.

Although appraisal or dissenters' rights commonly apply to close corporations, public companies may be subject to appraisal actions under some of the above circumstances. A common misperception exists that publicly held shares are not entitled to appraisal rights because of the existence in many states' appraisal statutes of a provision called the "market exception." This is discussed below in the section entitled "**Appraisal Rights in Publicly Traded Corporations: The Market Exception.**"

Oppression actions arise from shareholders of close corporations who assert that they have been treated unfairly or prejudicially by those in control and seek dissolution of the company or a buyout of their shares. Oppression remedies are available to these shareholders when they establish that the majority has excluded them from their proper share of the benefits accruing from the enterprise.[9] Oppression often involves egregious majority action targeting individual minority shareholders. It can include termination of compensation, employment, or dividends, and/or a siphoning of corporate assets for the benefit of the majority at the expense of the minority.

Oppression actions, like appraisal actions, are primarily based on state statutes. All but nine states have enacted oppression-triggered dissolution

---

[8] *Alabama By-Products Corp. v. Neal*, 588 A.2d 255, 256 (Del. 1991).

[9] "The terms 'majority' and 'minority' . . . distinguish those shareholders who possess the actual power to control the operations of the firm from those who do not." J.A.C. Hetherington & Michael P. Dooley, *Illiquidity and Exploitation: A Proposed Statutory Solution to the Remaining Close Corporation Problem*, 63 *Va. L. Rev.* 1, 5, n. 7 (1977).

statutes under which shareholders may petition for involuntary dissolution. Over time, alternative remedies to involuntary dissolution have arisen, and involuntary dissolution has come to be much less frequent. In fact, "'oppression' has evolved from a statutory ground for involuntary dissolution to a statutory ground for a wide variety of relief."[10]

In many states lacking oppression-triggered dissolution statutes, the courts have created another way for oppressed minority shareholders to seek redress. These courts have emphasized that a fiduciary duty of good faith and loyalty exists between the majority and the minority shareholders; other courts have even extended fiduciary duty obligations to exist between one shareholder and another. By so doing, these courts have permitted the "oppressed" shareholder to sue, asserting breach of fiduciary duty. The failure of the control shareholders to fulfill their fiduciary duties to the minority can be deemed to be oppression.

In breach of fiduciary duty cases, the courts grant many of the same remedies, such as dissolution and compulsory buyouts, which are provided for in the state oppresion statutes. The court employs the same fair value standard used in oppression and appraisal actions to make its judicial determination of minority share value. Professor Douglas Moll writes:

> The development of the statutory and fiduciary duty actions reflect[s] "the same underlying concerns for the position of minority shareholders, particularly in close corporations after harmony no longer reigns." Because of the similarities between the two remedial schemes, it has been suggested that "it makes sense to think of them as two manifestations of a minority shareholder's cause of action for oppression." In the close corporation context, therefore, it is sensible to view the parallel development of the statutory action and the fiduciary duty action as two sides of the same coin—i.e., the shareholder's cause of action for oppression.[11]

Delaware provides an example of courts acting under their own equitable authority in states where there is no specific oppression statute.[12] In Delaware, when the court believes there is a conflict of interest or

---

[10] Moll, "Minority Oppression and the Limited Liability Company: Learning (or Not) from Close Corporation History," 54 *Wake Forest L. Rev.* 883, 894 (2005).

[11] *Id.,* at 895, quoting Robert B. Thompson, "The Shareholder's Cause of Action for Oppression," 48 *Bus. Law.* 699, 739 (1993).

[12] Delaware is preeminent in establishing standards for corporate law because a majority of large publicly traded companies are incorporated in Delaware and because of Delaware's well-developed body of law regarding corporations.

oppressive behavior, it will allow a breach of fiduciary duty case for the minority shareholder. If the case is designated as one of "entire fairness," the Delaware courts will use the same standard of fairness, fair value, which its uses in Delaware appraisal cases to set the price for the minority's shares.

Importantly, defining fair value as a proportionate share of a company's value, as Delaware did in *Tri-Continental*, differentiates it from the other two standards of value—*fair market value* and *third-party sale value*.[13] It has been argued that the courts have made the best choice by selecting fair value as the appropriate standard and by rejecting fair market value and third-party sale value.[14] When fair market value is used in tax cases, for example, substantial discounts for the minority's lack of control and lack of marketability are often applied to the value of the minority shares. Courts have noted that a fair market value valuation based on such discounts would be less than the value of the minority shareholders' proportionate interest in the company. With a fair market valuation, the controller (or majority) would reap a windfall at the expense of the minority. Consequently, judicial interpretations and statutes in many states now reject minority or marketability discounts in the determination of fair value. However, a few states still allow the discounts either by precedent, at a court's discretion, or in special circumstances.[15]

On the other hand, if the courts used the standard of third-party sale value, those shares would receive a value, a *premium*, that would be higher than fair value. An augmented value would result because the third-party sale price could include additional elements of value resulting from the transaction, such as financial control and synergistic values. Minority shareholders would not be entitled to those additional values. Most appraisal statutes expressly instruct the judiciary to exclude from their determination of fair value the increases in value that resulted from the synergies accomplished by the transaction.

In order to further understand the issues and complexity surrounding fair value in appraisal and oppression cases, we will examine what elements of value are addressed by the courts in their determination of fair value. We look, as well, at how various courts address current valuation concepts and techniques.

---

[13] See "**Most States Now Reject Minority and Marketability Discounts**" below.

[14] Lawrence A. Hamermesh and Michael L. Wachter, "Rationalizing Appraisal Standards in Compulsory Buyouts," 50 *B.C. L. Rev.* 1021 (2009). In this chapter, we extensively cite the expert writings of Professors Hamermesh and Wachter in the area of appraisal and fair value.

[15] See "**Discounts at the Shareholder Level**" below.

THE APPRAISAL REMEDY FOR DISSENTING SHAREHOLDERS

History and Overview of the Appraisal Remedy

In the early nineteenth century, common law held that extraordinary corporate decisions were to be made unanimously, meaning 100% shareholder approval was required. The prevailing perspective on business was that the investment made by the minority shareholder contractually connected the corporation to the shareholder, and that shareholders should not be required to comply with fundamental changes they did not support. Therefore, any single shareholder could utilize his or her common law veto in order to prevent corporate action.[16]

This perspective could have a paralyzing effect on the decision-making process in a corporation. A minority shareholder could impulsively or arbitrarily threaten to reject a corporate action solely to collect a premium on an initial investment.[17] The advancing industrial revolution brought about an increasingly complex economy based on the nation's growing institutions and infrastructure, including the development of the transcontinental railroads. With these changes in commerce and finance, the corporations and the courts came to realize that a unanimity requirement was not efficient for forward movement and growth.[18]

In 1892, the Illinois Supreme Court turned away from the unanimity view of corporate management and affirmed majority rule and the role of the minority shareholder in *Wheeler v. Pullman Iron & Steel Co.*[19] The court decided that the fundamental law of corporations should be that the majority should control policy. It revised the concept of the minority shareholder's investment to mean that the minority shareholder, by investing in the corporation, agrees to abide by the decisions sanctioned

---

[16] Michael Aiken, "A Minority Shareholder's Rights in Dissension: How Does Delaware Do It and What Can Louisiana Learn?" 50 *Loyola L. Rev.* 231, 235 (Spring 2004).

[17] John D. Emory, "The Role of Discounts in Determining Fair Value under Wisconsin's Dissenter's Rights Statutes: The Case for Discounts," 1995 *Wisc. L. Rev.* 1155, 1163 (1995).

[18] Mary Siegel, "Back to the Future: Appraisal Rights in the Twenty-First Century," 32 *Harvard J. of Legislation* 79, 87 (Winter 1995).

[19] *Wheeler v. Pullman Iron & Steel Co.*, 32 N.E. 420, 423 (Ill. 1892): "Every one purchasing or subscribing for stock in a corporation impliedly agrees that he will be bound by the acts and proceedings done or sanctioned by a majority of the shareholders, or by the agents of the corporation [directors] duly chosen by such majority, within the scope of the powers conferred by the charter."

by the majority or the board of directors elected by the majority of the shareholders.[20]

Following the *Wheeler* decision, other state courts, recognizing the paralyzing effect of unanimity, generally became more sympathetic toward majority rule. Initially, majority rule was in place only in cases of insolvency, but later it was considered controlling in mergers, asset sales, and similar transactions, as long as the majority's decision was in the best interests of the corporation.[21] As a result, minority shareholders who disagreed with the actions of the majority were left without the power to challenge such corporate decisions or, if the shares were not publicly traded, the ability to exit the corporation. This in turn led to the development of appraisal rights for such minority shareholders.

An 1875 Ohio case was earlier evidence of the emergence of appraisal rights. In its decision, the Ohio Supreme Court stated:

> [O]ur legislature has seen proper to provide that stockholders in a railroad corporation shall not be carried into a new or consolidated company against their consent. From this provision it is plain that a stockholder not only can not be compelled to become a member of the consolidated corporation, but the consolidation can not proceed until he is paid the fair value of his stock. It is impossible to force upon him the liabilities and responsibilities attaching to the new corporation; it is impossible to change the character of the enterprise in which he agreed to embark his money, until he has been paid the fair value of his investment.[22]

Before the appearance of appraisal statutes, minority shareholders had to petition the courts to stop the corporation from pursuing a course of action until their desire to exit was satisfied. They had to sue for injunctive relief and for the cash value of their shares. The courts would award the fair value in cash to enable shareholders to escape forced membership in a new corporation.[23] Legislatures began to enact appraisal rights statutes that allowed the minority to dissent from a corporate transaction and receive a judicial determination of the fair value of their shares in the original

---

[20] Charles W. Murdock, "The Evolution of Effective Remedies for Minority Shareholders and Its Impact upon Valuation of Minority Shares," 65 *Notre Dame L. Rev.* 425, 429 (1990).

[21] Siegel, "Back to the Future," at 88.

[22] *Mansfield, Coldwater and Lake Michigan Railroad Co. v. Stout*, 26 Ohio St. 241, 1875 Ohio LEXIS 397 (Ohio 1875).

[23] Siegel, "Back to the Future," at 89.

corporation in cash.[24] The statutes prevented expensive and drawn-out injunction procedures and allowed corporations, during the dispute, to continue conducting business as usual.

The U.S. Supreme Court clarified the purpose of dissenters' rights statutes in its 1941 *Voeller* decision.[25] Justice Black cited a Securities and Exchange Commission (SEC) report describing the history and necessity of establishing majority rule and a remedy for minority shareholders:

> At common law, unanimous shareholder consent was a prerequisite to fundamental changes in the corporation. This made it possible for an arbitrary minority to establish a nuisance value for its shares by refusing to cooperate. To address this situation, legislatures authorized corporations to make changes by a majority vote. This, however, opened the door to victimization of the minority. To solve the dilemma, statutes permitting a dissenting minority to recover the appraised value of its shares were widely adopted.[26]

In 1927, the Uniform Business Corporation Act was introduced by the Commissioners for Uniform State Laws.[27] It was adopted only by Louisiana, Washington, and Kentucky, likely because most states were not comfortable with the implied inflexibility of uniform laws and wanted to reserve their own legislative rights.[28] Over the course of the first half of the twentieth century, nearly all states adopted an appraisal statute.[29]

---

[24] Barry M. Wertheimer, "The Shareholders' Appraisal Remedy and How Courts Determine Fair Value," 47 *Duke L. J.* 613, 619 (1998).

[25] *Voeller v. Neilston Warehouse Co.*, 311 U.S. 531 (1941).

[26] *Id.*, at 536, n. 6, citing *SEC Report on the Work of Protective and Reorganization Committees*, Part VII (Washington, D.C.: U.S. Government Printing Office, 1938), pp. 557, 590.

[27] The National Conference of Commissioners on Uniform State Laws was formed in 1892 for the purpose of providing states with nonpartisan, well-conceived, and well-drafted legislation that brings clarity and stability to critical areas of the law.

[28] Aiken, at 237.

[29] Robert B. Thompson, "Exit, Liquidity, and Majority Rule: Appraisal's Role in Corporate Law," 84 *Georgetown L. Rev.* 1 (1995), Appendix Table 2: New York 1890; Maine 1891; Kentucky 1893; New Jersey 1896; Delaware 1899; Connecticut and Pennsylvania 1901; Alabama, Massachusetts, Nevada, and Virginia 1903; Montana and New Mexico 1905; Ohio 1906; Tennessee 1907; Maryland 1908; Vermont 1915; Illinois and New Hampshire 1919; Rhode Island 1920; Arkansas, Florida, North Carolina, and South Carolina 1925; Minnesota and Oregon 1927; Louisiana 1928; Idaho and Indiana 1929; California, District of Columbia, and Michigan 1931; Washington 1933; Hawaii 1937; Georgia 1938; Arizona and Kansas 1939;

Appraisal Rights Today

Currently, the ABA and the ALI recognize various events that can trigger dissenters' rights. States have adopted triggering events in their statutes, and these may have developed differently from those of the RMBCA and the *Principles of Corporate Governance* because of each state's corporate law history. Some common triggers contained in the RMBCA and the state statutes include:

- Merger
- Share exchange
- Disposition of assets
- Amendment to the articles of incorporation that creates fractional shares
- Any other amendment to the articles from which shareholders may dissent
- Change of state of incorporation
- Conversion to a flow-through, unincorporated or non-profit entity

In practice, a substantial majority of appraisal cases today arise when control shareholders squeeze out minority shareholders for cash.

In fact, it has been convincingly argued by Professor Robert Thompson that the "conventional explanation [which] describes appraisal rights as part of a tradeoff implemented at the turn of the century to facilitate the growth of American business" provides an inadequate and incorrect understanding of the role of appraisal rights today.[30] This traditional view, set forth by Justice Black in *Voeller* and discussed by us above, explains that when appraisal rights were first granted, they were the tradeoff for the removal of the unanimity decision-making requirement. Thompson notes:

> Legislatures . . . passed statutes authorizing fundamental changes by a supermajority vote, and often included appraisal rights permitting the minority to exit from these changed enterprises. The focus was on facilitating desirable corporate changes while providing liquidity to those who chose not to continue in a business fundamentally different from the one in which they had originally invested.[31]

Colorado and Nebraska 1941; Missouri 1943; Iowa, Oklahoma, Wisconsin, and Wyoming 1947; Mississippi 1954; South Dakota and Texas 1955; Alaska and North Dakota 1957; Utah 1961; West Virginia 1974.

[30] Thompson, at 3. See discussion in Thompson at 3-5.

[31] *Id.*, at 3-4.

Thompson's argument, however, is that the original liquidity purpose of the appraisal remedy has almost completely disappeared. Instead, the remedy now "serves an entirely different purpose" of acting as a check against opportunism. He points out that "the overwhelming majority of appraisal cases …reflect this cash-out context" and "less than one in ten of …litigated cases illustrate the liquidity/fundamental change concern of the classic appraisal remedy."[32] Thompson states:

> Now the remedy serves as a check against opportunism by a majority shareholder in mergers and other transactions in which the majority forces minority shareholders out of the business and requires them to accept cash for their shares. In earlier times, policing transactions in which those who controlled the corporation had a conflict of interest was left to the courts through the use of fiduciary duty or statues that limited corporate powers. Today, that function is left for appraisal in many cases.[33]

Thompson makes the case that several statutory appraisal provisions which were deemed appropriate for liquidity purposes work counter to providing fairness in the modern opportunism context:

- excluding from the fair value calculation any appreciation or depreciation attributable to the merger transaction;
- requiring minority shareholders seeking appraisal to take four or more separate legal steps to perfect the remedy (and withdrawing relief if the actions are not perfect);
- excluding appraisal when shares are traded on a public market;[34] and
- making appraisal an exclusive remedy even when the valuation remedy does not include loss from breaches of fiduciary duty.[35]

Dissenters are required to follow precisely the complex timing and other requirements of state law in a process referred to as perfecting dissenters' rights. The process and timetable of these events vary from state to state,

---

[32] *Id.*

[33] *Id.*

[34] As discussed in "**Appraisal Rights in Publicly Traded Corporations: The Market Exception**" ahead, eight states deny appraisal rights to shareholders of companies that are publicly traded, and 27 states deny appraisal rights in most situations to shareholders of such companies who receive publicly traded shares in a stock-for stock transaction.

[35] *Id.*, at 4-5.

but in most cases are strictly enforced. A company's board of directors is required to give notice (commonly in a proxy or information statement) of a contemplated corporate action from which shareholders may dissent. Dissenters must then decline the consideration and demand payment of their shares in a notice to the board prior to the action. This dissent triggers an appraisal. Upon notice of dissent, dissenters relinquish all rights except the right to receive payment of the fair value of their shares, and will receive no payment until the conclusion or settlement of litigation. In some states, however, the company must put into escrow the amount that it contends to be fair value. Furthermore, dissenters become unsecured creditors of the company or its successor, which often is a highly leveraged entity.

Some modifications were suggested in 1978 when the Model Business Corporation Act (MBCA) provided that dissenting shareholders should be given notice of events from which they could dissent, and instituted guidelines as to how to dissent. Even with the MBCA's new procedural aids, there remain strict and onerous rules and procedures that dissenters must follow to perfect their rights.

Appraisal Rights in Publicly Traded Corporations: The Market Exception

There is a common misperception that publicly held shares are not entitled to appraisal rights because of a provision in many states' appraisal statutes called the *market exception*. The market exception denies appraisal rights in many circumstances for shareholders of companies whose shares are listed on a national market, or, in most states, have more than 2,000 shareholders.

Although it is true that shareholders of public companies, in contrast to shareholders of privately held companies, are often restricted in their ability to avail themselves of the appraisal remedy, there are conditions under which they may do so. Fifteen states permit appraisal rights to shareholders whether publicly traded or not while 35 states deny or materially limit the appraisal rights of publicly traded companies' shareholders under their market exceptions.[36] For example, the Arizona statute states:

Unless the articles of incorporation of the corporation provide otherwise, this [appraisal] section does not apply to the holders of

---

[36] Jeff Goetz, "A Dissent Dampened by Timing: How the Stock Market Exception Systematically Deprives Public Shareholders of Fair Value," 15 *Fordham J. of Fin. and Corp. L.* 771, 773 (2009). Two states (Colorado and Kansas) provide a market exception if the shares received are marketable even if the shares held by the investor before the transaction were not marketable.

shares of a class or series if the shares of the class or series were registered on a national securities exchange, were listed on the national market systems of the national association of securities dealers automated quotation system or were held of record by at least two thousand shareholders on the date fixed to determine the shareholders entitled to vote on the proposed corporate action.[37]

Although the 1969 MBCA included the market exception, the 1984 RMBCA deleted it because opponents argued that even when a liquid market existed, the market price might not reflect all relevant information. In addition, the market price is capped by the transaction price and "market value and fair value are not necessarily synonymous under all circumstances."[38] The 1999 RMBCA committee weighed these arguments and decided that it would again recommend a market exception provided that appraisals be available in conflict-of-interest transactions.[39]

Restrictions on appraisal rights break down as follows:

1. Arizona and seven other states do not permit appraisals of shares of public companies.
2. Twenty-seven states permit appraisals for shareholders of public companies under specified circumstances:
   a. Some permit appraisals unless the shareholder receives solely shares of a public company.
   b. Others permit appraisals if the shareholder receives anything but cash and/or shares of a public company, such as non-marketable shares, debt instruments, warrants, or contingent rights.
   c. Others permit appraisals in special circumstances.
3. Fifteen states and the District of Columbia have no market exception and extend appraisal rights without distinction as to whether the company is public or private.

Eight states (including Delaware) provide that shareholders of public companies have appraisal rights when the shareholder receives in consideration anything other marketable shares.[40] Delaware's statute states:

---

[37] Ariz. Rev. Stat. § 10-1302(D).

[38] Mary Siegel, "An Appraisal of the Model Business Corporation Act's Appraisal Rights Provisions," 74 *J. of Law and Contemporary Problems* 231, 247 (2011).

[39] *Id.*, at 248.

[40] In addition, Louisiana and Maryland provide for appraisal rights if shareholders receive anything but shares of the surviving corporation, but they do not specify that those shares must be listed.

Notwithstanding paragraph (b)(1) of this section [the market exception], appraisal rights under this section shall be available for the shares of any class or series of stock of a constituent corporation if the holders thereof are required . . . to accept for such stock anything except:

a. Shares of stock of the corporation surviving or resulting from such merger or consolidation, or depository receipts in respect thereof;
b. Shares of stock of any other corporation, or depository receipts in respect thereof, which shares of stock (or depository receipts in respect thereof) or depository receipts at the effective date of the merger or consolidation will be either listed on a national securities exchange or held of record by more than 2,000 holders.[41]

Fourteen states provide that the market exception is inapplicable and appraisal is permitted when the consideration includes anything other than cash and/or listed shares.[42] For example, the Florida statute provides:

Paragraph (a) [the market exception] shall not be applicable and appraisal rights shall be available pursuant to subsection (1) for the holders of any class or series of shares who are required by the terms of the corporate action requiring appraisal rights to accept for such shares anything other than cash or shares of any class or any series of shares of any corporation, or any other proprietary interest of any other entity, that satisfies the standards [of being publicly traded] set forth in paragraph (a) at the time the corporate action becomes effective.[43]

Two major states permit appraisals only in special circumstances. California allows dissent by holders of shares either when those shares are subject to transfer restrictions or when 5% of the outstanding shares of a class request appraisal.[44] Pennsylvania permits shareholders in a class other than common stock to dissent if the transaction does not require a majority vote of the class.[45]

---

[41] 8 Del. Code Ann. tit. 8, § 262(b)(2).
[42] In addition, the New Jersey statute reads similarly but specifies listed *securities* rather than *shares*. *Securities* is a broader term that includes debt and warrants.
[43] Fla. Stat. Ann. § 607.1302(2)(c).
[44] Cal. Corp. Code § 1300(b)(1).
[45] 15 Pa. Cons. Stat. § 1571(b)(2)(ii).

Exhibit 3.1 (on page 103) shows which jurisdictions apply the market exception, and gives an overview of those situations in which the shareholders of public companies will have appraisal rights and the exception does not apply.[46]

Fair Value Can Be Less Than Arms'-Length Price

Dissenting shareholders seek appraisal when they believe that the fair value of their shares is greater than the consideration that they were offered in the transaction. Dissenters have sometimes been awarded far more than the price they were originally offered, but this rarely happens when the buyer was a third party. When considering fair value, courts give substantial weight to a price negotiated in an arm's-length transaction:

> This fact that major shareholders . . . who had the greatest insight into the value of the company, sold their stock to [the third-party buyer] at the same price paid to the remaining shareholders also powerfully implies that the price received was fair.[47]

The Delaware Supreme Court reiterated this view in 1999, when it wrote that "a merger price resulting from arms-length negotiations where there are no claims of collusion is a very strong indication of fair value."[48] However, if the court determines that a third-party transaction was not arm's-length due to conflict of interest and/or improper actions by the buyer, the merger price is not credible evidence of fair value.[49] Because of synergies, as well as a buyer's ability to make changes in the operations and financial structure of a company, fair value is often less than third-party value.[50]

---

[46] In Exhibit 3.1, "listed" means listed on a national securities exchange (which now includes NASDAQ), and "NYSE" means the New York Stock Exchange and the NYSE MKT LLC (formerly the American Stock Exchange).

[47] *Cinerama, Inc. v. Technicolor, Inc.*, 663 A.2d 1134 (Del.Ch. 1994), *aff'd* in part, *Cede, Inc. v. Technicolor, Inc.*, 663 A.2d 1156 (Del. 1995). Similarly, a New Jersey court called market price a valuable tool for corroborating fairness (*Dermody v. Sticco*, 465 A.2d 948, 951 (N.J. Super. 1983)).

[48] *M.P.M. Enterprises, Inc. v. Gilbert*, 731 A.2d 790, 797 (Del. 1999).

[49] *Gearreald v. Just Care, Inc.*, 2012 Del. Ch. LEXIS 91, at *15, n.26.

[50] "Since the [appraisal] remedy provides going concern value and the shareholders [in an arms'-length transaction] are in fact receiving the higher amount, third-party sale value, the likely award in appraisal will be a lower amount than the dissenting shareholder will receive by voting in favor of the merger and taking the merger price." Hamermesh and Wachter, "The Fair Value of Cornfields in Delaware Appraisal Law," 31 *J. Corp. Law* 119, 142 (2005) (hereinafter, "Cornfields").

EXHIBIT 3.1 The Market Exception and When Appraisal Is Permitted Despite the Market Exception

	Market exception applies to:	When appraisal is permitted: (also see footnotes)
Alabama, Arkansas, D.C., Hawaii, Illinois, Kentucky, Massachusetts, Missouri, Montana, Nebraska, New Hampshire, New Mexico, Ohio, Vermont, Washington, Wyoming	No market exception	—
New York[a]	Shares of listed company	Shareholder receives anything but shares of listed company, or short form merger[g]
Delaware, Colorado, Kansas,[b] Oklahoma[c]	Shares of listed company or company with 2,000 shareholders	Shareholder receives anything but shares of listed company or company with 2,000 shareholders, or short form merger[g]
Georgia,[d] Texas	Shares of listed company or company with 2,000 shareholders	Shareholder receives anything but shares of listed company or company with 2,000 shareholders, or short form merger, or shareholder receives shares different in type or exchange ratio from shares offered to others of same class[g]
Utah	Shares of listed company or company with 2,000 shareholders	Shareholder receives anything but shares of listed company or company with 2,000 shareholders[g]
Michigan	If no shareholder vote required, shares of listed company	Shareholder receives anything but cash or shares of listed company
Minnesota, North Dakota	Shares of NYSE or NASDAQ company	Shareholder receives anything but cash or shares of NYSE or NASDAQ company

(*continued*)

EXHIBIT 3.1 (*Continued*)

	Market exception applies to:	When appraisal is permitted: (also see footnotes)
Nevada	Shares of listed company or company with 2,000 shareholders	Shareholder receives anything but *cash* or shares of listed company or company with 2,000 shareholders
Florida	Shares of NYSE or NASDAQ or company with 2,000 shareholders and market value of $10 million excluding shares held by senior executives, directors, and 10% beneficial shareholders	Shareholder receives anything but *cash* or shares of NYSE or NASDAQ company or company with 2,000 shareholders and market value of $10 million excluding shares held by senior executives, directors, and 10% beneficial shareholders
Idaho, Iowa,[e] Mississippi,[f] South Dakota, West Virginia	Shares of NYSE or NASDAQ company or company with 2,000 shareholders and market value of $20 million excluding shares held by senior executives, directors, and 10% beneficial shareholders	Shareholder receives anything but *cash* or shares of NYSE or NASDAQ company or company with 2,000 shareholders and market value of $20 million excluding shares held by senior executives, directors, and 10% beneficial shareholders, or transaction with interested party
Connecticut,[c] Maine, North Carolina,[f] Virginia[f]	Shares of company traded in an "organized market" [*not defined in statute*] or company with 2,000 shareholders and market value of $20 million excluding shares held by senior executives, directors, and 10% beneficial shareholders	Shareholder receives anything but *cash* or shares of company traded in an organized market or company with 2,000 shareholders and market value of $20 million excluding shares held by senior executives, directors, and 10% beneficial shareholders, or transaction with interested party
New Jersey	Shares of listed company or company with 1,000 shareholders	Shareholder receives anything but *cash* or securities of listed company or company with 2,000 shareholders

	Market exception applies to:	When appraisal is permitted: (also see footnotes)
California	Shares of listed company	Shares with transfer restrictions, or if more than 5% request appraisal
Louisiana	Shares of listed company	If not converted solely into shares of surviving corporation (but no public market requirement)
Maryland	Shares of listed company	If not converted solely into shares of surviving corporation (but no public market requirement); or if directors and executive officers were the beneficial owners, in the aggregate, of 5%; or if directors and executive officers receive stock on terms not available to all holders
Pennsylvania	Shares of listed company or company with 2,000 shareholders	Shares of any class unless transaction requires majority vote of the class
Alaska, Indiana, Oregon, South Carolina, Tennessee, Wisconsin	Shares of listed company	None
Arizona, Rhode Island	Shares of listed company or company with 2,000 shareholders	None

[a] Appraisal permitted in short-form merger; appraisal permitted if shares are not entitled to vote on transaction.
[b] Appraisal permitted in merger of subsidiary into parent.
[c] Appraisal permitted in short-form merger.
[d] Appraisal permitted if shareholder receives shares different in type or exchange ratio from shares offered to others of same class.
[e] Appraisal permitted in acquisition by beneficial owner of 20% of the voting rights or party with the right to elect 25% of directors.
[f] Appraisal permitted in interested party transactions.
[g] Cash for fractional shares does not trigger appraisal rights.

Importantly, dissenting shareholders have been awarded amounts lower than an arm's-length transaction price when the court determined that the transaction price included synergies and/or a control premium that should not have been included in fair value under Delaware law. A 2005 case concluded that the fair value of a company was $2.74 per share, even though the minority shares had been acquired for $3.31 in stock.[51] A 2003 decision awarded the petitioner "the value of the Merger Price net of synergies,"[52] which gave the dissenters only 86% of the merger price. In 2012, a company acquired by a competitor was also appraised at 86% of the purchase price, thus resulting in a minority shareholder value less than what the dissenters would have received in the transaction price.[53]

THE OPPRESSION REMEDY

Development of the Oppression Remedy

A remedy for oppressed shareholders emerged for reasons similar to the origin of dissenters' rights. As the courts moved to majority rule, which based decisions on the best interests of the corporation rather than the shareholders, minority shareholders could be frozen out or otherwise harmed without the intervention of the courts. Shareholders would have to bring suit for an injunction or to dissolve the corporation in order to recover their interest.

Illinois was the first state to codify oppression as a trigger for dissolution in the 1933 Illinois Business Corporation Act. The ABA later modeled the MBCA's dissolution statute after Illinois' example.[54] The 1953 MBCA stated that a shareholder could call for dissolution if "the acts of the directors or those in control of management are illegal, oppressive, or fraudulent."[55]

As oppression became more widely recognized over the course of the twentieth century, the courts needed to find ways to identify whether oppression had actually occurred. Some viewed oppression as akin to fraudulent or illegal acts. The Illinois court's 1957 decision in *Central Standard Life Insurance*[56] applied the term *oppression* more broadly than *fraudulent*

---

[51] *Finkelstein v. Liberty Media, Inc.*, 2005 Del. Ch. LEXIS 53 (Apr. 25, 2005), at *84.

[52] *Union Ill. 1995 Investment Ltd. P'ship v. Union Financial Group, Ltd.* 847 A.2d 340, 364 (Del. Ch. 2003).

[53] *Gearreald v. Just Care*, 2012 Del. Ch. LEXIS 91, at *1.

[54] Murdock, at 440.

[55] Comment, "Oppression as a Statutory Ground for Corporate Dissolution," 1965 *Duke L. J.*128, n. 2 (1965).

[56] *Central Standard Life Insurance v. Davis*, 141 N.E.2d 45, 51 (Ill. 1957).

or illegal activity despite finding in favor of the corporation. The term has come to include conduct by the majority that breaches fiduciary duty, denies the minority shareholder his or her reasonable expectations in acquiring shares and entering into a shareholder agreement, or is burdensome, harsh, and wrongful to minority shareholder interests. Oppressive acts by the majority can be very damaging to a minority shareholder; for example, a majority decision may eliminate a minority shareholder's ability to receive dividends or other types of benefits from a corporation.

Shareholder oppression now is seen to occur when the majority shareholders or the board of directors act in a manner that is detrimental to minority shareholders. New York's highest court described oppression in a 1984 decision:

> A shareholder who reasonably expected that ownership in the corporation would entitle him or her to a job, a share of corporate earnings, a place in corporate management, or some other form of security, would be oppressed in a very real sense when others in the corporation seek to defeat those expectations and there exists no effective means of salvaging the investment.[57]

Context of Oppression Remedy

Although dissent and oppression cases are sometimes grouped together, their nature is very different. Oppression is generally more personal. It often involves the loss of employment, exclusion from a close corporation that the stockholder may have helped build, or fallout between family members or business associates that results in the breaking up of a corporation. In contrast, dissent is generally less personal because it arises primarily from a financial decision in a corporation. Also dissenters' rights proceedings usually involve shareholders with small interests in a corporation.

There are some similarities between dissent and oppression cases. The primary similarity is that in most states they both use the fair value standard. Many courts understand the fair value definitions in the dissenters' rights statutes to carry over to the oppression statutes. Although the ALI asserts that fair value can be viewed differently for oppression and dissent, many courts disagree. For example, New Jersey's Supreme Court in *Balsamides*[58] agreed with Washington's Supreme Court in *Robblee*[59] that fair value in the oppressed shareholder context has the same meaning as

---

[57] *In re Kemp & Beatley, Inc.*, 473 N.E.2d 1173, 1179 (N.Y. 1984).

[58] *Balsamides v. Protameen Chemicals, Inc.*, 734 A.2d 721, 736 (N.J. 1999).

[59] *Robblee v. Robblee*, 841 P.2d 1289, 1294 (Wash. Ct. App. 1992).

in the dissenting shareholder context. In addition, many oppression and dissent cases cite each other for guidelines on how to deal with various elements of valuation.

Both oppression and dissent statutes and case law were developed to protect minority shareholders from being excluded or abused by the majority. In states where the oppression remedy is unavailable, oppressed shareholders may be entitled to exercise dissenters' rights. For example, reverse stock splits are often used to cash out minority shareholders by reducing the number of shares in a corporation so that certain members end up holding less than one share and are forced to sell it back to the corporation. The U.S. District Court for the Northern District of Illinois decided in *Connector Service Corp. v. Briggs* that the Delaware language governing reverse split cash-outs was similar to the language governing cash-out mergers and ordered the fair value of the oppressed shareholder's stock to be determined using the same criteria as in a cash-out merger.[60] This conclusion is consistent with the Delaware decision in *Metropolitan Life v. Aramark*, which granted a quasi-appraisal remedy in a reverse split.[61]

Closely held corporations present an unusual situation requiring departures from the corporate norm. Shareholders in large publicly held corporations necessarily relinquish their control over daily activities to the board of directors, and only function to elect the board and vote on fundamental transactions. Shareholders who disagree with corporate management may elect a new board or they may sell their shares in the open market. In contrast, in a closely held corporation, shareholders often serve as directors and officers of the corporation and minority shareholders do not have the alternative of selling their shares on the open market. Thus, shareholder agreements that set out the transfer of shares, voting rights, and election of directors are necessary safeguards for investors in close corporations. In addition, as a result of their small size, many close corporations operate without all of the strict formalities normally required in the operation of public corporations. In fact, the close corporation in many ways resembles a partnership.

One characteristic of a closely held corporation is that its shareholders often are also employees. Minority shareholders frequently invest with the expectation of receiving a salary from employment and of participating in the profits of the corporation. When an employee is frozen out of a

---

[60] *Connector Service Corp. v. Briggs*, 1998 U.S. Dist. Lexis 18864 (N.D. Ill., Oct. 30, 1998), at *18. Because appraisal and oppression cases are under state laws, federal courts follow state statutes and case law.

[61] *Metropolitan Life Ins. Co. v. Aramark Corp.*, 1998 Del. Ch. LEXIS 70 (Feb. 5, 1998).

corporation, it means that although he or she remains a shareholder, management eliminates that shareholder's job. Additionally, the majority may elect to eliminate the payment of dividends when applicable. Although the minority shareholder's ownership interest remains intact, that shareholder no longer receives the benefits he or she has received historically and expects as part of his or her investment.

Furthermore, there is no necessity for the company to buy out the minority shareholder, as it costs the company little to keep the shareholder locked in.[62] Alternatively, the minority shareholder may be compelled to accept an unfavorable price to gain liquidity.[63] If, however, the control shareholders do use their majority votes to force a squeeze-out merger, the minority shareholders will then have the option to exercise their dissenters' rights and seek appraisal.

Freeze-Outs and Squeeze-Outs[64] For public companies, freeze-outs are transactions in which minority shareholders are compelled to take cash for their shares, either in a cash merger or through a tender offer followed by a short-form merger. For private companies, the term *freeze-outs* covers compulsory buyouts as well as a broader range of actions by the controller. As Professor Moll wrote:

> Through this control of the board, the majority shareholder has the ability to take actions that are harmful to the minority shareholder's interests. Such actions are often referred to as "freeze-out" or "squeeze-out" techniques that "oppress" the close corporation minority shareholder. Standard freeze-out techniques include the refusal to declare dividends, the termination of a minority shareholder's employment, the removal of a minority shareholder from a position of management, and the siphoning off of corporate earnings through high compensation to the majority shareholder. Quite often, these tactics are used in combination. . . . Once the minority shareholder is faced with this "indefinite future with no return on the capital he or she contributed to the enterprise," the majority often proposes to purchase the shares of the minority shareholder at an unfairly low price.[65]

---

[62] Murdock, at 441.

[63] If the action to which the oppressed shareholder objects is a forced sale of his or her shares, the appraisal remedy may be available.

[64] The terms *freeze-out* and *squeeze-out* are commonly considered to be synonyms.

[65] Moll, "Minority Oppression and the Limited Liability Company," at 889–891.

Dissolution as a Remedy for Oppression

Presently, certain events trigger the right to call for judicial dissolution of a corporation.[66] Generally they fall under the categories of mismanagement, waste, fraud, or illegal acts by management and the board of directors. However, majority behavior does not necessarily have to be illegal or fraudulent to be unfair to a minority shareholder.

The shareholder oppression statutes are part of corporate dissolution statutes, which are the laws in place to provide guidelines for dissolving corporations. Dissolution statutes exist to provide procedures by which businesses may wrap up their business affairs and end their existence. Although, as noted above, most states use a combination of similar triggering events, the statutes are generally unique to each state.

Many states allow shareholder oppression as a triggering event for dissolution or a buyout of a claimant's shares.[67] Most states allow the oppressed minority shareholder to file for judicial dissolution; in those that do not, the oppressed shareholder must seek relief in other ways, such as a suit for breach of fiduciary duty.[68] Delaware does not include shareholder oppression in its dissolution statute.

Shareholder Buyouts as an Alternative Remedy

As long as dissolution was the primary remedy for oppressed minority shareholders, the courts were hesitant to find in favor of the minority share-

---

[66] The case law and concepts we address in this chapter deal exclusively with oppression in corporations and focus mainly on close corporations. Partnerships are not subject to the same remedies because of the withdrawal rights available by statute in most states. For LLCs, case law is in its infancy because of the relative newness of the corporate form. For more information on the remedies for minority mistreatment in all three corporate forms, see Moll, "Minority Oppression and the Limited Liability Company," at 892–895.

[67] An exception is Michigan, where an action citing oppression can be brought by the shareholder outside the dissolution statute, although dissolution (among others) may still be the remedy.

[68] Delaware and Indiana allow shareholder dissolution only in the case of deadlock. Kansas and Louisiana allow shareholder dissolution in the case of deadlock, but only if irreparable damage is being done to the corporation or shareholders. Massachusetts requires that no less than 40% outstanding shareholders can file for dissolution, but only in cases of shareholder or management deadlock. Michigan allows shareholders to file if they cannot agree on management and the corporation is not able to function properly. Nevada and Ohio allow shareholder dissolution only if petitioned by a majority. Oklahoma, Texas, and the District of Columbia do not allow shareholders to petition for dissolution.

holder. Oppressive conduct had to be egregious—a waste of assets or gross fraud or illegality. Dissolution is drastic because it results in the liquidation of the company and adversely affects employees, suppliers, and clients. An Alaska Supreme Court decision notes the problem:

> Liquidation is an extreme remedy. In a sense, forced dissolution allows minority shareholders to exercise retaliatory oppression against the majority. Absent compelling circumstances, courts often are reluctant to order involuntary dissolution. . . . As a result, courts have recognized alternative remedies based upon their inherent equitable powers.[69]

Dissolution remained the statutory remedy until the states began to institute buyout provisions for the shares of oppressed shareholders.[70] In 1941, California was the first state to institute a buyout provision; its statute[71] provided an option for a corporation to offer petitioning minority shareholders the fair cash value for their shares in lieu of dissolution.[72]

In 1973, the Oregon Supreme Court ruled that "for 'oppressive' conduct consisting of a 'squeeze out' or 'freeze out' in a 'close' corporation the courts are not limited to the remedy of dissolution, but may, as an alternative, consider other appropriate equitable relief."[73] The expressly permitted alternative is "[t]he ordering of affirmative relief by the entry of an order requiring the corporation or a majority of its stockholders to purchase the stock of the minority stockholders at a price to be determined according to a specified formula or at a price determined by the court to be a fair and reasonable price."[74] The decision proved highly influential, as many other states accepted the reasoning of the Oregon court and permitted buyouts as an alternative to dissolution.[75] A 1991 revision to the RMBCA introduced the compulsory buyout for shareholders filing for dissolution. By that time, the fair value buyout as an alternative remedy was already in use in some states, such as New York.

Several judicial remedies for the oppressed shareholder have emerged. If the court finds oppression, it can order a wide variety of remedies, including

---

[69] *Alaska Plastics, Inc. v. Coppock*, 621 P.2d 270, 274 (Alaska 1980).

[70] Murdock, at 453.

[71] 1941 Cal. Stat. 2058-59 (codified as amended at Cal. Corp. Code § 2000 (West 1977 & Supp. 1989)).

[72] Murdock, at 461.

[73] *Baker v. Commercial Body Builders, Inc.*, 507 P.2d 387, 395 (Ore. 1973).

[74] *Id.*, at 396.

[75] John H. Matheson and R. Kevin Maler, "A Simple Statutory Solution to Minority Oppression in the Closely Held Business," 91 *Minn. L. R.*, 657, 680–681 (2006).

an equitable distribution of the proceeds of a court-ordered liquidation or a compulsory buyout of the oppressed shareholder(s) shares at a court-determined fair value.[76] When the court orders a buyout, the price to be paid for the minority shares is judicially determined under the fair value standard.

If there is a chance the corporation will be found to have committed acts of oppression, fraud, mismanagement, abuse, or if the corporation anticipates dissolution being the outcome of the court proceeding, or if the corporation wants to avoid the court proceeding altogether, it may elect to purchase the petitioner's shares at their fair value within the statutory time

---

[76] The Oregon Supreme Court listed several "alternative remedies":

(a) The entry of an order requiring dissolution of the corporation at a specified future date, to become effective only in the event that the stockholders fail to resolve their differences prior to that date;

(b) The appointment of a receiver, not for the purposes of dissolution, but to continue the operation of the corporation for the benefit of all the stockholders, both majority and minority, until differences are resolved or "oppressive" conduct ceases;

(c) The appointment of a "special fiscal agent" to report to the court relating to the continued operation of the corporation, as a protection to its minority stockholders, and the retention of jurisdiction of the case by the court for that purpose;

(d) The retention of jurisdiction of the case by the court for the protection of the minority stockholders without appointment of a receiver or "special fiscal agent";

(e) The ordering of an accounting by the majority in control of the corporation for funds alleged to have been misappropriated;

(f) The issuance of an injunction to prohibit continuing acts of "oppressive" conduct and which may include the reduction of salaries or bonus payments found to be unjustified or excessive;

(g) The ordering of affirmative relief by the required declaration of a dividend or a reduction and distribution of capital;

(h) The ordering of affirmative relief by the entry of an order requiring the corporation or a majority of its stockholders to purchase the stock of the minority stockholders at a price to be determined according to a specified formula or at a price determined by the court to be a fair and reasonable price;

(i) The ordering of affirmative relief by the entry of an order permitting minority stockholders to purchase additional stock under conditions specified by the court;

(j) An award of damages to minority stockholders as compensation for any injury suffered by them as the result of "oppressive" conduct by the majority in control of the corporation.

Baker v. Commercial Body Builders, 507 P.2d 387, 395–396.

frame.[77] In this case, the dissolution proceeding will be put on hold (but not terminated) until an equitable settlement has been negotiated. One New York court pointed out that "once the corporation has elected to buy the petitioning stockholders' shares at fair value, the issue of majority wrongdoing is superfluous."[78] In addition, if the corporation elects the buyout, it may avoid the "equitable adjustments" the court might make in a case where wrongdoing is found, as well as other costs associated with a court proceeding.

In the buyout remedy, the company may elect to buy out the shareholder at fair value before a proceeding occurs, or the court can go forward with the proceeding. This leaves four scenarios when oppression is alleged:

1. If the company elects the buyout procedure after the oppressed minority shareholder has petitioned for dissolution, the company will pay fair value for the minority shares.
2. If the company does not elect the buyout option and the court finds that oppression has occurred, the company will ultimately pay fair value, plus any equitable adjustments the court requires.
3. If the court finds no oppression, the shareholder will likely not recover the fair value as a percentage of enterprise value, and the court may look to what the shareholder's share would bring on the open market, considering his or her minority status. This would imply the application of shareholder-level discounts.
4. If the court finds no oppression, there may be no buyout and the shareholder may be compelled to remain with the corporation.

As we have noted, in states with an election, if the election process does not succeed in reaching a value for the minority shares that is acceptable to both sides, the court may order a compulsory buyout of the minority shares. As Professor Moll describes it:

> Election provisions are designed to serve as a counterbalance to the dissolution-for-oppression statutes. Although an aggrieved investor is entitled to petition for dissolution of a company on the ground of oppressive conduct, shareholders who wish to continue the business may elect to buy out the petitioner's ownership stake to avoid any risk of dissolution. Thus, the purpose of the election provisions is to provide the remaining shareholders with a mechanism for continuing the business and, relatedly, to safeguard against

---

[77] Moll, "Shareholder Oppression and 'Fair Value,'" at 360.
[78] *In re Friedman*, 661 N.E. 2d 972, 976 (N.Y. 1985).

the risk of dissolution. In operation, an election usually circumvents any liability inquiry and converts an oppression lawsuit into a mere valuation proceeding. Indeed, because an election often occurs before a court has made a finding of oppression, the election statutes, in most instances, effectively create a no-fault "divorce" procedure. The company at issue continues as a going concern under the control of the majority shareholder, the allegedly aggrieved investor is cashed out of the business, and no finding of wrongdoing is made by the court.[79]

In cases of appraisal pursuant to a dissent action, an individual should receive the undiscounted proportionate value of the company as a going concern. In an oppression action, there are many other considerations caused by the degree of oppression and misconduct by the majority.

Exhibit 3.2 lists the states that have a buyout option in oppression cases and those that do not.

The generic terms *closely held corporation* or *close corporation* refer to privately held corporations formed under a state's regular business corporation statutes. A company is not a *statutory* close corporation unless it elects that status. As shown in Exhibit 3.2, the buyout option is offered only to statutory close corporations in some states, whereas in other states such an option is additionally available to all close corporations.

Statutory close corporations share the attributes of almost all close corporations: they are privately held, cannot make public offerings of stock, and shares are most often held by the owners/managers of the business and their families.[80] In addition, when shareholders die or wish to liquidate their interests, remaining shareholders or the company itself usually will purchase the shares.

---

[79] Moll, "Shareholder Oppression and 'Fair Value,'" at 69.

[80] Recognizing the unique issues presented by close corporations, 21 jurisdictions permit companies to elect statutory close corporation status. Four states— California, Maine, Ohio, and Rhode Island—permit corporations to elect statutory close corporation status pursuant to their regular corporation statutes. In addition,17 jurisdictions have enacted close corporation statutes permitting the election: Alabama, Arizona, Delaware, District of Columbia, Georgia, Illinois, Kansas, Maryland, Missouri, Montana, Nevada, Pennsylvania, South Carolina, Texas, Vermont, Wisconsin, and Wyoming. These entities can be run pursuant to their shareholder agreements, which is permitted to set forth and limit the duties and obligations of its shareholders.

Despite the ability to bypass some of the procedures required for close corporations, the great majority of corporations that otherwise would qualify to make a statutory close corporation election have not chosen to do so. Empirical studies have shown that only a very small percentage of corporations have ever registered

EXHIBIT 3.2 Availability of Buyout Remedy in Judicial Dissolution of Close Corporations by State

States	Buyout Available as Remedy
Alabama, Alaska, Arizona, California, Connecticut, District of Columbia, Florida,[a] Hawaii, Idaho, Illinois, Iowa, Maine, Michigan,[b] Minnesota, Mississippi, Montana, Nebraska, New Hampshire, New Jersey, New York, North Carolina,[c] North Dakota,[d] Rhode Island, South Carolina,[d] South Dakota, Utah, Virginia, West Virginia, Wyoming	Yes
Georgia, Maryland, Missouri, Oregon, Vermont, Wisconsin	Yes, but in statutory close corporation provision only
Arkansas, Colorado, Kentucky, New Mexico, Pennsylvania, Tennessee, Washington	No
Delaware, Indiana, Kansas, Louisiana, Massachusetts, Nevada, Ohio, Oklahoma, Texas	No statute providing for oppression as grounds for dissolution

a. The Florida dissolution statute applies only to companies with 35 or fewer shareholders.
b. In Michigan, once "illegal, fraudulent, or willfully unfair and oppressive" conduct has been established, the court may order dissolution, purchase at fair value, or other remedy provided for in the statute.
c. North Carolina allows the company to avoid dissolution by a buyout after the court decides that the situation merits dissolution.
d. In North Dakota and South Carolina, the court has equitable discretion to provide a buyout remedy.

---

as statutory close corporations. (Harwell Wells, "The Rise of the Close Corporation and the Making of Corporation Law," 5 *Berkeley Bus. L.J.* 263 (2008)).

To be eligible to elect statutory close corporation status in those states that provide that choice, corporations must meet certain criteria, such as size. To qualify, corporations cannot have more than a particular number of shareholders, typically a maximum of 30 or 50. In addition, shareholders usually must agree unanimously to statutory close corporation status and a written shareholders' agreement governing the affairs of the corporation must be drafted. It usually is also required that certain transfer restrictions appear on the corporation's stock certificates. Typically, where the close corporation statute, or shareholder agreement, is silent on a matter, the provisions of the state's regular business corporations statute will fill in the gaps.

Statutory close corporations are not heavily utilized, but the relevant statutes contain provisions that relate to the standard of value,[81] and they may differ from other closely held corporations both in those standards and in the remedies they provide. Only certain states provide statutory close corporation shareholders with dissolution as a remedy for oppressive or illegal conduct; others provide them with a buyout election in lieu of dissolution. Valuators involved in oppression cases need to work closely with counsel in the appropriate jurisdiction to understand the legal status of the entity in which they are valuing shares and to know what standard of value is applicable.

Examples of Oppression

Reasonable Expectations   More than 20 states use a "reasonable expectations" standard for oppression.[82] A breach of reasonable expectations was established as a fundamental determination of oppression based on the 1980 New York case *Topper v. Park Sheraton Pharmacy*,[83] one of the earliest cases in which the court ordered a buyout as an alternative remedy. In this case, the court found that the plaintiff's reasonable expectations were violated by an intentional freeze-out and ordered the buyout of his shares.

TOPPER V. PARK SHERATON PHARMACY

Three individuals operated two pharmacies in prominent Manhattan hotels, the New York Sheraton and the New York Hilton. The shareholder agreements were executed in early 1979. The agreements provided no method for transfer or purchase of shares, nor did they specify terms of employment. Topper associated himself with the other two individuals in the two corporations with the expectation of being an active participant in their operations. In order to participate, Topper ended a 25-year relationship with his prior employer and moved to New York, invested his life savings in the ventures, and executed personal guarantees of a lease extension and promissory notes for the purchase price of his stock interest.

---

[81] For example, Missouri explicitly provides statutory close corporation shareholders with dissenters' rights. § 351.870 R.S. Mo. (2012).

[82] Matheson and Maler, at 664.

[83] *Topper v. Park Sheraton Pharmacy*, 433 N.Y.S.2d 359 (N.Y. Supr. 1980).

The majority stockholders discharged Topper as an employee in February 1980, terminated his salary (after his salary had been raised from 150% in the first year), removed him as an officer and as a cosignatory on the corporate bank accounts, and changed the locks on the corporate office. Moreover, the corporations paid no dividends. The controlling shareholders claimed that the petitioner had suffered no harm, as his one-third interest remained intact.

The court deemed that the actions of the majority constituted a freeze-out and were oppressive because they violated Topper's reasonable expectations in joining the business. The court recognized that in a close corporation, the bargain of the participants is not necessarily reflected in the corporation's charter, bylaws, or other written agreement. In many small corporations, minority shareholders expect to participate in management and operations, and these expectations constitute the bargain of the parties by which subsequent conduct must be appraised.

The court also stated that New York's business corporation law determines that oppression of the "rights and interests" of minority shareholders in a close corporation is an abuse of corporate power. These rights are derived from the expectations of the parties underlying the formation of the corporation. The court awarded Topper the right to the fair market value[84] of his shares as of the day prior to the date of petition.

In a Connecticut case, the plaintiff sought to dissolve a corporation as tensions became high among the doctors in the corporation.[85] The plaintiff claimed she was entitled to a fair value of $338,000 as her share, but the shareholders' agreement stated that she was entitled to the net book value of the assets she had contributed to the corporation, a little over $13,000. No oppression was found by the court, and the court found it was *not* inequitable or unfair under the circumstances to look to the stockholders' agreement for a determination of value. This case indicates that maintenance of and adherence to a shareholders' agreement provides a certain amount of clarity

---

[84] It should be noted that although the courts were empowered to award fair value by N.Y. Statute § 1118, the court used the term *fair market value* as a substitute. It is unclear whether that substitution was intentional.

[85] *Stone v. R.E.A.L. Health, P.C.*, 2000 Conn. Super. LEXIS 2987 (Nov. 15, 2000).

as to shareholder expectations, as long as a particularly egregious breach of the agreement has not occurred.

Breach of Fiduciary Duty   The failure of the control shareholders to fulfill their fiduciary duties to the minority can be deemed to be oppression. According to Matheson and Maler, "twelve states have adopted a fiduciary duty approach that, for the most part, is expansive and could be employed to reach the same result as the reasonable expectations standard."[86] A landmark Massachusetts case offering relief to oppressed shareholders, *Donahue v. Rodd Electrotype*,[87] established that a breach of fiduciary duty (the obligation owed to minority shareholders by the majority) may determine whether shareholder oppression has occurred.[88]

DONOHUE V. RODD ELECTROTYPE OF NEW ENGLAND

In 1935, Harry C. Rodd began working for the Royal Electrotype Company of New England, Inc. ("Royal"). He became a director in 1936, and succeeded to the position of general manager and treasurer in 1946. Joseph Donahue was hired in 1936 as a "finisher" of electrotype plates. He became plant superintendent in 1946 and corporate vice president in 1955, but never participated in the management of the business.

Rodd and Donahue acquired 200 and 50 shares, respectively, of Royal at $20 per share. Another individual owned 25 shares and the parent company (Royal Electrotype of Pennsylvania) retained 725 shares.

In June 1955, Royal purchased all 725 shares from the parent company at a total price of $135,000. The 25 shares owned by the other individual were also purchased. The stock purchases left Harry Rodd as the 80% majority shareholder. Donahue was the only minority shareholder. The company subsequently was named Rodd Electrotype of New England.

Harry Rodd's sons assumed control of the company between 1959 and 1967. Harry Rodd also pursued a gift program by which he distributed his shares among his two sons and his daughter,

---

[86] Matheson and Maler, at 664.
[87] *Donahue v. Rodd Electrotype of New England*, 328 N.E.2d 505 (Mass. 1975).
[88] Massachusetts does not have a dissolution statute.

each child receiving 39 shares, with 2 shares being returned to the corporate treasury. In 1970, Harry Rodd was 77 and wished to retire, but he insisted that some financial arrangements be made regarding his remaining 81 shares. The directors decided that they would purchase 45 shares for $800 a share ($36,000). Following this, each child was gifted additional shares such that each held 51 shares. Donahue's heirs still owned 50 shares: his wife, Euphemia, owned 45 and his son, Robert, owned five.

In 1971, the Donahues learned that the corporation had purchased Harry Rodd's shares. The minutes of the meeting show that the stockholders unanimously voted to ratify the stock purchase agreement. However, the trial judge found that the Donahues did not vote affirmatively.

Euphemia Donahue offered her shares to the corporation on the same terms given to Harry Rodd. The corporation refused to purchase the shares as it was not in a financial position to do so.

As plaintiff, Euphemia characterized the purchase of Harry Rodd's shares as an unlawful distribution of corporate assets to controlling shareholders constituting a breach of fiduciary duty. The defendants claimed that the purchase was within the powers of the corporation and met the requirements of good faith and inherent fairness, and asserted that there is no right to equal opportunity in corporate stock purchases for the corporate treasury.

The court characterized the transaction as a preferential distribution of assets. The control shareholder had received an advantage over his fellow shareholders and had turned corporate funds to personal use. That action was inconsistent with the strict standard of fiduciary duty required in close corporations. The court ordered that either Harry Rodd remit the $36,000 with interest or that the plaintiff's 45 shares be purchased for $36,000 without interest.

Heavy-Handed, Arbitrary, or Overbearing Conduct Illinois uses the standard of heavy-handed and arbitrary or overbearing conduct to determine whether oppression has occurred. This definition leaves great discretion to the court's judgment on oppressive conduct. The standard was established by a 1972 Illinois case, *Compton v. Paul K. Harding Realty Co.*[89]

---

[89] *Compton v. Paul K. Harding Realty Co.*, 285 N.E.2d 574 (Ill. App 1972).

COMPTON V. PAUL K. HARDING REALTY CO.

Martha Compton was an officer and a shareholder of the Paul Harding Realty Corporation along with the defendant, Paul Harding. When they formed the business together in 1962, Harding led the discussions and planning on the formation of the corporation due to his more extensive experience in real estate.

Once the corporation was formed, Compton and Harding continued discussions in regard to an agreement between the shareholders. Compton testified that an agreement was drafted on yellow paper and later typed up by Harding. The provision that she had required was that the corporation was not to have any additional shareholders, other than Compton, Harding, and her brother, Forrest Leoty. The document was undated, but typed on letterhead and signed by Compton, Harding, and Leoty.

The record of the case states that from the beginning the corporation was loosely managed and shares were not distributed in accordance with the memorandum. Although the agreement stipulated that Harding's salary would be $100 per week, at the onset of business he received $175, soon raising it to $200. In the fall of 1964, the salary was raised to $250 per week. He also received commissions.

Compton contended that Harding was guilty of self-dealing and corporate mismanagement in raising his own salary without notice to the shareholders, contrary to the terms of the agreement. The court found that between incorporation and the trial, Harding had taken an amount in excess of his contractual salary, which was to be paid back to the corporation before liquidation, but it did not find that fraud had occurred. Harding claimed that the agreement he signed should have no effect, but the court stated that many close corporations have similar agreements and these have previously been recognized by the courts.

Last, and most significant with respect to the precedent set by this case, Harding claimed that there was no statutory basis by which the court could order liquidation because he had committed no fraud. The court looked to the statute indicating the availability of dissolution if the acts of the directors are illegal, oppressive, or fraudulent. The court referred to *Central Standard Life Insurance*, which held that oppression is not necessarily synonymous with illegal and fraudulent behavior and established the doctrine of heavy-handed, arbitrary, and overbearing conduct as a test for oppression, stating:

> We think there is ample evidence in the record showing an arbitrary, overbearing and heavy-handed course of conduct of the defendant Harding to justify the finding of oppression and the order of dissolution. Specific instances of such evidence include testimony regarding the failure of defendant Harding to call meetings of the board of directors or to consult with plaintiff Compton regarding management of corporate affairs, his imperious attitude when questioned about his salary and his dilatory reaction to the plaintiffs' requests.[90]

FAIR VALUE IS THE STANDARD OF VALUE IN APPRAISAL AND OPPRESSION IN ALMOST ALL STATES

Fair Value as Defined by Various Authorities and Statutes

Professors Lawrence Hamermesh and Michael Wachter write that in Delaware "the measure of 'fair value' in share valuation proceedings is superior, in both fairness and efficiency, to its two main competitors, [fair] market value and third-party sale value."[91] They posit that the fair value standard is fairer to opposing parties in a dispute than either fair market value or third-party sale value because fair value attempts to balance the dangers that lie in either direction: on one side, that of awarding a windfall to an opportunistic controller who has forced out the minority shareholders; on the other side, incentivizing litigation by minority shareholders attempting to capture value from controllers whose energies and abilities have resulted in increased company value through a synergistic transaction. These writers suggest that fair value strikes the best balance in the attempt to value what was taken from the minority by awarding them the pro rata share of the existing company's going-concern value. *Going-concern value* is the present value of the cash flows to be generated from the corporation's existing assets plus its reinvestment opportunities.[92]

Fair value is the standard of value for appraisal in 47 states and the District of Columbia.[93] State statutes vary, but most draw inspiration from

---

[90] *Id.*, at 581.

[91] Hamermesh and Wachter, "Rationalizing Appraisal Standards," at 1021.

[92] *Id.*, at 1022.

[93] Wisconsin uses *fair value* for all purposes other than business combinations, for which it uses *fair market value*. *Wis. Stat. Ann.*, §§ 180.1301, 180.1130(9)(a).

the MCBA (1969) and the later RMBCAs (1984 and 1999). In order to address the fair value standard, we look at the definitions in the various iterations. The 1969 MBCA set out that "fair value" was to be the measure by which the minority shareholder was to be paid for his or her shares, but it provided no details on fair value's definition. It stated that:

> [S]uch corporation shall pay to such shareholder, upon surrender of the certificate or certificates representing such shares, the fair value thereof as of the day prior to the date on which the vote was taken approving the proposed corporate action, excluding any appreciation or depreciation in anticipation of such corporate action.[94]

In 1984, the ABA issued the RMBCA, which added important additional concepts to the definition of fair value. It excluded from the value of minority shares the synergy value of the objected-to transaction "unless exclusion would be inequitable." It reads:

> The value of the shares immediately before the effectuation of the corporate action to which the dissenter objects, excluding any appreciation or depreciation in anticipation of the corporate action *unless exclusion would be inequitable* [added language in italics].[95]

The 1984 definition provides a guideline, however nonspecific, by which fair value should be determined. The company should be valued on the day before the corporate action occurs without any of the effects of the action unless their exclusion would be unfair. The passage does not give instructions on what method or valuation technique should be utilized to determine the fair value, nor does it define *inequitable*. Twenty-one states[96] currently use this exact definition of fair value. The intentional ambiguity in this definition allows for wide interpretation of the assumptions that underlie this standard of value. Comments published by the ABA explain that this definition leaves the matter to the courts to determine "the details by which fair value is to be determined within the broad outlines of the definition."[97]

---

[94] 1969 RMBCA.

[95] 1984 RMBCA.

[96] Alabama, Arizona, Arkansas, Colorado, Hawaii, Illinois, Indiana, Kentucky, Massachusetts, Michigan, Missouri, Montana, Nebraska, Nevada, New Hampshire, North Carolina, Oregon, South Carolina, Vermont, Washington, Wyoming.

[97] American Bar Association, *A Report of the Committee of Corporate Laws*, "Changes in the Revised Model Business Corporation Act: Amendments Pertaining to Close Corporations," 54 *Bus. Lawyer*, 209 (November 1998).

While insuring that the courts have wide discretion, this ambiguity can create confusion on the part of appraisers and appraisal users. Valuation professionals are well advised to discuss this with counsel so as to come to an understanding of the specific interpretation relevant to their state or appropriate jurisdiction.

Although most state statutes use the RMBCA's definition of fair value, six states have utilized the ALI's concept of fair value in case law.[98] In the *Principles of Corporate Governance*, published in 1992, the ALI defined fair value as:

> . . . the value of the eligible holder's proportionate interest in the corporation, without any discount for minority status or, absent extraordinary circumstances, lack of marketability. Fair value should be determined using the customary valuation concepts and techniques generally employed in the relevant securities and financial markets for similar businesses in the context of the transaction giving rise to appraisal.[99]

In 1999, following the development of substantial case law on dissent and oppression, as well as the publication of the ALI's *Principles of Corporate Governance*, the RMBCA was revised so that the definition of fair value reads:

> The value of the shares immediately before the effectuation of the corporate action to which the shareholder objects *using customary and current valuation concepts and techniques generally employed for similar businesses in the context of the transaction requiring appraisal,* and without discounting for lack of marketability or minority status *except, if appropriate, for amendments to the certificate of incorporation* [added language in italics].[100]

The 1999 RMBCA definition mirrors the ALI's *Principles of Corporate Governance* in that it adds two important concepts to the framework: the use of customary and current valuation techniques, and the rejection of the use of marketability and minority discounts except, "if appropriate, for amendments to the certificate of incorporation pursuant to section 13.02(a)(5)."[101] (The exception permitting discounts for

---

[98] Colorado, Minnesota, New Jersey, Arizona, Connecticut, Utah.

[99] ALI, *Principles of Corporate Governance*, at § 7.22.

[100] 1999 RMBCA.

[101] § 13.02(a)(5) of the 1999 RMBCA states that "any other amendment to the articles of incorporation, merger, share exchange or disposition of assets *to the extent*

amendments to the certificate of incorporation is minor in impact.)
The dissenters' rights statutes of 11 jurisdictions currently follow this
definition.[102]

Other states, including Delaware, have developed their own definitions
of fair value or have used different standards of value in their statutes. For
example, although New Jersey has used fair value as its statutory standard
for appraisal since 1968,[103] its oppression statute includes a clause that allows for "equitable adjustments."

Only three states—Louisiana, Ohio, and California—do not explicitly
use the phrase *fair value* for dissenters' rights. Louisiana and Ohio use *fair
cash value*, but with different meanings. Ohio's appraisal standard is unfavorable to dissenters, as discussed later in this chapter under "**Ohio's Unique
and Unfavorable Standard of Value in Appraisals.**" In contrast, the Louisiana statute's wording is favorable: "'[F]air cash value' means a value *not less
than the highest price paid* per share by the acquiring person in the control
share acquisition [emphasis added]."[104] Thus, a Louisiana court may determine that the value is higher than the transaction price, but the dissenter
cannot receive less.

California uses the term "fair *market* value" in dissent (but not in oppression). Its dissent statute states:

> The fair market value shall be determined as of the day before the
> first announcement of the terms of the proposed reorganization
> or short-form merger, excluding any appreciation or depreciation
> in consequence of the proposed action, but adjusted for any stock
> split, reverse stock split, or share dividend which becomes effective
> thereafter.[105]

---

*provided by the articles of incorporation, bylaws or a resolution of the board of
directors* [emphasis added]." The official comment to the 1999 RMBCA states that
if the corporation grants appraisal rights voluntarily for certain transactions that
do not affect the entire corporation, the court can use its discretion in applying
discounts.

[102] Connecticut, D.C., Florida, Idaho, Iowa, Maine, Mississippi, Nevada, South
Dakota, Virginia, West Virginia.

[103] *Balsamides*, 734 A.2d 721, 736.

[104] La. R.S. 12:140.2.C. (2012).

[105] 2010 Cal. Corp. Code, Chapter 13, Dissenters' Rights § 1303 (a). Given this definition, dissent does not appear to be an attractive option for shareholders, and it is
not surprising that there are no reported California dissent cases.

The dissolution statutes in California and Alaska permit payment of fair value in lieu of dissolution, and both state:

> The fair value shall be determined on the basis of the liquidation value as of the valuation date but taking into account the possibility, if any, of sale of the entire business as a going concern in liquidation.[106]

The term *fair value in liquidation*, as used in California and Alaska, is unusual since most states attempt to determine fair value in oppression circumstances under the assumption that the business will continue to operate as a going concern.

The diversity among states in their definitions of fair value combined with the complexity of each state's statutes compels valuation experts to consult with counsel for guidance before undertaking their fairness assessment.

As noted earlier, the majority of states use all or part of the RMBCA's definition of fair value. This definition involves several components, and in order to understand the requirements of the definition, it is important to break it down and understand each component separately.

THE VALUATION DATE—BEFORE THE EFFECTUATION OF THE CORPORATE ACTION TO WHICH THE SHAREHOLDER OBJECTS

In both appraisal and oppression cases, the valuation date is a critical component that can significantly affect a court's ultimate fair value assessment. This portion of the definition suggests a time frame for the valuation: it instructs the court to set a valuation date immediately prior to the corporate action from which the shareholder dissents. Most states follow the RMBCA and say that valuation should reflect the value on the day before the corporate action occurred or was voted on to which the shareholder dissents. This indicates that the shareholder should not suffer or benefit from the proceeds or effects of the transaction from which he or she dissented.

Valuation Date in Appraisal Cases

In appraisal cases, state statutes instruct the court as to the appropriate valuation date. Most states define the valuation date as the day of, or the day before, the effectuation of the corporate action from which the shareholder dissents. However, some states define the valuation date as the day of

---

[106] Cal. Corp. Code, § 2000(a); Alas. Stat. § 10.06.630(a).

or the day before the shareholder vote.[107] California is an anomaly: it uses day before the transaction was *announced* as the valuation date.

Although the date of effectuation of the corporate action is the valuation date in appraisal cases, what may be considered in the determination of fair value is often at issue. The general rule is that all information that is known *or knowable* as of the valuation date is generally to be considered. The *Tri-Continental* case, more than 60 years ago, stated that "facts which were known or which could be ascertained as of the date of merger" must be considered, as these are essential in determining value.[108]

In a few cases, events occurring after the valuation date have been used as a "sanity test" to check the validity of the corporate transaction valuation date fairness calculation. For example, in *Lane v. Cancer Treatment Centers*, the court allowed postvaluation date discovery for a year after the action to test the assumptions underlying a pre-merger discounted cash flow (DCF) calculation.[109]

In *Lawson Mardon Wheaton*, the lower courts refused to consider a post-event acquisition price.[110] The New Jersey Supreme Court, recognizing that Delaware had allowed the use in appraisal of certain post-merger information in order to better determine fair value at the time of merger,[111] decided to permit the consideration of certain post-event information.[112] The dissenter's assertion was that the trial court's fair value of $41.50 per share in 1991 was questionable because, in 1996, an acquisition price of $63 per share was offered. The court reasoned that the value of $41.50 per share in 1991, when the company was doing well, should be questioned in light of an actual sale in 1996 at $63 per share when the company's performance was poorer.

Valuation Date in Oppression Cases

In oppression, similarly as in appraisal, the valuation date is crucial to the fair value determination.

---

[107] Alaska, Louisiana, Maryland, Michigan, Missouri, New Mexico, New York, Ohio, and Rhode Island.

[108] *Tri-Continental*, 74 A.2d 71, 72.

[109] *Lane v. Cancer Treatment Centers of America, Inc.*, 1994 Del. Ch. LEXIS 67 (May 25, 1994), at *10–11.

[110] *Lawson Mardon Wheaton v. Smith*, 716 A.2d 550 (N.J. Super. 1998), *rev'd*, 734 A.2d 738 (N.J. 1999).

[111] *Cede & CO. v. Technicolor*, 1990 Del. Ch. LEXIS 259 (Oct. 19, 1990), *aff'd in part and rev'd in part on other grounds*, 634 A.2d 345(Del. 1993).

[112] *Lawson Mardon Wheaton*, 734 A.2d 738, 751–52.

"The [court's] determination of fair value [in oppression cases] is also critically influenced by the choice of the valuation date. . . . The question is of enormous consequence to the relevant parties, as a company's value is affected by internal and external factors that can materially change over a short period of time. The designation of the valuation date therefore is an important inquiry in and of itself, as the choice of date can significantly affect a court's ultimate fair value conclusion."[113]

The issues concerning the valuation date differ, but are equally important to the relief or the remedies for the oppressed shareholder. The valuation date for fair value will be the same when (a) the state statute or court permits the company or its majority shareholders to attempt to avoid trial by electing to purchase the dissenter's shares, or (b) no such election is made (or statutorily permitted) and the court finds oppression and orders a compulsory buyout as a remedy.

The RMBCA suggests that the court should "determine the fair value of the petitioner's shares as of the day before the date on which the [dissolution] petition . . . was filed or as of such other date as the court deems appropriate under the circumstances."[114] Three types of valuation dates may be used, and there are debates as to which is appropriate and under what circumstances. The date used in a substantial majority of fair value determinations is the date of filing (or the preceding day).[115] This date not only has the virtue of clarity and simplicity—it also embodies the notion that the minority shareholder has kept his shareholder status in the company as long as he chose to do so before feeling compelled to exit because of oppressive majority behavior.

The second most frequently used valuation date is the date of oppression, which may be much more difficult to determine. Since oppressive conduct usually occurs not on a single date but over a period of time, the court may have to assess when the most severe acts of oppression occurred in order to select a valuation date. Although this complicates the date of oppression, Moll posits that courts are competent to evaluate the evidence and to choose a date when the most damaging oppressive conduct occurred.[116]

---

[113] Moll, "Shareholder Oppression and 'Fair Value,'" at 366–367. For a comprehensive and informative discussion on valuation dates in oppression cases, see the commentary entitled "The Valuation Date," at 366–381.

[114] RMBCA § 14.34(d).

[115] New York uses the day before the date the petition was filed and Rhode Island uses the date of filing. California and New Jersey suggest the date of filing, but leave the door open for the court to designate an alternative date if more equitable.

[116] Moll, "Shareholder Oppression and 'Fair Value,'" at 371.

The third alternative is a post filing valuation date (i.e., the trial date, the judgment date, or the date a buyback order is issued). Moll points out the flaws in using a post-filing valuation date:

> A presumptive post filing valuation date is problematic, however, because the parties' actions will be influenced by the litigation context. In addition, . . . if the valuation period extends through (and potentially beyond) the date of trial, experts may be unable to draw final conclusions about a company's value by the time their reports are due, by the time their deposition testimony is required, and perhaps even by the time their trial testimony is needed.[117]

The arguments among these different valuation dates differ depending on whether election is permitted in the state in which the oppression occurred. When the company or majority is permitted to elect to buy out dissenters' shares, the argument for the use of the date of filing is strong. As Moll explains:

> [S]hareholders who wish to continue the business may elect to buy out the petitioner's ownership stake to avoid any risk of dissolution. . . . [B]ecause an election often occurs before a court has made a finding of oppression, the election statutes, in most instances, effectively create a no-fault "divorce" procedure. . . . [T]he allegedly aggrieved investor is cashed out of the business, and no finding of wrongdoing is made by the court.[118]

In nonelection cases, the arguments on balance are more persuasive for using the date of oppression. Since the majority has frustrated the oppressed shareholder's reasonable expectations and forced him or her into a non participatory role, it can be argued that adverse changes in the company's value post-freeze-out (or other oppressive act) should not be borne by the oppressed shareholder. Moll writes:

> The logical consequence of this argument is that a court should set the valuation date as close as possible to when the oppressive exclusion from management occurred, as that date signifies when the majority decided that the minority's participation would cease.[119]

---

[117] *Id.*, at 372–373.

[118] *Id.*, at 369.

[119] *Id.*, at 375.

In a variation of setting the valuation date as the date of oppression, some courts view the date of a specific act of oppression as the appropriate valuation date. When this has been done, it has depended on the specific facts and circumstances of the case. For example, a Washington court ruled that "'fair value' means the shares' value at the moment just before the majority committed misconduct."[120] A federal court concluded, "In cases of minority stockholder oppression, the date of ouster seems appropriately used."[121]

However, in nonelection cases, Moll argues that the use of the filing date can be justified as a means of allowing an oppressed shareholder the ability to benefit from increases in the value of the business:

[T]he date of filing is defensible as the presumptive valuation date to the extent that it is deemed to reflect the "unofficial" end of a plaintiff's shareholder status. Up until that point, the oppressed investor was entitled, as a shareholder, to participate in any changes in the company's value. It is important to note that this rationale can work both for and against a plaintiff shareholder, as changes in the company's value from the date of oppression to the date of filing can encompass losses as well as gains.[122]

[However,] no one will ever know with certainty what would have happened because the majority oppressively denied the minority an opportunity to participate. Because this uncertainty stems from the majority's conduct, it is appropriate to resolve the uncertainty against the majority's interests. If a company experienced post oppression losses, a court could legitimately presume that the minority's managerial participation would have prevented the decline. On this basis, a court could decide that the minority does not have to share in the losses.[123]

Although valuation dates vary not only among states but sometimes within states where the courts may use their discretion, "the date of filing of the oppression action is usually designated as the presumptive valuation date."[124]

---

[120] *Prentiss v. Wesspur, Inc.*, 1997 Wash. App. LEXIS 637 at *1–2 (Apr. 28, 1997).

[121] *Hendley v. Lee*, 676 F. Supp. 1317, 1327 (D.S.C. 1987).

[122] Moll, "Shareholder Oppression and 'Fair Value,'" at 373.

[123] *Id.*, at 377.

[124] *Id.*, at 368.

CUSTOMARY AND CURRENT VALUATION TECHNIQUES

As a result of numerous fair value cases, a considerable body of law suggesting various methodologies to arrive at fair value emerged in the twentieth century. One such well-known methodology is the Delaware block method. Midway through the twentieth century, the Delaware block method was often used for determining value in the context of appraisal rights,[125] and was relied on almost exclusively by the Delaware courts until 1983. This method was also adopted in several other states that tended to rely on Delaware cases related to corporate law.

The Delaware block method weights a company's *investment value* (based on earnings and dividends), *market value* (usually based on its public trading price, guideline public company information, or guideline transaction information), and *asset value* (usually the net asset value based on current value of the underlying assets). These individual values are determined and then assigned a weight selected by the valuator to compute the fair value.[126] Many viewed the Delaware block method as mechanistic and not reflective of the techniques regularly employed by those in the financial community.

In 1983, the Delaware Supreme Court's landmark *Weinberger* decision[127] enunciated the concept that a company could be valued using alternative methods customarily employed by the financial community, rather than relying on the long-established Delaware block method.

WEINBERGER V. UOP, INC.

UOP, Inc. was a diversified industrial company that engaged in petroleum and petrochemical services, construction, fabricated metal, transportation, chemicals, plastics, and other products and services. Its stock was publicly held and traded on the New York Stock Exchange. Signal Corporation, Inc. was a diversified technology company operating through various subsidiaries, including the Garrett Corporation and Mack Trucks, Inc.

---

[125] *In re General Realty & Utilities Corp.*, 52 A.2d 6, 11 (1947).

[126] Gilbert E. Matthews and M. Mark Lee, "Fairness Opinions and Common Stock Valuations," in *The Library of Investment Banking*, Vol. IV, R. Kuhn, ed. (Homewood, IL: Dow Jones Irwin, 1990), at 386.

[127] *Weinberger v. UOP, Inc.*, 457 A.2d 701 (Del. 1983) (*"Weinberger"*).

In 1975, negotiations took place and through tender offer and direct purchase, Signal obtained its 50.5% interest in UOP at $21 per share, while the stock was trading at slightly under $14. At UOP's annual meeting, Signal elected 6 members to the 13-member board. When the chief executive officer (CEO) of UOP retired in 1975, Signal replaced him with an executive of the Garret Corporation, who took the old CEO's position on the board as well.

UOP then went through some difficult years financially. During that time, Signal performed a study of the feasibility of acquiring the 49.5% balance of UOP's shares. The study indicated that acquiring the shares at any price under $24 would be a good value. Signal's executive committee proposed a merger by which the remaining shares would be cashed out at $21 per share. UOP's shares were trading at $14.50 the day prior to the announcement of the merger.

At the annual meeting, the merger was voted on, and 56% of the minority shares were voted. Of these, 2,953,812 voted in favor of the merger and 254,850 voted against it. In May 1978, UOP became a wholly owned subsidiary of Signal Companies, and UOP's former minority shareholders were cashed out at $21 per share for their former interests in UOP.

In a class action, the plaintiff claimed that the $21 price was grossly inadequate and unfair to UOP's minority shareholders. He asked that the minority shareholders be awarded damages or the appropriate value for their shares based on the substantial assets of the company. There were additional charges of abuse of authority, misleading shareholders, and a breach of fiduciary duty for failure to argue for a higher value of the shares.

The defendants held that their purpose was in no way illegal. They asserted that the $21 per share price, which was a 40% premium over market price, was more than fair to the minority.

Plaintiff's expert used a comparative analysis based on an analysis of the premium paid over market in 10 other tender-offer merger combinations and a discounted cash flow method. By these methods, he concluded that the value of the shares was no less than $26 per share. The defendant's expert used the Delaware block method and weighted the market value, net asset value, and investment value to come to the conclusion that the $21 share price was fair to minority shareholders. The trial court agreed with the defendant's expert, consistent with the precedent of utilizing the Delaware block method to value shares. The Court of Chancery ruled that the merger met the entire fairness standard. It decided that UOP's failure to obtain appraisals of all property and assets was not a breach of fiduciary duty because the appraisals would have no bearing on the fairness of the merger.

Upon appeal, the Delaware Supreme Court overturned the ruling, stating that there were misrepresentations made by the directors in the failure to supply sufficient information to shareholders, including a study conducted by Signal itself concluding that $24 would be a good price to acquire the additional shares.

> Until the $21 price is measured on remand by the valuation standards mandated by Delaware law, there can be no finding at the present stage of these proceedings that the price is fair. Given the lack of any candid disclosure of the material facts surrounding establishment of the $21 price, the majority of the minority vote, approving the merger, is meaningless.
>
> . . . On remand the plaintiff will be permitted to test the fairness of the $21 price by the standards we herein establish, in conformity with the principle applicable to an appraisal—that fair value be determined by taking "into account all relevant factors."[128]

The court relied on a 1981 amendment to the state's dissent statute referencing fair value that directs the court to "take into account all relevant factors." The court concluded that there was a legislative intent to fully compensate shareholders for their loss.

The Supreme Court decided that the Delaware block method excluded other generally accepted techniques used in the financial community and the courts, and was therefore outmoded. It stated that the standard should no longer be the exclusive technique used in valuation.

> We believe that a more liberal approach must include proof of value by any techniques or methods which are generally considered acceptable in the financial community and otherwise admissible in court, subject only to our interpretation of 8 Del. C. § 262(h).[129]

---

[128] *Id.*, at 714.
[129] *Id.*, at 713.

The Court of Chancery's findings that both the circumstances of the merger and the price paid to the minority shareholder were fair were overturned, and the matter was remanded for further proceedings. Upon remand, members of the plaintiffs' class were awarded an additional $1.00 per share in damages plus interest.[130]

Weinberger did not immediately do away with the use of the Delaware block method, but it is now rarely used in practice either in Delaware or elsewhere. *Weinberger* allowed widely accepted alternative valuation procedures to be used, as well as industry-appropriate valuation techniques. The appropriate valuation method is not the same in every case. It is likely that a court will use the most relevant evidence presented to it to determine value. As customary techniques have evolved, so has the case law. The Delaware block method looked only at historical data, and the courts now prefer forward-looking approaches in determining fair value. As a result, the discounted cash flow method is widely used in dissenting shareholder cases.

The ALI's *Principles of Corporate Governance* and the ABA's model statutes recommend that fair value be determined using the customary valuation concepts and techniques generally employed for similar businesses in financial markets. As corporations have different underlying assets, no universal technique of measurement can cover all industries. Therefore, it is necessary to allow flexibility in valuation so that the valuation professional and the courts can use their best judgment to find equitable outcomes.[131]

Exhibit 3.3 addresses the statutory guidance provided for determining fair value (or other standard of value) in states whose statutes include the use of *customary and current valuation concepts and techniques, all relevant factors,* or other guidance relating to the method of valuation.

The *Weinberger* court's directive that all methods typically used by the financial community be considered in these matters resulted in courts permitting the use of a number of methodologies recognized by the financial community. The primary methods that have been considered include:

- *Discounted cash flow (DCF)—the income approach. Weinberger* used the discounted cash flow method in its departure from the standard

---

[130] *Weinberger v. UOP, Inc.,* 1985 Del. Ch. LEXIS 378 (Jan. 30, 1985), at *31; *aff'd,* 497 A.2d 792 (Del. 1985).

[131] ALI, *Principles of Corporate Governance,* at 318.

EXHIBIT 3.3 Guidance Provided by Statutory Language with Respect to Valuation Techniques

State	Guidance Provided by Statutory Language as to Valuation Techniques[a]
Delaware § 262(h) Kansas § 17-6712(h) Oklahoma § 18-1091(H)	. . . the fair value of the shares exclusive of any element of value arising from the accomplishment or expectation of the merger or consolidation. . . . In determining such fair value, the Court shall take into account *all relevant factors.*
Connecticut § 33-855 District of Columbia § 29-311.01(4) Idaho § 30-1-1301(4) Iowa § 490.1301(4) South Dakota § 47-1A-1301(4) Virginia § 13.1-729 West Virginia § 31D-13-1302(5)(a) Wyoming § 17-16-1301(a)(iv)	. . . using customary and *current valuation concepts and techniques* generally employed for similar businesses in the context of the transaction requiring appraisal and without discounting for lack of marketability or minority status except, if appropriate, for amendments to the certificate of incorporation.
Maine § 1301(4) Mississippi § 79-4-13.01(4) Nevada § 92A.320	. . . using *customary and current valuation concepts and techniques* generally employed for similar businesses in the context of the transaction requiring appraisal, and without discounting for lack of marketability or minority status.
Alaska (appraisal) § 10.06.580(c) New York § 623(h)(4)	. . . the *concepts and methods then customary in the relevant securities and financial markets* for determining fair value of shares of a corporation engaging in a similar transaction under comparable circumstances and all other relevant factors.
Alaska (oppression) § 10.06.630(a)	Fair value shall be determined on the basis of the *liquidation value,* taking into account the possibility of *sale of the entire business as a going concern* in a liquidation.

134

Jurisdiction	Description
California (appraisal) § 1300(a)	The fair market value shall be determined the day before the first announcement of the terms of the proposed reorganization or short-form merger excluding any appreciation or depreciation in consequence of the proposed action, but adjusted for any stock split, reverse stock split, or share dividend which becomes effective thereafter.
California (oppression) § 2000(a)	The fair value shall be determined on the basis of the *liquidation value* as of the valuation date but taking into account the possibility, if any, of the *sale of the entire business as a going concern* in a liquidation.
Florida § 607.1301 (4)	Using *customary and current valuation concepts* and techniques generally employed for similar businesses in the context of the transaction requiring appraisal, excluding any appreciation or depreciation in anticipation of the corporate action. . . . For a corporation with 10 or fewer shareholders, without discounting for lack of marketability or minority status.
Illinois § 805 ILCS 5/11.70(j)(1)	The proportionate interest of the shareholder in the corporation, without discount for minority status or absent extraordinary circumstance, lack of marketability . . .
Louisiana § 12:140:2	A value not less than the highest price paid per share by the acquiring person in the control share acquisition.
New Jersey (appraisal) § 14A. 11-3	. . . "fair value" shall exclude any appreciation or depreciation resulting from the proposed action.
New Jersey (oppression) § 14A:12-7(8)(a)	Fair value as of the date of the commencement of the action *or such earlier or later date deemed equitable by the court, plus or minus any adjustments deemed equitable by the court* if the action was brought in whole or in part under paragraph 14A:12-7(1)(c) .

(continued)

135

EXHIBIT 3.3 (*Continued*)

State	Guidance Provided by Statutory Language as to Valuation Techniques[a]
Ohio § 1701.85(C) (corporations); § 1705.42(B) (LLCs); § 1782.437(B) (LPs)	The amount that a *willing seller* who is under no compulsion to sell would be willing to accept and that a *willing buyer* who is under no compulsion to purchase would be willing to pay, but in no event shall the fair cash value of a share exceed the amount specified in the demand of the particular shareholder. In computing fair cash value, any appreciation or depreciation in market value resulting from the proposal submitted to the directors or to the shareholders (merger, consolidation, or conversion) shall be excluded.
Pennsylvania § 1572	. . . taking into account all relevant factors, but excluding any appreciation or depreciation in anticipation of the corporate action.
Texas § 10.362(a)	Consideration must be given to the value of a domestic entity as a going concern without including in the computation of value any control premium, any minority discount, or any discount for lack of marketability.
Wisconsin § 180.130(4)	"Fair value", with respect to a dissenter's shares other than a business combination, means the value of the shares immediately before the effectuation of the corporate action to which the dissenter objects, excluding any appreciation or depreciation in anticipation of the corporate action unless exclusion would be inequitable. "*Fair value*", *with respect to a dissenter's shares in a business combination, means market value.*
Wisconsin § 180.1130(9)	"Market value" means . . . If the shares are listed . . . the highest closing bid per share quoted on the system during the valuation period. If the shares are listed . . . but no transactions are reported during the valuation period or if the shares are [not] listed . . . and if at least 3 members of [FINRA] are market makers for the securities, the highest closing bid per share . . . during the valuation period. If no report or quote is available [or in] the case of property other than cash or shares, the fair market value of the property on the date in question as determined in good faith by the board of directors of the corporation.

a. Emphasis added by authors.

Delaware block method. The DCF methodology is widely used in the determination of fair value, especially in Delaware. In the 1995 *Kleinwort Benson* decision, the Delaware court concluded that DCF was a better way of determining the value of a corporation than a market-based approach, and it stated that the DCF method should have greater weight because it values the corporation as a going concern, rather than comparing it to other companies.[132] In *Grimes v. Vitalink*, the Court of Chancery stated that the "discounted cash flow model [is] increasingly the model of choice for valuations in this Court,"[133] and in *Gholl v. eMachines, Inc.*, it pointed out that DCF "is widely accepted in the financial community and has frequently been relied upon by this Court in appraisal actions."[134]

- *Guideline methods—the market approach.* These methods involve valuing a privately held company based on multiples generated from the market prices of guideline public companies' traded shares (the *guideline* or *comparable company* method) or from guideline transactions involving both public and private companies (the *guideline* or *comparable transaction* method).[135] Those values can vary greatly depending on the selection of companies and on their similarity to the subject company. Although courts often rely more heavily on DCF, the market approach continues to be widely used.

- *Asset value.* Asset value is seldom used in appraisals. *Paskill* prohibited using a net asset value method alone for purposes of an appraisal of a going concern in Delaware because a going concern's liquidation value cannot be considered in appraisal.[136] However, asset value may be given an appropriate weight in limited circumstances. For example, a real estate company was valued primarily on its asset value in *Ng v. Heng Sang Realty Corp.*[137]

- *Excess earnings method.* The excess earnings method has rarely been employed in fair value cases. In *Balsamides*, however, the excess earnings method was used by the plaintiff's expert, who stated that the defendants would not provide the information needed to employ any other method.[138] The excess earnings method has not been addressed in Delaware.

---

[132] *Kleinwort Benson Limited,* 1995 Del. Ch. LEXIS 75 (June 15, 1995), at *28.

[133] *Grimes v. Vitalink Communications Corp.,* 1997 Del. Ch. LEXIS 124 (Aug. 26, 1997), at *3.

[134] *Gholl v. eMachines, Inc.,* 2004 Del. Ch. LEXIS 171 (July 7, 2004), at *20.

[135] When guideline transactions are utilized, adjustments are necessary to eliminate the effect of impermissible premiums.

[136] *Paskill Corp. v. Alcoma Corp.,* 747 A.2d 549 (Del. 2000).

[137] *Ng v. Heng Sang Realty Corp.,* 2004 Del. Ch. LEXIS 69 (Apr. 22, 2004).

[138] *Balsamides,* 734 A.2d 721, 730.

■ *Rules of thumb.* Rules of thumb are seldom accepted by courts as a valuation method. There are rare exceptions: For example, in a Delaware case, the court accepted value per recoverable ton of coal reserves as a valuation method;[139] a Louisiana court valued an alarm company at a multiple of its monthly revenues.[140]

It is common for courts to consider more than one method. In the U.S. District Court's *Steiner* decision (applying Nevada law),[141] the court weighted various methods in order to find a fair value of the stock. First, it looked to find enterprise value, weighting a DCF valuation 30% and what it called a mergers-and-acquisitions method 70%. To find market value, the guideline company method was considered. Then enterprise value and market value were weighted 75% and 25%, respectively.

The Delaware Court of Chancery has explicitly used weighting in some cases as well. For example, the court in *Andaloro* weighted DCF at 75% and comparable companies at 25%.[142] In *U.S. Cellular*, the weighting was 70% DCF, 30% comparable acquisitions.[143] In *Dobler,* the court gave a 30% weight to DCF, 5% to comparable companies, and 65% to comparable acquisitions.[144]

Courts tend to prefer analyses that use more than one valuation approach. A valuation supported by several independent indicia of value is considered more reliable than one by an expert who "does not even attempt to perform reasonableness checks upon his valuation."[145] In *Hanover Direct*, the court criticized an expert who used only DCF and stated, "If a discounted cash flow analysis reveals a valuation similar to a comparable companies or comparable transactions analysis, I have more confidence that both analyses are accurately valuing a company."[146]

---

[139] *Neal v. Alabama By-Products Corp.*, 1990 Del. Ch. LEXIS 127 (Aug. 1, 1990), at *36, *aff'd, Alabama By-Products Corp. v. Neal*, 588 A.2d 255 (Del. 1991).

[140] *Yuspeh v. Klein*, 840. So.2d 41, 53 (La. App. 2003).

[141] *Steiner Corp. v. Benninghoff*, 5 F. Supp. 2d 1117 (D. Nev. 1998).

[142] *Andaloro v. PFPC Worldwide, Inc.*, 2005 Del. Ch. LEXIS 125 (Aug. 19, 2005), at *78.

[143] *In re U. S. Cellular Oper. Co.*, 2005 Del. Ch. LEXIS 1 (Jan. 6, 2005), at *77.

[144] *Dobler v. Montgomery Cellular Holding Co.*, 2004 Del. Ch. LEXIS 139 (Oct. 4, 2004), at *73; *aff'd in part, rev'd in part on other grounds, Montgomery Cellular Holding Co. v. Dobler*, 880 A.2d 206 (Del. 2005).

[145] *Cede & Co. v. Technicolor*, 2003 Del. Ch. LEXIS 146 (Del. Ch. Dec. 31, 2003), at *13–14.

[146] *In re Hanover Direct, Inc. Shareholders Litig.*, 2010 Del. Ch. LEXIS 201 (Sept. 24, 2020), at *6.

Courts have often used the guideline company method when DCF could not be utilized because of the unavailability of adequate projections. In *Borruso,* the court was limited to using a multiple of comparable companies' revenues, as there was insufficient information to adequately apply any other multiple or method.[147] In *Doft,* the court rejected both experts' DCF analyses because the projections were unreliable[148] and relied on the EBIT-DA multiples and P/E ratios of comparable companies.[149] The U.S. District Court, applying Delaware law in *Connector Service,* noted that a multiple of EBITDA was a better method than DCF because the EBITDA multiple was based on the multiples used by the subject company itself in two prior acquisitions.[150]

The MBCA excludes "any appreciation or depreciation in anticipation of the corporate action."[151] Delaware prescribes that fair value excludes "any element of value arising from the accomplishment or expectation of the merger or consolidation."[152] This requires valuing the company as if the corporate action had not taken place.

FAIR VALUE IN DELAWARE

Delaware Fair Value Standards

Fair value for both appraisal and entire fairness in Delaware is a pro rata portion of the value of the company as a going concern. The Delaware Supreme Court developed the standards for valuations in appraisal and entire fairness cases in four seminal cases: *Tri-Continental* (1950),[153] *Sterling v. Mayflower* (1952),[154] *Weinberger* (1983),[155] and *Cavalier Oil Corp. v. Harnett* (1989).[156]

---

[147] *Borruso v. Communications Telesystems Intl.,* 753 A.2d 451, 455 (Del. Ch. 1999).

[148] *Doft & Co. v. Travelocity.com, Inc.,* 2004 Del. Ch. LEXIS 75 (May 21, 2004), at *21.

[149] *Id.,* at *44.

[150] *Connector Service Corp.,* 1998 U.S. Dist. LEXIS 18864, at *4–7.

[151] Some statutes add the phrase "unless exclusion would be inequitable."

[152] 8 Del. C. § 262(h).

[153] See discussion of *Tri-Continental* in "**Fair Value as Defined by Various Authorities and Statutes**" above.

[154] *Sterling v. Mayflower Hotel Corp.,* 93 A.2d 107 (Del. 1952).

[155] See discussion of *Weinberger* in "**Customary and Current Valuation Techniques**".

[156] *Cavalier Oil Corp. v. Harnett,* 564 A.2d 1137 (Del. 1989) ("*Cavalier* "). See discussion of *Cavalier* in "**Fair Value Is Proportionate Share of Equity Value**" ahead.

- *Tri-Continental* described fair value as that which has been taken from the shareholder and stated that fair value should be determined based on facts known or knowable at the valuation date.
- *Sterling v. Mayflower* stated that the proper test of fairness was whether the "minority stockholder will receive *the substantial equivalent in value of the shares he held* [emphasis added]."[157]
- *Weinberger* permitted the use of valuation techniques customarily accepted in the financial community and endorsed forward-looking valuation approaches.
- *Cavalier* confirmed that discounts for lack of marketability or minority interest should not be applied in calculating fair value.

Subsequent case law is based on these principles. Numerous decisions interpreting Delaware's appraisal statute[158] have further clarified how fair value is to be determined and have explained which factors should be considered and excluded. We discuss these developments in this section.

Entire Fairness in Delaware

When a minority shareholder believes that he/she has been treated unfairly and/or that there is a conflict of interest, such as in a freezeout conducted by an opportunistic controller, the minority shareholder may file a breach of fiduciary duty "entire fairness" action against the majority (the controlling shareholder(s)). Simply put, entire fairness cases are transactions in which the controllers have breached their fiduciary duties to shareholders, often in squeeze-out mergers. Hamermesh and Wachter point out that "the 'fair price' component of the 'entire fairness' standard mirrors the definition of 'fair value' as articulated in the appraisal cases" and that the Delaware courts generally use the same valuation analysis for evaluating entire fairness that they use for appraisals.[159]

Delaware does not have a shareholder oppression statute, but the failure of control shareholders to fulfill their fiduciary duties to the minority is, in many ways, analogous to oppression. Thus, in Delaware, the legal action is not governed by an oppression statute but is addressed by the courts in fairness cases. If the Delaware Court finds that the controlling shareholder breached his fiduciary duties by being conflicted and obtaining benefits for himself that were not shared with the minority shareholders, such as being

---

[157] *Sterling v. Mayflower*, 93 A.2d 107, 110.
[158] 8 Del. C. § 262.
[159] Hamermesh and Wachter, "Rationalizing Appraisal Standards," at 1030, citing *Rosenblatt v. Getty Oil Co.*, 493 A.2d 929, 940 (Del. 1985).

on both sides of a deal or negotiating a special price for himself or some group, the court will impose a very strict scrutiny review in its consideration of whether the transaction was fair to the minority shareholders. This standard is called the *entire fairness standard* ("entire fairness") and is "Delaware's most onerous standard."[160]

The court will proceed to examine the transaction by looking at how the majority treated the minority in regard to two prongs of fairness: fair price and fair dealing. Entire fairness thereby encompasses not only "'fair price' but also 'fair dealing'—the timing and structure of negotiations and the method of approval of the transaction."[161] *Weinberger* states:

> The concept of [entire] fairness has two basic aspects: fair dealing and fair price. The former embraces questions of when the transaction was timed, how it was initiated, structured, negotiated, disclosed to the directors, and how the approvals of the directors and the stockholders were obtained. The latter aspect of fairness [fair price] relates to the economic and financial considerations of the proposed merger, including all relevant factors: assets, market value, earnings, future prospects, and any other elements that affect the intrinsic or inherent value of a company's stock.[162]

When the Court is asking whether the majority engaged in "fair dealing," it is focusing on procedural fairness. The Court of Chancery, in deciding whether the majority has acted with procedural fairness and can thereby satisfy the "fair dealing" prong of an entire fairness review, assesses whether it meets three requirements:

> (a) a disinterested and independent special committee, which has sufficient authority and opportunity to hire its own independent advisors and to bargain on behalf of the minority stockholders, must recommend the transaction, and
> (b) the transaction must be subject to a non-waivable condition of approval by a majority of the minority stockholders based on

---

[160] George P. Young, Vincent P. Circelli, and Kelli L. Walter, "Fiduciary Duties and Minority Shareholder Oppression from the Defense Perspective: Differing Approaches in Texas, Delaware, And Nevada," *2012 Securities Regulation and Business Law Conference*, February 9–10, 2012 (available at http://www.haynesboone.com/files/Uploads/Documents/Attorney%20Publications/Minority_Shareholder_Oppression_Young.pdf).

[161] *Kahn v. Lynch Communication Systems, Inc.*, 669 A.2d 79, 84 (1995).

[162] *Weinberger*, 457 A.2d 701, 711.

disclosure that contains no material misstatements or omissions, and

(c) the controlling stockholder must not have engaged in threats, coercion, or fraud.[163]

A judicial determination of lack of entire fairness means that the controllers and/or directors have violated the duty they owed to the shareholders. If the shareholders establish that the board has violated the duty of fairness, the consequences are that the Delaware courts may decide whether to include adjustments or damage claims along with their determination of fair value. In such cases, the measure of damages may exceed the determination of fair value.[164] The *Weinberger* court looked at the case of damages in fair value through the perspective of the appraisal statutory requirement of "all relevant factors."[165] It stated:

> When the trial court deems it appropriate, fair value also includes any damages, resulting from the taking, which the stockholders sustain as a class. If that was not the case, then the obligation to consider "all relevant factors" in the valuation process would be eroded.[166]

Weinberger points out that the key difference between the appraisal remedy and the remedy in a fairness case is that an appraisal award must be in cash, while the Court of Chancery may award "any form of equitable and monetary relief as may be appropriate" in a fairness case.[167] It may, as damages or equitable remedies, order (or permit) payment in stock, grant rescission, or provide other forms of equitable compensation and relief.

The following two cases, *Seagraves v. Urstadt Property*[168] and *Bomarko v. International Telecharge*,[169] deal with decisions based on the corporation's lack of entire fairness to minority shareholders.

---

[163] *In re John Q. Hammons Hotels Inc. Shareholder Litig.*, 2009 Del. Ch. LEXIS 174 (Oct. 2, 2009), at *40–41.

[164] *ONTI, Inc. v. Integra Bank,* 751 A.2d 904, 930 (Del. Ch. 1999).

[165] *Weinberger,* 457 A.2d 701, at 713.

[166] *Id.* The subsequent enactment of Del. Code § 102b(7) allows a corporate charter provision to limit or eliminate the personal monetary liability of directors.

[167] *Weinberger,* 457 A.2d 701, 714.

[168] *Seagraves v. Urstadt Property Co., Inc.,* 1996 Del. Ch. LEXIS 36 (April 1, 1996).

[169] *Bomarko, Inc. v. International Telecharge, Inc.,* 794 A.2d 1161 (Del. Ch. 1999), *aff'd, International Telecharge, Inc. v. Bomarko, Inc.,* 766 A.2d 437 (Del. 2000).

SEAGRAVES V. URSTADT PROPERTY CO., INC.

A group of plaintiffs brought a class action suit against Urstadt Property Co. that would ultimately involve many more plaintiffs than those who had asserted their dissenters' rights. The company requested that it be allowed to pay the amount due under an appraisal remedy in order to avoid a class action trial which could result in defendants facing a much greater award to plaintiffs. The court denied the request and held the transaction to entire fairness review, stating that the company had not sought a fairness opinion at the time of the merger, nor had it established an independent committee to safeguard the interests of the minority shareholders. The court pointed out:

> Delaware law recognizes, however, that appraisal may not provide an adequate remedy to minority stockholders where "fraud, misrepresentation, [or] self-dealing ... are involved." The appraisal remedy also may not afford an adequate remedy for disclosure-based claims, such as in cases where material misdisclosures or nondisclosures might warrant injunctive relief. [170]

BOMARKO, INC. V. INTERNATIONAL TELECHARGE, INC.

The court found that the control shareholder had breached his duty of loyalty to International Telecharge. The court determined that the controller was liable for damages and wrote:

> [U]nlike the more exact process followed in an appraisal action, the "law does not require certainty in the award of damages where a wrong has been proven and injury established. Responsible estimates that lack mathematical certainty are permissible so long as the Court has a basis to make a responsible estimate of damages." [171]

(continued)

---

[170] *Seagraves*, at *12, citing at *Weinberger*, at 714.

[171] *Bomarko*, at 1184, citing *Red Sail Easter Limited Partners, L. P. v. Radio City Music Hall Prods., Inc.*, 1992 Del. Ch. LEXIS 203 (Sept. 29, 1992), at *19.

> The court awarded the plaintiffs fair value of $1.27 per share plus a pro rate share of the maximum recovery that the corporation could have received in a pending lawsuit by the corporation against the control shareholder. Plaintiffs received $1.51 per share (plus interest) as opposed to the $0.30 they had been offered in the merger.

Components of Fair Value in Delaware

Fair Value Is Proportionate Share of Equity Value

The Delaware appraisal statute states:

> [T]he Court shall determine the fair value of the shares exclusive of any element of value arising from the accomplishment or expectation of the merger or consolidation. . . . In determining such fair value, the Court shall take into account all relevant factors.[172]

Interpreting the statute, the Delaware Court of Chancery ruled in 1988 that a dissenting shareholder was entitled to a pro rata share of the equity value of the company:

> Under §262 [of the Delaware General Corporation Law], the dissenting shareholder is entitled to his proportionate interest in the overall fair value of the corporation, appraised as a going concern. The amount of the holdings of a particular dissenting stockholder is not relevant, except insofar as they represent that shareholder's proportionate interest in the corporation's overall "fair value." That a particular dissenting stockholde`r's ownership represents only a minority stock interest in a corporation is, therefore, legally immaterial in determining the corporation's "fair value."[173]

The Delaware Supreme Court upheld the lower court's *Cavalier* decision in 1989, pointing out that if minority shareholders were not to receive "the full proportionate value," the majority shareholders would "reap a windfall."[174]

---

[172] 8 Del. Code Ann. tit. 8, § 262(h).

[173] *Cavalier Oil Corp. v. Harnett*, 1988 Del. Ch. LEXIS 28 (Feb. 22, 1988), at *27; *aff'd*, 564 A.2d 1137 (Del. 1989).

[174] *Cavalier*, 564 A.2d 1137, 1145.

[T]o fail to accord to a minority shareholder the full proportionate value of his shares imposes a penalty for lack of control, and unfairly enriches the majority shareholders who may reap a windfall from the appraisal process by chasing out a dissenting shareholder, a clearly undesirable result.[175]

The two *Cavalier* decisions support the pro rata share concept that in an appraisal the minority shareholder should not receive a lesser price for his shares because he does not share in the exercise of control of the corporation. Giving proportionate value to minority shareholders means that the controller cannot benefit disproportionately from forcing out the minority at a diminished price. This thinking explains Delaware's position that fair value permits neither a discount for lack of marketability nor a minority discount.

Fair Value Is Going-Concern Value   The Delaware courts have consistently held that the best measure of fair value is *going-concern value*.[176] In Delaware, the concept of going-concern value is based on earnings from existing assets *plus the value of anticipated reinvestment opportunities*.

[G]oing concern value must include not only the discounted free cash flow to be generated by the corporation's current assets, but also the discounted free cash flow to be generated by the reinvestment opportunities anticipated by the corporation.[177]

A Delaware company is appraised as it exists at the transaction date, inclusive of its anticipated reinvestments. This concept of going-concern value is often referred to as *operative reality*. Recently, in *Just Care* (2012), the court wrote:

A company "must be valued as a going concern based upon the 'operative reality' of the company as of the time of the merger." In an appraisal proceeding, "the corporation must be valued as a going concern based upon the 'operative reality' of the company as of the time of the merger."[178]

---

[175] *Id.*

[176] Hamermesh and Wachter, "Rationalizing Appraisal Standards," at 1022.

[177] *Id.*

[178] *Gearreald v. Just Care, Inc.*, 2012 Del. Ch. LEXIS 91 (Apr. 30, 2012), at *21, citing *M.G. Bancorp., Inc. v. Le Beau*, 737 A.2d 513, 525 (Del. 1999) and *U.S. Cellular*, 2005 Del. Ch. LEXIS 1, at *56.

Going-Concern Value Is Based on How the Company Is Being Managed Prior to Merger An important part of operative reality is how the company is being managed at the time of the transaction. A company being appraised is valued "as is" under its current management, not as it might be run by a different party:

> The company, with all of its warts and diamonds, is valued in terms of the discounted free cash flow generated by the company's assets and reinvestment opportunities. In measuring the value of the warts and diamonds, the warts are valued as warts and the diamonds as diamonds. The minority shareholders cannot claim that if the company was run differently, or if a third party owned it, the warts would become diamonds. That may be correct as a factual matter, but it is irrelevant to the valuation issue. The minority's claim is equal to the value of the shares into the future, and that value is a mix of the existing warts and diamonds.[179]

However, it is important to note that some "warts" can be disregarded as discussed later in this section in "**Fair Value Includes Changes Contemplated by Management**" ahead.

Management's plans, not those of an independent acquirer, are a company's operative reality. When a third-party buyer projected a higher growth rate for the target than did the target's management, the court determined that the appropriate input for the court's DCF calculation in an appraisal was the growth rate expected by the target's CEO and principal shareholder, not the buyer's expectation.[180] Similarly, a company should be valued on its existing capital structure rather than on an optimal capital structure or the buyer's plans.[181]

Actions planned by existing management prior to a squeeze-out merger are part of operative reality. Although Delaware normally excludes actions planned by a *third-party acquirer* before it acquires control, there is an important exception. If control actually changes hands before a second-stage merger (a merger that squeezes out any minority shareholders whose shares were not acquired in an initial tender or exchange offer), the new control party's plans may be taken into account. In the long-running *Technicolor* case, the Supreme Court ruled in 1996 that dissenting shareholders were entitled to benefit from changes being made or planned by a new

---

[179] Hamermesh and Wachter, "Cornfields," at 143–144.

[180] *Crescent/Mach I Partnership, L.P. v. Dr Pepper Bottling Co. of Texas*, 2007 Del. Ch. LEXIS 63 (May 2, 2007), at *16–17 and *38.

[181] *In re Radiology Assocs., Inc. Litig.*, 611 A.2d 485, 493 (Del. Ch. 1991).

management that had assumed control prior to the valuation date.[182] The non-tendering shareholders were bought out in the second-stage merger at the same price that had been paid for the bulk of the shares in November 1982 pursuant to a friendly tender offer by MacAndrews & Forbes. By the time the squeeze-out merger was consummated in January 1983, MacAndrews & Forbes had taken operating control. The Supreme Court ruled that MacAndrews & Forbes's plan, which involved disposing of certain unprofitable operations and increasing profit margins, was the operative reality and that the projections based on that plan should be the basis for the valuation.

The Court of Chancery relied on the 1996 *Technicolor* decision in *Delaware Open MRI*, writing, "The expansion plans for Delaware III were clearly part of the operative reality of Delaware Radiology as of the merger date and under *Technicolor* and its progeny must be valued in the appraisal."[183] It ruled:

> The decision of [the control group] to cash out the [dissenters] at a price that did not afford it any of the value of the gains expected from [the additional MRI Centers] clearly bears on the fairness of the merger. Not only that, if the concept of opening [them] was part of the business plans of Delaware Radiology as of the merger date, then the value of those expansion plans must be taken into account in valuing Delaware Radiology as a going concern.[184]

The court added that "when a business has opened a couple of facilities and has plans to replicate those facilities as of the merger date, the value of its expansion plans must be considered in the determining fair value."[185]

The court may, however, reject the projected benefits of a planned expansion if it deems the project to be too speculative. In a case appraising a company that operated a prison health-care facility in South Carolina, the financial projections included renovating a Georgia prison as a medical detention facility. The Court of Chancery distinguished this expansion from *Delaware Open MRI* and rejected the portion of the projection that related to the Georgia facility:

> I find that the Georgia Case was too speculative to be included in the valuation of the Company as of the merger date. . . .[E]ven

---

[182] *Cede & Co. v. Technicolor*, 684 A.2d 289, 298-9 (Del. 1996).

[183] *Delaware Open MRI*, 898 A.2d 290, 316 (Del. Ch. 2006).

[184] *Id.*, at 313.

[185] *Id.*, 314-5.

if the new facility was successful, there was a risk that Georgia would move its prisoners currently housed at the Columbia Center back to Georgia, thereby reducing the value of the Columbia Center.[186]

Just Care could not undertake the expansion unilaterally without a decision by Georgia to move forward. The fact that the Company was focused on expanding into Georgia and had taken actions in furtherance of that goal is insufficient to make the Georgia Case part of Just Care's operative reality.[187]

The court did accept Just Care's planned expansion of its existing South Carolina facility but probability-weighted the calculated DCF value because of the uncertainty as to whether the state's Department of Correction would proceed with the project. To risk-adjust the planned expansion, the court deducted 33.3% from the calculated value.[188]

Fair Value Excludes Synergies Resulting from the Transaction but Includes Synergies Obtainable by Current Controller

In Delaware, the fair value standard does not permit the benefits of synergies resulting from a transaction to be included in a going-concern valuation:

[S]ynergies dependent on the consummation of an arm's-length acquisition or combination may not contribute to "fair value" in appraisal proceedings. Similarly, we conclude that operating efficiencies that arise from the acquirer's new business plans are not properly included in determining "fair value," as long as they are not operationally implemented before the merger, even though they derive solely from the enterprise's own assets.[189]

The Delaware Supreme Court has stressed that the value of synergies imbedded in a third-party purchase price should be excluded:

In performing its valuation, the Court of Chancery is free to consider the price actually derived from the sale of the company being valued, *but only after the synergistic elements of value are excluded from that price* [emphasis added].[190]

---

[186] *Gearreald v. Just Care*, 2012 Del. Ch. LEXIS 91, at *21–22.

[187] *Id.*, at *24.

[188] *Id.*, at *30.

[189] Hamermesh and Wachter, "Cornfields," at 151.

[190] *Montgomery Cellular*, 880 A.2d 206, 220.

Under the going-concern "operative reality" concept, the court did not include the benefits to a near-bankrupt airline of the transaction's cancellation of preferred stock, a debt restructuring, and a planned capital infusion. The court declined to credit the existing shareholders for benefits that could not have been achieved without the transaction. The acquirer's future plans and projections assumed the closing of the merger, which was conditioned on concessions from creditors and the infusion of new capital. The court followed the practice of excluding from fair value any gains that would not occur but for the transaction. The court noted:

[T]he Concessions were not being implemented—and thus were not an "operative reality"—as of the merger date. On that date the only "operative reality" was that the parties had entered into a contract which provided that the Concessions would become operative if and when the merger closed.[191]

Another example of a situation where the dissenter could not benefit from the consequences of the transaction was when shareholders of a real estate corporation were squeezed out in order to convert a C corporation into an S corporation. The prospective tax benefits from the conversion were excluded from fair value because they could not have been achieved without the transaction:

Heng Sang's conversion to an S corporation cannot be considered for valuation purposes, because without Ng's consent it was not possible for Heng Sang to convert to subchapter S status before the merger, and Ng never granted his consent.[192]

In contrast, if the controller can achieve the benefits without the transaction, the court may include the present value of those benefits in fair value. In the 2004 *Emerging Communications* decision, the court concluded that the substantial post-transaction benefits that defendants attributed to the merger were in fact contemplated and achievable before the transaction. It ruled that the control shareholder could have achieved the benefits without the merger by other means, such as entering into a contract between his wholly owned private company and the public company he controlled:

---

[191] *Allenson v. Midway Airlines Corp.*, 789 A.2d 572, 583 (Del. Ch. 2001).

[192] *Ng v. Heng Sang Realty Corp.*, at *18. The benefits of conversion to an S corporation were also excluded in *In re Sunbelt Beverage Corp. Shareholder Litig.*, 2010 Del. Ch. LEXIS 1 (Jan. 5, 2010), at *53.

The cost savings attributed to the consolidation were properly includable in the June projections, because they were contemplated well before the going private merger and could have been achieved without it. Prosser had identified potential consolidation savings before the Privatization occurred. Because Prosser controlled both ECM and ICC, *he had the power to accomplish those savings without a business combination, such as by intercompany contractual arrangements* [emphasis added]. To put it differently, the value achieved by Prosser's existing pre-merger ability to effect those cost savings was an asset of ECM at the time of the Privatization merger.[193]

The court decided that the fact that the controller's ability to accomplish the cost savings before the merger was an asset of the public company at the merger date and that all shareholders were entitled to share pro rata in that benefit.

Fair Value Includes Changes Contemplated by Management

If management is contemplating changes in the company at the time the relevant transaction is completed, or if new management has begun implementing its plans prior to a squeeze-out merger, the Court of Chancery will deem these changes to be operative reality. Professors Hamermesh and Wachter explain certain adjustments that Delaware will recognize in an appraisal:

[I]n appropriate circumstances in which a controlling shareholder is acquiring the minority shares, the courts have interpreted "fair value" to include elements of value that arise from assets or plans that were not in place operationally at the time of the merger. Those three areas . . . involve:

(1) pro forma inclusion of assets not formally owned by the corporation at the time of the merger, but constructively attributed to the corporation because they had represented a corporate opportunity wrongfully usurped prior to the merger;
(2) projections of post-merger returns in which actual costs are disregarded and excluded because they represent improper benefits to the controlling shareholder; and
(3) operating improvements that the controlling shareholder implements following the merger but that do not depend causally upon the consummation of the merger.[194]

---

[193] *In re Emerging Communications, Inc. Shareholders Litig.*, 2004 Del. Ch. LEXIS 70 (Del. Ch. May 3, 2004), at *48–49.
[194] Hamermesh and Wachter, "Cornfields," at 159.

This section discusses the three categories listed by Hamermesh and Wachter. We then discuss examples of adjustments rejected by the court as unacceptable under the fair value standard in Delaware appraisals, even though they might be considered by a financial buyer under the third-party sale value standard. Then we will discuss cases where plans in place at the merger date were considered.

Usurped Corporate Opportunities If a corporate opportunity is wrongfully usurped prior to the transaction, the court will constructively attribute the corporate opportunity to the corporation and adjust fair value to reflect this misconduct. Misappropriation of a corporate opportunity by a control share-holder has been addressed in appraisal cases when the misconduct was not known to the dissenters until after the transaction that triggered the appraisal.

In its seminal 1989 *Cavalier* decision, the Supreme Court discussed a diversion of assets to a related company and stated:

> The . . . corporate opportunity claim, if considered on its deriva-tive merits, would inure almost entirely to the benefit of the alleged wrongdoers, an inequitable result at variance with the fair value quest of the appraisal proceeding. . . . [T]he Vice Chancellor found that [petitioner] did not have knowledge of the basis for the corporate opportunity claim prior to the institution of the appraisal proceed-ing and that, as a matter of credibility, those claims were based on misrepresentations by the principal shareholders. We conclude that, under the unusual configuration of facts present here, the corporate opportunity claim was assertable in the [appraisal] proceeding.[195]

ONTI v. Integra Bank also involved an abuse of corporate opportunity. Within days of closing the squeeze-out cash merger, the control shareholder merged his company with a publicly traded company. Plaintiffs asked that the appraisal valuation take into consideration their pro rata portion of the market value of shares that the defendant received in the later merger. The court ruled in favor of the plaintiffs, stating, "I think it is clear that it is 'not the product of speculation' that the [subsequent] Transaction was effectively in place at the time of the Cash-Out Mergers."[196]

Improper Benefits to Control Shareholders The court may make adjust-ments to eliminate the agency costs of improper actions by a control party that were not known to shareholders before the transaction and that affect

---

[195] *Cavalier*, 564 A.2d 1137, 1143-44.
[196] *ONTI*, 751 A.2d 904, 917-18.

current and future cash flow. For example, in *ONTI*, the court adjusted the projection underlying the DCF calculation by doubling the fees receivable from an affiliate of the controller, which had been paying less than the contractual rate.[197]

In another case, the court accepted adjustments to eliminate the adverse consequences of "excessive management fees, an unexplained intercompany loan, an unexplained corporate allocation, and an overcharge by a vendor"[198] as well as "the sale and leaseback of Montgomery's cell sites and towers," which "was clearly an inappropriate exaction by [the control party] due to its corporate control."[199]

The court may also make adjustments when it can be shown that payments to shareholders were not for services rendered. In 1991, the court accepted a DCF analysis in which officers' salaries were adjusted to exclude a portion which, because compensation was proportional to equity ownership, was deemed to be a return on equity.[200] That decision was cited in a recent case where the court pointed out that "Delaware law on fair value . . . empower[s] a court to make normalizing adjustments to account for expenses that reflect controller self-dealing when the plaintiff/petitioner provides an adequate evidentiary basis for the adjustment." [201]

Claims relating to the control shareholder's improper conduct that were known prior to a squeeze-out—and thus could have been challenged prior to the squeeze-out—have been excluded from consideration in Delaware appraisals. For example, in two cases where the petitioners claimed that improperly issued shares had diluted their interests, the court determined that it could not address these claims in an appraisal context.[202]

Improvements Not Dependent on Merger   The court considers future events that were not speculative as part of going-concern value under the fair value standard. The court decided in a 2005 appraisal of a cellular telephone company that it was not speculative to consider the prospective conversion of its network to higher future industry standards, so that the

---

[197] *Id.*, at 910.

[198] *Dobler*, 2004 Del. Ch. LEXIS 139, at *69 (footnotes omitted). The court stated, "The management fee charged by [parent] can be reasonably interpreted to be a corporate charade by which the parent removed money from its subsidiary."

[199] *Id.*, at *71.

[200] *In re Radiology Assocs.*, 611 A.2d 485, 491-2.

[201] *Reis v. Hazelett Strip-Casting Corp.*, 28 A.3d 442, 472 (Del. Ch. 2011).

[202] *Cavalier*, 564 A.2d 1137, 1146; *Gentile v. SinglePoint Financial*, 2003 Del. Ch. LEXIS 21 (Del. Ch. Mar. 5, 2003), at *17–21.

requisite capital expenditures were part of the company's operative reality. It ruled that the expert "should have incorporated the effects of this expected capital improvement in his projections."[203]

Hamermesh and Wachter summarize this concept:

> In fact, we believe that both finance theory and Delaware case law are consistent with our view that minority shareholders have a right to "fair value" that incorporates not only current assets *but also future reinvestment opportunities, so long as those reinvestment opportunities reflect pre-merger plans or policies of the corporation and its controlling shareholder* [emphasis added]. . . . These reinvestment opportunities will not have been taken at the time of the merger, because they are to be funded with future free cash flow. Consequently, the assets purchased as part of the reinvestment opportunities will not exist at the time of the merger. However, these assets are as much a part of the present value of the corporation as are the value of the existing assets.[204]

Consistent with this view and with customary valuation practice, income should be normalized so that nonrecurring items should be excluded from valuation calculations.[205] The Court of Chancery has faulted an expert for not normalizing earnings data, pointing out, "The earnings figures used to derive the earnings base should be adjusted to eliminate non-recurring gains and losses."[206]

Pro Forma Adjustments Rejected by the Court   In 1997, the Delaware Supreme Court rejected petitioner's claim that earnings and projections should be adjusted because the control shareholder had been and continued to be materially overpaid. It noted that there was no plan prior to the merger to adjust that compensation. The court ruled that "in the absence of a derivative claim attacking excessive compensation, the underlying issue of whether such costs may be adjusted may not be considered in an appraisal proceeding."[207] It concluded that "going business value of the corporation at the moment before the merger . . . does not include the capitalized value

---

[203] *U.S. Cellular*, 2005 Del. Ch. LEXIS 1, at *56.

[204] Hamermesh and Wachter, "Cornfields," at 158.

[205] Normalizing adjustments include not only items classed as "extraordinary" under GAAP, but also nonrecurrent items in the income account such as gains or losses from litigation and (if truly nonrecurrent) restructuring costs.

[206] *Reis*, 28 A.3d 442, 470.

[207] *Gonsalves v. Straight Arrow Publishers*, 701 A.2d 357, 363 (Del. 1997).

of possible changes which may be made *by new management* [emphasis added]."[208]

A recent decision rejected an adjustment to earnings premised on the assertion that that the company was overspending on research. The Court of Chancery ruled, "Because a reduction in R&D expense only could be made by a new controller of Hazelett Strip-Casting, adjustments to reflect those changes would generate a third-party sale value, not going concern value."[209] The court stated that its conclusion was based on "the well-established principle of Delaware law that minority shareholders have no legal right to demand that the controlling shareholder achieve—and that they be paid—the value that might be obtained in a hypothetical third-party sale."[210]

Taxes Are Considered Only If They Are "Operative Reality"

The operative reality concept has also been used to justify the exclusion of deferred taxes on investment assets that management does not currently intend to sell. In *Paskill*, the Supreme Court ruled:

> The record reflects that a sale of its appreciated investment assets was not part of Okeechobee's operative reality on the date of the merger. Therefore, the Court of Chancery should have excluded any deduction for the speculative future tax liabilities that were attributed by Alcoma to those uncontemplated sales.[211]

This differs from the Supreme Court's ruling that accepted deferred taxes in *Technicolor* because Technicolor's management had already decided to sell the relevant assets. The expected gain on that asset sale was the operative reality on the date of the merger.[212]

In a 2006 decision, the Court of Chancery used the operative reality concept when it accepted taxes and other expenses paid as a result of an asset sale directly related to a merger. Carter-Wallace sold the assets of its consumer products business simultaneously with the merger into MedPointe Healthcare of its health-care business. Each transaction was contingent on the other. The asset sale resulted in substantial capital gains taxes and expenses. The petitioner unsuccessfully argued that the taxes and expenses should not be deducted in determining appraisal value because the asset sale was not completed prior to the date of the merger. The court said, "There is

---

[208] *Id.*

[209] *Reis,* 28 A.3d 442, 471.

[210] *Id.,* quoting Hamermesh and Wachter, "Cornfields," at 154.

[211] *Paskill,* 747 A.2d 549, 552.

[212] *Cede & Co. v. Technicolor,* 684 A.2d 289, 298.

no principled distinction between an asset sale occurring a few hours before the merger and a sale on the day before the merger," and based its appraisal of Carter-Wallace on the company's value after the asset sale, giving effect to all related expenses including taxes on the asset sales.[213]

A 2011 decision rejected the deduction of potential taxes and selling expenses and "add[ed] the full appraised value of the non-operating real estate" that the company had no current intent to sell.[214] Moreover, since the company expected to utilize its net operating losses, the Court of Chancery also added the potential tax benefit of the carry forward:

> Hazelett Strip-Casting has a history of generating taxable earnings, and the capitalized earnings valuation anticipates that it will continuing doing so in a manner that will enable the Hazelett family to take advantage of the NOL. I therefore add $258,000, representing the full value of the NOL.[215]

OHIO'S UNFAVORABLE STANDARD OF VALUE IN APPRAISALS

The Ohio statute's definition of "fair cash value" is unfavorable to dissenting shareholders in public and private companies:

> The fair cash value of a share for the purposes of this section is the amount that a willing seller, under no compulsion to sell, would be willing to accept, and which a willing buyer, under no compulsion to purchase, would be willing to pay, but in no event shall the amount thereof exceed the amount specified in the demand of the particular shareholder.[216]
>
> In computing . . . fair cash value, any appreciation or depreciation in market value resulting from the proposal submitted to the directors or to the shareholders shall be excluded.[217]

---

[213] *Cede & Co., Inc. v. MedPointe Healthcare*, 2004 Del. Ch. LEXIS 124 (Aug. 16, 2004), at *29 ("The inquiry here is not one of hours, but of whether one two-step transaction, with all components occurring in a certain order and substantially simultaneously, may (or must) be divided for valuation purposes.")

[214] *Reis*, 28 A. 3d 442, 476.

[215] *Id.*

[216] Ohio Rev. Code Ann. §1701.85(b).

[217] Ohio Rev. Code Ann. §1701.85(c).

Importantly, *fair cash value* is to be determined as of the day prior the shareholders' vote.[218] Under the Ohio statute, if there is an active market for a company's shares, the value for an appraisal will be no more than the market price.[219] In addition, the market price must be adjusted to reflect any impact on the market in reaction to the merger proposal.[220] In the landmark *Armstrong* case, the Ohio Court of Appeals conceded that shareholders seeking appraisal would likely receive less than shareholders who accepted the merger terms:

> [I]t is apparent that [appraisal] is likely to produce a fair cash value to be paid dissenting shareholders different from that received by assenting shareholders unless the fundamental corporate change is found to have had absolutely no effect on the market price of the stock, an unlikely possibility.[221]

The appraisal remedy in Ohio is unlike any other state. One commentator described the hapless position of an Ohio dissenting public company shareholder as follows:

> The [*Armstrong*] court thereby rendered the appraisal remedy useless to minority shareholders of publicly traded corporations, and guaranteed that it will not be invoked in this context in the future. No matter how low the merger price, it will invariably exceed the prevailing market price prior to the announcement of the merger; thus no sensible shareholder would elect to dissent, and the appraisal remedy in Ohio has been rendered largely impotent by judicial construction.
>
> To make matters worse, the Ohio Supreme Court has held that the appraisal remedy is the exclusive remedy available to minority shareholders complaining about the fairness of a merger price. See *Stepak v. Schey*, 553 N.E.2d 1072, 1075 (Ohio 1990); *Armstrong*, 513 N.E.2d at 798. *The appraisal remedy in Ohio is thus both useless and exclusive.* [emphasis added] In effect, as long as the controlling shareholder pays any amount over the prevailing market price, it is free to cash out the minority shareholders and

---

[218] *Id.*

[219] Steven D. Gardner, "Note: A Step Forward: Exclusivity of the Statutory Appraisal Remedy for Minority Shareholders Dissenting from Going-Private Merger Transactions," 53 *Ohio St. L. J.* 239, 246 (1992).

[220] *Armstrong v. Marathon Oil Co.*, 513 N.E.2d 776, 784 (Ohio 1987).

[221] *Armstrong v. Marathon Oil Co.*, 583 N.E.2d 462, 467 (Ohio App. 1990).

appropriate to itself any value not accurately reflected in the market price.[222]

Moreover, Ohio's fair cash value standard negatively impacts shareholders of private companies because it allows discounts that would not be permitted in calculating fair value. Using the willing buyer–willing seller approach, Ohio has concluded that minority and marketability discounts are appropriate. In an oppression case, the Ohio Court of Appeals concluded:

> The cases that appellant cites in support of his public policy argument [opposing discounts] are distinguishable because they all are from foreign jurisdictions where statutory law provides that a dissenting shareholder is entitled to the "fair value" of his or her shares. The concept of "fair value" is far different from the "fair cash value" concept.[223]

FAIR VALUE NORMALLY EXCLUDES DISCOUNTS AND PREMIUMS

Most States Now Reject Minority and Marketability Discounts

An issue in many fair value cases is whether discounts and/or premiums are applicable. If applicable, the issue becomes the magnitude of such discounts and/or premiums. The primary issue is shareholder-level discounts. The debate for the courts is whether minority shares should be valued at a pro rata portion of enterprise or by valuing the shares themselves based on their minority status. The debate is important because the use of discounts or their nonuse can result in the unfair enrichment of one of the parties.

For *fair* value, the issue centers on the definition of what the minority shareholders had prior to the valuation date and what they have lost because of the transaction. When the standard of value focuses on what was lost (i.e., a pro rata share of enterprise value), discounts would be detrimental to the minority shareholders.

If, instead, the standard of value becomes what the investor could reasonably realize in the market for a minority position (*fair market value*), then

---

[222] Wertheimer, "Shareholders' Appraisal Remedy," at 656, n. 207.

[223] *English v. Artromick Intl., Inc.*, 2000 Ohio App. LEXIS 3580 (Aug. 10, 2000), at *14.

discounts for lack of control and lack of marketability would commonly be considered. The minority shares would have less value because buyers normally consider liquidity and the lack of control before purchasing minority shares. The argument for the use of fair market value is that if minority shareholders were to sell in the open market, they would receive a discounted price for their shares and that, in fact, these shareholders were aware of the minority status of their shares when they initially acquired them. The advocates of discounts assert that the failing to consider marketability and minority discounts unfairly enriches minority shareholders.

Probably the most popular argument *against* discounts for minority shareholders involves the original purpose of appraisal, which is to compensate minority shareholders for what was taken from them. If the appraisal statutes were created to protect minority shareholders from controlling and/or opportunistic shareholders, a minority discount would be contrary to logic, as the majority shareholders would obviously benefit from a reduction in the amount they would have to pay the minority after a squeeze-out.

With respect to marketability discounts, the argument against applying a discount for lack of marketability is that the judicial proceeding itself creates a market for the shares, and therefore no marketability discount is applicable. If the minority shareholders were to lose a pro rata portion of the corporation's value because they were forced out, penalizing the minority would reward rather than deter the controller. Indeed, controllers would be encouraged to engage in freeze-outs if by doing so, they could buy out the minority at a diminished price and thereby receive a premium for mistreating the minority.

On the other hand, adding control premiums to valuations of minority shares would enrich the minority at the expense of the majority. As Hamermesh and Wachter explain:

> Control value does not exist in a corporation owned by a fluid, disaggregated mass of shareholders. Rather, it is created by the aggregation of shares. Such aggregation of shares entails a reduction in agency costs, resulting in the creation of ***value that fairly belongs to the entity aggregating the shares*** [emphasis added].[224]
>
> Excluding value associated with control from the measurement of fair value does not impose a "minority discount"; it simply denies shareholders value that does not inhere in the firm in which they are invested. Thus, third-party sale value is an inappropriate standard for determining the fair value of dissenting shares because

---

[224] Hamermesh and Wachter, "Rationalizing Appraisal Standards," at 1023–1024.

it incorporates elements of value—associated with acquisitions of control by third parties—that do not belong to the acquired enterprise or to shares of stock in that enterprise.[225]

Thus, in a majority of states, fair value in an appraisal now excludes any discount for lack of marketability or minority interest and any premium for control. Delaware explicitly took this position in *Cavalier*, and most states now concur.

Levels of Value

Levels of value have been presented and explained by two leading valuation authorities in recent editions of their books: Shannon Pratt's *Valuing a Business*[226] and Christopher Mercer's *Business Valuation: An Integrated Theory*.[227] Pratt's levels-of-value chart shows five levels of value for publicly traded companies: synergistic (strategic) value, value of control shares, market value of freely traded minority shares, value of restricted stock, and value of nonmarketable shares.[228] Mercer describes the levels of value as *strategic control value, financial control value, marketable minority value,* and *nonmarketable minority value.*[229]

Discounts and premiums should also be viewed in light of the type of valuation methodology used and the resultant level of value arrived at based on that method. If indeed shareholder-level discounts (or premiums) are applicable, they should be applied after the valuation of the corporation itself.[230]

The levels of value are described as follows:

- *Synergistic value or strategic control value*—This is the highest value that would be paid for control shares by a buyer who expects to benefit from synergies.

---

[225] *Id.,* at 1038.

[226] Shannon P. Pratt, *Valuing a Business: The Analysis and Appraisal of Closely Held Companies,* 5th ed. (New York: McGraw Hill, 2008), at 384.

[227] Z. Christopher Mercer and Travis W. Harms, *Business Valuation: An Integrated Theory,* 2nd ed. (Hoboken, NJ: John Wiley & Sons, 2007).

[228] Pratt, *Valuing a Business,* 5th ed., at 384. The restricted stock level (which is not shown separately by Mercer) is for shares that are not currently marketable but will become marketable with the passage of time.

[229] Mercer and Harms, at 71.

[230] David Laro and Shannon P. Pratt, *Business Valuation and Taxes: Procedure, Law and Perspective* (Hoboken, NJ: John Wiley & Sons, 2005), at 266.

■ *Value of control shares or financial control value*—This value does not include anticipated synergies, but includes "the ability of a specific buyer to improve the existing operations or run the target company more efficiently."[231]

■ *Marketable minority value*—The next level is minority shares that may be publicly traded. Although lacking control, a marketable minority share is easily liquidated. For example, shares traded on the New York Stock Exchange are marketable minority shares.

■ *Nonmarketable minority value*—The lowest level of value is the nonmarketable minority share of a privately held company. This share does not have control over management, the board of directors, or a company's direction without cooperation from the majority. The nonmarketable minority share is not traded on a public exchange, and, therefore, is not easily liquidated.[232]

The levels of value represent a conceptual framework, and the levels can in fact overlap. For example, unless one can extract more cash flow, the so-called minority marketable shares may be trading at or close to control value. As discussed ahead, many commentators believe that actively traded minority shares often trade at or close to financial control value. Indeed, Mercer's book presents a levels-of-value diagram that shows marketable minority value overlapping financial control value,[233] as does a widely cited article by Mark Lee.[234]

Discounts at the Shareholder Level

As previously mentioned, the courts have frequently rejected the notion of discounting shares because of minority status in fair value cases. The courts generally view the appraisal as protecting the value of those minority shares in situations where that value is intentionally being diminished by the controlling shareholders.

As discussed earlier, *Tri-Continental* stated in 1951 that "under the appraisal statute . . . the stockholder is entitled to be paid . . . his proportionate interest in a going concern." The Iowa Supreme Court cited *Tri-Continental* in its 1965 *Woodward v. Quigley* decision when it concluded that there

---

[231] Mercer and Harms, at 73.

[232] Restricted stock moves from nonmarketable to marketable when the restriction is lifted.

[233] Mercer and Harms, at 83.

[234] Mark Lee, "Control Premiums and Minority Discounts: The Need for Economic Analysis," *Business Valuation Update*, August 2001, p. 4.

should be no minority discount in an appraisal.[235] *Woodward* also cited a 1942 Iowa decision that said, "[E]ach share is worth the figure found by dividing the net value of the corporate property by the total shares outstanding at the time of the arbitration."[236] In the same vein, the Missouri appellate court in *Dreiseszun* stated in 1979, "The statute does not . . . intend that a minority stockholder be in any way penalized for resorting to the remedy afforded thereunder."[237]

As discussed earlier, the Delaware Supreme Court rejected shareholder-level discounts in *Cavalier* in 1989.[238] The Maine Supreme Judicial Court cited *Cavalier* in *McLoon Oil*[239] and explained why it rejected discounts:

> In the statutory appraisal proceeding, the involuntary change of ownership caused by a merger requires as a matter of fairness that a dissenting shareholder be compensated for the loss of his proportionate interest in the business as an entity. The valuation focus under the appraisal statute is not the stock as a commodity, but rather the stock only as it represents a proportionate part of the enterprise as a whole. The question for the court becomes simple and direct: What is the best price a single buyer could reasonably be expected to pay for the firm as an entirety? The court then prorates that value for the whole firm equally among all shares of its common stock. The result is that all of those shares have the same fair value.
>
> Our view of the appraisal remedy is obviously inconsistent with the application of minority and nonmarketability discounts.[240]

Some states reject discounts when shareholders are squeezed out by means of a reverse stock split. Kansas held in 1999 that minority and marketability discounts should not be applied when the fractional share resulted from a 1-for-400 reverse stock split intended to eliminate a minority shareholder's interest in the corporation.[241] Iowa took the same position in 2001.[242]

Several states that previously permitted discounts have reversed their positions in recent years. For example, the Georgia Court of Appeals in

---

[235] *Woodward v. Quigley*, 133 N.W.2d. 38, 44-45 (Iowa 1965).

[236] *First National Bank v. Clay*, 2 N.W.2d 85, 92-93 (Iowa 1942).

[237] *Dreiseszun v. FLM Indus., Inc.*, 577 S.W.2d 902, 906 (Mo. App. 1979).

[238] See "**Fair Value Is Proportionate Share of Equity Value**" above.

[239] *In re Val. of Common Stock of McLoon Oil Co.*, 565 A.2d 997, 1005 (Me. 1989).

[240] *Id.*, at 1004.

[241] *Arnaud v. Stockgrowers State Bank*, 992 P.2d 216, 217 (Kan. 1999).

[242] *Rolfe State Bank v. Gunderson*, 794 N.W.2d 561, 569(Iowa 2011).

1984 had permitted minority and marketability discounts;[243] the same court in 2000 changed its position and reversed a lower court decision that permitted these discounts:

> [T]he majority of other jurisdictions with similar [appraisal] statutes have held that minority and marketability discounts should not be applied when determining the fair value of dissenting shareholders' stock. These courts have reasoned that using discounts injects speculation into the appraisal process, fails to give minority shareholders the full proportionate value of their stock, encourages corporations to squeeze out minority shareholders, and penalizes the minority for taking advantage of the protection afforded by dissenters' rights statutes.[244]

The Colorado Supreme Court reversed precedent in 2001, ruling that marketability discounts could no longer be applied in appraisal cases.[245] Similarly, a 1982 Kentucky appellate decision had permitted a discount for lack of marketability,[246] but a 2011 Kentucky Supreme Court decision overruled this precedent, ruling, "Once the entire company has been valued as a going concern, . . . the dissenting shareholder's interest may not be discounted to reflect either a lack of control or a lack of marketability."[247]

In addition, several states, such as Connecticut, Florida, Illinois, Mississippi, Nevada, and South Dakota, have amended their appraisal statutes in recent years to bar discounts.

New York rejects minority discounts but accepts marketability discounts. The 1985 New York *Blake* case rejected minority discounts:

> Business Corporation Law §1104 [a dissolution statute] was enacted for the protection of minority shareholders, and the corporation should therefore not receive a windfall in the form of a discount because it elected to purchase the minority interest pursuant to Business Corporation Law §1118 [election to purchase]. Thus, a minority interest in closely held corporate stock should not be discounted solely because it is a minority interest.[248]

---

[243] *Atlantic States Construction, Inc. v. Beavers*, 314 S.E.2d 245 (Ga. App. 1984).

[244] *Blitch v. Peoples Bank*, 540 S.E.2d 667, 669 (Ga. App. 2000).

[245] *Pueblo Bancorp. v. Lindoe, Inc.*, 63 P.3d 353 (Colo. 2003).

[246] *Ford v. Courier-Journal Job Printing Co.*, 639 S.W.2d 553 (Ky. App. 1982).

[247] *Shawnee Telecom Resources, Inc. v. Brown*, 354 S.W.3d 542, 564 (Ky. 2011).

[248] *Blake v. Blake Agency,*107 A.D.2d 139, 148.

Discounts for lack of marketability are often accepted in New York. In a 1987 New York case approving a buyout to avoid dissolution, the appellate court considered *Blake,* as well as decisions in other states that rejected discounts, but nonetheless allowed a marketability discount in determining the fair value of the minority shares. It stated, "A discount for lack of marketability accurately reflects the lesser value of shares that cannot be freely traded, whether they be a minority or a majority of the shares, and as such is an appropriate adjustment."[249] However, it added, "The companies' expert's proposed discount of 35% contains an element of discount for minority status and is excessive. A discount for lack of marketability of no more than 10% is appropriate in this case."[250]

Other shareholder-level discounts that are customarily weighed in determining fair market value in non-appraisal cases are blockage (or illiquidity) discounts and discounts for nonvoting or low-vote shares. However, if the court awards the dissenting shareholder a pro rata portion of the value of a company, these discounts would not be relevant to fair value.

The "Implicit Minority Discount"

Several Delaware decisions have applied the impact of an "implicit minority discount"[251] (IMD) to guideline company valuations, thereby adjusting them upward. In an article criticizing the court's use of IMD, Hamermesh and Wachter described the concept:

> The financial/empirical assertion of the IMD is quite simple: no matter how liquid and informed the financial markets may be, all publicly traded shares persistently and continuously trade in the market at a substantial discount relative to their proportionate share of the value of the corporation. This discount, it is said, arises because the stock prices on national securities markets represent "minority" positions, and minority positions trade at a discount to the value of the company's equity. The consequence of the IMD in appraisal proceedings is limited in scope, but substantial in scale: in applying a valuation technique . . . comparable company analysis . . . that estimates subject company value by reference to market trading multiples observed in shares of comparable publicly traded firms, the result must be adjusted upward by adding a premium to

---

[249] *Raskin v. Walter Karl, Inc.,* 129 A.D.2d 642, 644 (A.D.2d Dept. 1987).

[250] *Id.*

[251] Also called *implied* or *inherent* or *embedded* minority discount.

offset the "implicit minority discount" asserted to exist in the comparable companies' share prices.[252]

The Court of Chancery accepted an IMD for the first time in *Spectrum Technology* (1992), where the respondent's expert added a 30% adjustment for an IMD adjustment in her guideline company valuation.[253] The Chancery Court's next appraisal that accepted a guideline company analysis was *Kleinwort Benson* in 1995. Petitioner's expert added an 86% premium and respondent's expert testified that a minority discount of 10% to 15% was reasonable; the court applied a 12.5% adjustment.[254] The court noted that although it had rejected an IMD in *Interstate Bakeries*,[255] "our different conclusions result from differences in the [testimony] presented by the parties in the respective cases."[256]

Since 2000, Delaware has adjusted guideline company valuations for an IMD whenever both sides did so, most often applying a 30% premium. In one case, the Court of Chancery added a premium where neither expert did so.[257] Only once has Delaware adjusted for IMD over the respondent's objection.[258] Otherwise, when neither side's valuation addressed IMD, Delaware has applied no adjustment for an IMD.

There are few decisions in other states regarding IMDs. New Jersey rejected an IMD, commenting, "Our research suggests that the concept of an inherent, or embedded, minority discount is not a concept generally accepted in the financial community."[259] The concept was also rejected in Nevada,[260] but accepted in Maine.[261]

The first published challenge to the assumption that publicly traded share prices necessarily include an IMD preceded any Delaware cases using

---

[252] Lawrence A. Hamermesh and Michael L. Wachter,, "The Short and Puzzling Life of the 'Implicit Minority Discount' in Delaware Appraisal Law," 156 *U. Pa. L. Rev.* 1, 5–6 (2007).

[253] *Hodas v. Spectrum Technology, Inc.*, 1992 Del. Ch. LEXIS 252 (Dec. 7, 1992).

[254] *Kleinwort Benson Ltd. v. Silgan Corp.*, 1995 Del. Ch. LEXIS 75 (June 15, 1995), at *12.

[255] *Salomon Brothers Inc. v. Interstate Bakeries Corp.*, 1992 Del. Ch. LEXIS 100 (May 1, 1992).

[256] *Kleinwort Benson*,1995 Del. Ch. LEXIS 75, at *9.

[257] *Doft*, 2004 Del. Ch. LEXIS 75, at *46.

[258] *Prescott Group Small Cap, L.P. v. Coleman Co.*, 2004 Del. Ch. LEXIS 131 (Sept. 8, 2004).

[259] *Lawson Mardon Wheaton*, 716 A.2d 550 (N.J. Super. 1998).

[260] *Steiner*, 5 F. Supp.2d 1117, 1124.

[261] *In re: Val. of Common Stock of Penobscot Shoe Co.*, 2003 Me. Super. LEXIS 140 (May 30, 2003), at *63.

IMDs. Eric Nath posited in 1990 that the freely traded market prices of a company already incorporated the company's financial control positives or negatives and therefore reflected control value.[262]

Decisions since 2000 that adjusted for IMDs relied on citations that were outdated and that expressed views that the writers had modified or abandoned. When the Court of Chancery applied a control premium in *Le Beau* (1998), it cited then-current books by Shannon Pratt and Chris Mercer.[263] By 1999, Pratt had expressed a different view, writing, "Valuation analysts who use the guideline public-company valuation method and then automatically tack on a percentage 'control premium' . . . had better reconsider their methodology."[264] Pratt had included this comment in the fourth edition of *Valuing a Business* in 2000, but the Court of Chancery apparently was not aware of this change, as it again cited Pratt's 1996 third edition in its 2001 *Agranoff* decision. Indeed, *Andaloro* (2005) cited the *third* edition as support for IMD,[265] even though the same decision cited the *fourth* edition in discussing DCF.[266]

In 2001, Pratt further clarified his position in the first edition of *Business Valuation Discounts and Premiums*. Pratt quoted an article by Mark Lee[267] and then wrote that "given the current state of the debate, one must be extremely cautious about applying a control premium to public market values to determine a control level of value."[268] Similarly, Mercer's 2004

---

[262] Eric Nath, "Control Premiums and Minority Interest Discounts in Private Companies," 9 *Bus. Val. Rev.*59 (1990).

[263] *Le Beau v. M.G. Bancorp., Inc.,* 1998 Del. Ch. LEXIS 9 (Jan. 29, 1998), at *25, n. 15, citing Shannon P. Pratt, Robert F. Reilly, and Robert P. Schweihs, *Valuing a Business: The Analysis and Appraisal of Closely Held Companies,* 3rd ed. (Chicago: Irwin, 1996), pp. 194–195 and 210, as well as Christopher Mercer, *Valuing Financial Institutions* (Homewood, IL: Dow Jones Irwin, 1992), pp. 198–200 and Chapter 13.

[264] Pratt, "Control Premiums? Maybe, Maybe Not: 34% of 3rd Quarter Buyouts at Discounts," *Business Valuation Update* (Jan. 1999), pp. 1–2; Pratt, Reilly, and Schweihs, *Valuing a Business: The Analysis and Appraisal of Closely Held Companies*, 4th ed. (New York: McGraw Hill, 2000), at 357 (citing Pratt's 1999 article).

[265] *Andaloro,* 2005 Del. Ch. LEXIS 125, at *65. See the discussion of this case in Matthews, "A Review of Valuations in Delaware Appraisal Cases, 2004–2005," 25 *Bus. Val. Rev.* 44, 59–60 (2006), comparing the discussion of control premiums in the third and fourth editions of *Valuing a Business*. Hamermesh and Wachter compare those two editions in "The Short and Puzzling Life" at 51–53.

[266] *Id.,* at *36.

[267] Lee, "Control Premiums and Minority Discounts," p. 4.

[268] Pratt, *Business Valuation Discounts and Premiums* (Hoboken, NJ: John Wiley & Sons, 2001), at 40.

book agreed with Nath's 1990 article[269] and explained that "unless there are cash flow–driven differences between the enterprise's financial control value and its marketable minority value, there will be no (or very little) minority interest discount."[270]

Several professors of corporate law have questioned the assumption that most market prices include an IMD. Professor Richard Booth wrote in 2001 that "it is not necessarily the case that actual market price is always less than fair market price."[271] Professor William Carney argued in 2003 against assuming that market prices of most publicly traded shares include a significant IMD, concluding, "Even if all values, both present and potential, are valued in the market price for the firm's shares, one would not expect to find a discernible control premium in a widely held firm that is well managed and appears to offer little probability of a transfer of control."[272]

The 2007 Hamermesh and Wachter article argued that premiums paid in acquisitions are not justification for assuming that market prices include IMD, stating, "[N]ot a single piece of financial or empirical scholarship affirms the core premise of the IMD—that public company shares systematically trade at a substantial discount to the net present value of the corporation."[273] They also pointed out the inconsistency of applying IMDs to guideline company valuations but not to terminal value multiples used in DCF analyses.[274]

Although Delaware courts have adjusted guideline company valuations for IMD on numerous occasions, they have never applied an IMD adjustment to a terminal value calculated by using guideline companies' multiples. The Court of Chancery has used multiples to calculate terminal value in four appraisal opinions, but no adjustments for IMDs were proposed by petitioners' experts in any of these cases.[275] The inconsistency between adjusting for the IMD in guideline company valuations and not adjusting terminal values

---

[269] Mercer, *The Integrated Theory of Business Valuation* (Memphis, TN: Peabody, 2004), at 101.

[270] *Id.*, at 108.

[271] Richard A. Booth, "Minority Discounts and Control Premiums in Appraisal Proceedings," 57 *Bus. Lawyer* 127, 130 (2001).

[272] William J. Carney and Mark Heimendinger, "Appraising the Nonexistent: The Delaware Courts' Struggle with Control Premiums," 152 *U. Pa. L. Rev.* 845, 860 (2003).

[273] Hamermesh and Wachter, "The Short and Puzzling Life," at 5–6.

[274] *Id.*, at 6.

[275] *Gilbert v. MPM Enterprises, Inc.*, 709 A.2d 663 (Del. Ch. 1997), *aff'd MPM Enterprises, Inc. v. Gilbert*, 731 A.2d 790 (Del. 1999); *Grimes v. Vitalink Communications Corp.*, 1997 Del. Ch. LEXIS 124 (Aug. 26, 1997); *Gray v. Cytokine*

based on multiples derived from guideline companies was acknowledged in 2006, when the court stated that "an exit multiple based on minority trading data . . . [is] a less favored technique [for determining terminal value] that raises questions about whether it embeds a minority discount."[276]

Later in 2007, Vice Chancellor Lamb recognized that there is a debate about the IMD, citing the Hamermesh/Wachter and Booth articles, which both "argu[e] that the implicit minority discount has not gained general acceptance in the financial community,"[277] as well as a contrary 1999 article by John Coates[278] that argued that adjusting for an IMD is sometimes appropriate.

IMDs was criticized from a business valuation point of view in *Business Valuation Review* in 2008. The article concluded, "The default assumption should be that publicly traded shares sell at a company's going-concern value. If petitioner's expert concludes that an IMD is appropriate in a given situation, its magnitude should be based on a comparison between acquisition multiples and market multiples."[279]

No Premiums Are Applicable to DCF Values

When using control cash flows in a DCF valuation method, a control premium is not warranted. Delaware rejected a control premium in *Radiology Associates* because "[t]he discounted cash flow analysis, as employed in this case, fully reflects this value without need for an adjustment."[280] The view that the DCF value of a company should not be adjusted for a control premium is consistent with generally accepted practice in the financial community. Pratt explains that a DCF value based on projected cash flows does not require the addition of a control premium.[281]

Pharmasciences, Inc., 2002 Del. Ch. LEXIS 48 (Apr. 25, 2002); *U.S. Cellular*, 2005 Del. Ch. LEXIS 1.

[276] *In re PNB Holding Co. Shareholders Litigation*, 2006 Del. Ch. LEXIS 158 (Aug. 18, 2006), at *114–115. The court chose to use respondent's growth model rather than petitioner's exit multiple for determining terminal value.

[277] *Highfields Capital, Ltd. v. AXA Financial, Inc.*, 2007 Del. Ch. LEXIS 126 (June 27, 2007), at *67.

[278] John C. Coates IV, "'Fair Value' as an Avoidable Rule of Corporate Law: Minority Discounts in Conflict Transactions,"147 *U. Pa. L. Rev.*, at 1251 (1999).

[279] Matthews, "Misuse of Control Premiums in Delaware Appraisals," 27 *Bus. Val. Rev.*, at 107, 118 (2008).

[280] Radiology Assocs., 611 A.2d 485, 494.

[281] Pratt, *Valuing a Business*, 5th ed., at 228; Pratt, *Business Valuation Discounts and Premiums*, 2nd ed. (Hoboken, NJ: John Wiley & Sons, 2009), at 26.

It is undisputed in Delaware that no premium should be applied when terminal value is determined using a growth model (the academically preferred approach). Premiums to DCF valuations using growth models were explicitly rejected in 2004 in both *Dobler* and *Lane,* even though the court adjusted for IMDs in its guideline company valuations in both cases.[282] The court in *Dobler*, citing Pratt, said:

> [DCF] value should represent the full value of the future cash flows of the business. Excluding synergies, a company cannot be worth a premium over the value of its future cash flows. Thus, it is improper and illogical to add a control premium to a DCF valuation.[283]

It added, "A DCF is a final valuation that does not need any additional correction, such as a control premium."[284]

Discounts at the Corporate Level

Corporate-level discounts are those that apply to the company as a whole. Since they apply to the company as a whole, corporate-level discounts should be deducted from the corporate valuation before considering shareholder-level discounts and premiums.[285] The New Jersey Supreme Court stated in *Balsamides*, "Discounting at the corporate level may be entirely appropriate if it is generally accepted in the financial community in valuing businesses."[286]

The Delaware courts have historically understood the necessity of corporate-level adjustments in certain limited circumstances. In *Tri-Continental*, the company being valued was a closed-end investment company. Because of this structure, shareholders of the company had no right to demand their proportionate share of the company's assets. For this reason and due to the company's various leverage requirements, the market value of the corporation as a whole was lower than its net asset value. The court therefore applied a discount at the corporate level before valuing the minority shares.

---

[282] *Dobler*, 2004 Del. Ch. LEXIS 139, at *72 and *65–66; *Lane,* 1994 Del. Ch. LEXIS 67, at *117–118 and *129.

[283] Pratt, *The Lawyer's Business Valuation Handbook* (ABA, 2000), at 359, quoting Matthews, "Delaware Court Adds Control Premium to Subsidiary Value," *Business Valuation Update,* May 1998, p. 9.

[284] *Dobler*, 2004 Del. Ch. LEXIS 139, at *72.

[285] Laro and Pratt, *Business Valuation and Taxes*, at 266.

[286] *Balsamides*, 734 A.2d 721,733.

Several corporate-level discounts may be applied in a fair value determination. The valuator may consider, when applicable, application of a trapped-in capital gains discount, a portfolio (nonhomogeneous assets) discount, a contingent liabilities discount, or a key-man discount. In *Hodas v. Spectrum Technology*, a 1992 Delaware appraisal action, the court accepted the 20% key-man discount determined by the company's expert, concluding that the founder's "departure would mean the demise of the company."[287] The court rejected a 40% corporate-level lack of marketability discount applied by the appraiser because of the purported lack of a readily available market for the company as a whole.

Control Premiums at the Corporate Level

Most states reject control premiums in appraisals. Although several decisions discuss applying control premiums, a careful reading of most of these decisions leads to the conclusion that the courts are not actually adding a control premium to their valuations, but rather are merely making an adjustment to eliminate a perceived IMD. They are attempting to avoid applying an impermissible minority discount and often do so by making an adjustment by considering premiums paid in other transactions.

Only three states (Vermont, New Jersey, and Iowa) have actually applied control premiums at the corporate level in appraisals, and then only in certain cases. These cases effectively use third-party value.

Vermont courts have applied control premiums in two cases. In *Trapp Family Lodge*, the Vermont Supreme Court ruled:

> [T]o find fair value, the trial court must determine the best price a single buyer could reasonably be expected to pay for the corporation as an entirety and prorate this value equally among all shares of its common stock.[288]

The control premium that was applied was based on comparable acquisitions of other hotels and motels. Another Vermont decision cited *Trapp Family Lodge* when it approved a control premium[289] and noted that "the projected cash flow . . . was not adjusted to reflect decisions by a controlling purchaser."[290]

---

[287] *Hodas v. Spectrum Technology*, 1992 Del. Ch. LEXIS 252, at *14.

[288] *In re 75,629 Shares of Common Stock of Trapp Family Lodge, Inc.*, 725 A.2d 927, 931 (Vt. 1999).

[289] *In re Shares of Madden, Fulford and Trumbull*, 2005 Vt. Super. LEXIS 112 (May 16, 2005), at *35.

[290] Id., at *25.

The New Jersey Superior Court supported a limited control premium in *Casey v. Brennan*, concluding that "in a valuation proceeding a control premium should be considered in order to reflect market realities, provided it is not used as a vehicle for the impermissible purpose of including the value of anticipated future effects of the merger."[291]

The 2007 Iowa Supreme Court decision in *Northwest Investment* permitted a control premium in a bank appraisal "[b]ecause the minority shareholders presented credible evidence the corporation could obtain a significant control premium in the event of a sale"; the court affirmed a control premium applied by the lower court.[292] Interestingly, none of the other six appraisal decisions by the Iowa Supreme Court in the past two decades discussed control premiums.

Although no reported New Mexico appraisal has applied a control premium, the state's Supreme Court, stated that a control premium is a question of fact to be determined on a case-by-case basis assessment.[293]

Delaware does not apply control premiums at the parent company level. However, in its anomalous 1992 *Rapid-American* decision, the Delaware Supreme Court ruled that control premiums should be applied to the valuations of the holding company's subsidiaries.[294] Rapid-American was a holding company whose three subsidiaries operated in widely different industries. The Delaware Supreme Court concluded that since the Court of Chancery had used guideline companies to value the subsidiaries, it had "treated Rapid as a minority shareholder in its wholly-owned subsidiaries." The Supreme Court stated that guideline market prices "do not reflect a control premium," but the inherent value of the parent included the control value of its subsidiaries.[295] On remand, the Court of Chancery applied control premiums to each subsidiary based on petitioners' expert's testimony as to "the average p/e ratios of companies in the industry as well as the average p/e ratios of all companies and the average control premium applicable to companies in the industry and to all companies."[296] During the 1990s, control premiums were twice more applied to Delaware valuations of subsidiaries.[297]

---

[291] *Casey v. Brennan*, 780 A.2d 553, 571 (N.J. Super. 2001).

[292] *Northwest Investment Corp. v. Wallace*, 741 N.W.2d 782 (Iowa 2007).

[293] *New Mexico Banquest Investors Corp. v. Peters Corp.*, 159 P.3d 1117, 1124 (N.M. App. 2007), *aff'd*, *Peters Corp. v. New Mexico Banquest Investors Corp.*, 188 P.3d 1185 (N.M. 2008).

[294] *Harris v. Rapid-American Corp.*, 603 A.2d 796 (Del. 1992).

[295] *Id.*, at 804.

[296] *Harris v. Rapid-American Corp.*, 1992 Del. Ch. LEXIS 75 (Apr. 1, 1992), at *9.

[297] *Le Beau*, 1998 Del. Ch. LEXIS 9, aff'd, *M.G. Bancorp.*, 737 A.2d 513; *Hintmann v. Fred Weber, Inc.*, 1998 Del. Ch. LEXIS 26 (Feb. 17, 1998).

However, there is no apparent reason for the value of an operating business to be higher if it operates as a subsidiary rather than as a division. This distinction elevates form over substance.[298] In 2001, Vice Chancellor (now Chancellor) Leo Strine discussed expressed concern about this discrepancy, commenting, "It seems a fine point to conclude that the value of the entity as a going concern includes the potential to sell controlled subsidiaries for a premium but not the potential to sell the entity itself."[299]

Hamermesh and Wachter criticized the discrepancy in a 2007 article:

> It takes little imagination to see that this rationale, carried to its logical conclusion, compels the inclusion of a control premium, measured by a hypothetical third-party sale value, in all share valuation cases, not just in situations in which the corporation owns its operating assets through controlled subsidiaries. A corporation's control of directly owned assets is at least as great as it would be if those assets were held through controlled subsidiaries.[300]

Since 1998 there have been no cases that have explicitly applied a control premium to a subsidiary, despite the fact that several subsequent Delaware appraisal cases valued holding companies. Indeed, no control premiums were added to subsidiary values even in cases where several subsidiaries were separately valued by the court.[301]

Some States Permit Considering Extraordinary Circumstances in Determining Whether to Apply Discounts

Some states permit the application of a discount for lack of marketability in *extraordinary circumstances*. This requires more than just a lack of a public market, for the shares. The court will apply a discount only if merited by the specific facts and circumstances of the case. An example of an extraordinary circumstance is when an award would harm the *continuing* shareholders. In *Advanced Communication Design*, a minority shareholder sought dissolution as a counterclaim to the closely held company's suit against him for breach of fiduciary duty.[302] The Minnesota

---

[298] Matthews, "Delaware Court Adds Premium to Control Valuation," *Business Valuation* Update (May 1998), at 10.

[299] *Agranoff v. Miller*, 791 A.2d 880, 898 n. 45(Del. Ch. 2001).

[300] Hamermesh and Wachter, "The Short and Puzzling Life," at 15.

[301] E.g., *Highfields Capital*, 2007 Del. Ch. LEXIS 126; *Gesoff v. IIC Industries Inc.*, 902 A.2d 1130 (Del. Ch. 2006).

[302] *Advanced Communication Design, Inc. v. Follett*, 615 N.W.2d 285 (Minn. 2000).

Supreme Court chose not to apply a bright-line rule as to marketability discounts. It decided that not applying a marketability discount in this case would be unfair to the company because it would place unrealistic financial demands on it, resulting in an unfair wealth transfer from the remaining shareholders to the dissenter. Financial data presented in the record led to the conclusion that in all probability, the unfair wealth transfer would strip appellant corporation of necessary cash flow and earnings for future growth.

Devivo v. Devivo, a Connecticut oppression case, cited *Advanced Communication Design* when the court applied a 35% marketability discount to the value of a 50% interest because of the company's large debt, its required capital expenditures, and its declining growth rate.[303]

Another extraordinary circumstance is when a minority shareholder attempts to game the system. The ALI offers the example of a dissenting shareholder withholding approval of a merger in an attempt to exploit the appraisal-triggering transaction in order to divert value to the dissenter at the expense of other shareholders. In that case, the court may determine that the dissenter is entitled to an amount less than a pro rata portion on the company's value.[304]

Extraordinary circumstances are subject to review. In *Lawson Mardon Wheaton*,[305] the New Jersey Supreme Court reversed the trial court's holding that an extraordinary circumstance existed in that the dissenters had exploited a change that they had previously supported. The Supreme Court stated that the dissenters wanted to sell their stock back to the corporation because they had no confidence in the new management and it decided that these stockholders were validly exercising their right to dissent. The court held that to find extraordinary circumstances in this case would be inconsistent with the purpose of the statute.

Court Decisions Have Moved toward Rejecting Discounts

The treatment of discounts is largely addressed by each state individually. Some states prohibit discounts in their statutes, and others leave the decision on discounts to the judgment of the courts. Precedents set by case law are not, however, set in stone and, as discussed earlier, some states have reversed earlier decisions regarding the application of minority or marketability discounts at the shareholder level.

---

[303] *Devivo v. Devivo*, 2001 Conn. Super. LEXIS 1285 (May 8, 2001), at *34.

[304] ALI, *Principles of Corporate Governance*, at 325.

[305] *Lawson Mardon Wheaton*, 716 A.2d 550, 558.

Exhibit 3.4 summarizes many of the significant state and federal court decisions on the application of discounts. The published opinions that have addressed these issues vary considerably from state to state. Some reject discounts by statute, others by case law. Some apply discounts consistently, others on a case-by-case basis, depending on the specific circumstances of each case. Because appraisals and buyouts in oppression cases are under state law, federal courts follow state statutes and case law.

The decisions summarized in Exhibit 3.4 show that several states which formerly permitted discounts now reject them.[306] No states have moved in the other direction. A few states have no published court decisions concerning shareholder-level discounts in dissent or oppression cases.[307]

EXHIBIT 3.4 Significant Court Decisions Regarding Discounts

Alabama:
James Offenbecher v. Baron Services, Inc., 874 So.2d 532 (Ala. Civ. App. 2002), *aff'd, Ex parte Baron Services, Inc.*, 874 So.2d 545 (Ala. 2003).
The corporation merged into a new company in a stock-for-stock merger that was substantively equivalent to a reverse split. The dissenting shareholder was left with just under the required amount of shares to remain a shareholder in the successor corporation and demanded the fair value of his shares. The trial court applied a 50% discount for lack of marketability. The appellate court looked to the 1999 changes in the MBCA and the Georgia decision in *Blitch v. People's Bank* as indicative of the trend against applying discounts and overturned the lower court's application of discounts. The Alabama Supreme Court affirmed the appellate decision.
Arizona:
Pro Finish USA, Ltd. v. Johnson, 63 P.3d 288 (Ariz. App. 2003)
Dissenting shareholders objected to sale of a company's assets to a third party. The trial court declined to apply minority and marketability discounts. The appellate court, after looking to the ALI's *Principles of Corporate Governance* and the trend in Delaware for disallowing discounts, upheld the trial court's valuation.

(continued)

---

[306] Colorado, Georgia, Illinois, Indiana, Kansas, Kentucky, Missouri, and New Mexico.

[307] Alaska, Hawaii, Michigan, New Hampshire, Maryland, North Dakota, Pennsylvania, and Tennessee, have no cases or statute regarding discounts. The District of Columbia and West Virginia have no cases regarding discounts but have a statute barring discounts.

EXHIBIT 3.4   *(continued)*

California:
Brown v. Allied Corrugated Box Co., 154 Cal. Rptr. 170 (Cal. App. 1979)
After minority shareholders in a closely held corporation sought dissolution, the control shareholder asked the court to ascertain the value of the minority shares. The court ordered that an appraisal be conducted by three commissioners. One commissioner's report diverged markedly from the other two. The court confirmed the report of the majority commissioners, which included a minority discount. The appellate court held that devaluing minority shares in closely held corporations for lack of control had little validity when the shares were to be purchased by the controller. The court pointed out that under the majority commissioners' approach, a controlling shareholder could avoid the proportionate distribution that would follow from an involuntary dissolution simply by invoking the buyout provisions.
Colorado:
Pueblo Bancorp. v. Lindoe, Inc., 37 P.3d 492 (Colo. App. 2001), *aff'd*, 63 P.3d 353 (Colo. 2003)
A company converted from a C corporation to an S corporation. The dissenting shareholder was itself a C corporation and thus ineligible to be a shareholder of the new company. The trial court applied minority and marketability discounts. The appellate court noted that the dissenter was entitled to a proportionate share of going-concern value and that no minority discount and, except under extraordinary circumstances, no marketability discount was to be applied. The Colorado Supreme Court affirmed the Court of Appeals' decision in a split decision, and ruled that, as to permitting marketability discounts, prior cases were overruled.
M Life Ins. Co. v. Sapers & Wallack Ins. Agency, 40 P.3d 6 (Colo. App. 2001)
The trial court determined that neither a minority discount nor a marketability discount was applicable as a matter of law. The appellate court agreed that a minority discount was not applicable as matter of law, but cited *WCM Indus. v. Trustees of the Harold G. Wilson 1985 Revocable Trust*, 948 P.2d 36 (Colo. App. 1997), which stated that a discount for lack of marketability should be considered case by case.
Connecticut:
Devivo v. Devivo, 30 Conn. L. Rptr. 52 (2001), 2001 Conn. Super. LEXIS 1285 (May 8, 2001)
A minority shareholder in a motor transportation company sought dissolution due to oppression and a deadlock of management. Here, although a marketability discount normally would not be allowed, this was viewed by the court as an extraordinary circumstance because of the corporation's existing debt and market conditions that would limit further growth. The court applied a marketability discount of 35% because of the extraordinary circumstance.
(This decision preceded the relevant statute barring discounts.)

EXHIBIT 3.4 (*continued*)

Delaware:
Cavalier Oil Corp. v. Harnett, 1988 Del. Ch. LEXIS 28 (Feb. 22, 1988); *aff'd*, 564 A.2d 1137 (Del. 1989)
The court stated that minority and marketability discounts are improper under Delaware law.
Florida:
Cox Enterprises, Inc. v. News-Journal Corp., 510 F.3d 1350 (11th Cir. 2007)
The District Court noted the finding in *Munshower* that Florida courts may apply marketability discounts. Provided with no means to determine the shares' illiquidity, the trial court did not apply a marketability discount. The U.S. Court of Appeals found no abuse of discretion and affirmed the District Court's finding. (*The initiation of the litigation preceded the relevant statute barring discounts.*)
Munshower v. Kolbenheyer, 732 So.2d 385 (Fla. App. 1999) The minority shareholder brought a dissolution proceeding and the corporation elected to purchase the minority shares in lieu of dissolution. The court noted that a discount for lack of marketability is generally necessary because shares of a closely held corporation cannot be readily sold. (*This decision preceded the relevant statute barring discounts.*)
Georgia:
Blitch v. People's Bank, 540 S.E.2d 667 (Ga. App. 2000).
In a dissenters' rights proceeding, the appraiser applied both minority and marketability discounts. The appellate court reversed precedent and rejected the minority and marketability discounts. It held that "the term 'fair value' under the statute encompasses the modern view expressed by the Revised Model Business Corporation Act." [p. 670]
Atlantic States Construction, Inc. v. Beavers, 314 S.E.2d 245, 251 (Ga. Ct. App. 1984)
The trial court refused to apply either a minority or marketability discount. The appellate court ruled that discounts are allowable but must be applied with caution. The case was remanded and the trial court was instructed to determine from the evidence whether these discounts had any bearing on a stock's fair value.
Idaho:
Hall v. Glenn's Ferry Grazing Assn., 2006 U.S. Dist. LEXIS 68051 (D. Ida. Sept. 21, 2006)
This federal case cited Comment 4(b) to *Idaho Code 30-1-1434(4)* ("In cases where there is dissension but no evidence of wrongful conduct, 'fair value' should be determined with reference to what [the shareholder] would likely receive in a voluntary sale of shares to a third party, taking into account his minority status."). [p. *20] Therefore, the court applied a minority discount.

(*continued*)

EXHIBIT 3.4   *(continued)*

Illinois:
Brynwood Co. v. Schweisberger, 913 N.E.2d 150 (Ill. App. 2009)
The court explained that shareholder level discounts (i.e., discounts for lack of marketability and lack of control) should generally be disallowed because they inequitably harm the minority shareholder.
Jahn v. Kinderman, 814 N.E.2d 116 (Ill. App. 2004)
The Illinois Court of Appeals, First Division, affirmed the lower court's decision denying a marketability discount in determining fair value in a buyout election. The court found that the substantial dividends and employment opportunities presented by stock ownership in the subject company offset any potential impact on marketability presented by a shareholders' agreement. Also, the court concluded that applying discounts is contrary to the current trend seen in other courts. *(This decision preceded the relevant statute barring discounts.)*
Weigel Broadcasting Co. v. Smith, 682 N.E.2d 745 (Ill. App. Ct. 1996), *appeal denied*, 689 N.E.2d 1147 (Ill. 1997)
The appellate court held that it is within the trial court's discretion to apply minority and marketability discounts.
Laserage Technology Corp. v. Laserage Laboratories, Inc. 972 F.2d 799 (7th Cir. 1992)
The federal appellate court, applying *Stanton*, concluded that in Illinois the determination of fair value is vested in the sound discretion of the fact finder. In contrast to *Stanton*, in this case discounts were rejected.
Stanton v. Republic Bank of South Chicago, 581 N.E.2d 678 (Ill. 1991)
The Illinois Supreme Court ruled that trial court acted within its discretion when it applied a 5% minority discount and a 5% illiquidity discount.
Independence Tube Corp. v. Levine, 535 N.E.2d 927 (Ill. App. 1989)
The appellate court accepted the discounts applied and stated that the trial court had properly considered both the minority and illiquidity factors.
Indiana:
Wenzel v. Hopper & Galliher, P.C., 779 N.E.2d 30 (Ind. App. 2002)
A law firm requested the determination of fair value of shares owned by a shareholder who was leaving the company. The appellate court cited numerous decisions in other states that rejected discounts and stated that reliance on *Perlman* and other fair market value cases was misplaced. The appellate court reversed the trial court, noting that discounts would unfairly benefit the buyer of the shares and that the purchase of shares created a readymade market for those shares.

EXHIBIT 3.4 *(continued)*

Perlman v. Permonite Mfg. Co., 568 F. Supp. 222 (N.D. Ind. 1983), *aff'd*, 734 F.2d 1283 (7th Cir. 1984)
The federal court decided that in an appraisal under Indiana law, discounts for minority interest and lack of marketability were proper.
Iowa:
Rolfe State Bank v. Gunderson, 794 N.W.2d 561 (Iowa 2011)
The court investigated legislative intent and found that Iowa code intended to extend the use of discounts to bank holding companies but not to banks engaged in reverse stock splits. It affirmed the decision not to apply discounts.
Northwest Investment Corp. v. Wallace, 741 N.W.2d 782 (Iowa 2007)
The Iowa Supreme Court provided the definition of fair value from Iowa Code § 490.1301(4), which is based on the MBCA's 1999 definition and prohibits the use of minority and marketability discounts. The court noted the MBCA's opinion that the fair value of a shareholder's interest should generally be calculated as the shareholder's pro rata share of the value of the entire corporation. The court affirmed a control premium applied by the lower court because credible evidence showed that the company could obtain a significant control premium in a sale.
Sieg Co. v. Kelly, 568 N.W.2d 794 (Iowa 1997)
In a shareholder dissent case, the Iowa Supreme Court reversed a trial court that had allowed a marketability discount, pointing out that Iowa law was clear that a marketability discount was not permitted. *(This decision preceded the relevant statute barring discounts except for banks and bank holding companies.)*
Security State Bank v. Ziegeldorf, 554 N.W.2d 884, 889 (Iowa 1996)
The Iowa Supreme Court refused to allow discounts for minority interest, citing *Woodward v. Quigley*, 794 N.W.2d 561.
Richardson v. Palmer Broadcasting Co., 353 N.W.2d 374 (Iowa 1984)
The Iowa Supreme Court reversed precedent and ruled that under Iowa law, minority discounts were contrary to the spirit of determining fair value for dissenters.
Woodward v. Quigley, 794 N.W.2d 561 (Iowa 1965)
The Iowa Supreme Court rejected a minority discount in an appraisal, explaining, "It is contrary to the purpose of the statute to discount the minority interest because it is a minority. This in effect would let the majority force the minority out without paying it its fair share of the value of the corporation." [p. 43]
Kansas:
Arnaud. v. Stockgrowers State Bank of Ashland, Kansas, 992 P.2d 216 (Kan. 1999)
The Kansas Supreme Court ruled that minority and marketability discounts are not appropriate when the purchaser of stock is the corporation or the majority.

(continued)

EXHIBIT 3.4   (*continued*)

Moore v. New Ammest, Inc., 630 P.2d 167 (Kan. Ct. App. 1981)
The appellate court ruled that trial court's acceptance of appraiser's valuation, which included a minority discount, was not improper.
Kentucky:
Shawnee Telecom Resources, Inc. v. Brown, 354 S.W.3d 542 (Ky. 2011)
The Kentucky Supreme Court noted the trend among courts to find shareholder-level minority and marketability discounts impermissible in an appraisal. It held that shareholder-level minority and marketability discounts cannot be applied to a dissenting shareholder's interest.
Brooks v. Brooks Furniture Mfgrs., Inc., 325 S.W.3d 904 (Ky. App. 2010)
The court ruled that giving a dissenting shareholder less than his proportionate share of the value of the corporation as a going concern would enable windfall profits to majority shareholders in the context of a squeeze-out merger and as a result encourage squeeze-outs. The appellate court adopted the ALI's view that marketability discounts should not be applied unless exceptional circumstances exist. It reversed the lower court's use of a marketability discount, overruling prior Kentucky case law, which generally allowed for discounts.
Ford v. Courier-Journal Job Printing Co., 639 S.W.2d 553 (Ky. App. 1982)
The court accepted a 25% marketability discount.
Louisiana:
Cannon v. Bertrand, 2 So.3d 393 (La. 2009)
The Louisiana Supreme Court reversed the appellate court's approval of a minority discount. It noted that the trend is away from applying discounts and stated, "Minority discounts and other discounts, such as for lack of marketability, may have a place in our law; however, such discounts must be used sparingly and only when the facts support their use." [p. 396]
Maine:
Kaplan v. First Hartford Corp. 603 F. Supp. 2d 195 (D. Me. 2009)
The federal court cited *McLoon Oil*, which barred minority and marketability discounts. It determined fair value by taking the market value reflected in the Pink Sheets and adjusting to reverse built-in minority and marketability discounts.
In re Val. of Common Stock of Penobscot Shoe Co., 2003 Me. Super. LEXIS 140 (May 30, 2003)
The court cited the Maine Supreme Court's prohibition in *McLoon Oil* against applying discounts to the fair value of a dissenting shareholder's interest. It adjusted for the presumptive minority discount in comparable companies.

EXHIBIT 3.4   (*continued*)

Re Valuation of Common Stock of McLoon Oil Co. 565 A.2d 997 (Me. 1989)
Dissenting minority shareholders demanded the fair value of their stock in a closely held family corporation after their father sought to merge it into another company where he would have sole voting control. The court held that the shareholder who disapproves of a proposed merger gives up his right of veto in exchange for the right to be bought out, not at market value, but at fair value. Therefore, the court stated that as a matter of law, the dissenting shareholders should receive their proportionate share of the corporation's value without any discounts.
Maryland:
Pittsburgh Terminal Corp. v. Baltimore and Ohio Railroad, 875 F.2d 549 (5th Cir. 1989)
Minority shareholders argued that the consideration they received was considerably less than an outsider would bid for a controlling interest in the corporation. Upon review, the federal court found that the controlling parties had effective control even before the merger and, therefore, it would not be appropriate to apply a control premium.
Massachusetts:
Spenlinhauer v. Spencer Press, Inc., 959 N.E.2d 436 (Mass. App. 2011)
The appellate court rejected any premiums or discounts and affirmed the trial court.
BNE Mass Corp. v. Sims, 588 N.E.2d 14 (Mass. App. 1992)
The trial court valued a bank holding company by giving equal weight to market value, earnings, and book value. The appellate court stated that the task assigned to a court by the statute was to determine what a willing buyer would pay for the enterprise as a whole on the valuation date, as opposed to the per-share value. That way, the minority stockholders could be assured that controlling shareholders may not purchase the enterprise at a price less than they would receive in the open market. The court cited Maine's *McLoon Oil* decision, which posited that any rule of law giving the shareholders less than their proportionate value would produce a transfer of wealth from the minority to the controller. The case was remanded to the trial court because it gave excessive weight to the market price of a very thinly traded stock.
Minnesota:
Helfman v. Johnson, 2009 Minn. App. Unpub. LEXIS 212 (Feb. 24, 2009)
The trial court applied a marketability discount at the corporate level rather than a minority or marketability discount at the shareholder level. The Minnesota Court of Appeals upheld the trial court's decision.
Advanced Communication Design, Inc. v. Follett, 615 N.W.2d 285 (Minn. 2000)
A minority shareholder sought dissolution as a counterclaim to the closely held company's suit against him for breach of fiduciary duty. The Minnesota Supreme

(continued)

EXHIBIT 3.4   (*continued*)

Court chose not to apply a bright-line rule as to marketability discounts. It decided that not applying a marketability discount in this case would be unfair to the company because it would place unrealistic financial demands on it, resulting in an unfair wealth transfer from the remaining shareholders to the dissenter. Financial data presented in the record led to the conclusion that, in all probability, the unfair wealth transfer would strip appellant corporation of necessary cash flow and earnings for future growth.
Foy v. Klapmeier, 992 F.2d 774 (8th Cir. 1993)
The 8th Circuit, applying Minnesota law, decided that U.S. District Court had erred in applying a minority discount, noting that rejecting discounts is "in accordance with the approach of the majority of states which have addressed" the issue.
MT Properties, Inc. v. CMC Real Estate Corp., 481 N.W.2d 38 (Minn. Ct. App. 1992)
The court held that the aim of the statute was to protect the dissenting shareholder and, therefore, minority discounts must be prohibited.
Mississippi:
Dawkins v. Hickman Family Corp., 2011 U.S. Dist LEXIS 63101 (N.D. Miss. June 11, 2011)
The court noted that Mississippi law prohibits minority and marketability discounts "except, if appropriate, for amendments to the articles" and accepted an expert's valuation that had been adjusted to remove a minority discount.
Hernando Bank v. Huff, 609 F. Supp. 1124, 1126 (N.D. Miss. 1985), *aff'd*, 796 F.2d 803 (5th Cir. 1986)
The federal court reviewed Mississippi law and concluded that a minority discount was proper in the case.
(*This decision preceded the relevant statute barring discounts.*)
Missouri:
Swope v. Siegel-Robert, Inc., 243 F.3d 486, 492 (8th Cir. 2001)
The federal appellate court, applying Missouri law, rejected both marketability and minority discounts. It stated, "The marketability discount is incompatible with the purpose of the appraisal right, which provides dissenting shareholders with a forum for recapturing their complete investment in the corporation after they are unwillingly subjected to substantial corporate changes beyond their control." It added, "The application of a minority discount undermines the purpose of a fair value appraisal statute by penalizing minority shareholders for their lack of control and encouraging majority shareholders to take advantage of their power."

EXHIBIT 3.4 (*continued*)

Hunter v. Mitek Indus., 721 F. Supp. 1102 (E.D. Mo. 1989)
The federal court declined to apply minority or marketability discounts, but noted that, under Missouri law, the imposition of such discounts is within the discretion of the trier of fact.
King v. F.T.J., Inc., 765 S.W.2d 301 (Mo. Ct. App. 1988)
The appellate court held that the application of minority and marketability discounts is within trial court's discretion. It applied a minority discount only to that portion of the corporation's value attributable to its "non-saleable assets" and affirmed the trial court's rejection of a discount for lack of marketability.
Montana:
Hansen v. 75 Ranch Co., 957 P.2d 32 (Mont. 1998)
The Montana Supreme Court reversed a lower court's determination of fair value. It rejected the application of a minority discount as inappropriate when the shares are purchased by the company or an insider.
Nebraska:
Camino, Inc. v. Wilson, 59 F. Supp. 2d 962 (D. Neb. 1999)
The federal court noted that the Nebraska Supreme Court barred minority and marketability discounts in *Rigel Corp. v. Cutchall*, which assumed that the company would continue as a going concern and not be liquidated. The court awarded dissenting shareholders a proportionate share of equity value.
Rigel Corp. v. Cutchall, 511 N.W.2d 519 (Neb. 1994)
A minority shareholder dissented from a merger in order to recover the fair value of his shares. The trial court allowed a minority discount. The Nebraska Supreme Court reviewed case law and recent trends and decided that, in the event of a merger, neither a minority discount nor a deduction for lack of marketability was allowed in determining the fair value.
Nevada:
American Ethanol Inc. v. Cordillera Fund, L.P., 252 P.3d 663 (Nev. 2011)
Defendant argued that the district court abused its discretion by not determining fair value according to *Steiner*. The Nevada Supreme Court cited the 2009 amendment to Nevada statute declaring that the fair value of a dissenter's shares is to be determined without applying minority or marketability discounts. The district court's rejection of discounts was affirmed.
Steiner Corp. v. Benninghoff, 5 F. Supp. 2d 1117 (D. Nev. 1998)
The federal court rejected a minority discount but applied a 25% discount for illiquidity.
(*This decision preceded the relevant statute barring discounts.*)

(*continued*)

EXHIBIT 3.4   *(continued)*

New Jersey:
Casey v. Brennan, 780 A.2d 553 (N.J. Super. 2001)
The lower court had ruled that control premiums were prohibited as a matter of law. The appellate court reversed the lower court, stating that "in a valuation proceeding a control premium should be considered in order to reflect market realities, provided it is not used as a vehicle for the impermissible purpose of including the value of anticipated future effects of the merger." [p. 571] The appellate court ruled that a control premium should be applied to the bank's value.
Balsamides v. Protameen Chemicals, Inc., 734 A.2d 721 (N.J. 1999)
A shareholder claimed oppression and brought a dissolution action. The trial court ordered the other shareholder to sell his interest in the company to the petitioner. The New Jersey Supreme Court accepted a 35% marketability discount to ensure that the oppressing shareholder being bought out was not unjustly enriched by the undiscounted valuation of his shares because the oppressed shareholder would incur the potential effects of the diminished value if he were ultimately to sell the company to an outside investor.
Lawson Mardon Wheaton Inc. v. Smith, 734 A.2d 738 (N.J. 1999)
On the same day as *Balsamides*, the court ruled against a marketability discount in an appraisal case. Although the trial court had considered this an extraordinary circumstance because of the actions of the dissenters, the New Jersey Supreme Court concluded that the stockholders were only exercising their right to dissent, which did not warrant application of a marketability discount.
New Mexico:
Peters Corp. v. New Mexico Banquest Investors Corp., 188 P.3d 1185 (N.M. 2008)
New Mexico law supports a case-by-case assessment of whether fair value should be adjusted for a control premium. In this case, a control premium was rejected.
McMinn v. MBF Operating Acq. Corp., 164 P.3d 41 (N.M. 2007)
A shareholder objected to a cash-out merger and brought suit against the corporation. The New Mexico Supreme Court noted the undefined status of "fair value" in the New Mexico statute, but stated that revisions to the MBCA, including the barring of minority and marketability discounts, guide interpretation of the statute.
McCauley v Tom McCauley & Son, Inc., 724 P.2d 232 (N.M. 1986)
The trial court, finding oppression, applied a 25% minority discount in a closely held family corporation. Plaintiff appealed, arguing that had the court ordered liquidation, she would have received her proportionate share of the company's assets. The New Mexico Supreme Court noted that the trial court was not bound simply to order dissolution, but to choose from a variety of available remedies, and it found that it was within the trial court's discretion to apply a minority discount.

EXHIBIT 3.4 *(continued)*

New York:
Giaimo v. Vitale, 2012 N.Y. App. Div. LEXIS 8706 (Dec. 20, 2012)
The appellate court ruled that the "increased costs and risks associated with corporate ownership of the real estate … ha[s] a negative impact on how quickly and with what degree of certainty the corporations can be liquidated, which should be accounted for by way of a discount." [p. *3] The court "conclude[d] that a 16% DLOM against the assets of both corporations is appropriate and should be applied." [p. *4]
Application of Zulkofske, 2012 N.Y. Misc. LEXIS 3088 (N.Y. Supr., June 28, 2012)
In lieu of dissolution, the parties agreed to a statutory appraisal. The trial court rejected a liquidity discount because the plaintiff owned 50% of the company.
Murphy v. United States Dredging Corp., 74 A.D.3d 815 (N.Y. App. Div. 2010)
A corporation elected, in lieu of dissolution, to purchase the interests held by several minority shareholders. The appellate court cited *Blake v. Blake Agency* and held that New York law prohibits minority discounts but allows marketability discounts. The court affirmed the trial court's application of a marketability discount because of the entity's classification as a close corporation. Further, the court rejected the shareholder's argument that New York law limits marketability discounts to goodwill.
Application of Jamaica Acquisition, Inc., 901 N.Y.S.2d 907 (N.Y. Supr. 2009)
The court rejected a minority discount but applied a discount for lack of marketability. The court rejected the argument that the discount for lack of marketability should be applied only to goodwill, concluding that the cases cited by petitioners did not support this limitation.
Blake v. Blake Agency, Inc., 486 N.Y.S.2d 341 (N.Y. App. Div. 1985)
The court held that a minority interest in closely held corporate stock should not be discounted solely because it is a minority interest.
North Carolina:
Vernon v. Cuomo, 2010 NCBC LEXIS 7 (N.C. Super. March 15, 2010)
The court rejected marketability and minority discounts under the facts of the case.
Garlock v. Southeastern Gas & Power, Inc., 2001 NCBC LEXIS 9 (N.C. Super., Nov. 14, 2001)
The court determined that oppression had occurred. The court-appointed appraiser had applied a lack of marketability discount and a minority discount, but the Court ruled that under the circumstances of the case it would been inequitable to impose a discount for lack of control or for lack of marketability.
Royals v. Piedmont Elec. Repair Co, 1999 NCBC LEXIS 1 (N.C. Super. 529 Mar. 3, 1999), *aff'd*, S.E.2d 515 (N.C. App 2000)

(continued)

EXHIBIT 3.4 (*continued*)

"The statute clearly does not contemplate such a windfall for majority shareholders, nor should it be interpreted in such a way as to provide an incentive for majority shareholders to oppress minority shareholders and force them to sell. The Court believes that North Carolina law does not favor application of discounts for lack of control or lack of marketability under these circumstances and will not apply discounts in this case." [p. *39]
Ohio (Fair Cash Value):
Martin v. Martin Bros. Container & Timber Products Corp., 241 F. Supp. 2d 815 (N.D. Ohio 2003)
The federal court applied the Ohio standard of willing seller and willing buyer, citing *Armstrong*. Minority and marketability discounts were accepted.
English v. Artromick Intl., Inc., 2000 Ohio App. LEXIS 3580 (Aug. 10, 2000)
An owner and employee of a close corporation refused a monetary offer for his stock and requested a judicial determination of value. The trial court concluded that a pro rata valuation of appellant's stock was inappropriate. Instead, the trial court applied the willing buyer–willing seller approach and determined that minority and marketability discounts were appropriate. The appellate court upheld the application of the discounts.
Armstrong v. Marathon Oil Co., 553 N.E.2d 462 (Ohio App. 1990)
The trial court had concluded that the appraisal process should consider the per-share value of all shares of the corporation on the basis of a hypothetical sale of all of its shares. This approach was rejected by Ohio Court of Appeals. It concluded that, since there was an active trading market for the stock, appraisal should be based on market price adjusted to eliminate any effects from the proposed transaction. Adjusting the market price for the impact effect of the pending merger limited the dissenters to Marathon Oil's pre-announcement market price.
Oklahoma:
Woolf v. Universal Fidelity Life Ins. Co., 849 P.2d 1093 (Okla. App. 1992)
An insurance company proposed changes to its articles of incorporation, and some shareholders pursued their dissenters' rights. The trial court applied a 12% minority discount to the value of their shares. The appellate court ruled that as the Oklahoma dissenters' rights statute was based on Delaware's, it should apply Delaware's understanding of fair value. Thus, it rejected the application of discounts.
Oregon:
Marker v. Marker, 242 P.3d 638 (Ore. App. 2010)
A minority shareholder alleged oppressive conduct and brought action against the majority shareholder. The trial court ordered a buyout of the minority shareholder and accepted a valuation without minority and marketability discounts. The Oregon Court of Appeals affirmed.

EXHIBIT 3.4 (*continued*)

Hayes v. Olmsted & Associates, Inc. 21 P.3d 178 (Ore. App. 2001)
A shareholder alleged oppression and the firm agreed to purchase his shares. The court cited *Chiles*, ruling that neither a minority nor a marketability discount was appropriate in determining the fair value of the stock of an oppressed shareholder's stock.
Chiles v. Robertson, 767 P.2d 903 (Ore. App. 1989)
The appellate court affirmed the trial court's refusal to apply minority or marketability discounts, commenting that "applying those discounts would give plaintiffs less than they would receive on a dissolution after defendants had made the [companies] whole for the damage they suffered, a result that would not be appropriate in light of our finding of defendants' oppressive conduct." [p. 926] The court distinguished this case from *Columbia Management* (which was a merger transaction) because defendants in this case were required to purchase the shares due to a breach of fiduciary duty.
Columbia Management Corp. v. Wyss, 765 P.2d 207 (Ore. App. 1988)
The appellate court held that the trial court correctly applied a marketability discount but that it should not have applied a minority discount. The court decided that including a minority discount would penalize the shareholder while allowing the corporation to buy his shares cheaply. It stated that a marketability discount "reflect[s] the potential volatility in Columbia's enterprise value and the fact that its asset value is considerably less than the enterprise value, as well as the marketability problems that affect the shares of all closely held corporations." [p. 213]
Rhode Island:
DiLuglio v. Providence Auto Body, Inc., 755 A.2d 757 (R.I. 2000)
The minority shareholder cited a breach of fiduciary duty and filed for dissolution. The lower court ordered a buyout at an undiscounted price. The majority shareholder claimed that a marketability discount could be applied at the corporate level instead of the shareholder level. Reviewing prior cases, the Supreme Court rejected the appeal, accepting the trial court's reasoning that because the purchaser was obligated to buy, the lack of public market for the shares was irrelevant.
Charland v. Country View Golf Club, Inc., 588 A.2d 609, 612 (R.I. 1991)
The court adopted a rule that in a buyout remedy, shares should not be discounted simply due to minority status.
South Carolina:
Morrow v. Martschink, 922 F. Supp. 1093 (D. S.C.1995)
An action was brought for the dissolution of a closely held realty corporation. The parties agreed to allow the court to determine the fair value for the purpose of a buyout. Applying South Carolina law, the U.S. District Court found that discounts were not applicable in intra-family transfers in closely held company or in a forced sale situation.

(*continued*)

EXHIBIT 3.4 *(continued)*

South Dakota (2005):
First Western Bank of Wall v. Olsen, 621 N.W.2d 611 (S.D. 2001)
In a dissenting shareholder matter involving a regional bank with branches in four cities, the South Dakota Supreme Court concluded that the proper standard of value in a dissenting shareholder action is fair value. It further concluded that discounts for minority interest and lack of marketability were improper under this standard of value.
(This decision preceded the relevant statute barring discounts.)
Texas:
Ritchie v. Rupe, 339 S.W.3d 275 (Tex. App. 2011)
A minority shareholder claimed shareholder oppression after management refused to meet with potential third-party buyers of the shareholder's interest. The district court ordered a buyout at "fair value" as determined by a jury. Appellants argued that the court erred by instructing the jury not to apply minority or marketability discounts. The Texas Court of Appeals held that a pro rata portion of corporate value is generally appropriate where the oppressed shareholder has no desire to exit. However, since the minority shareholder had attempted to sell her interest, the amount awarded should be fair market value. Therefore, the Court of Appeals ruled that minority and marketability discounts should apply in this instance.
Utah:
Hogle v. Zinetics Medical, Inc., 63 P.3d 80 (Utah 2002)
The Utah Supreme Court rejected discounts and stated that dissenting shareholders are entitled to a proportionate share of equity value with no discount for minority status or, absent extraordinary circumstances, lack of marketability.
Vermont:
In re Shares of Madden, Fulford and Trumbull, 2005 Vt. Super. LEXIS 112 (May 16, 2005)
A control premium was applied because it "is appropriate to account for the value of control in owning the corporation as a whole [citing *Trapp Family Lodge*] . . . and because the projected cash flow . . . was not adjusted to reflect decisions by a controlling purchaser." [p. *35]
Waller v. American Intl. Distrib. Corp., 706 A.2d 460 (Vt. 1997)
The Vermont Supreme Court affirmed the lower court's valuation concluding that a minority discount was inapplicable in cases where oppression has been found.

EXHIBIT 3.4 *(continued)*

In re 75,629 Shares of Common Stock of Trapp Family Lodge, Inc., 725 A.2d 927 (Vt. 1999)
"[T]o find fair value, the trial court must determine the best price a single buyer could reasonably be expected to pay for the corporation as an entirety and prorate this value equally among all shares of its common stock." [p. 931] A control premium was applied based on comparable acquisitions of other hotels and motels.
Virginia:
U.S. Inspect, Inc. v. McGreevy, 57 Va. Cir. 511 (2000), 2000 Va. Cir. LEXIS 524 (Nov. 27, 2000)
A minority shareholder dissented from a merger of a corporation into its inactive subsidiary. Her stock was valued based on her proportionate interest in the corporation as if the proposed merger had not taken place. The court found that it was not appropriate to apply either a minority or marketability discount to valuation of the shareholder's interest, nor was the shareholder entitled to a control premium.
Washington:
Matthew G. Norton Co. v. Smyth, 51 P.3d 159 (Wash. App. 2002)
The court noted that fair value did not include shareholder-level discounts under the dissenters' rights statute. However, a discount for built in gains could be applied to the company assets at the corporate level if property was scheduled to be sold.
Robblee v. Robblee, 841 P.2d 1289 (Wash. App. 1992)
The appellate court rejected a "fair market value minority discount" in a valuation performed pursuant to a private division-of-assets agreement, analogizing to appraisal law.
Wisconsin:
Edler v. Edler, 745 N.W.2d 87 (Wisc. App. 2007)
After a court-ordered buyout resulting from findings of breach of fiduciary duty, the majority shareholder appealed the court's valuation. The appellate court ruled that the trial court's exclusion of minority and marketability discounts was within its discretion.
HMO-W Inc. v. SSM Health Care System, 611 N.W.2d 250 (Wisc. 2000)
The Wisconsin Supreme Court considered, as an issue of first impression, whether a minority discount could be applied in determining the fair value of a dissenter's shares. The court employed statutory interpretation and noted that the majority of other courts had rejected minority discounts because the minority shareholder, who already lacks control, is then penalized for this lack of control. The court found that applying a minority discount is impermissible because doing so is inconsistent with the equitable statutory purpose of protecting minority shareholders. The court held that the fair value is the shareholder's proportionate interest in the corporation as a going concern.

(continued)

EXHIBIT 3.4 *(continued)*

Wyoming:
Brown v. Arp and Hammond Hardware Co., 141 P.3d 673 (Wyo. 2006).
The trial court did not apply a marketability discount but applied a minority discount to dissenters' shares. On appeal, the Wyoming Supreme Court found that applying a minority discount would be inconsistent with the dissenters' rights statute's compensation of a minority shareholder involuntarily stripped of his or her interest. The court concluded that a minority discount may not be applied to a dissenting shareholder's interest, and the case was remanded.

EQUITABLE ADJUSTMENTS TO FAIR VALUE

Consideration of Wrongdoing in Calculating Fair Value

In states that have both dissenters' rights and oppression statutes, the definition of fair value is usually stated in the dissenters' rights statute unless the oppression statute differs in valuation standard of value in oppression is different.[308] Although fair value in dissent and oppression cases is often thought of as being the same, the valuation can be impacted by how the state's statute is written and how the court determines what is fair. For example, New Jersey's dissolution statute permits equitable adjustments to fair value in cases of oppression, but not for appraisal.

The RMBCA's definition of fair value asserts that although the new definition denies the application of discounts, fair value in appraisal should be seen as different from fair value in dissolution because of the differing circumstances of majority conduct in oppression and dissent cases. The RMBCA's comment to § 14.34 (oppression) states:

> The two proceedings [appraisal and oppression] are not wholly analogous . . . and the court should consider all relevant facts and circumstances of the particular case in determining fair value. For example, liquidating value may be relevant in cases of deadlock but an inappropriate measure in other cases. *If the court finds that the value of the corporation has been diminished by the wrongful conduct of controlling shareholders, it would be appropriate to include as an element of fair value the petitioner's proportional claim for any compensable corporate injury* [emphasis added]. In cases where there is dissension but no evidence

---

[308] As shown in Appendix B, Alaska, California, and New Jersey have different definitions for dissent and oppression, and Wisconsin has different definitions for business combinations than for other transactions.

of wrongful conduct, fair value should be determined with reference to what the petitioner would likely receive in a voluntary sale of shares to a third party, taking into account his minority status. If the parties have previously entered into a shareholders' agreement that defines or provides a method for determining the fair value of shares to be sold, the court should look to such definition or method unless the court decides it would be unjust or inequitable to do so in light of the facts and circumstances of the particular case.[309]

The comment suggests that in contrast to an appraisal proceeding (where a dissenter receives an undiscounted proportionate value of the company as a going concern), an oppression action permits consideration of the degree and circumstances of oppression and misconduct by the majority.

The corporation may elect to buyout dissenters' shares at their fair value within the statutory time frame if it fears liability for oppression, abuse, fraud, or mismanagement, or if the corporation anticipates a court-ordered dissolution, or if it simply wishes to avoid any legal proceeding.[310] The dissenters' dissolution proceeding will be stayed until an equitable settlement has been negotiated. Electing a buyout may also help the corporation avoid the "equitable adjustments" the court might make in a case where wrongdoing is found, as well as other costs associated with a court proceeding. For example, the corporation in a Connecticut case avoided equitable adjustments by electing to purchase the petitioners' shares. The family members who were 30.83% minority owners had petitioned to company. The court agreed that there was dissension but found there was no oppression. It determined that the failure to continue the employment of family members was not oppressive because they continued to receive compensation and benefits.[311]

An equitable adjustment may be the award of damages, expert fees, and attorney fees. In other circumstances, the courts may adjust a fair value determination by using discounts and premiums to raise or lower the value of the shares to achieve what is perceived to be an equitable result. In attempting to reach an equitable conclusion, the court may or may not strictly adhere to all of the underlying assumptions that valuation professionals commonly associate with fair value.

---

[309] ABA, *A Report of the Committee of Corporate Laws*, "Changes in the Revised Model Business Corporation Act: Appraisal Rights," 54 *Bus. Lawyer* 209 (1998).

[310] Moll, "Shareholder Oppression and 'Fair Value,'" at 321.

[311] *Johnson v. Johnson*, 2001 Conn. Super. LEXIS 2430 (Aug. 15, 2001), at *16.

The New Jersey dissolution statute[312] allows the court to adjust the valuation date or make inclusions or exclusions of certain elements in the calculation of fair value. In *Balsamides*,[313] a marketability discount was used to reduce the value of the shares in the corporation because the oppressed shareholder would be remaining with the corporation. The very same day, however, a complementary decision handed down in a dissenting shareholder case, *Lawson Mardon Wheaton*, rejected all discounts.[314] In both cases, the court considered the equities of the circumstances before making its decision.

BALSAMIDES V. PROTAMEEN CHEMICALS, INC.

Emanuel Balsamides and Leonard Perle went into business together over 25 years before the suit was filed. Balsamides had been a purchasing agent for Revlon and acted as the rainmaker for the corporation due to his many contacts. He was also responsible for advertising, marketing, and insurance. Perle, having a chemistry background, was responsible for the technical and administrative portion of the business. By mid-1995, gross sales exceeded $19 million, and each man had an annual income of between $1 and $1.5 million.

In the late 1980s, each brought two sons into the business, expecting eventually to hand over management. Balsamides' sons worked in sales and received commissions, expense accounts, and company cars, as did other Protameen salesmen. Perle's sons started in administrative and office management positions. Perle believed his sons should receive the same compensation as Balsamides' sons, and hostilities ensued.

In the early 1990s, Perle's sons moved into sales. However, the feuding already had gone so far as to cause conditions at the company to deteriorate to the point where the families could no longer conduct business together. In June 1995, Balsamides sought relief as an oppressed minority shareholder. Perle answered by denying the allegations and seeking the sale of Protameen to a third party. The court directed Balsamides to cooperate.

---

[312] N.J. Statute 14(A):12-7(8)(a).

[313] *Balsamides*, 734 A.2d 721, 736.

[314] *Lawson Mardon Wheaton v. Smith*, 734 A.2d 738, 752.

Despite many claims and counterclaims, all but the breach of fiduciary duty by Perle were dismissed. The court found that Balsamides was an oppressed shareholder and was entitled to buy out Perle in lieu of dissolution or sale. The court found both families at fault, but concluded that Perle conducted himself in a way that was harmful to the business of Protameen and his partner.

The fair value that was accepted by the trial court was that of Balsamides' expert, Thomas Hoberman, using an excess earnings method of valuation with a 35% marketability discount. Perle's expert, Robert Ott, valued the company using a combination of market and income approaches without any marketability discount because the court was creating a market for the shares by ordering the buyout.

Ott's valuation was specifically rejected by the trial court, as it looked not to determine the value of Protameen in light of a buyout but to determine the intrinsic value[315] of the business, which does not change simply because the court directed a buyout.

On appeal, the appellate court was concerned about the trial court's application of the 35% marketability discount in valuing Perle's stock. The appellate court stated that the shares were not being sold to the public, nor would they later be sold to the public. Therefore, any discount for marketability would be inappropriate as Balsamides would maintain 100% ownership. In addition, the court recognized that the IRS frowns on the excess earnings method of valuation, and Revenue Ruling 68-609 states that this method should be used to value intangible assets only if there is no better basis available.

Although Hoberman claimed that there was no better basis available, Ott claimed that he was able to use an income approach and verify his results with a market approach. The appellate court found that Hoberman was not given enough information to execute a valuation better than the excess earnings method allowed, and that this was due to Perle's noncooperation. Moreover, the only reason why Ott could calculate the income approach was because Perle provided him with more information than he provided Hoberman.

(*continued*)

---

[315] It should be noted that although the language the court used is "intrinsic value," it appears that in this instance *intrinsic value* was used synonymously with *fair value*.

There was also discussion of the 30% capitalization rate that Hoberman used. This rate was based on the lack of a full-time chemist, the projected decline in the market for the company's animal-and mineral-based chemicals over the coming years, the use of purchasing policies that placed priority on price over quality, the potential cancellation of a big contract, the reliance on six customers who account for 27% of sales, and the generation of nearly half the company's sales by Balsamides. The appellate court suggested that these items could be corrected with the corporation under Balsamides' management and should not contribute to such a high capitalization rate, but that the potential competition from Perle and his sons should be taken into consideration. Although the 30% was deemed high considering the factors offered by Hoberman, the existence of competition could merit the high rate if on remand the trial court decided to uphold its original acceptance of the 30% rate.

When the New Jersey Supreme Court reviewed the lower court's decision, it found that the appellate decision had not abused its discretion on most issues. However, in addressing the marketability discount, the Supreme Court pointed out the distinction between applying a discount at the corporate level versus the shareholder level and stated that the former may be appropriate if generally accepted in the financial community. It further cited the New Jersey dissolution statute, which directs the court to determine the fair value plus or minus any adjustments deemed equitable by the court. This statute gives the court substantial discretion to adjust the buyout price.

Balsamides claimed that by not applying a discount, if he chose to sell the corporation at a later time, he would have to absorb the full reduction for the lack of marketability of a close corporation. The appellate court thought it would not be fair or equitable for the surviving shareholder to obtain the remaining interest at a discount, dismissing the idea that Balsamides would sell at a later time. The New Jersey Supreme Court, however, called this an erroneous assumption, as there was a reality to the illiquidity of Protameen, and if the marketability discount were not applied at the buyout, Balsamides would incur the full brunt of the illiquidity if and when he tried to sell the corporation at a later date.

The valuator needs to be aware that discounts may be considered by the court because of improper conduct, as in *Balsamides*, or where a damage claim for the loss of a job or other forms of wrongdoing can be brought in conjunction with the judicial valuation. Accordingly, the practitioner should consult with counsel and obtain direction as to the applicability of extraordinary adjustments in connection with a claim of improper conduct.

Although sometimes employed as punishment in oppression cases, discounts are generally a poor calibration of what the actual recompense for damages should be. Some commentators have suggested that there are more appropriate punishments for malfeasance, such as payment of court fees, the award of damages, or the use of injunctions.[316]

Damage Claims

The loss of salary can be a significant issue in many oppression cases. Since a characteristic of a closely held business is that its shareholders are often its key employees, those shareholders have the expectation of income from employment (salary and benefits) as well as the benefits associated with ownership. In such a case, behavior by the majority to eliminate that job might be more damaging to the minority shareholder's interest than the elimination of the profits from the ownership. Here we are referring only to the difference between the amount paid to the shareholder-employee and the salary that would be paid for similar work at a comparable company if such work is available. For example, consider a situation where a shareholder-employee of a corporation earned a salary of $175,000 and perks worth $25,000. A nonshareholder employee with a comparable position at a comparable company would earn $125,000. The termination of the shareholder-employee causes him or her to lose the ability to receive an incremental $75,000 per year. If the fair value of the shareholder's investment included compensation for the loss of his or her job, he or she would have to receive the $75,000 annual difference from the time of termination to the time of the trial. In addition, that $75,000 may continue for a given or specified period of years after the date of trial, depending on the judgment of the court.[317]

Several cases have addressed the fact that minority shareholders often rely on their salary as the principal return on their investment.[318] The vio-

---

[316] Moll, "Shareholder Oppression and 'Fair Value,'" at 360.

[317] *Id.*, at n. 180.

[318] *Wilkes v. Springside Nursing Home, Inc.*, 353 N.E.2d 657, 662 (Mass. 1976); *Exadaktilos v. Cinnaminson Realty Co.*, 400 A.2d 554, 561 (N.J. Super. Ct. Law Div. 1979).

lation of the shareholder's expectation to continue employment in a close corporation may be sufficient to incur damages, back pay, or other adjustments to the value of his or her shares.[319] It is often difficult to ascertain the appropriate value and it may largely become a judgment call for the court.[320] The New Jersey Superior Court, for instance, in *Musto v. Vidas*[321] suggested that after the petitioning shareholder's termination, the shareholder should continue to receive the same compensation as the defendants, as provided for in the initial shareholder agreement, for a period of two years after the shareholder was frozen out.

SUMMARY

We have traced the development of fair value from the time when majority rule was instituted in place of the unanimity requirement that had previously existed. While fair market value evolved to mean the value arrived at in a hypothetical transaction between willing participants, fair value was created for the purpose of shareholder dissent and oppression in order to protect a minority shareholder and to compensate the shareholder for that which has been taken.

The attempt to establish exactly what has been taken is the basis for the controversy over fair value. The ABA, the ALI, state legislatures, case law, and the valuation profession itself all provide guidance for the valuation professional. As we have discussed, in many cases these sources also specify certain elements of the valuation, such as choice of valuation date and the application of discounts and premiums, that must be followed. However, the valuator must still determine the type of economic enterprise he or she is valuing, the context in which the valuation arises, and the best methods to perform the valuation.

Although dissenters' and oppressed shareholders' rights have developed throughout the twentieth century, fair value litigation was infrequent until Delaware's 1983 *Weinberger* decision. That seminal decision established that DCF and other customary valuation techniques, rather than a formula based solely on historic data, should be used for valuing a business under the relevant statutes. In the past three decades, fair value litigation has substantially increased in both appraisal and oppression cases.

Delaware's courts' appraisal and other corporate law decisions have significantly influenced courts in other states. Since the Delaware Supreme

---

[319] Mark A. Rothstein, et al., *Employment Law*, §9.24, at 593 (1994).

[320] Moll, "Shareholder Oppression and Fair Value," at 344, n. 185.

[321] *Musto v. Vidas*, 658 A.2d 1305 (N.J. Super. Ct. App. Div., 2000), at *1312.

Court's 1989 *Cavalier* decision, many states have adopted Delaware's position that dissenting shareholders are entitled to going-concern value, a pro rata share of enterprise value, with no minority or marketability discounts and no control premium. A Delaware appraisal values a company based on the way the company is currently being run, not on how an acquirer might run it. However, normalizing adjustments to eliminate the impact of usurped opportunities and improper benefits to controllers are permitted. Dissenters are not entitled to any benefit from cost savings and synergies that could not be achieved without the transaction.

Only three states do not currently use fair value as a standard. Definitions and treatments of fair value differ somewhat, but the Delaware standards are increasingly accepted in other jurisdictions. State courts now generally accept and utilize contemporary valuation techniques in appraisal and oppression cases.

When a court reviews the facts and circumstances of a case, it attempts to compensate the parties involved equitably. Courts' concern with equity is the underlying basis for "extraordinary circumstances," the award of damages, and any "adjustments" to value that would not normally be applied. Ultimately, a court may not be as concerned with strict adherence to the assumptions underlying fair value and, instead, may simply intend to find a means of fairly compensating the minority shareholder for that which has been taken.

CHAPTER 4

Standards of Value for Partnership and Limited Liability Company Buyouts

Noah J. Gordon

INTRODUCTION

As with the corporations discussed in Chapter 3, the issue of the appropriate standard of value arises in connection with a buyout, for whatever reason. This includes dissent and oppression in partnerships (general partnerships, limited partnerships, and limited liability partnerships (LLPs)) and limited liability companies (LLCs). These forms of business organizations have become increasingly popular. As they are increasingly used, especially for closely held businesses, understanding the application of the proper standard of value to partnership and LLC buyouts is becoming increasingly important.

The starting point for a determination of the applicable standard of value for these entities is the applicable state statute. As discussed in greater detail in the sections that follow, some state statutes provide for the buyout of an LLC or partnership member's interest upon the partner's or member's dissociation from the entity. As in the corporate context, state statutes may also provide for the buyout of a partner's or member's interest in lieu of dissolution, whether triggered by oppression or other conditions. In addition, a small minority of states provide for partners' or members' dissenters' rights that are similar to those enjoyed by shareholders in a corporation. In some instances, where a state statute provides for buyout, the statute also specifies the standard of value to be applied in determining the value of the interest that will be purchased.

Because some states have adopted some versions of the uniform laws promulgated by the National Conference of Commissioners on Uniform State Laws (NCCUSL), it is also helpful to look to the Uniform Laws for guidance.

Because LLCs and partnerships are primarily creatures of contract, where the owners determine most of the business's governing rules by contract in partnership agreements, operating agreements, or articles of organization, many states do not have a statutory scheme that provides the default rules for buyout or dissent. In the absence of such default rules, and in the absence of governing contractual provisions, case law may provide the appropriate standard of value, and, in some instances, it is arguable that the standard of value used in an analogous corporation statute should be used.

BUYOUT UPON DISSOCIATION

Dissociation is a legal term of art used by a number of LLC and partnership statutes. The term refers to the change in the relationships among the dissociated member or partner, the company, and the other members or partners caused by a member's or partner's ceasing to be associated in the entity's business.[1] In some cases, the dissociation of the member or partner can terminate all of the rights and responsibilities that attach to that member's or partner's interest. In other cases, dissociation will result in the termination of a member's right to participate in the business of the LLC or partnership or to exercise any of the rights of a member or partner other than the right to share in the LLC's or partnership's profits, losses, and distributions.[2] Events that may trigger dissociation include the member's or partner's voluntary withdrawal, bankruptcy, expulsion, termination, death, or the sale of the member's or partner's entire interest.

In some states, members or partners are entitled to receive payment for the value of their interest upon their dissociation (i.e., buyout), whereas in some states dissociation does not trigger buyout rights. Some states providing for a buyout specify that the applicable standard of value is fair value, and some states specify the factors that a court should consider when determining value under some other standard of value.

---

[1] See Uniform Limited Liability Company Act, § 601 comment (1996; available at https://www.law.upenn.edu/library/archives/ulc/fnact99/1990s/ullca96.htm).

[2] See, e.g., Susan Kalinka, "Dissociation of a Member from a Louisiana Limited Liability Company: The Need for Reform," 66 *La. L. Rev.* 365 (Winter 2006).

BUYOUT IN LIEU OF DISSOLUTION

As with corporations, most states authorize judicial dissolution of partnerships or LLCs upon the occurrence of certain triggering events. However, unlike many corporation statutes, many statutes governing partnerships and LLCs do not expressly provide for buyout in lieu of dissolution, or, if they do, they do not specify the standard of value under which a buyout must occur.

For general partnerships, in some states a partnership may be dissolved upon application of a partner if a court determines that the economic purpose of the partnership is likely to be unreasonably frustrated; another partner has engaged in conduct relating to the partnership business that makes it not reasonably practicable to carry on the business in partnership with that partner; or it is not otherwise reasonably practicable to carry on the partnership business in conformity with the partnership agreement. Moreover, dissociation almost always causes dissolution in states that have adopted the Uniform Partnership Act (UPA), and is an important cause of dissolution under the Revised Uniform Partnership Act (RUPA) as well. Dissolution in turn results generally in winding up, liquidation, and distribution of the proceeds to the partners. However, even in situations that seem to call for liquidation upon dissolution, courts have permitted buyout rather than compelling liquidation, especially under UPA.[3] Because liquidation and dissolution involve substantial costs and are a last-resort remedy, a strong argument can be made that, in the usual situation, the partnership entity and business continue after withdrawal of a partner and that liquidation occurs only in particular circumstances, such as a majority or unanimous vote of the partners for dissolution, or when judicial dissolution is appropriate.[4] Moreover, when there is dissolution under the limited partnership statutes (under which limited partnerships are much less dissolvable than general partnerships), the partnership business may be continued by sale as a going concern to some of the partners of the dissolved partnership, to third parties, or through a buyout of some partners (or their estates) by partners who continue the business.[5]

For LLCs, judicial dissolution may be triggered in the event of deadlock, oppressive behavior, illegal conduct, other stated misconduct, or on the grounds that it is not reasonably practicable to carry on business. However,

---

[3] Alan R. Bromberg and Larry E. Ribstein, *Bromberg and Ribstein on Partnership*, § 7.11(f) (2012).

[4] *Id.*, at §§ 7.01(d), 7.11(h).

[5] *Id.*, at § 17.11(a).

most—but not all—LLC statutes are silent with regard to the specific remedy of a buyout or its valuation methodology.[6]

DISSENTERS' RIGHTS

A small minority of states also afford investors in limited partnerships and LLCs dissenters' rights similar to those available to shareholders in corporations.

PARTNERSHIPS AND LIMITED LIABILITY PARTNERSHIPS (LLPs)

This section addresses the buyout provisions in the state partnership/LLP statutes. We begin with the NCCUSL, commonly referred to as the U.S. Uniform Law Commission. This is a nonprofit, unincorporated association headquartered in Chicago, which proposes uniform acts that are then posed to the states as model legislation. The NCCUSL is best known for its work on the Uniform Commercial Code (UCC) drafted in conjunction with the American Law Institute.[7] The NCCUSL put forth the UPA in 1914. This act was adopted in every state except Louisiana. UPA's provisions governing a partner's withdrawal were modeled on what is known as the *aggregate theory*. Under this theory of partnerships, the partnership is viewed "as a collection of sole proprietors engaged in the same business. For example, where one or another general partner is held fully liable for any obligation of the partnership, the partnership is being treated as an aggregation of individuals."[8] Under the aggregate theory, whenever a partner departs, the partnership is legally terminated. If the remaining partners want to continue the partnership, they have to create a new partnership. Under UPA, some courts prohibit a buyout and required a forced sale of assets following dissolution of the partnership, since UPA provided in §38(1) that any partner has a right to compel liquidation of partnership assets in order to receive his share.[9] Under UPA, such a compelled liquidation occurred through a sale of all the partnership

---

[6] Sandra K. Miller, "Discounts and Buyouts in Minority Investor LLC Valuation Disputes Involving Oppression or Divorce," 13 *U. Pa. J. Bus. L.* 607, pp. 618–620 (Spring 2011).

[7] The National Conference of Commissioners on Uniform State Laws. Uniform Law Commission. (2012; www.uniformlaws.org).

[8] Burton J. DeFren, *Partnership Desk Book* (Minnetonka, MN: Olympic Marketing Corp., June 1978), at 103.

[9] Unif. P'ship Act § 38(1) (1914).

assets at an auction—at fair market value. This differs from a buyout, where the dissociating partner's interest is bought at a negotiated or predetermined price by the non-dissociating partners who wish to continue the partnership. Other courts, however, permitted a buyout under UPA on equitable grounds, out of a concern that liquidation would result in a loss of value because of the nature of the asset, market conditions, or the costs and risks of sale.[10]

In 1992, the NCCUSL proposed a revised UPA, to be known as the RUPA, which was approved by the states. Although many of RUPA's provisions were similar to UPA's provisions, RUPA was based on an *entity theory* of partnership, as opposed to an aggregate theory. Under RUPA, dissociation of a partner does not terminate the partnership, but triggers a buyout by the partnership of the dissociating partner's interest. Dissolution under RUPA is identical to dissolution under UPA.[11] As under UPA, some courts interpreting RUPA permit a buyout to prevent dissolution, whereas other courts mandate a compelled liquidation. Subsequent revisions to RUPA occurred in 1993, 1994, 1996, and 1997, culminating with the 1997 version of RUPA. Wyoming, Montana, and Texas adopted the 1992 version of RUPA. Connecticut, Florida, and West Virginia adopted variations on the 1994 version. In all, the 1997 Act has been adopted in 37 states and the District of Columbia.[12]

Limited Liability Partnerships

The 1996 Amendments to UPA added the option for partnerships to become LLPs upon registration, thereby providing limited liability for all partners similar to the limited liability enjoyed by shareholders in a corporation. Partners in a general partnership are personally liable for all partnership obligations, so that they may be required to discharge partnership obligations from their own personal assets once partnership assets are exhausted.

---

[10] Alan R. Bromberg and Larry E. Ribstein, *Bromberg and Ribstein on Partnership*, § 7.11(f) (1988 & Supp. 2007).

[11] Tiffany A. Hixson, "Note, The Revised Uniform Partnership Act—Breaking Up (Or Breaking Off) Is Hard To Do: Why the Right to 'Liquidation' Does Not Guarantee a Forced Sale upon Dissolution of the Partnership," 31 *W. New Eng. L. Rev.*, 797, 799.

[12] Nicole Julal, *Legislative Fact Sheet: Partnership Act*, Uniform Law Commission (2012; www.uniformlaws.org/LegislativeFactSheet.aspx?title=Partnership%20Act). States that have enacted RUPA are: Alabama, Alaska, Arizona, Arkansas, California, Colorado, Connecticut, Delaware, District of Columbia, Florida, Hawaii, Idaho, Illinois, Iowa, Kansas, Kentucky, Maine, Maryland, Minnesota, Mississippi, Montana, Nebraska, Nevada, New Jersey, New Mexico, North Dakota, Ohio, Oklahoma, Oregon, South Dakota, Tennessee, Texas, Utah, Vermont, Virginia, Washington, West Virginia, and Wyoming.

In a LLP a partner is immune from personal liability for any partnership obligations other than those individually incurred by the partner. A partner who personally incurs an obligation in the conduct of partnership business is fully liable.

In addition to having to register upon election to become a LLP, a partnership that elects to become an LLP must also identify itself as an LLP to those with whom it does business. The registration and identification requirements are to provide clear notice of its limited liability status to those who do business with the partnership.

Notwithstanding LLP status, the partnership is subject to UPA's (*RUPA*) laws. Therefore, rules that govern such matters as partners' obligations to each other, distributions, dissociation from the partnership, dissolution of the partnership, buyout, and so forth remain the same for LLPs as they do for general partnerships governed by UPA (RUPA).[13]

As set forth in the following, § 701 of RUPA added a buyout provision, because under the entity theory, dissociation and dissolution are separate pathways following a partner's withdrawal. Section 801 specifies the events that will trigger dissolution. Otherwise, a buyout is mandatory. Thus, in all instances when a partner exits the partnership, either the partnership will be dissolved or the partner will be bought out. Under § 701, a dissociated partner whose dissociation does not result in dissolution under § 801 has the right to a buyout of his or her partnership interest by the remaining partners. Unless the partnership agreement provides otherwise, a buyout is obligatory. The default buyout price governed by § 701(b) provides the dissociated partner with the greater of either "the liquidation value or the value based on a sale of the entire business as a going concern without the dissociated partner." The policy behind valuing the partnership assets this way is to provide the dissociating partner with fair compensation whether the business assets are put up for public sale or there is a buyout by the partnership. The Act also allows for payment of damages as reduction from the amount due to the departing partner.

SECTION 701. PURCHASE OF DISSOCIATED PARTNER'S INTEREST.[14]

If a partner is dissociated from a partnership without resulting in a dissolution and winding up of the partnership business under Section 801, the partnership shall cause the dissociated partner's interest

---

[13] Nicole Julal, *Legislative Fact Sheet: Partnership Act*, Uniform Law Commission (2012; www.uniformlaws.org/LegislativeFactSheet.aspx?title=Partnership%20Act).
[14] National Conference of Commissioners on Uniform State Laws, RUPA § 701, Purchase of Dissociated Partner's Interest (2012; www.uniformlaws.org).

in the partnership to be purchased for a buyout price determined pursuant to subsection (b).

The buyout price of a dissociated partner's interest is the amount that would have been distributable to the dissociating partner under Section 807(b) if, on the date of dissociation, the assets of the partnership were sold at a price equal to the greater of the liquidation value or the value based on a sale of the entire business as a going concern without the dissociated partner and the partnership were wound up as of that date. Interest must be paid from the date of dissociation to the date of payment.

Damages for wrongful dissociation under Section 602(b), and all other amounts owing, whether or not presently due, from the dissociated partner to the partnership, must be offset against the buyout price. Interest must be paid from the date the amount owed becomes due to the date of payment.

These comments provide guidance on the standard of value for the buyout price to be paid to a departing partner. As can be seen, RUPA purposely did not use the terms *fair value* and *fair market value*, but instead used the term *buyout price*. This term appears to be enterprise value without minority discounts, but with marketability discounts and other discounts such as key-person discounts, if appropriate. However, the comments to § 701 state as follows:[15]

3. Subsection (b) provides how the "buyout price" is to be determined. The terms "fair market value" or "fair value" were not used because they are often considered terms of art having a special meaning depending on the context, such as in tax or corporate law. "Buyout price" is a new term. It is intended that the term be developed as an independent concept appropriate to the partnership buyout situation, while drawing on valuation principles developed elsewhere.

Under subsection (b), the buyout price is the amount that would have been distributable to the dissociating partner under § 807(b) if, on the date of dissociation, the assets of the partnership were sold at a price equal to the greater of liquidation value or going concern value without the departing partner. Liquidation value is not intended to mean distress sale value. Under general principles of valuation, the hypothetical selling price in either case should be the price that a willing and informed buyer would pay a willing and informed seller, with neither being under any compulsion to deal. The notion of a minority discount in determining the buyout

---

[15] *Id.*

price is negated by valuing the business as a going concern. Other discounts, such as for a lack of marketability or the loss of a key partner, may be appropriate, however.

The comments further explain that:

the § 701 rules are merely default rules. The partners may, in the partnership agreement, fix the method or formula for determining the buyout price and all of the other terms and conditions of the buyout right. Indeed, the very right to a buyout itself may be modified, although a provision providing for a complete forfeiture would probably not be enforceable.[16]

Opponents of buyouts argue that a private sale does not provide partners with the fair market value of the assets because of the prospect of a higher return at a public auction. This concern can be partially eliminated by ordering judicial supervision of the sale to ensure a fair price. In addition, a buyout is an effective counterbalance to the risk of exploitation brought on by a right to liquidation, where a dissociated partner may compel liquidation simply to freeze out other partners and appropriate the partnership business for herself at less than fair market value.[17]

Twenty-nine states follow the definition set forth in RUPA that the buyout price of a dissociated partner's interest is the amount that would have been distributable to the dissociating partner if, on the date of dissociation, the assets of the partnership were sold at a price equal to the greater of the liquidation value or the value based on a sale of the entire business as a going concern without the dissociated partner and if the partnership were wound up as of that date. Interest must be paid from the date of dissociation to the date of payment.[18]

To this, Montana and Wyoming add that in either case (liquidation value or going-concern value) the selling price of the partnership assets must be determined on the basis of the amount that would be paid by a willing buyer to a willing seller, neither being under any compulsion to buy or sell, and with knowledge of all relevant facts (i.e., appearing to apply a fair market value standard of value).[19] However, note that this language is followed in the comment section set forth earlier by the statement, "The notion of a

---

[16] National Conference of Commissioners on Uniform State Laws, RUPA § 701, Purchase of Dissociated Partner's Interest (2012; www.uniformlaws.org).

[17] See Hixson, *supra* note 11, at 806–807.

[18] See, e.g., Alaska Stat. § 32.06.701(b) (2012); N.D. Cent. Code, § 45-19-01 (2012).

[19] Mont. Code Anno., § 35-10-619(2)(b) (2011).

minority discount in determining the buyout price is negated by valuing the business as a going concern. Other discounts, such as for a lack of marketability or the loss of a key partner, may be appropriate, however."

Fifteen states use the phrase *value of his interest* in the definition of value, although using different verbiage in the definition. Colorado uses the phrase *value of the partners' interest*. Louisiana employs the phrase *the value that the share of the former partner had at the time membership ceased*.

A few states provide for the buyout at fair value. Delaware provides that the buyout price is an amount equal to the fair value of such partner's economic interest as of the date of dissociation based upon such partner's right to share in distributions from the partnership.[20] Alabama[21] and Texas[22] simply provide for buyout at fair value as of the date of dissociation. New Jersey provides that *buyout price* means the fair value as of the date of withdrawal based upon the right to share in distributions from the partnership unless the partnership agreement provides for another fair value formula.[23] Oregon specifies that the buyout price of a dissociated partner's interest is an amount equal to the fair value of the dissociated partner's interest in the partnership on the date of the dissociation, but adds that if the dissociated partner has a minority interest in the partnership, the buyout price of the dissociated partner's interest may not be discounted as a result of such minority interest.[24]

Exhibit 4.1 on the next page presents the provisions related to the buyout of a disassociated partner in all 50 states and the District of Columbia. For ease of reference, we have presented the definition of value in bold.

---

[20] 6 Del. C. § 15-701(b) (2012).

[21] Code of Ala. § 10A-8-7.01(b) (2012).

[22] Tex. Business Organizations Code § 152.602(a) (2012).

[23] N.J. Stat. § 42:1A-34(b) (2012).

[24] ORS § 67.250(2) (2011).

EXHIBIT 4.1 Individual States' Definitions of Value under Partnership Statutes

States/Territories	Definition of Value
Alaska, § 32.06.701 Arizona, § 29-1061 Arkansas, § 4-46-701 California, § 16701 Connecticut, § 34-362 District of Columbia, § 29-607.01 Florida, § 620.8701 Hawaii, § 425-133 Idaho, § 53-3-701 Illinois, § 805 ILCS 206/701 Iowa, § 486A.701 Kansas, § 56a-701 Kentucky, § 362.1-701 Maine, § 1071 Maryland, § 9A-701 Minnesota, § 323A.0701 Mississippi, § 79-13-701 Nebraska, § 67-434 Nevada, § 87.4346 New Mexico, § 54-1A-701 North Dakota, § 45-19-01 Ohio, § 1776.54 Oklahoma, § 1-701 South Dakota, § 48-7A-701 Tennessee, § 61-1-701 Vermont, § 3261 Virginia, § 50-73.112 Washington, § 25.05.250 West Virginia, § 47B-7-1	(a) If a partner is dissociated from a partnership without resulting in a dissolution and winding up of the partnership business, the partnership shall cause the dissociated partner's interest in the partnership to be purchased for a buyout price determined under (b) of this section. (b) The buyout price of a dissociated partner's interest is **the amount that would have been distributable to the dissociating partner under . . . if, on the date of dissociation, the assets of the partnership were sold at a price equal to the greater of the liquidation value or the value based on a sale of the entire business as a going concern without the dissociated partner and if the partnership were wound up as of that date.** Interest must be paid from the date of dissociation to the date of payment. (c) Damages for wrongful dissociation and all other amounts owing, whether or not presently due, from the dissociated partner to the partnership, must be offset against the buyout price. Interest must be paid from the date the amount owed becomes due to the date of payment.
Montana, § 35-10-619 Wyoming, § 17-21-701	(1) If a partner is dissociated from a partnership without resulting in a dissolution and winding up of the partnership business, the partnership shall cause the dissociated partner's interest in the partnership to be purchased for a buyout price determined pursuant to subsection (2). (2)(a) The buyout price of a dissociated partner's interest is the amount that would have been distributable to the dissociating partner if, on the date of dissociation, the assets of the partnership were **sold at a price equal to the greater of: (i) the liquidation value; or (ii) the value based on a sale of**

States/Territories	Definition of Value
	the entire business as a going concern without the dissociated partner and the partnership were wound up as of that date.
	(b) In either case, the selling price of the partnership assets must be determined on the basis of the amount that would be paid by a willing buyer to a willing seller, neither being under any compulsion to buy or sell, and with knowledge of all relevant facts. Interest must be paid from the date of dissociation to the date of payment.
	(3) Damages for wrongful dissociation and all other amounts owing, whether or not presently due, from the dissociated partner to the partnership must be offset against the buyout price. Interest must be paid from the date the amount owed becomes due to the date of payment.
Indiana, § 23-4-1-42 Massachusetts, § 42 Michigan, § 449.42 Missouri, § 358.420 Nevada, § 87.420 New Hampshire, § 304-A:42 New York, § 73 North Carolina, § 59-72 Pennsylvania, § 8364 Rhode Island, § 7-12-53 South Carolina, § 33-41-1080 Utah, § 48-1-39 Wisconsin, § 178.37	When any partner retires or dies, and the business is continued under any of the conditions set forth . . . without any settlement of accounts as between him or his estate and the person or partnership continuing the business, unless otherwise agreed, he or his legal representative as against such persons or partnership may have **the value of his interest** at the date of dissolution ascertained, and shall receive as an ordinary creditor an amount equal to the value of his interest in the dissolved partnership with interest, or, at his option or at the option of his legal representative, in lieu of interest, the profits attributable to the use of his right in the property of the dissolved partnership; provided that the creditors of the dissolved partnership as against the separate creditors, or the representative of the retired or deceased partner, shall have priority on any claim arising under this section.
Georgia, § 14-8-42	When any partner withdraws or dies, and the business is continued under any of the conditions set forth in subsection (a) of Code Section 14-8-41 or paragraph (2) of subsection (b) of Code Section 14-8-38, without any settlement of accounts as between the withdrawn partner or the legal representative of the estate of a deceased partner and the persons or partnership continuing the business, unless otherwise agreed:

(Continued)

EXHIBIT 4.1 (*Continued*)

States/Territories	Definition of Value
	(1) Such persons or partnership shall obtain the discharge of the withdrawn partner or the legal representative of the estate of the deceased partner, or appropriately hold him harmless from all present or future partnership liabilities, and shall ascertain **the value of his interest** at the date of dissolution; and (2) The withdrawn partner or legal representative of the estate of the deceased partner shall receive as an ordinary creditor an amount equal to **the value of his interest** in the dissolved partnership with interest, or, at his option, in lieu of interest, the profits attributable to the use of his right in the property of the dissolved partnership, provided that the creditors of the dissolved partnership as against the separate creditors, or the representative of the withdrawn or deceased partner, shall have priority on any claim arising under this Code section, as provided by subsection (d) of Code Section 14-8-41.
Colorado, § 7-64-701	(1) If a partner is dissociated from a partnership without resulting in a dissolution and winding up of the partnership business under section 7-64-801, the partnership shall cause the dissociated partner's interest in the partnership to be purchased for a buyout price determined pursuant to subsection (2) of this section. (2) The buyout price of a dissociated partner's interest is an amount equal to the **value of the partner's interest** in the partnership. Interest shall be paid from the date of dissociation to the date of payment. (3) Damages for wrongful dissociation under Section 7-64-602(2), and all other amounts owing, whether or not presently due, from the dissociated partner to the partnership, shall be offset against the buyout price. Interest shall be paid from the date the amount owed becomes due to the date of payment.
Louisiana, Art. 2823; Art. 2824	2823. The former partner, his successors, or the seizing creditor is entitled to an amount equal to **the value that the share of the former partner had at the time membership ceased.**

States/Territories	Definition of Value
	2824. If a partnership continues to exist after the membership of a partner ceases, unless otherwise agreed, the partnership must pay in money the amount referred to in Article 2823 as soon as that amount is determined together with interest at the legal rate from the time membership ceases.
Delaware, § 15-701	(a) If a partner is dissociated from a partnership without resulting in a dissolution and winding up of the partnership business or affairs under Section 15-801, the partnership shall cause the dissociated partner's interest in the partnership to be purchased for a buyout price determined pursuant to subsection (b). (b) The buyout price of a dissociated partner's partnership interest is an amount equal to the **fair value** of such partner's economic interest as of the date of dissociation based upon such partner's right to share in distributions from the partnership. Interest must be paid from the date of dissociation to the date of payment. (c) Damages for wrongful dissociation under Section 15-602(b), and all other amounts owing, whether or not presently due, from the dissociated partner to the partnership, must be offset against the buyout price. Interest must be paid from the date the amount owed becomes due to the date of payment.
Alabama, § 10A-8-7.01	(a) If a partner is dissociated from a partnership without resulting in a dissolution and winding up of the partnership business under Section 10A-8-8.01, the partnership shall cause the dissociated partner's interest in the partnership to be purchased for a buyout price determined pursuant to subsection (b). (b) The buyout price of a dissociated partner's interest shall be the **fair value** of the dissociated partner's interest in the partnership as of the date of dissociation. (c) Damages for wrongful dissociation under Section 10A-8-6.02(b), and all other amounts owing, whether or not presently due, from the dissociated partner to the partnership, must be offset against the buyout price. Interest must be paid from the date the amount owed becomes due to the date of payment.

(Continued)

EXHIBIT 4.1 (*Continued*)

States/Territories	Definition of Value
Texas, § 152.601; § 152.602	Redemption If Partnership Not Wound Up: The partnership interest of a withdrawn partner automatically is redeemed by the partnership as of the date of withdrawal in accordance with this subchapter if: (1) the event of withdrawal occurs under Sections 152.501(b)(1)--(9) and an event requiring a winding up of partnership business does not occur before the 61st day after the date of the withdrawal; or
	(2) the event of a withdrawal occurs under Section 152.501(b)(10). Redemption Price: (a) Except as provided by subsection (b), the redemption price of a withdrawn partner's partnership interest is **the fair value of the interest** on the date of withdrawal. (b) The redemption price of the partnership interest of a partner who wrongfully withdraws before the expiration of the partnership's period of duration, the completion of a particular undertaking, or the occurrence of a specified event requiring a winding up of partnership business is the lesser of: (1) the **fair value of** the withdrawn partner's partnership interest on the date of withdrawal; or (2) the amount that the withdrawn partner would have received if an event requiring a winding up of partnership business had occurred at the time of the partner's withdrawal. (c) Interest is payable on the amount owed under this section.
New Jersey, § 42:1A-34	(a) If a partner is dissociated from a partnership without resulting in a dissolution and winding up of the partnership business under Section 39 of this Act, except as otherwise provided in the partnership agreement, the partnership shall cause the dissociated partner's interest in the partnership to be purchased for a buyout price as determined pursuant to subsection (b) of this section. (b) As used in subsection (a) of this section, "buyout price" means the **fair value** as of the date of withdrawal **based upon the right to share in distributions from the partnership unless the**

States/Territories	Definition of Value
	partnership agreement provides for another fair value formula. (c) Damages for wrongful dissociation under subsection (b) of Section 32 of this Act, and all other amounts owing, whether or not presently due, from the dissociated partner to the partnership, shall be offset against the buyout price. Interest shall be paid from the date the amount owed becomes due to the date of payment.
Oregon, § 67.250	(1) If a partner is dissociated from a partnership without resulting in a dissolution and winding up of the partnership business under ORS 67.290 (Events causing dissolution and winding up of partnership business), the partnership shall cause the dissociated partner's interest in the partnership to be purchased for a buyout price determined pursuant to subsection (2) of this section. (2) The buyout price of a dissociated partner's interest is an amount equal to the **fair value** of the dissociated partner's interest in the partnership on the date of the dissociation. If the dissociated partner has a minority interest in the partnership, the buyout price of the dissociated partner's interest **shall not be discounted as a result of such minority interest.** Interest must be paid from the date of dissociation to the date of payment. (3) Damages for wrongful dissociation under ORS 67.225 (Partner's power to dissociate) (2) and all other amounts owing, whether or not presently due, from the dissociated partner to the partnership, must be offset against the buyout price. Interest must be paid from the date the amount owed becomes due to the date of payment.

Thirty-seven states and the District of Columbia allow for a buyout of the partner's interest upon any form of dissociation. Thirteen states limit the buyout to retirement or death. Practitioners should consult with their attorney to obtain a definition of *retirement* in this context.

Thus, for partnerships, as contrasted with corporations, in many states the buyout provision applies not only for matters akin to dissent and oppression, but for retirement or any other reason a partner may dissociate from the partnership.

General Partnership Standard of Value Cases

Louisiana   The following two cases from Louisiana show how the standard of value for partnerships follows the reasoning in corporate dissent and oppression cases. In the first matter, *Shopf v. Marina Del Ray Partnership*, a partner sought to be bought out of his partnership interest. He requested to be bought out at fair market value and the court applied a minority discount following the reasoning of fair market value. In the second matter, *Cannon v. Bertrand*, the court followed fair value reasoning and declined to apply a minority discount, arguing that the remaining partners would suffer no lack of control. We suggest that a practitioner consult with an attorney on the applicability of the buyout provision and the standard of value for partnership buyouts within their jurisdiction.

SHOPF V. MARINA DEL RAY PARTNERSHIP

A partner, fired from his position as general manager, brought suit for breach of his employment contract and sought damages. The partner notified the partnership of his intent to withdraw, and the remaining partners decided to buy out the withdrawing partner. The parties could not agree to a buyout price and the withdrawing partner filed for a judicial appraisal of his interest, pursuant to La. C.C. arts. 2823-2825 (the Louisiana partnership buyout provision). The trial court found the book value of the partnership to be negative on the day of the withdrawing partner's firing and therefore found his interest to have no value and ordered no payment. Upon appeal, the Court of Appeal, First Circuit, Parish of St. Tammany, found no error in the trial court's finding and affirmed. The Supreme Court of Louisiana accepted the withdrawing partner's application for certiorari to review the lower court's finding that his interest had no value.

The Supreme Court of Louisiana noted that the Louisiana code providing for judicial determination of the value of the withdrawing partner's interest did not define that value. The withdrawing partner contended that fair market value, rather than book value, was the appropriate valuation method, citing *Anderson v. Wadena Silo Co.*, 310 Minn. 288, 246 N.W.2d 45 (1976). The partnership agreed, but argued that the partnership's liabilities were greater than the fair market value of the withdrawing partner's interest, and that the interest therefore had no value.

The Supreme Court of Louisiana noted the applicable Civil Code (C.C.) provisions. "Once a partner has withdrawn from the partnership which continues to exist, he is not entitled to . . . "an amount equal to the value that the share of the former partner had at the time membership ceased," and the value of the share must be paid in money, unless otherwise agreed, together with legal interest from the time membership ceases. 9 La.C.C. art. 2823-24. When there is no agreement on the amount to be paid, any interested party may apply for a judicial determination of the value of the share and for a judgment ordering its payment. 10 La. C.C. art. 2825.

The Supreme Court of Louisiana accepted the fair market value definition as "the price that a willing buyer would pay to a willing seller for a certain piece of property in an arm's-length transaction, neither being under any compulsion to buy or sell and both having reasonable knowledge of the relevant facts."

The court based its determination of the interest's fair market value on the per-point price that a remaining partner paid for a portion of a third partner's interest months before the withdrawal in the present case. This same price was offered to, although rejected by, the withdrawing partner in an attempt to resolve a conflict months before the withdrawal. The Supreme Court considered discounts and noted that a minority interest in a closely held business may be less valuable to an independent buyer than to a controlling shareholder because of its illiquidity. Therefore, the court applied a "minority interest discount," ordered payment of the resulting amount, and reversed the decisions of the two lower courts.

Source: *549 So.2d 833 (La. 1989).*

CANNON V. BERTRAND

In this case, the Louisiana Supreme Court followed the reasoning of fair value, stating that a minority discount was not applicable. A partner sought to withdraw from a three-member LLP in which each partner held a one-third interest, and filed suit in the district court for

(continued)

valuation of his share. The district court applied a 35% discount. The appellate court cited the Supreme Court of Louisiana's approval of minority discounts in *Shopf* and affirmed the district court. The withdrawing partner applied for a writ of certiorari. The Supreme Court of Louisiana interpreted the 35% discount to be a combination of minority and marketability discounts. The Supreme Court noted that in *Shopf* it discounted a majority shareholder's previous offer price for a minority interest in order to determine the fair market value of that interest. The rationale was that a minority share is worth more to a majority shareholder than to a third party.

The Supreme Court of Louisiana in *Canon* explained that the *Shopf* discount is different from a "minority discount," and established that *Shopf* should not be relied upon as precedent in this case. In *Canon*, the Supreme Court suggested that minority and marketability discounts may be legal when warranted by fact, but should be used sparingly. The court held, in *Canon*, that since the purchasers of the one-third partnership interest were the remaining two partners, they would suffer no lack of control. Accordingly, a minority discount would therefore be inappropriate. Further, the court held that such a discount would unfairly penalize the withdrawing partner for exercising his right to withdraw, and would provide undeserved profits for the remaining partners, and held the value of the withdrawing partner's share to be the value found by the district court before application of the minority discount.

Source: *2 So.3d 393; 2009 La. LEXIS 11.*

The issue of the buyout of an interest held by a deceased partner's estate arose in a New York case. The New York partnership statute (N.Y. Consolidated Law Service Partnership 73 (LexisNexis 2012)) provides that when a partner dies or retires and the business continues, the depository partner, or representative of his estate, has the right to receive the "value of his interests at the date of dissolution ascertained." The New York Appellate Court interpreted the value of his interest to be without minority and marketability discounts for a deceased partner. The court distinguished between the value for federal estate tax purposes where minority and marketability discounts would be applicable and the actual payment to the deceased partner's estate where they would not be applicable.

VICK V. ALBERT

Representatives of an estate sued for the recovery of a deceased partner's interest in two partnerships. The trial court awarded the representatives an amount for the two partnership interests and found that neither a minority nor a marketability discount was appropriate. The Supreme Court of New York, Appellate Division (First Department), affirmed the trial court decision. Further, the Appellate Division found that since "the purposes of estate tax valuation and partnership interest valuation differ, there is no basis here for deeming the representation in the estate tax return an admission as to value with regard to the partnership interest." The court reasoned that application of the discounts would yield amounts less than the value of the deceased partner's interest in the partnerships as going concerns and found minority and marketability discounts to be unavailable.

Source: *2008 N.Y. App. Div. LEXIS 310*

CONTI V. CHRISTOFF

The district court disagreed with a magistrate's valuation of a withdrawing partner's interest and instructed the magistrate to use fair cash value. The withdrawing partner appealed the district court's reversal, and the Court of Appeals of Ohio cited *Bromberg & Ribstein on Partnership (2001 Supp.)*, 7:188–189, § 7.13(b)(1), stating that the value of a withdrawing partner's interest should take into account relevant factors such as minority and marketability discounts. The court upheld the trial court's use of discretion among valuation methods and its remanding of the case to the magistrate.

Ohio thus follows the definition of value in RUPA, but in remanding the case, the appellate division found that the magistrate should consider minority and marketability discounts.

Source: *2001 Ohio 3421; 2001 Ohio App. LEXIS 4534 (Oct. 2, 2001)*

Limited Partnerships

Limited partnerships are partnerships that have limited partners who have little control over the partnership and general partners who exercise strong centralized, entrenched management over the partnership. Although limited partnerships are governed to some degree by the law of contracts, property, agency, equity, and trust, they are primarily governed by state statute.[25] Most of the states have generally adopted one or more iterations of uniform limited partnership acts promulgated by the NCCUSL.

The first of these, the Uniform Limited Partnership Act (ULPA), was promulgated in 1916, and, with the UPA, has been the basic law governing partnerships in the United States. The first revision of ULPA after 1916 occurred in 1976, and there were further amendments in 1985. The 1975 Act along with the 1985 amendments thereto is commonly referred to as the Revised Uniform Limited Partnership Act (RULPA).[26] Further changes were made in 2001 to modernize the Act. This included changes that addressed the modern needs of estate planning arrangements, by accommodating the so-called family limited partnership (FLP). That version is commonly referred to as ULPA 2001, although some refer to it as "Re-RULPA."[27] Here, we refer to it as ULPA 2001. When the states adopt any of these uniform acts, they are free to enact nonuniform language and provisions, so some states' acts may vary from the uniform acts.

Significantly, ULPA 2001 is a standalone act, delinked from both the original general partnership act (UPA) and the RUPA. ULPA 2001 incorporates many provisions from RUPA and some from the Uniform Limited Liability Company Act (ULLCA).[28] Linkage refers to the concept of filling gaps in limited partnership law with rules governing general partnerships. Both ULPA and RULPA link to general partnership law. Delinkage of the law began with RUPA, which excluded from its scope the limited partnership. Even though ULPA 2001 delinked from UPA and RUPA, only a minority of states have adopted it.[29] ULPA and RULPA were adopted in 49 states

---

[25] Alan R. Bromberg and Larry E. Ribstein, *Bromberg and Ribstein on Partnership*, § 11.01(a) (2003).

[26] See http://uniformlaws.org/ActSummary.aspx?title=Limited%20Partnership%20 Act (this is the official website of the NCCUSL).

[27] See, e.g., Elizabeth S. Miller, "Closely-Held Business Symposium: The Uniform Limited Partnership Act: Linkage and Delinkage: A Funny Thing Happened to Limited Partnerships When the Revised Uniform Partnership Act Came Along," 37 *Suffolk U. L. Rev.*, 891 (2004).

[28] *Id.*

[29] ULPA 2001 has been adopted in: Alabama, Arkansas, California, District of Columbia, Florida, Hawaii, Idaho, Illinois, Iowa, Kentucky, Maine, Minnesota,

(except Louisiana), the District of Columbia, and the U.S. Virgin Islands.[30] A few states enacted RULPA without repealing ULPA. Thus, some limited partnerships may be governed by ULPA, RULPA, or ULPA 2001.[31]

Limited partnerships should be distinguished from LLPs, discussed previously. The LLP, called a *registered limited liability partnership* in some states, is a form of general partnership in which general partners are not personally liable for some or all kinds of partnership debts and obligations.[32] ULPA 2001 also provides for limited liability limited partnership (LLLP) status, which is expressly available to provide a full liability shield to all general partners of a limited partnership.

Effect of Dissociation   RULPA §§ 603 and 604 permitted a limited partner to withdraw on six months' notice and receive the fair value of the limited partnership interest, unless the partnership agreement provided the limited partner with some exit right or stated a definite duration for the limited partnership. However, under ULPA 2001 § 505, "[a] person does not have a right to receive a distribution on account of dissociation." Instead, a partner that dissociates becomes a transferee of its own transferable interest under §§ 602(a)(3) (person dissociated as a limited partner) and 605(a)(5) (person dissociated as a general partner), although this default rule may be altered in the partnership agreement. Under this default rule, blocking the limited partners' exit allows the members to claim a valuation discount for estate tax purposes.[33] Limited partnerships that provide for a general partner's right to dissociate arguably can be expected also to provide for buyout rights in the agreement.[34]

Montana, Nevada, New Mexico, North Dakota, Oklahoma, Utah, and Washington (http://www.uniformlaws.org/LegislativeFactSheet.aspx?title=Limited%20Partnership%20Act).

[30] http://www.uniformlaws.org/LegislativeFactSheet.aspx?title=Limited%20Partnership%20Act.

[31] For a thorough discussion of linkage issues, see Elizabeth S. Miller, "Closely-Held Business Symposium: The Uniform Limited Partnership Act: Linkage and Delinkage: A Funny Thing Happened to Limited Partnerships When the Revised Uniform Partnership Act Came Along," 37 *Suffolk U. L. Rev.*, 891 (2004).

[32] *Bromberg and Ribstein on Partnership*, § 11.01(a) (2003).

[33] Alan R. Bromberg and Larry E. Ribstein, *Bromberg and Ribstein on Limited Liability Partnerships, the Revised Uniform Partnership Act, and the Uniform Limited Partnership Act*, § 9.505 (2012); 26 U.S.C. § 2704.

[34] *Id.*, at § 9.605.

Dissent   California provides partners in a limited partnership with dissenters' rights similar to those enjoyed by shareholders in a corporation.[35] The standard of value for determining the value of a partner's interest in California is fair market value.[36] Florida also provides limited partnerships with appraisal rights. For this purpose, in Florida, *fair value* means the value of the limited partner's partnership interests determined: (a) immediately before the effectuation of the appraisal event to which the partner objects; (b) using customary and current valuation concepts and techniques generally employed for similar businesses in the context of the transaction requiring appraisal, excluding any appreciation or depreciation in anticipation of the transaction to which the partner objects unless exclusion would be inequitable to the limited partnership and its remaining partners; (c) for a limited partnership with 10 or fewer limited partners, without discounting for lack of marketability or minority status.[37]

Dissolution   The vast majority of states provide that on application by a partner, a court may order dissolution of a limited partnership if it is not reasonably practicable to carry on the activities of the limited partnership in conformity with the partnership agreement.[38]

Michigan provides for dissolution of a limited partnership on application of a partner where it is established that the acts of the general partners or those of the general partners in control of the limited partnership are illegal, fraudulent, or willfully unfair and oppressive to the limited partnership or to the partner.[39]

Texas, while not specifying oppression as a ground for dissolution, provides that dissolution may be had where another partner has engaged in conduct relating to the partnership's business that makes it not reasonably practicable to carry on the business in partnership with that partner—ostensibly covering situations of illegality or oppression.[40]

Distribution upon Partner's Withdrawal   Some states provide that, if not otherwise provided in the partnership agreement, the withdrawing partner is entitled to receive, within a reasonable time after withdrawal, the fair value

---

[35] Cal. Corp. Code § 15911.22(a) (2012).

[36] Cal. Corp. Code § 15911.22(c) (2012).

[37] Fla. Stat. § 620.2113(4) (2012); for a discussion of Florida's treatment of discounts in this context, see Rebecca C. Cavendish and Christopher W. Kammerer, "Determining the Fair Value of Minority Ownership Interests in Closely Held Corporations: Are Discounts For Lack of Control and Lack of Marketability Applicable?" 82 *Fla. Bar J.*, 10 (Feb. 2008).

[38] See, e.g., Md. Corporations and Associations Code Ann. § 10-802 (2012); ALM GL ch. 109, § 45 (2012); Minn. Stat. § 321.0802 (2012).

[39] MCLS § 449.1802 (2012).

[40] Tex. Business Organizations Code § 11.314(1)(B) (2012).

of his or her interest in the limited partnership as of the date of withdrawal based upon the withdrawing partner's right to share in distributions from the limited partnership. These include Alaska,[41] Colorado,[42] Connecticut,[43] Delaware,[44] Georgia,[45] Indiana,[46] Kansas,[47] Maryland,[48] Massachusetts,[49] Michigan,[50] Mississippi,[51] Montana,[52] Nebraska,[53] New Hampshire,[54] New Jersey,[55] New York,[56] North Carolina,[57] Ohio,[58] Oregon,[59] Pennsylvania,[60] Rhode Island,[61] South Carolina,[62] South Dakota,[63] Tennessee,[64] Texas,[65] Vermont,[66] West Virginia,[67] Wisconsin,[68] and Wyoming.[69]

Missouri, while also using a fair value standard of value, provides that if the partnership agreement does not provide for a distribution to which a withdrawn partner is entitled, the withdrawn partner becomes an assignee of the partner's interest, but the partnership may thereafter purchase the withdrawn partner's interest in the partnership, for the fair value of the

---

[41] Alaska Stat. § 32.11.270 (2012).

[42] C.R.S. 7-62-604 (2011).

[43] Conn. Gen. Stat. § 34-27d (2012).

[44] 6 Del. C. § 17-604 (2012).

[45] O.C.G.A. § 14-9-604 (2012).

[46] Burns Ind. Code Ann. § 23-16-7-4 (2012).

[47] K.S.A. § 56-1a354 (2011).

[48] Md. Corporations And Associations Code Ann. § 10-604 (2012).

[49] ALM GL ch. 109, § 34 (2012).

[50] MCLS § 449.1604 (2012).

[51] Miss. Code Ann. § 79-14-604 (2011).

[52] Mont. Code Anno., § 35-12-1004 (20101).

[53] R.R.S. Neb. § 67-266 (2012).

[54] RSA 304-B:34 (2012).

[55] N.J. Stat. § 42:2A-42 (2012).

[56] N.Y. CLS Partn. § 121-604 (2012).

[57] N.C. Gen. Stat. § 59-604 (2012).

[58] ORC Ann. 1782.34 (2012).

[59] ORS § 70.260 (2011).

[60] 15 Pa.C.S. § 8554 (2012).

[61] R.I. Gen. Laws § 7-13-34 (2012).

[62] S.C. Code Ann. § 33-42-1040 (2011).

[63] S.D. Codified Laws § 48-7-604 (2012).

[64] Tenn. Code Ann. § 61-2-604 (2012).

[65] Tex. Business Organizations Code § 153.111 (2012).

[66] 11 V.S.A. § 3454 (2012).

[67] W. Va. Code § 47-9-34 (2012).

[68] Wis. Stat. § 179.54 (2012).

[69] Wyo. Stat. § 17-14-704 (2012).

EXHIBIT 4.2   Limited Partnerships

States/ Territories	Standard of Value	Basis for Statutory Definition	Individual States' Definition of Value under Dissenters'/ Appraisal Rights Actions
New Hampshire	Fair Value	1984 RMBCA definition adopted	§ 304-B:16-c(II) (LPs): The value of the dissenter's partnership interest of a limited partnership immediately before the effective date of the limited partnership action, excluding any appreciation or depreciation in anticipation of the limited partnership action.
Florida	Fair Value	Definition similar to 1999 RMBCA with minor changes	§ (Ltd. partnerships): Using customary and current valuation concepts and techniques generally employed for similar businesses in the context of the transaction requiring appraisal, excluding any appreciation or depreciation in anticipation of the corporate action unless exclusion would be inequitable to the LP and its remaining partners. For an LP with 10 or fewer partners, without discounting for lack of marketability or minority status.
Ohio	Fair Cash Value	Unique to statute	§ 1782.437(B) (limited partnerships): The amount that a willing seller who is under no compulsion to sell would be willing to accept and that a willing buyer who is under no compulsion to purchase would be willing to pay, but in no event shall the fair cash value of a share exceed the amount specified in the demand of the particular partner. In computing fair cash value, any appreciation or depreciation in market value resulting from the proposal submitted to the directors or to the shareholders (merger, consolidation, or conversion) shall be excluded.

withdrawn partner's interest in the partnership as of the date of withdrawal based upon such withdrawn partner's right to share in distributions from the partnership as an ongoing business.[70] Oregon, which also applies a fair value standard of value, provides that the fair value of the withdrawing partner's interest is determined by assuming that any distribution to which the withdrawing partner is otherwise entitled has been made.[71]

Exhibit 4.2 (on page 220) shows examples of the standard of value set forth in certain state statutes.

Limited Partnership Cases Rejecting Discounts   The courts in Arkansas, Kansas, and Maryland have rejected the use of discounts in the valuation of a withdrawing partner's interest.

WINN. V. WINN ENTERPRISES

The court held that the "fair value" received by withdrawing partners ought not to include minority or marketability discounts, and it reversed and remanded the circuit court's decision.

Source: 265 S.W.3d 125 (Ark. App 2007).

ESTATE OF HJERSTED

The Court of Appeals of Kansas considered whether the district court, in incorrectly valuing the transfer as a transfer of corporate shares rather than as a transfer of a majority interest in a limited partnership, erred by not applying discounts. The court provided multiple reasons for why it found minority and marketability discounts unnecessary. However, per the Kansas Supreme Court, if transfers represent legitimate estate and business planning, "discounts for lack of control and lack of marketability can appropriately be applied to interests in family limited partnerships." However, the Supreme Court of Kansas also decided that "Kansas joins the majority of states holding that minority and marketability discounts should not be applied when the fractional share resulted from a reverse stock split intended to eliminate a minority shareholder's interest in the corporation."

Source: 175 P.3d 810 (Kan. App. 2008).

---

[70] § 359.351 R.S.Mo. (2012).
[71] ORS § 70.260 (2011).

WELCH V. VIA CHRISTI HEALTH PARTNERS, INC.

Limited partners objected to the fair value determined by the general partner's expert in a merger agreement as compensation for their partnership interests. Upon appeal, the Supreme Court of Kansas noted that the general partner did interfere with the valuation expert but did so to convince the expert not to apply minority or marketability discounts, and did not consider this interference sufficient, under *Weinberger v. UOP,* 457 A.2d 701, 711 (Del. 1983), to warrant inquiry into the fairness of the valuation. The court affirmed.

Source: 133 P.3d 122 (Kan. 2006).

EAST PARK L.P. V. LARKIN

The court found that the fair value of a limited partnership's interests is a question of fact and that according to Md. Code Ann., Corps. & Ass'ns § 10-604, the withdrawing partner's interest is sold to the partnership, not on the open market, and therefore applying discounts to that interest is generally inappropriate. The court affirmed the lower court's finding of fair value.

Source: 893 A.2d 1219 (Md. App. 2006).

LIMITED LIABILITY COMPANIES, GENERALLY

A limited liability company (LLC) is a flexible form of enterprise that blends elements of partnership and corporate structures, thereby providing limited liability to its investors, who are referred to as *members* rather than shareholders or partners. Members are also afforded favorable partnership tax treatment and extensive freedom to contractually arrange the business. Whereas LLC statutes provide default rules for the operation of LLCs, LLCs are primarily creatures of contract, and LLC operating agreements and other agreements typically can alter the default rules on most issues.[72] In the United States, the LLC form of organization dates back to 1977, although

---

[72] See, e.g., 6 Del. C. § 18-1101(b) (2012) ("It is the policy of this chapter to give the maximum effect to the principle of freedom of contract and to the enforceability of limited liability company agreements.").

it did not receive significant attention until disadvantageous federal income tax treatment to which it had been subject in its early years was changed in 1988.[73] In recent years, the LLC has emerged as the favored business structure for many closely held enterprises, and LLC filings have been soaring.[74] However, to date there is no uniform or consensus framework for LLCs, even though all jurisdictions have enacted LLC statutes. Thus, in generalizing about the laws that apply to LLCs, it is useful to use the uniform LLC acts propounded by the National Conference of Commissioners on Uniform State Laws (NCCUSL) as a framework and starting point, even though such uniform acts have not been widely adopted.

Uniform Acts

In 1996, the NCCUSL approved and recommended for enactment in all the states the Uniform Limited Liability Company Act (ULLCA) to govern LLCs. ULLCA was enacted in Alabama, Hawaii, Illinois, Montana, South Dakota, and the U.S. Virgin Islands.[75] Ten years later, in 2006, the NCCUSL approved the Revised Uniform Limited Liability Company Act (RULLCA). As of the time of publication of this book, RULLCA was enacted in District of Columbia, Idaho, Iowa, Nebraska, New Jersey (effective March 18, 2013, for newly formed LLCs and March 2014 for all LLCs including existing LLCs formed under New Jersey's current LLC statute),[76] Utah (effective July 1, 2013), and Wyoming, and it had been legislatively introduced in California, Kansas and Minnesota.[77] Whereas ULLCA had not provided a statutory remedy for oppressive behavior, RULLCA does. Its oppression remedy appears in the section concerning dissolution. Section 701(a)(5) authorizes a court to dissolve a limited liability company:

> on application by a member, . . . on the grounds that the managers or those members in control of the company:
>
> (A) have acted, are acting, or will act in a manner that is illegal or fraudulent; or

---

[73] Larry E. Ribstein and Robert R. Keatinge, *Ribstein and Keatinge on Limited Liability Companies 1:1*, at 1-1 (2nd ed. 2004).

[74] Sandra K. Miller, "Discounts and Buyouts in Minority Investor LLC Valuation Disputes Involving Oppression or Divorce," 13 *U. Pa. J. Bus. L.*, 607 (Spring 2011).

[75] http://uniformlaws.org/LegislativeFactSheet.aspx?title=Limited%20Liability%20 Company%20%281995%29%281996%29.

[76] N.J. Stat. § 42:2C-48 (2012).

[77] http://uniformlaws.org/LegislativeFactSheet.aspx?title=Limited%20Liability%20 Company%20%28Revised%29.

(B) have acted or are acting in a manner that is oppressive and was, is, or will be directly harmful to the applicant.[78]

Section 701(b) authorizes a court to "order a remedy other than dissolution."[79] The operating agreement cannot alter § 701(a)(5) but may limit or even eliminate subsection (b).[80] Thus, the default remedy is dissolution, but RULLCA provides a possible, less draconian alternative to dissolution. If the members in their operating agreement choose to override this alternative, provided in § 701(b), they will effectively limit the court and themselves to the all-or-nothing remedy of dissolution. A frequently used alternative to dissolution has been buyout in lieu of dissolution. As the drafting committee of RULLCA noted: "In the close corporation context, many courts have reached this position without express statutory authority, most often with regard to court-ordered buyouts of oppressed shareholders. The Drafting Committee preferred to save courts and litigants the trouble of re-inventing that wheel in the LLC context."[81]

Buyout in Lieu of Dissolution

Thus, under RULLCA and the statutes of many states, once a court has determined that there has been unfairly prejudicial or oppressive conduct on the part of a majority owner, or when it is "no longer reasonably practicable" to carry on the business of the LLC or management is deadlocked, a court-ordered buyout will often be the court's remedy of choice, as typically such a remedy is less draconian than dissolution. "Oppression" and similar grounds of prejudicial or illegal conduct have evolved from statutory grounds for involuntary dissolution to statutory grounds for a wide variety of relief, including buyout.[82] Unless a controlling LLC agreement establishes guidelines for determining a buyout price, the court will be faced with the issue of valuing the oppressed member's interest. This may occur more often than not, given the low likelihood that the operating agreement will provide buyout

---

[78] Revised Uniform Limited Liability Company Act § 701(a)(5).

[79] *Id.*, at § 701(b).

[80] Daniel S. Kleinberger and Carter G. Bishop, "The Next Generation: The Revised Uniform Limited Liability Company Act," 62 *Bus. Law.*, 515 (February 2007), noting that whereas § 110(c)(7) provides that an operating agreement may not "vary the power of a court to decree dissolution in the circumstances specified in Section 701(a) . . . (5))," § 110(c) does not mention § 701(b), so that the operating agreement has plenary power over that provision.

[81] RULLCA, 2005 Annual Meeting Draft, § 701(b), Reporters' Notes.

[82] Douglas K. Moll, "Minority Oppression and the Limited Liability Company: Learning (Or Not) from Close Corporation History," 40 *Wake Forest L. Rev.*, 883 (Fall 2005).

guidance. Although the LLC structure is likely to produce some ex ante bargaining between the members, this is no guarantee that effective planning for dissension will occur,[83] let alone for how to value members' interests.[84] Thus, the judicial role is likely to continue to be significant in buyout disputes.

New Jersey does not provide for the buyout of an oppressed minority member. Under RULLCA Article 7 (Dissolution and Winding Up)[85]

> RULLCA provides remedies for oppressed minority owners. RULLCA permits a member to seek a court order dissolving the company on the grounds that the managers or those members in control of the company have acted or are acting in a manner that is oppressive and was, is, or will be directly harmful to the member. RULLCA also permits a member to seek (or, in its equitable discretion, a court to order in lieu of dissolution) a less drastic remedy such as the appointment of a custodian.

Article 7 also provides for the sale of the members interest to either the LLC, or any other member or members of the LLC, if the court deems it fair and equitable to all parties.

However, because LLCs are a relatively new form of business organization, there is not much statutory or case law guidance for the proper approach to making such valuations.[86] In the absence of precedent addressing LLC buyouts, the court may want to look for guidance in the jurisdiction's case law interpreting buyout provisions in the state's corporate and partnership statutes. Some commentators argue that the most appropriate standard of value to apply in these cases is fair value without the application of minority or marketability discounts, reasoning that such buyouts are coercive, there is a need to deter oppressive majority conduct, and the discounts inject uncertainty into the valuation process. They further reason

---

[83] *Id.*, at 955.

[84] See Sandra K. Miller, "What Buy-Out Rights, Fiduciary Duties, and Dissolution Remedies Should Apply in the Case of the Minority Owner of a Limited Liability Company?," 38 *Harv. J. on Legis.*, 413, at 416–417, 421 (2001) (indicating that operating agreements do not typically provide minority owners with certain buyout and dissolution rights). See also Sandra K. Miller, "A New Direction for LLC Research in a Contractarian Legal Environment," 76 *S. Cal. L. Rev.*, 351 (2003) (indicating that many LLC agreements are based on form agreements that are not extensively negotiated, and providing empirical data that even many attorneys lack familiarity with default buyout rights of LLC members).

[85] N.J. Stat. § 42:2C-48 (2012).

[86] See generally, Sandra K. Miller, "Discounts and Buyouts in Minority Investor LLC Valuation Disputes Involving Oppression or Divorce," 13 *U. Pa. J. Bus. L.*, 607 (Spring 2011).

that the goal of such buyouts is not to closely simulate a market sale, but rather to provide a sensible remedy for the deprivation of an investment that the LLC owner would have otherwise continued to own.[87] In any event, as previously discussed, the state's LLC statutes are not uniform in their treatment of the standard of value to be applied in buyout situations, with many not addressing the issue at all.

In a majority of states, an LLC may be dissolved in a proceeding by or for a member or manager of the LLC if it is established that it is not reasonably practicable to carry on the business of the LLC in conformity with the operating agreement. Many also provide for dissolution if management is deadlocked or subject to internal dissention, dissolution is reasonably necessary for the protection of the rights or interests of the complaining members, or the business of the LLC has been abandoned.

Some states permit dissolution on application by or for a member where the members or managers of the LLC have acted or are acting in a manner that is illegal or fraudulent with respect to the LLC's business. These include Arizona,[88] California,[89] the District of Columbia,[90] Idaho,[91] Iowa,[92] Kansas,[93] Maine,[94] Minnesota,[95] Montana,[96] Nebraska,[97] New Hampshire,[98] New Jersey,[99] North Dakota,[100] South Carolina,[101] South Dakota,[102] Utah,[103] Vermont,[104] West Virginia,[105] Wisconsin,[106] and Wyoming.[107]

---

[87] *Id.*, at 651.

[88] A.R.S. § 29-785(3) (2012).

[89] Cal. Corp. Code § 17351(5) (2012).

[90] D.C. Code § 29-807.01(a)(5)(A) (2012).

[91] Idaho Code § 30-6-701(e)(i) (2012).

[92] Iowa Code § 489.701 1.e.(1) (2012).

[93] K.S.A. § 17-76, 117(a) (2011).

[94] 31 M.R.S. § 1595 1.E. (2011).

[95] Minn. Stat. § 322B.833 Subd. 1(2)(ii) (2012).

[96] Mont. Code Anno., § 35-8-902(1)(e) (2011).

[97] R.R.S. Neb. § 21-147(a)(5)(A) (2012).

[98] RSA 304-C:51(IV) (2012).

[99] N.J. Stat. § 42:2C-48 (2012).

[100] N.D. Cent. Code, § 10-32-119 1.b.(2) (2012).

[101] S.C. Code Ann. § 33-44-801(4)(e) (2011).

[102] S.D. Codified Laws § 47-34A-801(a)(4)(iv) (2012).

[103] Utah Code Ann. § 48-3-701(5) (2012).

[104] 11 V.S.A. § 3101(5)(E) (2012).

[105] W. Va. Code § 31B-8-801(5)(v) (2012).

[106] Wis. Stat. § 183.0902(3), (4) (2012).

[107] Wyo. Stat. § 17-29-701(a)(iv)(A), (a)(v)(A) (2012).

Some states also provide for dissolution on application by or for a member where the other members or managers have engaged in oppression or have acted in a manner unfairly prejudicial toward one or more members or managers. These include the District of Columbia,[108] Idaho,[109] Iowa,[110] Minnesota,[111] Montana,[112] Nebraska,[113] New Hampshire,[114] New Jersey,[115] North Carolina,[116] North Dakota,[117] South Carolina,[118] Utah,[119] Vermont,[120] West Virginia,[121] Wisconsin,[122] and Wyoming.[123] Of the states providing for dissolution of an LLC based on member oppression, Minnesota,[124] Nebraska,[125] North Carolina,[126] North Dakota,[127] and Utah[128] provide for a buyout election in lieu of dissolution, or for a court-ordered buyout in lieu of dissolution.

---

[108] D.C. Code § 29-807.01(a)(5)(B) (2012).

[109] Idaho Code § 30-6-701(e)(ii) (2012).

[110] Iowa Code § 489.701 1.e.(2) (2012).

[111] Minn. Stat. § 322B.833 Subd. 1(2)(ii) (2012).

[112] Mont. Code Anno., § 35-8-902(1)(e) (2011).

[113] R.R.S. Neb. § 21-147(a)(5)(B) (2012).

[114] RSA 304-C:51(VII) (2012) (where oppression is specified as a ground for judicial dissolution in the LLC agreement).

[115] N.J. Stat. § 42:2C-48 (2012).

[116] N.C. Gen. Stat. § 57C-6-02(2)(ii) (2012) (where liquidation is reasonably necessary for the protection of the rights or interests of the complaining member) or N.C. Gen. Stat. § 57C-6-02(2)(iv) (2012) (where the articles of organization or a written operating agreement entitles the complaining member to dissolution of the LLC).

[117] N.D. Cent. Code, § 10-32-119 1.b.(2) (2012) (where the governors or those in control of the LLC have acted in a manner unfairly prejudicial toward a member).

[118] S.C. Code Ann. § 33-44-801(4)(e) (2011).

[119] Utah Code Ann. § 48-3-701(5) (2012).

[120] 11 V.S.A. § 3101(5)(E) (2012).

[121] W. Va. Code § 31B-8-801(5)(v) (2012).

[122] Wis. Stat. § 183.0902 (3), (4) (2012).

[123] Wyo. Stat. § 17-29-701(a)(v)(B) (2012).

[124] Minn. Stat. § 322B.833 Subd. 2 (2012).

[125] R.R.S. Neb. § 21-147(b) (2012).

[126] N.C. Gen. Stat. § 57C-6-02.1(d) (2012) (after dissolution has been okayed by court).

[127] N.D. Cent. Code, § 10-32-119(2) (2012) (it is within court's discretion whether to order buyout).

[128] Utah Code Ann. § 48-3-702 (2012).

California[129] and Utah[130] provide for buyout in lieu of dissolution (for whatever reason) at fair market value. In California, if the parties are unable to agree on the buyout price, the court is directed to appoint three disinterested appraisers to appraise the value of the interest to be bought out. Utah provides that the court may make the valuation based on the factors the court determines to be appropriate.

In Illinois, in addition to being triggered by other factors, dissolution may be triggered if a dissociating member is not paid his or her distributional interest if the member's dissociation would not otherwise result in a dissolution and winding up of the company's business.[131] Thus, to avoid dissolution in such an instance, the distributional interest must be paid at fair value, with the court considering among other relevant evidence the going-concern value of the company, any agreement among some or all of the members fixing the price or specifying a formula for determining value of distributional interests for any other purpose, the recommendations of any appraiser appointed by the court, and any legal constraints on the company's ability to purchase the interest.[132]

Withdrawal and Buyout

There is no uniform way the states handle the withdrawal or resignation of an LLC member. Under ULLCA, the LLC is required to purchase a dissociated member's interest for its "fair value" if the member's dissociation does not result in a dissolution and winding up of the company's business.[133] If a member is dissociated by an LLC that is not entered into for a term (an *at-will LLC*), the member's interest must be purchased for its fair value as determined as of the date of the member's dissociation.[134] If the LLC is entered into for a term (a *term LLC*), the member's interest must be purchased at the expiration of the specified term that existed on the date of the member's dissociation and for its fair value as of the date of the expiration of the LLC's term (unless the dissociation causes the LLC to dissolve).[135] Although the ULLCA does not define the term *fair value*, if a dissociated member and the LLC cannot reach an agreement as to the fair value of the interest,

---

[129] Cal. Corp. Code § 17351(b) (2012).

[130] Utah Code Ann. § 48-2c-1214(4) (2012) (effective until July 1, 2013, when it is replaced with Utah Code Ann. § 48-3-702).

[131] 805 ILCS 180/35-1 (2012).

[132] 805 ILCS 180/35-65(1) (2012).

[133] Uniform Limited Liability Company Act § 701(a).

[134] Uniform Limited Liability Company Act § 701(a)(1).

[135] Uniform Limited Liability Company Act § 701(a)(2).

such value may be judicially determined.[136] A court is authorized to consider, among other relevant evidence, the going-concern value of the LLC, any agreement among some or all of the members fixing the price or specifying a formula for determining the value of the LLC interests for any other purpose, the recommendations of any appraiser appointed by the court, and any legal constraints on the LLC's ability to purchase the interest.[137] The default value is "fair value," and the court is free to determine the fair value of an LLC interest on a fair market, liquidation, or any other basis deemed appropriate under the circumstances. A fair market value standard is not used because it is too narrow, often inappropriate, and assumes a willing buyer and a willing seller, which is a factor not contemplated by ULLCA.[138]

Some states provide that upon withdrawal or disassociation, a withdrawing or disassociated member is entitled to receive any distribution to which the member is entitled under the articles of organization or operating agreement, and, if not otherwise provided in the articles of organization and operating agreement, the withdrawing/disassociated member is entitled to receive, within a reasonable time after withdrawal, the value of the withdrawing member's interest in the LLC as of the date of resignation based upon the member's right to share in distributions from the LLC. Included among these states are Florida (fair value),[139] Louisiana (fair market value),[140] Massachusetts (fair value),[141] Michigan (fair value),[142] Mississippi (fair value),[143] Missouri (fair value, determined by excluding business goodwill),[144] Montana (fair value),[145] Nevada (fair market value),[146] New Mexico (fair market value),[147] New York (fair value),[148] North Carolina (fair value),[149] Pennsylvania (fair value),[150] South Carolina (fair value),[151] Tennessee (fair

---

[136] Uniform Limited Liability Company Act § 701(d), (e).

[137] Uniform Limited Liability Company Act § 702(a)(1).

[138] Uniform Limited Liability Company Act § 702, comment.

[139] Fla. Stat. § 608.427(2) (2012).

[140] La.R.S. 12:1325(C) (2012).

[141] ALM GL ch. 156C, § 32 (2012).

[142] MCL § 450.4305 (2012).

[143] Miss. Code Ann. § 79-29-603 (2011).

[144] § 347.103 2(1) R.S.Mo. (2012).

[145] Mont. Code Anno., § 35-8-808(1) (2011).

[146] Nev. Rev. Stat. Ann. § 86.331(2) (2012).

[147] N.M. Stat. Ann. § 53-19-24 (2012).

[148] N.Y. CLS LLC § 509 (2012).

[149] N.C. Gen. Stat. § 57C-5-07 (2012).

[150] 15 Pa.C.S. § 8933 (2012).

[151] S.C. Code Ann. § 33-44-701(a) (2011).

value;[152] however, for LLCs formed prior to 1999, the lesser of the fair market value of the withdrawing or terminating member's interest determined on a going-concern basis or the fair market value of the withdrawing member's interest determined on a liquidation basis[153]), Texas (fair value),[154] Vermont (fair value),[155] West Virginia (fair value),[156] and Wisconsin (fair value).[157]

In Illinois,[158] Montana,[159] South Carolina,[160] Tennessee,[161] Vermont[162] and West Virginia,[163] in determining fair value, the court must consider the going-concern value of the company, any agreement among some or all of the members fixing the price or specifying a formula for determining value of distributional interests for any other purpose, the recommendations of any appraiser appointed by the court, and any legal constraints on the company's ability to purchase the interest.

In Mississippi, the fair value of the member's financial interest must be determined using customary and current valuation concepts and techniques generally employed for similar businesses in the context of the transaction requiring appraisal, and without discounting for lack of marketability or minority status.[164]

In New Jersey, under RULLCA,

> a resigning owner is no longer entitled to receive the fair values of his or her LLC interest as of the date of resignation. Rather, upon resignation, the resigning owner is dissociated as a member and only has the rights of an economic interest holder.[165]

In Kansas, if not otherwise provided in the operating agreement, the resigning member is not entitled to receive the fair value of the member's

---

[152] Tenn. Code Ann. § 48-249-505(c) (2012).

[153] Tenn. Code Ann. § 48-216-101(e) (2012).

[154] Tex. Business Organizations Code § 101.205 (2012).

[155] 11 V.S.A. § 3091(a) (2012).

[156] W. Va. Code § 31B-7-701(a) (2012).

[157] Wis. Stat. § 183.0604 (2012).

[158] 805 ILCS 180/35-65 (2012).

[159] Mont. Code Anno., § 35-8-809(1)(a) (2011).

[160] S.C. Code Ann. § 33-44-702(a)(1) (2011).

[161] Tenn. Code Ann. § 48-249-506(3)(B)(ii) (2012).

[162] 11 V.S.A. § 3092(a)(1) (2012).

[163] W. Va. Code § 31B-7-702(a)(1) (2012).

[164] Miss. Code Ann. § 79-29-603 (a), (b) (2011).

[165] N.J. Stat. § 42:2C-48 (2012).

limited liability company interest until the dissolution and winding up of the limited liability company.[166]

Other states, for example, New Hampshire,[167] Ohio,[168] and Rhode Island,[169] provide that upon the withdrawal of a member, except as otherwise provided in writing in an operating agreement, the withdrawn member and his or her legal representatives, successors, and assigns do not have the right to receive any distribution by reason of the withdrawal but have only the rights of an assignee to receive distributions as to the withdrawn member's interest during any continuation of the business of the limited liability company and upon completion of winding up less any damages recoverable against the withdrawn member if the event of withdrawal violated the limited liability company's operating agreement.

Dissenters' Rights

As LLCs have become increasingly used business entities, states increasingly have endowed LLCs with rights similar to those enjoyed by corporations. Thus, a minority of states provide LLC members with dissenters' rights akin to those enjoyed by shareholders of corporations.

Typically, the states define the standard of value for dissenters' rights of LLC members in the same manner as they define that standard for corporation shareholders. This is the case in Florida,[170] Georgia,[171] Minnesota,[172] North Dakota,[173] Ohio,[174] Tennessee,[175] and Washington.[176] In New Hampshire, while the definition is similar to that used for corporations, the definition for LLCs does not provide an exception for exclusion of appreciation or depreciation in anticipation of the limited liability action, whereas for corporations such an exception is made if exclusion would be inequitable.[177] In California, where LLC dissenters are paid for their interests at fair

---

[166] K.S.A. § 17-76,107 (2011).

[167] RSA 304-C:41 (2012).

[168] ORC Ann. 1705.12 (2012).

[169] R.I. Gen. Laws § 7-16-29 (2012).

[170] Fla. Stat. § 608.4351(5) (2012).

[171] O.C.G.A. § 14-11-1001(3) (2012).

[172] Minn. Stat. § 322B.386 subd. 1(c) (2012).

[173] N.D. Cent. Code, § 10-32-55(1)(a) (2012).

[174] ORC Ann. § 1705.42(B) (2012).

[175] Tenn. Code Ann. § 48-231-101(2) (2012).

[176] Rev. Code Wash. (ARCW) § 25.15.425(3) (2012).

[177] RSA 304-C:22-a(II) (2012).

market value,[178] the exception where exclusion would be inequitable is made for LLCs, but not corporations.[179] The New Jersey statute is silent on dissenter rights.

Professional LLCs

For LLCs used for performing professional services, some states provide a standard of value for certain distributions. In Alabama, a terminated professional is entitled to the fair value of the professional's interest upon disqualification or death, with the same rules applying to professional LLCs as to professional corporations.[180] In Mississippi, the disqualified member is entitled to judgment for the fair value of the disqualified person's membership interest determined by the court as of the date of death, disqualification, or transfer. Fair value is determined using the 1999 RMBCA standard—namely, fair value means the value of the membership interest of the professional limited liability company determined using customary and current valuation concepts and techniques generally employed for similar businesses in the context of the transaction requiring appraisal and without discounting for lack of marketability or minority status.[181] In Virginia, absent a provision specifying the value to be paid to the terminated professional member, the LLC must pay the book value of the interest, determined as of the end of the month immediately preceding the event that terminated the membership of the former member.[182]

Exhibit 4.3 presents examples of the standard of value followed in certain states.

---

[178] Cal. Corp. Code § 17604 (2012).

[179] Cal. Corp. Code § 17601(a) (2012).

[180] Code of Ala. § 10A-5-8.01 (2012).

[181] Miss. Code Ann. § 79-29-913(4), (6) (2011).

[182] Va. Code Ann. § 13.1-1117(C) (2012).

EXHIBIT 4.3 Limited Liability Company

States/ Territories	Standard of Value	Basis for Statutory Definition	Individual States' Definition of Value under Dissenters'/ Appraisal Rights Actions
New Hampshire	Fair Value	1984 RMBCA definition adopted	§ 304-C:22-a(II) (LLCs): Immediately before the effective date of the limited liability action, excluding any appreciation or depreciation in anticipation of the limited liability action.
Minnesota, North Dakota	Fair Value	1984 RMBCA definition partially adopted (Minnesota)	(i) Value of the shares immediately before the effectuation of the LLC action to which the shareholder objects.
Florida	Fair Value	Definition similar to 1999 RMBCA with minor changes	§ 608.4351(4)(LLCs): Using customary and current valuation concepts and techniques generally employed for similar businesses in the context of the transaction requiring appraisal, excluding any appreciation or depreciation in anticipation of the corporate action unless exclusion would be inequitable to the LLC and its remaining members. For an LLC with 10 or fewer members, without discounting for lack of marketability or minority status.
Ohio	Fair Cash Value	Unique to statute	§ 1705.42(B) (LLCs): The amount that a willing seller who is under no compulsion to sell would be willing to accept and that a willing buyer who is under no compulsion to purchase would be willing to pay, but in no event shall the fair cash value of a share

(continued)

EXHIBIT 4.3 (*Continued*)

States/ Territories	Standard of Value	Basis for Statutory Definition	Individual States' Definition of Value under Dissenters'/ Appraisal Rights Actions
			exceed the amount specified in the demand of the particular member. In computing fair cash value, any appreciation or depreciation in market value resulting from the proposal submitted to the directors or to the shareholders (merger, consolidation, or conversion) shall be excluded.

LLC Decisions

While there are not a great deal of published decisions on the buyout of member interests in LLCs, in the following two cases, the courts in Rhode Island and New Jersey rejected minority and marketability discounts.

MARSH. V. BILLINGTON FARMS LLC.

Two 25% owners of an LLC filed a complaint against the other two owners alleging breach of fiduciary duty. The four owners agreed to avoid dissolution via a buyout. In determining the fair value of the complaining owners' interests, the court cited *Charland v. Country View Golf Club,* 588 A.2d 609, 613 (R.I. 1991), which rejected the use of minority and marketability discounts. The *Marsh* court declared that the owners should receive their proportionate share of the fair value of the LLC.

Source: 2007 R.I. Super. LEX IS 105 (Aug. 2, 2007).

DENIKE V. CUPO.

In response to a complaint from the other owner, a 50% owner of a limited liability company counterclaimed for the fair value of his interest. The trial court accepted the court-appointed expert's valuation and agreed that, since the interest was to be acquired by the remaining owner, neither a minority nor a marketability discount should be applied. The appellate court affirmed and agreed with the expert's opinion that minority and marketability discounts should be excluded where there is neither a transfer of shares nor a sale of the whole entity.

Source: 926 A.2d 869 (N.J. Super. 2007).

SUMMARY

As explained in this chapter, partnerships, including limited liability partnerships, limited partnerships, and limited liability companies, are being increasingly used as business vehicles in lieu of corporations. To address the issues of governance including buyouts, the NCCUSL established model laws for each of these entities. In turn, many states address the buyout of disassociating owners in their statutes. Lastly, a body of case law is beginning to develop on these issues. As always, practitioners should seek guidance from these sources and the attorney with whom they are working to determine the applicable standard of value for the specific situation.

CHAPTER 5

Standards of Value in Divorce

INTRODUCTION

In this chapter, we address the theory and application of the standards of value used in divorce. As in stockholder oppression and dissent cases, the standards of value in matrimonial matters are state specific and often case specific.

As one commentary has indicated:

> Matrimonial actions are unique types of litigation. While people in litigation are people in conflict, people in matrimonial litigation are involved in conflicts that go to the very root of their existence.[1]

Divorce cases are often acrimonious and adversarial. It is the task of business valuation professionals to sort through these issues and evaluate a business based on the objective application of valuation methodology that is consistent with the laws of a given state.

In the absence of statutory guidance, the application of the standard of value is left to the courts within the individual states. These courts can often inconsistently apply the underlying assumptions of a standard of value, to achieve what they believe to be equitable solutions consistent with the policy expressed in each state's statutes.

When we compare the way valuation issues are viewed in the U.S. Tax Court to the way they are viewed in many matrimonial courts, we often find significant differences. In the Tax Court, precedents have fashioned a consistent premise, value in exchange, and a consistent standard, fair market value, and have provided guidance to practitioners as to the application of

---

[1] Gary N. Skoloff and Laurence J. Cutler, *New Jersey Family Practice*, 10th ed. (New Brunswick, NJ: New Jersey Institute for Continuing Legal Education, 2001), at 1.11.

this standard. Because of this consistency, experts can differ in methodology but not on the premise or standard of value. For instance, valuation practitioners can opine on the size of the applicable discount for an interest lacking control, but not, in most instances, on its applicability.

In the same manner, fair value is the standard applied most often in stockholder dissent and oppression matters in most states. Again, the premise of value is a value in exchange, and the standard is fair value. In these matters, the most frequent valuation controversy involves the applicability of lack of control and marketability discounts. As we explained in Chapter 3, legal associations such as the American Law Institute (ALI) and the American Bar Association (ABA) have weighed in on the applicability of lack of control and marketability discounts under this standard of value.

As will be explained further in this chapter, we have found that there has been no consistent application of the premises and standards of value in divorce matters. In fact, even though the ALI has opined on certain valuation issues concerning divorce, its opinions have not been cited in matrimonial cases as frequently as in dissenters' and oppressed shareholder matters.

In divorce, the standard of value for each state is established by court cases that implement that state's marital dissolution statutes. Each state's legislature sets forth the property distribution policy in the statute. The courts attempt to implement the policy through their individual decisions. Generally, the statutes provide little guidance on valuation; one has to divine it from case law. Therefore, to more clearly understand the standards of value in this context, one needs to understand the definition of property in the particular state statute and the treatment of business and intangible value in that state's case law. In our analysis, we address the implied or stated standard of value as it is expressed in the court opinions regarding the treatment of assets such as enterprise and personal goodwill, the application of lack of control and marketability discounts, and the weight accorded buy–sell agreements.

We begin with a general background and history of the treatment of marital and separate property and then analyze the identification of marital and separate property. We then discuss the premises of value, the standards of value, and their theoretical underpinnings as stated or implied by statute or case law.

Premises of value are assumptions based on the set of actual or hypothetical circumstances applicable in a valuation. Standards of value represent the type of value being sought.[2] In determining a premise of value, one must ask whether the business or business interest should be valued in

---

[2] Shannon P. Pratt and Alina Niculita, *Valuing a Business: The Analysis and Appraisal of Closely Held Companies*, 5th ed. (New York: McGraw-Hill, 2008), at 41.

a hypothetical exchange between a willing buyer and willing seller, or as a business in the hands of its current owners with no consideration of such an exchange.

In our view, standards of value in divorce can be seen to fall under two general basic premises: value in exchange and value to the holder. Value in exchange is the value arrived at in a hypothetical sale, with assumptions ranging from the seller departing immediately and competing with his or her former business, to the seller staying on to help transition management. Underlying value in exchange are two general standards: fair market value, where discounts for lack of control and lack of marketability, also referred to as shareholder-level discounts, are generally considered, and fair value, where the value of a fractional interest is generally seen to be, except under extraordinary circumstances, as its pro rata share of the enterprise without minority or lack of marketability discounts. The value to the holder premise is based on the assumption that the business or business interest will not be sold. Although frequently not articulated, the standard of value most often associated with the value to the holder is investment value, which in this context is also referred to as *intrinsic value.*

After a general discussion of the assumptions implicit in the two premises and three standards, we discuss the value in exchange premise and how personal and enterprise goodwill, shareholder-level discounts, and buy–sell agreements are viewed. Similarly, in states where these issues are addressed using a value to the holder premise, we discuss such issues as the difference between goodwill and earning capacity, the inclusion of such marital assets as a professional degree or license, enhanced earning capacity, celebrity status, and the issue of double dipping. We eventually use the premise and standard of value implied by the treatment of personal and enterprise goodwill, lack of control and marketability discounts, and the weight accorded buy–sell agreements to move toward a standard of value classification system.

Using these elements, we build a continuum of value that addresses the way courts view property by their treatment of goodwill, the application of shareholder-level discounts, and the adherence to buy–sell agreements, all under a stated or implied standard and premise of value. Note that this continuum is based on our view of the issues implicit in business valuations for the purpose of divorce, and that the lines between these classifications are not always clear. In some cases, even a state that appears to adhere strictly to one standard may use elements of another to achieve what the court believes to be an equitable result. Moreover, we are reviewing statutes and cases as valuation practitioners, not lawyers, and applying our suggested classifications to premises and standards of value in ways that are consistent with generally accepted valuation theory but may not have been contemplated by courts, the attorneys, and even many experts.

Marital Property: General Background and History

The varying nature of the divorce laws of the states can be traced back to the turn of the twentieth century, when the National Conference of Commissioners for Uniform State Laws[3] sought to unify divorce laws across the nation. The common sentiment at the time, endorsed by the public, the clergy, and even President Theodore Roosevelt, was that the unsettling increase in the divorce rate across the land had to be checked. Thus, in the same way the commissioners later attempted to create uniform triggering events for dissenting shareholders, they proposed certain laws that would create a uniform standard by which a married couple could get divorced. The states, however, wanted autonomy, as several already had more stringent grounds for divorce in place. For example, in New York, adultery was the only grounds for divorce. In South Carolina, divorce was not permitted on any grounds. Accordingly, despite being adopted by five states, the uniform divorce laws were viewed as a massive failure.[4]

It is generally agreed that the law of marital property in the United States has its origins in English common law. However, influenced by their French or Spanish heritage, eight states adopted the continental system of community property. Those original eight community property states are Arizona, California, Idaho, Louisiana, Nevada, New Mexico, Texas, and Washington.[5] Later the total increased to ten, when both Alaska and Wisconsin chose to treat marital property as community property.

Initially, most common law states looked exclusively to property law where title dictated ownership. This left the non-titled spouse at a severe disadvantage. In 1973, the Uniform Marriage and Divorce Act set an example for the states by abandoning the traditional treatment of property by common law and moved toward a system that would give the court discretion over how to divide property. Over the next 10 years, this principle was adopted by the remaining 41 common law states and the District of Columbia in their statutes as equitable distribution. This new standard for distribution divided marital property according to some principle of need or equity, without particular regard to title or ownership as determined by common law rules.[6]

---

[3] The National Conference of Commissioners on Uniform state laws was formed in 1892 for the purpose of providing states with nonpartisan, well-conceived, and well-drafted legislation that brings clarity and stability to critical areas of the law (www .uniformlaws.org/Narrative.aspx?title=About%20the%20ULC).

[4] James J. White, "Symposium: One Hundred Years of Uniform State Laws: Ex Proprio Vigore," 89 *Michigan Law Review*, (August 1991), at 2106.

[5] *Id* .

[6] Mary Ann Glendon, "Symposium: Family Law: Family Law Reform in the 1980s," 44 *Louisiana Law Review*, 1553 (July 1984).

By the early 1990s, all states had enacted statutes that provided for the distribution of property acquired during the marriage in accordance with equitable distribution or the continental system of community property. Equitable distribution states endeavor to divide marital property fairly, but not necessarily equally. Community property states more often seek to divide marital property equally, but in many cases also prefer an equitable arrangement for distribution.[7]

Marriage is now generally considered to be an economic partnership where title is irrelevant and property is acquired and maintained by the marital unit rather than separately by the individuals. In both community property and equitable distribution states, property acquired during the marriage through the time, skill, and labor of either spouse is considered part of the marital estate. Typically, anything acquired by gift or inheritance or acquired before or after the marriage is considered to be the separate property of the owner.

The states that adopted the equitable division method of property distribution now look to equitably distribute assets defined as marital property. As such, all states, whether by equitable distribution or community property, recognize that the noneconomic contribution of the non-titled spouse has value and the state legislatures have enacted statutes that provide for the fair distribution of property acquired during the marriage.

Dividing marital property as part of a divorce involves a three-step process:

1. Identify marital assets.
2. Value them.
3. Then distribute them.

There is an interrelationship among the three steps, with the term *value* mostly left undefined by statute. In fact, only the statutes of Arkansas and Louisiana explicitly address the standard of value to be used. Arkansas's statute, for example, establishes the standard of value only for certain assets:

When stocks, bonds, or other securities issued by a corporation, association, or government entity make up part of the marital

---

[7] California requires an equal division. Idaho and Nevada both require equal division unless compelling reasons exist to divide property differently. Alaska, Arizona, and Washington require equitable division. New Mexico, Texas, and Wisconsin leave the details of division to the court's discretion. Louisiana does not include direction on division in their statutes.

property, the court shall designate in its final order or judgment the specific property in securities to which each party is entitled, or after determining the fair market value of the securities, may order and adjudge that the securities be distributed to one (1) party on condition that one-half (1/2) the fair market value of the securities in money or other property be set aside and distributed to the other party in lieu of division and distribution of the securities.[8]

Louisiana requires that the parties to a divorce list their community assets at their fair market value for distribution.[9] No other state statute addresses the value of closely held businesses and business interests with even that much specificity. Some states refer to a particular standard in their case law; others suggest a certain standard by their treatment of certain elements of value. Often a case in a particular state may name one standard of value but attribute to it characteristics more commonly associated with another standard of value.

Identification of Marital Property and Separate Property

In our view, the ambiguity as to the appropriate standard of value in a state often is the result of differing interpretations of what constitutes property in general and marital property in particular. In fact, property is quite often undefined in most statutes. Community property states, typified by the statute in Arizona, define community property as:

> All property acquired by either husband or wife during the marriage, except that which is acquired by gift, devise or descent is the Community Property of the husband and wife.[10]

Alternatively, an equitable distribution state, such as Pennsylvania, defines marital property as:

> (a) all property acquired by either party during the marriage; (b) including the increase in value, until the day of final separation of non-marital property acquired by gift, bequest, devise or descent; and (c) the increase in value of property owned prior to the

---

[8] Arkansas Statute § 9-12-315(4).
[9] Louisiana Statute § 9:2801.
[10] Arizona Statute 25-211.

marriage or property acquired in exchange for property owned prior to the marriage until the date of final separation.[11]

As can be seen, the definition of *property* is rather ambiguous, regardless of the property distribution scheme. This can lead to controversy with respect to certain assets that can be difficult to identify and value.

This ambiguity is most clearly seen in the treatment of intangible property. Identifying intangible assets can involve the valuation of an expected (or future) income stream, which may not be transferable and/or may require the continued efforts of a spouse after the end of the marriage. The courts in each state decide whether these types of assets may or may not be included as assets to be distributed. Their decisions will rely on their interpretation of the term *marital property*.

The identification of tangible assets acquired during the marriage does not stir the same controversy as the identification of intangible assets. Essentially, tangible assets are physical things—things that may be valued based on use (the value one receives from owning an asset) or in exchange (the value at which it may be sold to a third party). Either way, with these assets, identification typically is not an issue.

Identification issues relating to intangible assets, the most common of which is often labeled *goodwill*, can be much more difficult. The controversies are manifold, but the main issue in the identification of marital assets becomes whether the intangible asset, if one exists, belongs to the person or the enterprise and whether that intangible asset was developed during the marriage. In order to understand the treatment of these assets in a given state, we must understand the nature of these assets and how they were developed.

Ultimately, a valuation professional determines the value of property based on valuation principles and analysis coupled with professional judgment, the guidelines set by the statutes, and the precedents set by the courts interpreting those statutes. From there, the courts will determine what is fair and equitable in distribution. Aside from the states that mandate equal distribution, the final outcome of "who gets what and how much" is left to the judgment of the courts.

Regarding the distribution of assets, a Michigan court stated:

The only requirement [for an award of marital assets in a divorce action] is that the award result in a fair and equitable distribution of the marital assets.[12]

---

[11] Pennsylvania Divorce Code § 3501.

[12] *Hatcher v. Hatcher* (1983), 129 Mich. App. 753; 343 N.W.2d 498; 1983 Mich. App. LEXIS 3397.

As sound as these societal principles may be, they offer the valuation expert little guidance as to the application of valuation principles to a particular situation.

The standard of value varies from state to state and may vary even within a state. Some courts do not define and follow any one standard of value consistently. As will be seen, the courts often use the term *fair market value* and attribute to it elements and attributes more closely related to investment value. The courts may not fully understand the assumptions that underlie the particular standard that they are applying or even intend to apply a certain standard of value at all. They are identifying and distributing assets in a manner they consider to be fair and equitable. As another commentator stated:

> No single standard could possibly encompass the multitude of considerations necessary for equitably dividing marital assets.[13]

In addition to the division of property acquired during the marriage, most states have statutes that address spousal support (alimony) and child support and a body of case law that implements those statutes. There is a relationship between alimony and property distribution, and the combination of these remedies is used by the courts, which, in theory, look to be fair and equitable, without a requirement to adhere strictly to the underlying assumptions of a given standard of value. Courts often have the opportunity to adjust alimony or the percentages of the property distribution to achieve what they view as a fair outcome for the parties involved. The judge may start with a certain standard of value in mind, but may end at a completely different standard based on his or her interpretation of the facts and circumstances of the case. Moreover, the courts generally adhere to their interpretation of the law and the equities in the particular case more rigorously than they adhere to the assumptions inherent in or classification associated with a particular standard of value.

Relationship between Valuation and Identification of Intangible Assets

While one may suspect that a business has intangible assets (goodwill in particular), often there is no way to know that goodwill exists until the business is valued or sold. In matrimonial matters, frequently used methodologies

---

[13] John McDougal and George Durant, "Business Valuation in Family Court," 13 *South Carolina Lawyer*, No. 14 (September/October 2001), at 2.

for valuing goodwill can include excess earnings[14] or finding the sale price above the net asset value of a business.[15]

The Washington case of *In re: Hall,*[16] which addressed the valuation of goodwill in a medical practice, provides an example of several methods that the courts may recognize in valuing goodwill. According to the case, three of the methods are: (1) the capitalization of excess earnings method; (2) the straight capitalization method; and (3) the IRS variation on the capitalization of excess earnings method. The other two methods discussed in the case are: (4) the buy–sell agreement method; and (5) the open market approach.

Simply stated, some form of the capitalization of benefits (the first three methods) can be employed to determine whether an intangible asset exists. From a strictly legal point of view, these methods have been criticized for placing too much importance on future earnings, thereby including the future efforts of the owner.[17] Some experts contest this criticism, contending that the ability of the asset to continue to produce earnings in the future is attributable to the fruits planted during the marriage. Another criticism is that these methods may set high relative values for an unrealized intangible asset for which the titled professional gives up a tangible asset such as real property or cash. This could potentially overcompensate the non-titled spouse by trading liquid assets like cash and property for a relatively illiquid interest in the goodwill of a closely held business.

The fourth method referred to in the case, the utilization of a buy–sell agreement, is addressed later in this chapter. The utilization of a buy–sell agreement is often considered in the valuation of fractional interests in professional partnerships where an arm's-length agreement is in place. Courts may rely more heavily on a buy–sell agreement to determine value if transactions have been consummated under the terms of the agreement as partners have entered and exited the partnership. A court probably will not consider an agreement binding if it was signed shortly prior to divorce,

---

[14] The *excess earnings* method for valuing intangible assets consists of estimating the value of the tangible assets, estimating a reasonable rate of return on the tangible assets, and, to the extent that total returns of the business or practice exceed the reasonable return of the tangible assets, is the basis for finding the dollar value of the intangible assets. That is accomplished by dividing the excess returns by a rate called a *capitalization rate.*

[15] Mary K. Kistjardt, "Professional Goodwill in Marital Dissolution: The State of the Law," in *Valuing Professional Practices and Licenses,* Ronald L. Brown, ed. (2004 supplement).

[16] 692 P.2d 175 (Wash. Supr. Ct. 1984).

[17] Mary Kay Kistjardt, "Professional Goodwill in Marital Dissolution," December 31, 2008 at 2.04 p. 41. University of Missouri at Kansas City—School of Law.

or if partners have come and gone without exercising the explicit formula established by the agreement.[18]

The fifth method, the so-called open market approach, tries to establish value upon a hypothetical sale. In a value-in-exchange context, this is seen by some as the most relevant method for valuing goodwill, as a quantifiable asset that would be realizable upon the sale of the business.

Appreciation on Separate Property

Another central issue in many divorces is the treatment of separate property owned by a spouse prior to the marriage or gifted to, or inherited by, the spouse during the marriage. The majority of states do not include separate property as distributable assets.[19] However, special provisions may apply to appreciation on that property that occurs during the marriage. For example, the Pennsylvania statute mentioned earlier includes the increase in value of separate property over the course of the marriage. Divorce statutes generally include a description as to the circumstances where the appreciation of separate property can be included in distributable assets. The circumstances often relate to the cause of the appreciation during the marriage and the efforts of the spouse who owned the separate property. The cause of the appreciation is often classified as active or passive. Active appreciation is that which is caused by the efforts of one or both of the spouses; passive appreciation is that which is caused by external forces such as market fluctuations or the efforts of other partners.

On one extreme, there are state statutes that do not differentiate between active and passive appreciation on separate property, suggesting that neither is to be distributed.[20] For instance, Delaware's marital dissolution statutes state:

---

[18] *Id.*, at 1.04, p. 1–33.

[19] New Hampshire appears to be the only state that includes all property in the consideration for distribution, defining property in this way: § 458:16-a.I: "Property shall include all tangible and intangible property and assets, real or personal, belonging to either or both parties, whether title to the property is held in the name of either or both parties. Intangible property includes, but is not limited to, employment benefits, vested and non-vested pension or other retirement benefits, or savings plans. To the extent permitted by federal law, property shall include military retirement and veterans' disability benefits." However, the statute goes on to direct that the value of premarital or gifted property should be considered in the distribution of the marital estate. Other states may not recognize separate property, but they do not provide that direction by statute.

[20] Illinois also does not include appreciation, but includes a reimbursement provision for the non-owner spouse for his or her efforts contributing to an increase in value. The appreciation is not made marital property but is recognized by reimbursement.

(b)... For purposes of this chapter only, *"marital property" means all property acquired by either party subsequent to the marriage except:* (1) Property acquired by an individual spouse by bequest, devise or descent or by gift, except gifts between spouses, provided the gifted property is titled and maintained in the sole name of the donee spouse, or a gift tax return is filed reporting the transfer of the gifted property in the sole name of the donee spouse or a notarized document, executed before or contemporaneously with the transfer, is offered demonstrating the nature of the transfer. (2) Property acquired in exchange for property acquired prior to the marriage; (3) Property excluded by valid agreement of the parties; and *(4) The increase in value of property acquired prior to the marriage*[21] [emphasis added].

On the other extreme, the statutes do not specifically include or exclude a particular type of appreciation. Colorado, for instance, provides for this to be included in the marital pot:

(4) Subject to the provisions of subsection (7) of this section, *an asset of a spouse acquired prior to the marriage* or in accordance with subsection (2) (a) or (2) (b) of this section shall be considered as marital property, for purposes of this article only, to the *extent that its present value exceeds its value at the time of the marriage* or at the time of acquisition if acquired after the marriage[22] [emphasis added].

Most states deal with the issue between the extremes. In some states, the appreciation on separate property may be marital if that appreciation was a product of marital efforts (marital efforts being the contribution of either or both spouses to the increased value, not necessarily to the increased value of the asset itself, but to the marital partnership in raising children, keeping the home, etc.). This does not include appreciation on premarital property from dividends, interest, or general market conditions that occur without any action by either individual (passive appreciation). North Carolina, for instance, is one of these middle-ground states. The North Carolina statute specifically defines the circumstances that constitute active and passive appreciation:

Passive increases in value, such as those attributable to inflation or to market fluctuations, will be considered as part of the separate

---

[21] 13 Del. C. § 1513.
[22] Colorado Statute 14-10-113.

property, whereas *active* appreciation in the value of the property, such as that resulting from economic or noneconomic contributions by one or both of the spouses, is to be treated as part of the marital property[23] [emphasis added].

Additionally, the courts must make decisions on commingled property. *Commingling* refers to the mixing of separate and marital property. In the case of separate property, the issue is whether separate property has been mixed with marital property and whether this mixing causes the separate property to lose its character and become marital property. This is often referred to as *transmuted property*. Separate property can be transmuted to marital property by commingling. A few states have specific statutory provisions on commingled property. Missouri, for instance, states:

> Property which would otherwise be non-marital property shall not become marital property solely because it may have become commingled with marital property.[24]

The Alabama statute, however, includes property that may be separate but has benefited both spouses during the marriage as marital property:

> ... the judge may not take into consideration any property acquired prior to the marriage of the parties or by inheritance or gift unless the judge finds from the evidence *that the property, or income produced by the property, has been used regularly for the common benefit of the parties during their marriage* [emphasis added].[25]

Most states that have addressed commingling have done so in the courts. For instance, Alaska decided that commingling itself does not necessarily establish intent to hold property jointly, and therefore the court should consider the property's source when determining what assets are available for distribution.[26]

Going back to the definition of marital property, if an asset was created during the marriage, these issues are not addressed. However, if an asset preexisted the marriage, an appraiser may have to employ multiple

---

[23] Cheryl Lynn Daniels, "North Carolina's Equitable Distribution Statute," 64 *North Carolina Law Review*, Rev. 1395 (August 1986), at 1399.

[24] Arkansas Statute 2004 § 452.330, at 4.

[25] Code of Alabama 2005 § 30-2-51(a).

[26] *Julsen v. Julsen*, 741 P.2d 642 (Alaska 1987).

valuation dates[27] and determine the value of the asset at the beginning and the end of the marriage. The issues of active and passive appreciation, transmutation, and commingling arise somewhat independently from the premise or standard of value, but are nonetheless important considerations for the practitioner.

PREMISES AND STANDARDS OF VALUE IN DIVORCE

As mentioned, the valuation of marital assets falls under two basic premises that form the basis of a continuum of value: value in exchange and value to the holder.

Premises of Value

Value in Exchange   States following the value in exchange premise view the identification and valuation of marital assets in the context of a sale. Value in exchange presumes some sort of hypothetical transaction where the business or business interest is exchanged for cash or cash equivalent. To the extent that the conclusion of value depends on the continued efforts of one party, that portion of the value is excluded and viewed as separate property or not as property at all. States following a value in exchange premise reject the inclusion of intangible value reliant on an individual for several reasons, including the viewpoint that postmarital efforts are necessary to realize the value, and also that the "property" allegedly created is not capable of being separated from the person.

Value to the Holder   Value to the holder considers the value of a business or business interest in the hands of its owner, regardless of whether he or she intends to sell the business. It further assumes that the titled spouse will continue to enjoy the benefits generated by a business that was created or appreciated during the marriage, and contemplating a value upon sale would dilute the actual value that both spouses enjoyed during the marriage, as only the titled spouse would continue to benefit from that value after the marriage ends.

---

[27] As previously discussed, determining what caused the appreciation in value is an important element of the distribution of the increase in value. The valuation expert should consult with the retaining attorney to determine what, if any, role he or she has to opine on the economic reason for this increase.

Exhibit 5.1 shows the first level of the continuum of value for these two premises, which have different underlying assumptions involving a state's determination of what constitutes property and how it should be valued.

EXHIBIT 5.1   Continuum of Value: Premises of Value

Premise of Value	Value in Exchange	Value to the Holder

In our view, these two premises form a continuum of value under which businesses or business interests are identified, valued, and eventually distributed in a divorce. In determining a value in exchange, those elements of skill and reputation attributed to the owner spouse that cannot be distinguished from the individual (and would no longer benefit the business if he or she departed) are typically not considered to be marital and should be separated from the value. One values only the assets of the enterprise that could be sold to a hypothetical buyer at the date of a hypothetical sale.

Under value to the holder, these issues typically do not come into play, as the presumption is that no sale will take place, and, therefore, the effect of the owner leaving is not relevant. Standards of value fall under these two premises, from fair market value, which is value in exchange, to investment value, which is value to the holder. Thus, the continuum of value moves from valuing only assets that may be sold to valuing assets that may have limited or no marketability absent the continued participation of the owner spouse.

The standards of value most often used by courts to value marital assets are fair market value, fair value (more commonly referred to in oppression and dissent cases), and investment value (also called *intrinsic value* or, colloquially, *value to the holder*).

In the remainder of this chapter, we explain how we analyze the premises and standards of value and their stated or implied application. We can use value in exchange and value to the holder as a framework to better understand the theory and application of the common standards of value used in divorce cases.

Standards of Value

Although a court may use the name of a particular standard of value, the assumptions normally associated with that standard of value are often treated inconsistently or not addressed at all. This can be more readily seen in the varying treatment of goodwill, shareholder-level discounts, and the weight accorded to buy–sell agreements. The valuation professional has to be aware of the precedent-setting case law in each state, including the underlying facts and assumptions of each case in addition to the exact words in the decision.

Fair Market Value   Fair market value is widely applied in divorce valuations. Several states have asserted through case law that fair market value is the appropriate standard; others have implied that it is the standard they are using by their treatment of personal goodwill and the applicability of shareholder-level discounts. Fair market value is defined by the Estate Tax Regulations as:

> the price at which the property would change hands between a willing buyer and a willing seller when the former is not under any compulsion to buy and the latter is not under any compulsion to sell, both parties having reasonable knowledge of the relevant facts.[28]

Application of a fair market value standard for businesses or business interests in divorce focuses on those elements of the business value that are considered transferable. To a varying extent, the resulting value under this standard does not ordinarily include nontransferable elements such as personal goodwill. The extent to which this assumption applies varies in some states as to the consideration of the seller's participation in the transition. Some states view the application of fair market value as an immediate departure of the owner with an ability and willingness to compete. Other states consider a more orderly transition.

Simply stated, fair market value assumes a value in exchange: The buyer gets the asset and the seller gets cash or a cash equivalent. This value in exchange results in the identification and valuation of those elements that are normally transferable or capable of being transferred with no long-term participation on the part of the seller.

As we discussed in Chapter 2, certain assumptions are inherent in the application of the standard of fair market value. For example, since it falls within the value in exchange premise and contemplates a hypothetical sale of the business or business interests, discounts for lack of control and/or marketability are generally considered.

Fair Value   Fair value is defined mainly in connection with dissent and oppression cases in the corporation statutes and cases. Fair value in divorce is generally applied the same way as it is in dissent and oppression cases, in that it is a standard that is largely determined by case law.

---

[28] Estate Tax Regulation § 20.2031-1.

Fair value is different from fair market value and investment or intrinsic value. Fair market value assumes a willing buyer and a willing seller. Investment value assumes that the business will not be sold and the owner will continue to receive benefits from the business or business interest (unless a sale is really occurring). In one context, fair value can entail an exchange, but not necessarily from a willing seller. Fair value may also assert that a lack of intention to sell a business prevents its valuation as a value in exchange. As we will show, some fair value cases adhere more to a value in exchange premise; others adhere to a value to the holder premise. Generally, if a valuation takes a pro rata portion of the enterprise value without shareholder-level discounts, we considered it to be fair value.

The 1950 Delaware dissent case, *Tri-Continental v. Battye*,[29] defines fair value in this way:

> The basic concept of value under the appraisal statute is that the stockholder is entitled to be paid for that which has been taken from him, viz., his proportionate interest in a going concern. By value of the stockholder's proportionate interest in the corporate enterprise is meant the true or intrinsic value of his stock which has been taken by the merger. In determining what figure represents this true or intrinsic value, the appraiser and the courts must take into consideration all factors and elements which reasonably might enter into fixing the value.[30]

In this interpretation, the courts look to fairly compensate the departing party for that which has been unwillingly taken from him or her. To extrapolate this concept to divorce, under fair value, the courts may look to compensate the non-titled spouse for the value generated during the marriage but realized after the divorce. Most often, courts believe that absent extraordinary circumstances, it would be unfair in an oppression case to apply discounts to the value sought by the oppressing party, as the oppressed party has been mistreated and would otherwise be unwilling to sell. This would create an undeserved windfall for the oppressor. Similarly, in divorce (regardless of marital misconduct or fault), a court evaluating discounts may see the application of discounts as an unfair advantage to the party that will continue to enjoy the benefits of the asset.

In this respect, divorce and oppression may be similar in that they can both be seen in terms of the reasonable expectations of those entering into a

---

[29] 74 A.2d 71, 72 (Del. 1950).
[30] *Id.*

partnership or contract (business or marital). A shareholder has the expectation of sharing in the benefits of the business for the course of his or her life or the term of the contract. Should those expectations be breached, the court looks to fairly compensate that individual. Marriage is viewed as an economic partnership in which each party has an expectation of sharing the economic benefits generated during the marriage. In this case, the court may view discounts, which lower the value attributed to the owner, as unfairly benefiting the owner spouse at the expense of the non-owner spouse.

Investment Value Another widely used standard of value in divorce matters is investment value, which is often also referred to as intrinsic value. This standard commonly falls under the value to the holder premise. Application of this standard contemplates value not to a potential hypothetical buyer but rather to a particular buyer, which in the case of divorce is the current owner, hence, value to the holder. This standard also recognizes that there may or may not be an *intention* to sell or leave the business, and as it continues, the business will enjoy the benefits and the value derived from the owner's continued presence.

In this context, investment value differs from fair market value in that it will provide a going-concern value to the current owner, not a hypothetical buyer. Some courts refer to this standard as the value of a going concern to the owner. This standard of value identifies assets that have an inherent or intrinsic worth to the owner, which may not be transferable to another individual. Some argue that the existence of this asset, regardless of its transferability, was created or germinated during the marriage, and this value is partially attributable to the efforts of the non-owner spouse. During the marriage, both spouses benefited from that earning ability. After the marriage, only the owner will continue to benefit. Several states consider these types of assets marital; many do not. California's landmark case, *Golden v. Golden*,[31] for example, gives the reasoning behind using the characterization of property that leads to the application of an investment value standard:

> . . . in a matrimonial matter, the practice of the sole practitioner husband will continue, with the same intangible value as it had during the marriage. Under the principles of community property law, the wife, by virtue of her position of wife, made to that value the same contribution as does a wife to any of the husband's earnings and accumulations during marriage. She is as much entitled to be

---

[31] 270 Cal. App.2d 401; 75 Cal. Rptr. 735; 1969 Cal. App. LEXIS 1538.

recompensed for that contribution as if it were represented by the increased value of stock in a family business.[32]

There are various assumptions involved in a determination of investment value. For example, the transferability (and therefore marketability) of personal goodwill is often not at issue, as there is likely no intention to sell. To illustrate, we can look at the example of a law firm in New Jersey, when the clients (goodwill) of the law firm could not be sold to another lawyer.[33] Under a fair market value standard, the goodwill of a law firm in New Jersey at that time would have no value.[34] However, under an investment value standard, the ability to sell is not as important as it is under the fair market value standard in determining the business's ongoing value to its current owner. The use of the investment value standard suggests that the court is attempting to compensate the non-titled spouse for the economic benefits the titled spouse will receive in the future, regardless of whether that spouse can sell those benefits. This appears to be the reasoning followed in New Jersey's *Dugan v. Dugan.*[35]

Also, when determining the investment value, discounts are typically not taken because investment value does not contemplate an actual or hypothetical sale, but only the value to the current owners.

Exhibit 5.2 presents the continuum of value for the premise of value and standards of value.

EXHIBIT 5.2 Continuum of Value: Premises and Standards of Value

Premise of Value	Value in Exchange		Value to the Holder	
Standard of Value	Fair Market Value		Fair Value	Investment Value

---

[32] *Id.*, at 738.

[33] See *Dugan v. Dugan*, 92 N.J. 423; 457 A.2d 1; 1983 N.J. LEXIS 2351, at 21. DR 2-108(A) of the Disciplinary Rules of the Code of Professional Responsibility: "A lawyer shall not be a party to or participate in a partnership or employment agreement with another lawyer that restricts the right of a lawyer to practice law after the termination of a relationship created by the agreement, except as may be provided in a bona fide retirement plan and then only to the extent reasonably necessary to protect the plan."

[34] Today, the goodwill or client base of a law firm may be sold in New Jersey. This was not always the case.

[35] *Dugan v. Dugan* , 92 N.J. 423; 457 A.2d 1; 1983 N.J. LEXIS 2351.

Premises of Value Revealed through the Valuation of Insurance Agencies

Two cases involving captive State Farm insurance agencies demonstrate the difference between a value in exchange premise and a value to the holder premise. The Washington case of *In re: Zeigler*[36] presents a value in exchange, whereas the Colorado case of *In re: Graff*[37] reveals a value to the holder.

IN RE: ZEIGLER

Mr. Zeigler was the sole stockholder of a captive insurance agency of the State Farm Insurance Company. In his agreement with State Farm, he sold only State Farm–approved products; the names and book of business were owned by State Farm (and therefore Mr. Zeigler could not sell them). Mr. Zeigler controlled the organization and management of the agency. Upon termination of the agreement, Mr. Zeigler's agency could remain, retaining its name, staff, location, and so on, but would be prohibited from soliciting State Farm policyholders for one year, and for this agreement Mr. Zeigler would be paid 20% of the prior year's commissions for five years by State Farm.

Mr. Zeigler's expert testified that the goodwill of the agency was owned by State Farm, and because Mr. Zeigler had no personal interest in State Farm, he did not own any of the goodwill. The expert calculated no excess earnings and therefore no goodwill value to the agency.

Mrs. Zeigler's expert also applied an excess earnings methodology and adjusted Mr. Zeigler's salary to reflect industry averages, yielding a goodwill value of $231,000.

The trial court agreed with the assessment of Mr. Zeigler's expert, that the agency itself had no goodwill and any value to the firm above its assets was in the termination agreement. Additionally, any excess value to the business was associated with Mr. Zeigler's skill, knowledge, and hard work (what the court called earning capacity), rather than the expected public patronage based on business goodwill. Essentially, the business goodwill belonged to State Farm itself, not Mr. Zeigler's agency.

(continued)

---

[36] Wash. App. 602, 849 P.2d 695 (Wash. App. Div. 3, 1993).
[37] *In re: Marriage of Graff*, 902 P.2d 402 (Colo. App., 1994).

> The Appeals Court agreed that because of the captive status of the agency and the agreements in place, any goodwill resides with State Farm, not with Mr. Zeigler or his agency.

In this case, the business was seen as an entity independent from (but still reliant on) the products it sold. If Mr. Zeigler terminated his relationship with State Farm, the agency would have no goodwill value. Because the goodwill belonged to State Farm, Mr. Zeigler did not have any right to sell it, and therefore it had no value to him.

The opposite was seen to be true in the Colorado case *In re: Graff*. Shortly after the Zeigler decision, the Colorado Court of Appeals decided a case involving another State Farm agency, with a similar contract as the agency discussed in Zeigler.

IN RE: MARRIAGE OF GRAFF

Mr. Graff's expert argued largely the same points as did Mr. Zeigler's expert. He pointed out that the agency could not sell, assign, exchange, or mortgage the value represented by the agency's ability to generate income. Mrs. Graff's expert testified that the agency had value because Mr. Graff acted like the owner of a business. Mr. Graff set his own hours, decided the location of the office, hired and fired his own employees, set their salaries, purchased his own supplies, and characterized his interest in the firm as that of a business on Schedule C of his tax return. The value arrived at by the wife's expert was $131,500, including a value for goodwill.

The trial court looked at the transferability and termination agreements, the same as those in the Washington case, but found that because a transfer or termination was not contemplated, the husband's interest in the firm and the continuing involvement with State Farm constituted value.

The court of appeals agreed with the trial court, stating that:

> the value of goodwill is not necessarily dependent upon what a willing buyer would pay for such goodwill, rather the important consideration is whether the business has a value

> to the spouse over and above the tangible assets. . . . Good-
> will may be valued even though an agreement, as here, pre-
> vents the sale of an agency.[38]
>
> This statement shows a clear adherence to a value to the holder
> premise. Although the goodwill cannot be sold, it still has value to
> the owner who continues in place.

In the case of *Seiler v. Seiler*,[39] New Jersey also addressed the value of a captive insurance agency, in this case, an Allstate agency. The court found that there was no goodwill owned by the individual, as the husband was an employee of the firm, rather than a sole proprietor of his individual business. Any goodwill was associated with Allstate, rather than Mr. Seiler. As applied to the valuation of businesses and business interests, it appears that New Jersey is a fair value state,[40] as the courts regularly reject discounts but include the value of goodwill, even in businesses that cannot be sold. However, because Mr. Seiler was an employee of the firm rather than a sole proprietor or a stockholder, the court found that there was no business and no value to goodwill.

As this shows, two states may view the exact same business in very different ways. When approaching a valuation, one of the most important indicia of value is whether the asset in question qualifies as a business. As we explain, only in New York[41] is the value of goodwill in the form of a professional degree, license, enhanced earnings capacity, and celebrity status, without the associated business entity, considered divisible marital property.

Concepts of Value under the Two Premises

The continuum of value represented by the two premises, value in exchange and value to the holder, can be examined by looking at the treatment of goodwill and whether a particular state views this personal intangible asset as marital or separate property. Let us first look at value in exchange through

---

[38] *Id.*, at [**5].

[39] 308 N.J. Super. 474; 706 A.2d 249; 1998 N.J. Super. LEXIS 80.

[40] While the above applies to businesses and business interests, it appears that other marital assets, including real property, are valued at their fair market value.

[41] *O'Brien v. O'Brien* , 66 N.Y.2d 576; 489 N.E.2d 712; 498 N.Y.S.2d 743 (1985).

the prism of two closely related issues: personal and enterprise goodwill and the applicability of a covenant not to compete, or the right to compete.

Compete: An extreme view of value in exchange includes neither the participation of the owner to help transition the business nor the owner's agreement to refrain from competing with the buyer. This scenario would represent the value of the business if the seller were allowed to open up shop next door, participating in exactly the same business as he or she just sold. In this case, the income stream purchased will not include any value attributable to the personal goodwill of the seller and the value would have to consider the former owner's effect as a direct competitor. This is termed the *walk-away value*.

Cooperate: Another view of the value in exchange standard considers the situation where the seller is willing and therefore cooperates to maximize value. The seller would eventually leave, possibly signing a covenant not to compete to restrict his or her efforts. The seller might also agree to a consulting contract of limited duration, where he or she will help transition the goodwill of the business to the new owners. Generally, under a value in exchange, the value of this covenant, however, would not be included in the value of the business because it is inextricably tied to the owner and his or her future efforts.

These differing assumptions of the seller's post-sale behavior can result in significantly different values for the business. Moreover, with regard to the valuation of professional practices and other types of businesses under value in exchange, this view of the covenant not to compete will form one of the bases of the difference between personal and enterprise goodwill. Under value to the holder, a sale is not necessarily contemplated. Therefore, the owner's participation in the transition is moot.

In the case that an actual sale occurs (at or prior to divorce), the court would have to consider whether the covenant's value was marital property. As the covenant's value affects an individual's behavior, under value in exchange, it would not likely be included in marital property. Under value to the holder, the issue is rarely addressed as there is an assumption that there is no sale.

STANDARDS OF VALUE IN DIVORCE AMONG THE 50 STATES

Lack of Statutory Insight

As we have mentioned, there is a substantial lack of statutory insight as to the standard of value in divorce proceedings. In dissenter's rights and oppressed shareholder suits, there is little doubt that fair value is the generally accepted standard. When it comes to divorce, only two states, Arkansas and Louisiana, provide any statutory guidance as to the standard of value. The Arkansas statute says:

§ 9-12-315.(4)—When stocks, bonds, or other securities issued by a corporation, association, or government entity make up part of the marital property, the court shall designate in its final order or judgment the specific property in securities to which each party is entitled, or after determining the *fair market value* of the securities, may order and adjudge that the securities be distributed to one (1) party on condition that one-half (1/2) the fair market value of the securities in money or other property be set aside and distributed to the other party in lieu of division and distribution of the securities [emphasis added].

The Louisiana statute more generally applies the fair market value standard:

§ 9:2801—(1)(a) Within forty-five days of service of a motion by either party, each party shall file a sworn detailed descriptive list of all community property, the *fair market value* and location of each asset, and all community liabilities [emphasis added].

Further, Louisiana's statute prevents the valuation of personal goodwill in the distribution of community assets:

§ 9:2801.2—In a proceeding to partition the community, the court may include, in the valuation of any community-owned corporate, commercial, or professional business, the goodwill of the business. However, *that portion of the goodwill attributable to any personal quality of the spouse awarded the business shall not be included in the valuation of a business* [emphasis added].

Most states do not recommend or require any particular standard with which to value assets upon the dissolution of marriage. For example, New Jersey's equitable distribution provision states:

§ 2A:34-23h. In all actions where a judgment of divorce or divorce from bed and board is entered the court may make such award or awards to the parties, in addition to alimony and maintenance, to effectuate an Equitable Distribution of the *property*, both real and personal, which was legally and beneficially acquired by them or either of them during the marriage. However, all such *property*, real, personal or otherwise, legally or beneficially acquired during the marriage by either party by way of gift, devise, or intestate succession shall not be subject to Equitable Distribution, except that interspousal gifts shall be subject to Equitable Distribution [emphasis added].

Although the Arkansas statute is specific regarding the applicable standard of value in divorce, the New Jersey statute, along with the majority of others, states that property is to be distributed but does not state how the property is to be valued or the standard of value to be used in the process.

In the course of our research, we found that eight states made reference to fair market value in their equitable distribution statutes/community property statutes, but not with regard to the value of a closely held businesses or business interest. These states are: Montana, North Carolina, Oregon, Pennsylvania, Tennessee, Vermont, West Virginia, and Wisconsin.

Revealing Standard of Value through Case Law

Many states appear to view the valuation of marital property based on the circumstances of the case or the precedents previously set by the courts with respect to certain elements of value. Because of this, clarity about the applicable standard of value suffers from the valuation practitioner's point of view. We can begin to look at the decisions made by each state as a means of suggesting which standard or combination of standards may apply. Later we will further discuss the continuum of value as it applies to these decisions and the actual classification of states into standard and premise of value categories.

Whereas, with few exceptions, state statutes do not address the standard of value, a review of relevant case law can provide further insight as to the application of a standard of value in a particular state. A few states, including Hawaii, Florida, and Missouri, more clearly apply fair market value as the standard of value in their case decisions. For example, Hawaii's statute does not provide guidance on the standard of value:

§ 580-47—Upon granting a divorce, or thereafter if, in addition to the powers granted in subsections (c) and (d), jurisdiction of those matters is reserved under the decree by agreement of both parties or by order of court after finding that good cause exists, the court may make any further orders as shall appear just and equitable (1) compelling the parties or either of them to provide for the support, maintenance, and education of the children of the parties; (2) compelling either party to provide for the support and maintenance of the other party; (3) finally dividing and distributing the estate of the parties, real, personal, or mixed, whether community, joint, or separate; and (4) allocating, as between the parties, the responsibility for the payment of the debts of the parties whether community, joint, or separate, and the attorney's fees, costs, and expenses incurred by each party by reason of the divorce. In making these further orders, the court shall take into consideration: the respective merits of the parties, the relative abilities of the parties, the condition in which each party will be left by the divorce, the burdens imposed upon either party for the benefit of the children of the parties, and all other circumstances of the case.

Accordingly, the statute provides only a general outline for the dissolution of the marital estate. However, in the 1988 Hawaii case, *Antolik v. Harvey*,[42] the court clearly applies fair market value as the standard with which to value businesses.

ANTOLIK V. HARVEY

The husband was a licensed chiropractor and a sole proprietor of his business. As the business was premarital, the parties agreed that the wife was entitled to half of the increase in value of the practice from the date of marriage to the date of contemplation of divorce. The family court found the values at $8,000 and $48,000 respectively as of these dates, and the husband was ordered to pay the wife $20,000.

The husband's expert valued the practice based on an adjusted book value, arriving at a value of $8,000 at the start of the marriage in 1984, assuming a business loan for $18,675.99 was used for personal expenditures and excluding it from the valuation. He used a similar method to determine that the value of the husband's practice was $48,000 at the time of divorce in 1986, but included the remaining balance on the business loan previously discussed.

The wife's expert determined that the practice had gross receipts of $85,445 in 1985, $147,151.05 in 1986, and would generate $175,000 in 1987. The earnings of the practice in 1987 were estimated to be

(continued)

---

[42] 761 P.2d 305 (Haw. Interm. App. 1988).

$105,000. Using a reasonable compensation figure of $54,000, the expert concluded that the earnings of the business would be $51,000, and by using a 20% future earnings rate, valued the business at $255,000, plus the replacement value of its tangible assets, less liabilities.

The wife contended that the $48,000 value arrived at in the family court did not include a goodwill value. The appellate court discussed the nature of goodwill and determined it to be an attribute of a business in which there is a recognized value above the tangible assets of such entity. The court stated:

> When dividing and distributing the value of the property of the parties in a divorce case, the relevant value is, as a general rule, the fair market value (FMV) of the parties' interest therein on the relevant date. We define the FMV as being the amount at which an item would change hands from a willing seller to a willing buyer, neither being under any compulsion to buy or sell and both having reasonable knowledge of the relevant facts.

The court rejected the contention that the value of the sole proprietorship was the value to the professional operating it, as other assets are valued at their fair market value.

In determining the value of the practice at the date of marriage, the court concluded that the debt must be considered, and therefore the adjusted net book value of the business was $8,136.96.

For the date of divorce valuation, the family court concluded the value was $48,000 including a value of $2,310 for the patient charts.

The appellate court's review stated that the sale of the business including goodwill would be contingent upon the owner's cooperation and continued presence to transfer the existing patient base to a similarly productive chiropractor. Should the husband leave immediately, the goodwill could not be transferred. The family court did not contemplate the lack of a binding agreement that would prevent the husband from competing upon sale. However, the husband did not appeal the inclusion of the value of the book of business, so the appellate court affirmed the family court's 1986 valuation.

No state specifically uses the terms *investment value* or *fair value* as the standard of value in their statute, but various case decisions in a state might provide the insight so as to generally establish a given standard of value.

New Jersey's *Brown v. Brown*[43] (discussed in detail later) uses the language of fair value and refers to New Jersey dissent and oppression cases to determine fair value.

Similarly, in *Grelier v. Grelier*,[44] the Alabama Civil Appeals Court, in a case of first impression, referred to *Brown* in addressing whether a divorce court should use minority and marketability discounts when assessing the value of a divorcing spouse's interest in a closely held business organization. Coming to a conclusion that no discount for minority interest and lack of marketability should be applied and referring to *Brown* from New Jersey, the Alabama Civil Appeals Court indicated:

> Because the Alabama Supreme Court has adopted the same reasoning that is applied in New Jersey in dissenting-shareholder cases, it seems reasonable to conclude that it would follow the same reasoning in divorce cases involving minority ownership of closely held business organization.[45]

California's *Golden v. Golden*,[46] although never specifically mentioning investment value, clearly lays out what appears to be a value to the holder treatment of assets that embodies most of the elements found in investment value.

GOLDEN V. GOLDEN

After a seven-year marriage, the parties involved were divorced. The husband was a doctor, 31 years old, and the wife was 29 and a housewife who had previously worked as a teacher. In the distribution of community assets, the court included an allocation of $32,500 for the goodwill of the husband's medical practice.

On appeal, the husband argued that the trial court erred in finding goodwill to be a community asset, citing a previous California decision holding that upon the dissolution of law practices, no allowance could be made for goodwill because the reputation of the firm depends on the skill of each member. Additionally, tax cases held that goodwill was connected only with a going business.

(continued)

---

[43] 348 N.J. Super. 466; 792 A.2d 463; 2002 N.J. Super. LEXIS 105.

[44] 63 So.3d 668 (Alab. Civ. App. 2010).

[45] *Id.,*

[46] 75 Cal. Rptr. 735 (Cal. App. 1969).

Other cases, however, had found that salable goodwill exists in a professional business even if founded on personal skill and reputation, and upon the dissolution of the community, a professional's practice must be taken into account for evaluating the community estate. The court established what it called a better rule, as follows:

> We believe the better rule is that, in a divorce case, the good will of the husband's professional practice as a sole practitioner should be taken into consideration in determining the award to the wife. Where, as in Lyon, the firm is being dissolved, it is understandable that a court cannot determine what, if any, of the good will of the firm will go to either partner. But, in a matrimonial matter, the practice of the sole practitioner husband will continue, with the same intangible value as it had during the marriage. Under the principles of community property law, the wife, by virtue of her position of wife, made to that value the same contribution as does a wife to any of the husband's earnings and accumulations during marriage. She is as much entitled to be recompensed for that contribution as if it were represented by the increased value of stock in a family business.

The valuation therefore stood with the inclusion of goodwill in the calculation of value.

As Exhibit 5.3 shows, we begin with two premises of value and place the standards of value under the applicable premises. Fair market value is a value in exchange, and investment value is a value to the holder. Fair value may fall under either premise in that it may contain elements of both. The three cases we have mentioned in terms of the standard of value used are placed on the continuum as examples.

EXHIBIT 5.3 Continuum of Value: Standards of Value with Case Examples

Premise of Value	Value in Exchange		Value to the Holder
Standard of Value	Fair Market Value	Fair Value	Investment Value
Case Example	*Antolik v. Antolik*	*Brown v. Brown*	*Golden v. Golden*

Toward a Standard of Value Classification System

To perform this analysis, we first looked to the statutes of all 50 states and the District of Columbia for guidance on the standard of value applied in each jurisdiction. We found that only Arkansas and Louisiana provide direction in their statutes. We then moved to the case law in each jurisdiction, and through this review, we found clearer guidance in 24 additional states. Including Arkansas and Louisiana, 25 states direct the use of fair market value in their case law, and one state, Alabama, uses the term *fair value.*

The standard of value in the remaining 25 jurisdictions must be inferred from the use and application of certain concepts. In these jurisdictions, we examined the treatment of personal versus enterprise goodwill, shareholder-level minority and lack of marketability discounts, and the weight accorded buy–sell agreements. In value in exchange states, we looked at the language of cases and the use of discounts to determine whether a fair market value standard or a fair value standard was being followed. Additionally, by reviewing the language of the case and the treatment of goodwill and covenants not to compete, we have tried to determine whether a state followed a walk-away fair market standard or a more traditional fair market value standard.

In some states, the standard of value is less clear and the body of case law does not imply adherence to any particular standard or valuation principle, perhaps to intentionally allow the court a higher degree of flexibility to pass judgment based on the facts, circumstances, and equities of a given case.

Although the standard of value in each state is often not an absolute, for analytical purposes it is helpful to categorize states based on our earlier assumptions. Although this should not be seen as a hard-and-fast determination of the application of a specific standard of value, this classification system should provide a reasonable starting point from which to analyze how value is viewed in a particular state. As always, the valuator must be conscious of the nuances in any given case or state that may affect how value is determined.

We begin with the manner in which states view intangible value, specifically goodwill. The treatment of goodwill can be an indicator of how a court views marital property, the premise of value, and the standard of value. Just as the fair market value standard implies the exclusion of personal goodwill (because it cannot be transferred upon sale), prior case law demonstrating the consistent exclusion of personal goodwill implies that the state follows a value in exchange premise and the use of a fair market value standard.

The listed states, either through statute or specific language contained in case law, specifically mention the standard of value that should be used in a divorce valuation. Following this concept, we cite cases where the standard of value is specifically mentioned.

Alabama	FV	*Hartley v. Hartley*[47]
Alaska	FMV	*Fortson v. Fortson*[48]
Arkansas	FMV	Statute[49]
Connecticut	FMV	*Dahill v. Dahill*[50]
Florida	FMV	*Christians v. Christians*[51]
Hawaii	FMV	*Antolik v. Harvey*[52]
Indiana	FMV	*Nowels v. Nowels*[53]
Iowa	FMV	*Frett v. Frett*[54]
Kansas	FMV	*Bohl v. Bohl*[55]
Louisiana	FMV	*Trahan v. Trahan*[56]
Minnesota	FMV	*Berenberg v. Berenberg*[57]
Mississippi	FMV	*Singley v. Singley*[58]
Missouri	FMV	*Wood v. Wood*[59]
Nebraska	FMV	*Shuck v. Shuck*[60]
New Hampshire	FMV	*Martin v. Martin*[61]
New York	FMV	*Beckerman v. Beckerman*[62]
North Carolina	FMV	*Walter v. Walter*[63]
North Dakota	FMV	*Sommers v. Sommers*[64]
Oklahoma	FMV	*Traczyk v. Traczyk*[65]

[47] 50 So.3d 1102 (Alab. Civ. App. 2010).

[48] 131 P.3d 451(Ala. Supr. Ct. 2006).

[49] Arkansas Statute §9-12-315(4).

[50] 1998 Conn. Super. LEXIS 846.

[51] 732 So.2d 47 (Fla. App. 1999).

[52] 761 P.2d 305 (Haw. Interm. App. 1988).

[53] 836 N.E.2d 481; 2005 Ind. App. LEXIS 2039.

[54] LEXIS 694 (Iowa. App. 2004).

[55] 657 P.2d1106; (Kan. Supr. Ct. 1983).

[56] 43 So. 3d 218 (La. App. 2010).

[57] 474 N.W.2d 843 (Minn. Ct. App. 1991).

[58] LEXIS 283 (Miss. Supr. Ct. 2003).

[59] 361 S.W.3d 36 (Mo. App. 2011).

[60] 1806 N.W.2d 580 (Neb. App. 2011).

[61] LEXIS 275 (N.H. Supr. Ct. 2006).

[62] 126 A.D.2d 591(N.Y. Supr. Ct. App. 1987). New York also follows an investment value standard of value as evidenced by *O'Brien v O'Brien*, 489 N.E.2d 712 (N.Y. Ct. App. 1985).*Moll v. Moll*, 187 Misc. 2d 770 (N.Y. Supr. Ct. 2001).

[63] 561 S.E.2d 571, 577 (N.C. App. 2002).

[64] 660 N.W.2d 586 (N.D. Supr. Ct. 2003).

[65] 891 P.2d 1277 (Okla. Supr. Ct. 1995).

Oregon	FMV	*Marriage of Belt*[66]
South Carolina	FMV	*Hickum v. Hickum*[67]
South Dakota	FMV	*Fausch v. Fausch*[68]
Vermont	FMV	*Drumheller v. Drumheller*[69]
West Virginia	FMV	*May v. May*[70]
Wisconsin	FMV	*Herlitzke v. Herlitzke*[71]
Wyoming	FMV	*Neuman v. Neuman*[72]

For the remaining unclassified states, we can look at the manner in which certain issues are treated to reveal the standard of value. Additionally, we can look at the way the states that use specific language treat certain issues in their case law to make a more specific assessment of their standard of value.

First, we can look at whether a state chooses to follow a value in exchange or value to the holder premise by its treatment of goodwill. If nonmarketable or personal goodwill is excluded, the state falls under a value in exchange premise. If a state does not distinguish enterprise and personal goodwill in its case law (or specifically includes personal goodwill), we categorize it under a value to the holder premise.

Under this classification system, a value in exchange state may be either fair market value or fair value based on its consideration of goodwill, discounts, buy–sell agreements, and case-specific language.

In terms of case-specific language, some cases use concepts that imply fair value rather than fair market value, such as an unwilling buyer, unwilling seller, fairness, or instruction to take a pro rata share of the enterprise. Other cases use language of how much a willing buyer would pay or how much a willing seller would accept, indicating a fair market value standard. Courts seeking to determine a value to the holder often use language indicating that a sale is unlikely or the value of a business or business interest should be its value to its current holder.

Under the value in exchange premise, following a fair market value standard of value, the language used may further delineate fair market value into a so-called walk-away standard where very little, if any, goodwill is

---

[66] 672 P.2d 1205 (Ore. App. 1983).

[67] 463 S.E.2d 321 (S.C. Ct. App. 1995).

[68] 697 N.W.2d 748 (S.D. Supr. Ct. 2005) citing *First Western Bank Wall v. Olsen*, 2001 S.D. 16, P.17, 621 N.W.2d 611 617.

[69] 972 A.2d 176 (Vt. Supr. Ct. 2009).

[70] 589 S.E.2d 536 (W. Va. Supr. Ct. 2003).

[71] 724 N.W.2d 702 (Wisc. App.2006).

[72] 842 P.2d 575 (Wyo. Supr. Ct. 1992).

considered a marital asset. Similarly, a value to the holder state will reveal either fair value or investment value based on the same principles of language.

The application of discounts may also reveal the standard of value. If shareholder-level discounts are applied, the case generally falls under fair market value. Under a value in exchange, if discounts are rejected, the case generally falls under fair value. Under value to the holder, discounts are generally not contemplated. However, some cases include goodwill without distinguishing personal and enterprise goodwill and reject the application of discounts. This also suggests a fair value standard.

The analysis of the weight accorded buy–sell agreements depends more on the context and language in the decision. If the language in the decision indicates that great weight should be accorded the buy–sell agreement because it is the amount that the individual will actually receive, that would be a strong indication of value in exchange. If the language in the decision measures the weight associated with the buy–sell agreement in terms of its fairness, it indicates that the continuum is moving from value in exchange to value to the holder. If the language in the decision indicates that little or no weight should be accorded to the buy–sell agreement because there will be no sale, then that indicates a value to the holder standard.

Exhibit 5.4 presents these principles graphically.

Additionally, certain states contain elements that belong to both value in exchange and value to the holder. We consider these to be hybrid states. For example, New York looks to apply fair market value in some cases[73] while in other instances also having cases that clearly fall under value to the holder.[74] The list that follows classifies states according to our analysis of their treatment of goodwill, shareholder-level discounts, and the weight accorded buy–sell agreements.

Fair Market Value *(The rest of this list continues on page 270.)*

Alaska	*Fortson v. Fortson*[75]
Arkansas	*Tortorich v. Tortorich*[76]
Connecticut	*Dahill v. Dahill*[77]
Delaware (walk-away)	*S.S. v. C.S.*[78]
District of Columbia	*McDiarmid v. McDiarmid*[79]

---

[73] *Beckerman v. Beckerman* , 126 A.D.2d 591 (N.Y. Supr. Ct. App. 1987).

[74] *O'Brien v. O'Brien* , 489 N.E.2d 712 (N.Y. Ct. App. 1985).

[75] 131 P.3d 451 (Alas. Supr. Ct. 2006).

[76] 902 S.W.2d 247 (Ark. App. 1995).

[77] 1998 Conn. Super. LEXIS 846 (Conn. Super. Ct. 1998).

[78] LEXIS 213 (Del. Fam. Ct. 2003).

[79] 649 A.2d 810 (D.C. App. 1994).

EXHIBIT 5.4 Value in Exchange, Value to the Holder Flowchart

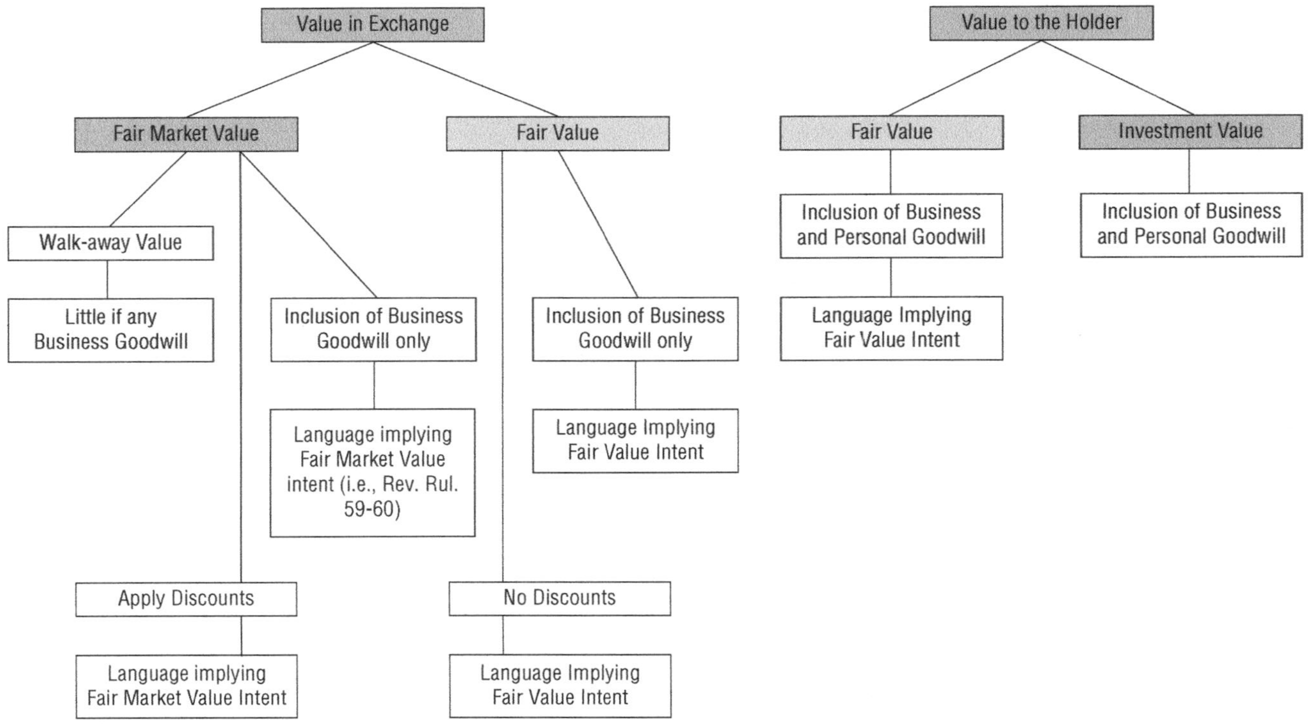

Fair Market Value *(continued from page 268)*

Florida (walk-away)	*Williams v. Williams*[80]
Georgia	*Miller v. Miller*[81]
Hawaii (walk-away)	*Antolik v. Harvey*[82]
Idaho	*Stewart v. Stewart*[83]
Illinois	*In re: Marriage of Heroy*[84]
Indiana	*Alexander v. Alexander*[85]
Iowa	*Frett v. Frett*[86]
Kansas (walk-away)	*Powell v. Powell*[87]
Kentucky	*Gaskill v. Robbins*[88]
Louisiana	La. Statute §9:2801-(1)(a)
Maine	*Ahern v. Ahern*[89]
Maryland	*Prahinski v. Prahinski*[90]
Minnesota	*Baker v. Baker*[91]
Mississippi (walk-away)	*Lewis v. Lewis*[92]
Missouri (walk-away)	*Hanson v. Hanson*[93]
Nebraska	*Shuck v. Shuck*[94]
New Hampshire	*In re: Watterworth*[95]
North Dakota	*Sommers v. Sommers*[96]
Ohio	*Bunkers v Bunkers*[97]
Oklahoma	*McQuay v. McQuay*[98]
Oregon	*Slater v. Slater*[99]
Pennsylvania	*Butler v. Butler*[100]

---

[80] 667 So.2d 915 (Fla. Dist. Ct. App. 1996).

[81] 288 Ga. 274 (Ga. Supr. Ct. 2010).

[82] 761 P.2d 305 (Haw, Interm. App. 1988).

[83] 152 P.3d 544 (Ida. Supr. Ct. 2007).

[84] 895 N.E.2d 1025 (Ill. App.2008).

[85] 927 N.E.2d 926 (Ind. App. 2010).

[86] LEXIS 694 (Iowa App. 2004).

[87] 648 P.2d 218 (Kan. Supr. Ct. 1982).

[88] 282 S.W.3d 306 (Ky. Supr. Ct. 2009).

[89] 938 A.2d 35 (2008)(Me. Supr. Ct. 2008).

[90] 582 A.2d 784 (Md. Ct. App. 1990).

[91] LEXIS 94 (Minn. App. 2007).

[92] 54 So.3d 216 (Miss. Supr. Ct. 2011).

[93] 738 S.W.2d 429 (Mo. Supr. Ct. 1987).

[94] 806 N.W.2d 580 (Neb. App. 2011).

[95] 821 A.2d 1107 (N.H. Supr. Ct. 2003).

[96] 660 N.W. 2d 586 (N.D. Supr. Ct. 2003).

[97] 2007 Ohio 561; LEXIS 523 (Ohio App. 2007).

[98] 217 P.3d 162 (Okla. Civ. App. 2009).

[99] 245 P.3d 676 (2010 Ore. Ct. App. 2010).

[100] 663 A.2d 148 (Pa.Supr. Ct. 1995).

Fair Market Value

Rhode Island	*Moretti v. Moretti*[101]
South Carolina (walk-away)	*Hickum v. Hickum*[102]
South Dakota	*Priebe v. Priebe*[103]
Texas	*Von Hohn v. Von Hohn*[104]
Utah	*Stonehocker v. Stonehocker*[105]
Vermont	*Goodrich v. Goodrich*[106]
West Virginia	*May v. May*[107]
Wisconsin	*McReath v. McReath*[108]
Wyoming	*Root v. Root*[109]

Fair Value

Alabama	*Grelier v. Grelier*[110]
Massachusetts	*Bernier v. Bernier*[111]
Virginia	*Howell v. Howell*[112]

Investment Value

Arizona	*Mitchell v. Mitchell*[113]
California	*Golden v. Golden*[114]
Nevada	*Ford v. Ford*[115]

---

[101] 766 A.2d 925 (R.I. Supr. Ct. 2001).

[102] 463 S.E.2d 321 (S.C. Ct. App. 1995).

[103] 556 N.W.2d 78 (S.D. Supr. Ct. 1996).

[104] 260 S.W.3d 631 (Tex. App. 2008).

[105] 176 P.3d 476 (Utah App. 2008).

[106] 613 A.2d 203 (Vt. Supr. Ct. 1992).

[107] 589 S.E.2d 536 (W. Va. Supr. Ct. 2003).

[108] 800 N.W.2d 399 (Wisc. Supr. Ct. 2011).

[109] 65 P.3d 41 (Wyo. Supr. Ct. 2003).

[110] 63 So.3d 668 (Alab. Civ. App. 2010).

[111] 873 N.E.2d 216 (Mass. Supr. Ct. 2007).

[112] 523 S.E.2d 514 (Va. App. 2000). Howell uses the term *intrinsic value*, which is a value to the holder/investment value definition, but does not allow personal goodwill as a marital asset. Therefore, we classify Virginia as a fair value state.

[113] 732 P.2d 208 (Ariz. Supr. Ct. 1987).

[114] 75 Cal. Rptr. 735 (Cal. Ct. App. 1969). Some argue that in California community assets considered marketable should be valued using the fair market value standard of value. They cite *In re: Marriage of Cream* (1993) 13 CA 4th, 81, 16 CR.2d 575 as the basis for the view that marketable assets should be valued at their fair market value and not under the investment value standard. What constitutes a *marketable asset* is undefined and in our view the issue is unsettled. The practitioner should discuss with counsel which standard to use or using both standards of value so that the issue will be delineated to the court.

[115] 782 P.2d 1304 (Nev. Supr. Ct. 1989).

Investment Value

New Mexico		*Mitchell v. Mitchell*[116]
Washington		*In re: Marriage of Hall*[117]

Hybrid

Colorado	FMV	*In re: Marriage of Thornhill*[118]
	IV	*In re: Marriage of Huff*[119]
Michigan	FMV	*Lemmen v. Lemmen*[120]
	IV	*Kowalesky v. Kowalesky*[121]
Montana	FMV	*DeCosse v. DeCosse*[122]
	IV	*In re: Marriage of Stufft*[123]
New Jersey	FV	*Brown v. Brown*[124]
	IV	*Dugan v. Dugan*[125]
New York	FMV	*Beckerman v. Beckerman*[126]
	IV	*Moll v. Moll*[127]
North Carolina	FMV	*Crowder v. Crowder*[128]
	IV	*Hamby v. Hamby*[129]
Tennessee	FMV	*McKee v. McKee*[130]
	FV	*Bertuca v. Bertuca*[131]

There are no states without decisions regarding the standard of value.

As with dissenter's rights and oppression proceedings, we can look to the law associations for guidance on the standard of value. The ALI's *Principles of the Law of Family Dissolution*[132] espouses a value in exchange premise, because it advocates excluding nonsalable goodwill attributable

---

[116] 719 P.2d 432 (N.M. Ct. App. 1986).

[117] 692 P.2d 175 (Wash. Supr. Ct. 1984).

[118] 232 P.3d 782 (Colo. Supr. Ct. 2010).

[119] 834 P.2d 244 (Colo. Supr. Ct. 1992).

[120] 809 N.W.2d(Mich. App.2010).

[121] 384 N.W.2d 112(Mich. App. 1986).

[122] 936 P.2d 821 (Mont. Supr. Ct. 1997).

[123] 950 P.2d 1373(Mont. Supr. Ct. 1997).

[124] 792 A.2d 463 (N.J. Super. Ct. App. Div. 2002).

[125] 457 A.2d 1 (N.J. Supr. Ct. 1983).

[126] 126 A.D.2d 591(N.Y. Supr. Ct. App. 1987).

[127] 187 Misc. 2d 770(N.Y. Supr. Ct. 2001).

[128] 556 S.E.2d 639(N.C. App. 2001).

[129] 547 S.E.2d 110 (N.C. App. 2001).

[130] LEXIS 524(Tenn. App. 2010).

[131] LEXIS 690(Tenn. App. 2007).

[132] ALI, "Principles of the Law of Family Dissolution: Analysis and Recommendations" (Philadelphia: Matthew Bender, 2002), at §4.07.

to the individual for assets subject to equitable distribution. The reasoning separates enterprise goodwill and personal goodwill from any value associated with an increased earning capacity. The ALI's *Principles of the Law of Family Dissolution* state:

> (1) Spousal earning capacity, spousal skills, and earnings from post-dissolution spousal labor, are not marital property.
> (2) Occupational licenses and educational degrees are not marital property.
> (3) Business goodwill and professional goodwill earned during marriage are marital property to the extent they have value apart from the value of spousal earning capacity, spousal skills, or postdissolution spousal labor.

In the explanation to this passage, the ALI endorses a market treatment for goodwill, indicating that it exists if and only if the market value of the practice exceeds the asset value.[133]

Although the *Principles of Corporate Governance* are cited continually in case law and legal scholarship with regard to fair value in dissenters' rights and shareholder oppression matters, the *Principles of the Law of Family Dissolution* are not often cited in marital dissolution matters. The states are generally more concerned with the case law precedents of their own or other states with respect to goodwill, discounts, earning capacity, and the like than with the suggestions of law associations.

To demonstrate how we arrived at the classification system, we can start by looking at Arkansas' *Wilson v. Wilson*[134] as an example of why Arkansas is categorized as a fair market value state. In this case, for goodwill to be marital property, it has to be a business asset with value independent of the presence or reputation of a particular individual.

California's *Golden v. Golden*, however, established that goodwill in a medical practice exists, and the individual practitioner's inability to sell it should not affect its consideration as an asset because the non-titled spouse contributed to its existence. This implies an investment value standard.

New Jersey's *Brown v. Brown* is a matrimonial case where there are continuing references to the fair value standard as used in dissenting and oppressed shareholder matters. Accordingly, fractional interests in businesses seem to be viewed the same way in matrimonial matters as in dissent and oppression matters in New Jersey.

---

[133] American Law Institute, "Principles of the Law of Family Dissolution" (2002).
[134] *Wilson v. Wilson*, 741 S.W.2d 640 (Ark. 1987).

New York is an example of a hybrid state. While seeming to base the valuation of businesses on the IRS's Revenue Ruling 59-60, including the application of shareholder-level discounts where appropriate (an indicia of fair market value), the state seems to fall closer to investment value with regard to other types of marital property. In fact, New York has gone so far as to assign a value to a license, professional degree, and enhanced earning capacity.

We next address the key issues and cases that help form the basis for our classification system. We begin with the treatment of goodwill, especially enterprise and personal goodwill, by the individual states.

VALUE IN EXCHANGE

As discussed, value in exchange assumes a hypothetical sale and looks to the value of the asset based on what would be realizable upon that sale at the valuation date. Several issues stem from the assumption of a hypothetical sale. We begin by looking at the differences in enterprise and personal goodwill, as a value in exchange would be concerned only with the elements of value that could be transferred to another owner as opposed to those that reside solely with the current owner.

Goodwill

Enterprise Goodwill Enterprise goodwill is the goodwill of the business. Therefore, it generally is a transferable asset, and it almost always is included in the valuation of the enterprise, even in those states that adhere to the narrowest interpretation of fair market value.[135] Upon selling a business, one has the ability to transfer enterprise goodwill to the buyer. Enterprise goodwill is defined by *Black's Law Dictionary* as "favorable consideration shown by the purchasing public to goods or services known to emanate from a particular source."[136] The existence of enterprise goodwill is based on the fact that customers return to an enterprise, based on its location, staff, telephone number, facilities, and the reputation of the overall entity.[137] Enterprise goodwill is found when there is an expectancy of repeat patronage attributable to the entity as distinguished from

---

[135] Enterprise goodwill in a professional practice may be treated differently because of the reliance on a particular owner.

[136] Bryan A. Garner, *Black's Law Dictionary*, 8th ed. (St. Paul, MN: Thompson West, 2004), at 694.

[137] Jay Fishman, "Personal Goodwill v. Enterprise Goodwill," *2004 AICPA National Business Valuation Conference*, Session 5, Orlando, FL, November 7, 2004.

the individual. An elegant description is found in the nineteenth-century English case *Cruttwell v. Lye:*[138]

> The good-will, which has been the subject of sale, is nothing more than the probability, that the old customers will resort to the old place.

An early twentieth-century New York commercial case makes a broader statement about goodwill, extending it not only to a particular place, but to a particular advantage that may be sold to another:

> Men will pay for any privilege that gives a reasonable expectancy of preference in the race of competition.[139]

These privileges might include a business's name, its phone number, its logo, or any facet of the business that might give it a continuing competitive advantage. Enterprise goodwill is the goodwill adhering to an entity regardless of the input of any specific individual.

Personal Goodwill

Personal goodwill is goodwill that adheres to an individual. It consists of personal attributes of an individual, including personal relationships, skill, personal reputation, and various other factors. It is usually not transferable and, therefore, states with a value to the holder premise usually do not require it be distinguished from enterprise goodwill. Justice Joseph Story, Associate Justice of the Supreme Court serving from 1812 to 1845, builds on the idea of goodwill adhering not only to a location, but to the reputation or celebrity of the establishment that causes customers to resort to a particular behavior.

> Goodwill may be properly enough described to be the advantage or benefit, which is acquired by an establishment, beyond the mere value of the capital, stock, funds, or property employed therein, in consequence of the general public patronage and encouragement which it receives from constant or habitual customers, on account of its local position, or common celebrity, or reputation for skill or affluence, or punctuality, or from other accidental circumstances or necessities, or even from ancient partialities or prejudices.[140]

---

[138] 34 Eng. Rep. 129, 134 (1810).

[139] *In re: Brown* , 150 N.E. 581, 583 (N.Y. 1926).

[140] Joseph Story, "Commentaries on the Law of Partnerships," § 99, at 170 (6th ed., 1868).

The basic question surrounding the issue of personal goodwill comes from whether certain abilities, relationships, qualities, and attributes of individuals that generate income (including their reputation) can or should be distributed as marital property. Additionally, are these personal assets transferable within some reasonable time frame to the entity through an individual's cooperation?

A useful working definition of personal goodwill is "[the] part of increased earning capacity that results from the reputation, knowledge and skills of individual people, and is nontransferable and unmarketable."[141] Simply, personal goodwill is that which would make a doctor's patients follow him even if he changed his location, staff, and phone number.

California's *In re: Marriage of Lopez*[142] is an example of an early case where the court suggested a list of factors to be considered in valuing goodwill. Those five factors are:

1. The age and health of the professional
2. The professional's demonstrated earning power
3. The professional's reputation in the community for judgment, skill, and knowledge
4. The professional's comparative professional success
5. The nature and duration of the professional's practice, either as a sole proprietor or as a contributing member of a partnership or professional corporation

Upon careful review, it is clear that at least four of the five factors deal with personal attributes. Typically, the age and health of the professional is of little concern to the buyer, unless they have impacted the historical performance of the practice or are used as a negotiating ploy. The reliance on these factors implies that California falls under a value to the holder premise, as there appears to be no explicit attention drawn to the difference between the professional and the practice. In a value in exchange state, most of the five factors would be used to determine how much goodwill is dependent on the individual and should therefore be excluded from value.

Owner's Compensation   There is often an interrelationship between enterprise goodwill, personal goodwill, and the amount paid to the owner employee. One characteristic of a closely held business is that typically its owners are

---

[141] Helga White, "Professional Goodwill: Is It a Settled Question or Is There 'Value' in Discussing It?" 15 *Journal of the American Academy of Matrimonial Lawyers*, (1998), Vol. No. 2 at 499.

[142] 113 Cal. Rptr. 58, 38 Cal. App.3d 1044 (1974).

also its key employees. As a result, there is a merging of a return on labor (wages) and return on capital (profits/dividends). The valuation professional is tasked with the responsibility of separating these two returns into wages paid to the employee on an arm's-length basis and the profits generated by the business. This is a difficult task under ordinary circumstances; it becomes even harder when the enterprise is indistinguishable from the individual. The separation of these two returns is necessary under both a value in exchange and a value to the holder premise. Assuming one can estimate compensation for the replacement proxy, it is important to understand whether the resulting profits, if any, are attributable to the enterprise and therefore part of the business or merely the earning capacity of the individual.

The case of *Dugan v. Dugan*[143] laid out several factors that should be considered in an assessment of reasonable compensation, including age, experience, education, expertise, effort, and locale. In a value in exchange state, to the extent these excess profits are generated by some unique inchoate attribute, the profits in excess of the reasonable compensation, if any, are considered personal goodwill and not includable as a marital asset. In a value to the holder state, typically, the individual attributes are not explicitly excluded but are considered in the selection of reasonable compensation and in the capitalization rates used in the valuation methodology.[144]

Goodwill versus Going Concern   The Pennsylvania case *Gaydos v. Gaydos*[145] may further illuminate the character of personal goodwill. The husband, a sole-proprietor dentist, argued that the difference between the fire-sale value and the court's value (found using the average income method) was personal goodwill. The trial court said that this was simply the going-concern value of the business and, therefore, was marital property. On appeal, the Appellate Court decided that the husband, not the practice, was responsible for the net income of the business, and that going-concern value was contingent upon his continued participation, not that of another dentist at the same practice in place of him. (The appellate court was saying that the value was personal to the practitioner.)

Going-concern value, as indicated by the *Gaydos* court, is not the same as goodwill. Going-concern value refers to the intangible elements that

---

[143] 92 N.J. 423; 457 A.2d 1; 1983 N.J. LEXIS 2351.

[144] There is much debate on the methodologies to be used to determine reasonable compensation; however, that is beyond the scope of this book. For such a study, see *Dugan v. Dugan*, 92 N.J. 423; 457 A.2d 1; 1983 N.J. LEXIS 2351, or Jay E. Fishman, Shannon P. Pratt, and J. Clifford Griffith, "PPC's Guide to Business Valuation" (Thompson PPC, 2004), at 11–12.

[145] 693 A.2d (Pa. Super. Ct. 1993).

result from factors such as having a trained work force, an operational plant and the necessary licenses, systems and procedures in place. It is also based on the concept that a business enterprise is expected to continue operations into the future.[146] Business goodwill is not concerned with physical assets; instead, it can be viewed as the excess earnings the business produces due to (among other things) its reputation and skill.[147] Personal goodwill concerns the excess earnings reliant on the practitioner's personal attributes.

Exhibit 5.5 builds on the continuum of value with an additional layer showing the types of intangible value and where they fall over the full continuum. In the next section, we address the intangible values included in marital property under value in exchange, and how those are differentiated from value to the holder intangibles. Later, we will address the most inclusive intangibles under our analysis of value to the holder concepts.

EXHIBIT 5.5 Continuum of Value: Intangible Assets

Premise of Value	Value in Exchange			Value to the Holder	
Standard of Value	Fair Market Value		Fair Value		Investment Value
Intangible Value	Enterprise Goodwill May Be Minimal or Nonexistent	Enterprise Goodwill Only	Enterprise and Personal Goodwill		Personal Intangible Value
Underlying Assumption	Walk Away and Compete / Covenant Not to Compete Excluded from Value	Covenant Not to Compete Included / Covenant Not Addressed	Court's Decision	Going Concern Value Assuming Owner Will Continue Ownership	Enhanced Earnings Capacity

Distinguishing Personal and Enterprise Goodwill   Typically, commercial goodwill that has been institutionalized is considered marital property. It is when there is a question as to whether the goodwill adheres to an individual or to a business that identification and valuation of goodwill can be problematic. The requirement to distinguish between personal and enterprise goodwill often can be used as a litmus test to establish how that particular state

---

[146] "Valuations in the Business Setting: International Glossary of Business Valuation Terms" (2000). *William & Mary Annual Tax Conference.* Paper 184. <http://scholarship.law.wm.edu/tax/184>.

[147] Kathryn J. Murphy, "Business Valuations in Divorce," Dallas Chapter Texas Society of Certified Public Accountants, *1998 Divorce Conference*, September 22, 1998, at 19.

views value. In those states where a value to the holder premise is employed, the issue is almost never explicitly addressed, as there is no requirement to distinguish between transferable enterprise goodwill and nontransferable personal goodwill. Generally enterprise goodwill, the institutionalized expectancy of repeat patronage, is considered marketable. Personal goodwill, the goodwill associated with the person, generally is not marketable without the continued post-marital participation of that person.[148]

In a value in exchange state, transferable enterprise goodwill must be separated from nontransferable personal goodwill, but this is not always an easy distinction. The line between an individual's contribution to the success of a business and the success of the business itself is not necessarily clear. However, any state using fair market value or some other variation of a value in exchange premise requires the valuation practitioner to distinguish between the two concepts.

The seminal Florida case of *Thompson v. Thompson*[149] provides insight as to how that state views the distinction between personal and enterprise goodwill, in this case, in a professional practice.

THOMPSON V. THOMPSON

The Thompsons were married for 23 years. During that time, Mr. Thompson finished college, attended law school, and became an attorney specializing in personal injury and medical malpractice while Mrs. Thompson maintained the home and raised their children.

The trial court awarded Mrs. Thompson permanent periodic alimony, lump-sum alimony paid over 10 years, child support, and other real and personal property, which to some extent represented a credit for the goodwill of Mr. Thompson's sole shareholder interest in a professional association. On appeal, Mr. Thompson argued that the trial court improperly included goodwill of the professional practice as distributable marital property. The court stated that, typically, a nonprofessional spouse's efforts during the marriage increase the professional spouse's earning power and that this should be compensated with higher alimony. The court then acknowledged that if

(continued)

---

[148] Alica Brokers Kelly, "Sharing a Piece of the Future Post-Divorce: Toward a More Equitable Distribution of Professional Goodwill," 51 *Rutgers Law Review*, (Spring 1999), at 588.

[149] 576 So.2d 267 (Fl. Supr. Ct. 1991).

indeed professional goodwill exists and was developed during the marriage, it should be included in the marital estate upon dissolution.

The court had defined goodwill as the advantage or benefit a business has beyond the value of its property and capital. The court then reviewed the treatment of professional goodwill in various states, finally settling in agreement with the Missouri case, *Hanson v. Hanson*,[150] which stated that professional goodwill is property that attaches to and is dependent upon an existing business entity. Any personal component, including a person's reputation and skill, however, are not components of goodwill in a professional practice and therefore are not subject to equitable distribution.

The Missouri court went on to define goodwill as the value of the practice that exceeds tangible assets that is dependent on clients returning to the business irrespective of the participation of the individual practitioner. If goodwill depends on the practitioner, it is not marketable, and represents probable future earning capacity, which may be relevant to determining alimony but not property distribution.

The Thompson court directed that fair market value was the clearest method by which to value a business, and directed that it should be the exclusive method of measuring the goodwill in a professional association.

Unfortunately, *Thompson* refers to fair market value as a method of value and not a standard of value. While approaches and methods can be used to establish fair market value, the term *fair market value* is a standard under which various approaches and methods are employed.

In some practices, the viability of the practice may be dependent on the continued participation of an individual practitioner, making it difficult to distinguish between enterprise goodwill and the individual practitioner's reputation. Courts that look for a transactional value have in some cases excluded the consideration of goodwill in a professional practice altogether because of either its lack of marketability or its reliance on a particular individual. Other courts have acknowledged that goodwill in a professional practice may have elements of both personal and enterprise goodwill, suggesting that there would be a value to the enterprise in the sale of the business to another individual. At the other end of the continuum, courts in states that favor a value to the holder premise will likely not differentiate

---

[150] 738 S.W.2d 429, 434 (Mo. Supr. Ct. 1987).

between personal and enterprise goodwill as no transaction is contemplated and therefore the transferability issue is not as relevant.

Because of the service aspect of their operations, professional practices and other service businesses are where the personal/enterprise goodwill issue is most evident. A group or partnership type of professional practice might have less reliance on personal goodwill, as it may involve several individuals providing the service and transferability in the form of partners buying in or out of a practice. Other commercial enterprises, including manufacturing, retailing, and wholesaling, may not be as reliant on an individual; therefore, personal goodwill may be less prevalent, depending on the nature of the firm and its management structure. Of course, these are all flexible concepts that will vary based on the circumstances of any given enterprise.

Either the stated or implied standard of value in a given state probably will have the largest effect on the elements of goodwill of a professional practice that are identified as marital property. Indiana's *Yoon v. Yoon*[151]is a case where a court attempted to distinguish personal and enterprise goodwill in a professional corporation.

YOON V. YOON

Upon dissolution of marriage, the court ordered Dr. Yoon to pay child support to his wife and divided the marital estate 55% to his spouse. The value of the estate included Yoon's medical practice. Former Indiana case law had established that the goodwill of a professional practice could be included in the marital estate. Dr. Yoon appealed the valuation of this goodwill, as he asserted it represented his future earning capacity that had already been used as a reason to unequally divide property (55% versus 45%) for the benefit of his wife.

The court established that goodwill in a professional practice may be attributable to the business by virtue of arrangements with suppliers, customers, or others, and its anticipated future customer base. However, it may also be attributable to the owner's personal skill, training, or reputation. The court recognized that case law from other jurisdictions has recognized enterprise goodwill as a divisible asset. However, reviewing previous Indiana case law, the court viewed personal goodwill as indivisible future earning capacity. In order to determine whether goodwill should be included in the
(continued)

---

[151] 711 N.E.2d 1265; 1999.

estate, the court must determine what portion of it is attributable to the individual and exclude that value.

As to the valuation, the wife's expert used an "intrinsic value" in determining the value "to the physician." The court determined that this value was the physician's future earning capacity. In its decision, the court explained that enterprise goodwill was subject to equitable distribution, whereas personal goodwill could affect only the relative distribution of property, stating the following:

> . . . before including the goodwill of a self-employed business or professional practice in a marital estate, a court must determine that the goodwill is attributable to the business as opposed to the owner as an individual. If attributable to the individual, it is not a divisible asset and is properly considered only as future earning capacity that may affect the relative property division. In this respect, the future earning capacity of a self-employed person (or an owner of a business primarily dependent on the owner's services) is to be treated the same as the future earning capability and reputation of an employee.

The court considered whether any value was actually attributed to the value of the practice rather than Yoon's reputation and remanded the valuation to the lower court to remove the value of personal goodwill. On remand, the case was settled before the lower court issued an opinion.

Following *Yoon*, the case of *Bobrow v. Bobrow*[152] discussed the enterprise goodwill of the accounting firm Ernst & Young. In this business, the facts of the case established that no individual owner had any personal goodwill in the entity and therefore only enterprise goodwill existed.

BOBROW V. BOBROW

In a divorce action, the husband had a partnership interest in a division of the Big Four accounting firm Ernst & Young (E&Y).

---

[152] State of Indiana, Hamilton Superior Court No. 29D01-0003-DR-166.

Although there was a partnership agreement limiting the owner's interest to the value of the capital account, thereby excluding goodwill, the partner, Mr. Bobrow, conceded that the agreement applied only to a transaction of his partnership interest (resignation, retirement, or death).

Based on the finding in *Yoon*, the court recognized that the assets of E&Y were not personal to the partner but belonged to the institution of which each partner had a share. These institutional assets included such intangible assets as E&Y's trade name. Specifically, E&Y, the entity, has a favorable business reputation and name recognition. E&Y owns the methods and tools that provide value to the firm. E&Y has relationships with suppliers. All these items were transferable to an outside purchaser. This case contrasts with the case of *Yoon*, where all these assets were associated with the doctor himself rather than the entity and the court found that they could not be transferred to another individual.

Ultimately, because of the Indiana law as interpreted by *Yoon*, the court included the value of enterprise goodwill in valuing E&Y and awarded Mrs. Bobrow a share of the value of Mr. Bobrow's partnership interest in E&Y based on his pro rata share of the value of the enterprise.

Because of its conclusion of value as the pro rata share of the enterprise value, *Bobrow* may be construed as a fair value case under the value in exchange premise. Despite a buy–sell agreement that specified only payment of what was in the capital account, the court valued Mr. Bobrow's ownership at his pro rata share of the enterprise, similar to the way it would be treated under a fair value standard in a dissenting or oppressed shareholders' case. The asset can be sold, enterprise goodwill may be valued, and no personal goodwill is involved. However, were this to be viewed under the fair market value standard, typically discounts would be considered for both lack of control and lack of marketability. We discuss this distinction later on in the chapter.

There has also been substantial debate as to whether the value of goodwill in a sole proprietorship should be treated in the same manner as an interest in a partnership or a closely held corporation. In a sole proprietorship, the value of the business may be inherently more dependent on the proprietor than it would be for a business owned and managed by several operators working together. The Pennsylvania case *Beasley v. Beasley*[153] noted this difference by stating:

> A sole proprietor can be distinguished from a partnership, or a professional corporation, to which an ascertainable value can be ascribed for the purpose of buying into or withdrawing from the relationship: but it is the association, or some share of it, that is valued and not the individual partner upon which the value is placed. . . . When a sole proprietor terminates his activity, the lights go out, the value of the sole proprietorship is extinguished and is non-transferable.

A number of states follow Pennsylvania's *Beasley* in recognizing that goodwill exists in a professional practice, but typically not in a sole proprietorship. These include Alaska,[154] Connecticut,[155] Maryland,[156] Nebraska,[157] Oklahoma,[158] Minnesota,[159] Louisiana,[160] Ohio,[161] Tennessee,[162] and Utah.[163]

Nebraska's *Taylor v. Taylor*[164] commented on the dependence of goodwill on the continued efforts of a particular individual. This comment was later cited in Florida's *Thompson v. Thompson*[165] in determining whether personal goodwill should be included in the value of a professional practice. The *Taylor* court indicated that:

> If goodwill depends on the continued presence of a particular individual, such goodwill, by definition, is not a marketable asset distinct from the individual. Any value which attaches to the entity solely as a result of personal goodwill represents nothing more than probable future earning capacity, which, although relevant

---

[153] 518 A.2d 545 (Pa. Super. Ct., 1986).

[154] *Moffitt v. Moffitt*, 813 P.2d 674 (Al. Supr. Ct. 1991).

[155] *Cardillo v. Cardillo* , 1992 WL 139248 (Conn. Super. Ct 1992).

[156] *Prahinski v. Prahinski* , 540 A.2d 833 (Md. Spec. App. 1988).

[157] *Taylor v. Taylor* , 386 N.W.2d 851 (Neb. 1986).

[158] *Travis v. Travis*, 795 P.2d 96 (Okla. 1990).

[159] *Roth v. Roth* , 406 N.W.2d 77 (Minn. App. 1987).

[160] *Depner v. Depner*, 478 So.2d 532 (La. App. 1985).

[161] *Burma v. Burma* , No. 65062 (Ohio App. 8 Dist. Sept. 29, 1994).

[162] *Smith v. Smith* , 709 S.W.2d 588 (Tenn. App. 1985).

[163] *Sorenson v. Sorenson* (769 P.2d 820 (Utah App. 1989), *aff'd* 839 P.2d 774 (Utah 1992).

[164] *Taylor v. Taylor* , 386 N.W.2d 851 (Neb. 1986).

[165] 576 So.2d 267; 1991 Fla. LEXIS.

in determining alimony, is not a proper consideration in dividing marital property in a dissolution proceeding.[166]

Walk-Away Value   In the Florida case *Held v. Held*,[167] the trial court relied on the opinion of one expert who claimed that a non-solicitation agreement was part of enterprise goodwill. On appeal, the court ruled that the lower court impermissibly valued personal goodwill in the non-solicitation agreement and remanded, directing the trial court to use only the adjusted book value in determining the fair market value of the business. Similarly, as discussed earlier, the court in Hawaii's *Antolik v. Harvey*[168] criticized the lower court for not considering that the chiropractor would compete upon the sale of his business.

Under this fairly narrow view of fair market value, the assumption is that the seller could and would compete with the buyer, thereby taking nearly all of the otherwise transferable goodwill. In these instances, the business's value would most likely be close to the net tangible assets of the business. Under a more conventional interpretation of fair market value, the seller would cooperate, to some extent, with the buyer. For this reason, some refer to states that apply the more narrow view of fair market value in this fashion as walk-away value states.

The following states have cases that use language implying the walk-away standard.

State	Source
Delaware	*S.S. v. C.S.*[169]
Florida	*Williams v. Williams*[170]
Hawaii	*Antolik v. Harvey*[171]
Kansas	*Powell v. Powell*[172]
Mississippi	*Singley v. Singley*[173]
Missouri	*Taylor v. Taylor*[174]
South Carolina	*Hickum v. Hickum*[175]

---

[166] *Id.*

[167] 912 So.2d 637 (Fla. App. 2005).

[168] 761 P.2d 305(Haw. Interm. App. 1988).

[169] LEXIS 213 (Del. Fam. Ct. Aug. 22, 2003).

[170] 667 So.2d 915 (Fla. Dist. Ct. App. 1996).

[171] 761 P.2d 305(Haw. Interm. App. 1988).

[172] 648 P.2d 218 (Kan. Supr. Ct. 1982).

[173] LEXIS 283 (Miss. Supr. Ct. 2003).

[174] 736 S.W.2d 388 (Mo. Supr. Ct. 1987).

[175] 463 S.E.2d 321 (S.C. Ct. App. 1995).

Merging of Personal and Practice Goodwill There may also be instances when the value of the personal goodwill merges with the enterprise goodwill. This normally results from the professional's choice to grow the practice and surround him- or herself with capable people and institutionalize the personal goodwill. As an example of institutionalization, the Mayo Clinic is a business whose personal goodwill has merged with its practice goodwill. It is fairly obvious that no one goes to the Mayo Clinic to be treated by someone named Mayo, but the reputation of the practice is such that people will travel from around the country to be treated there.[176] The enterprise goodwill could (and normally does) exceed the value of the personal goodwill when the personal goodwill has been institutionalized.

Covenant Not to Compete The lack of transferability of personal goodwill is part of the reason why many courts will exclude it as marital property. However, some elements of personal goodwill may be transferred over time by an individual who will participate in the transition by, at a minimum, signing a covenant not to compete.[177]

> Neither an editor nor lawyer, nor a physician, can transfer to another his style, his learning, or his manners. Either however, can add to the chances of success and profit of another who embarks in the same business in the same field, by withdrawing as a competitor. So that the one sells and the other buys something valuable . . . the one sells his prospective patronage, and the other buys the right to compete with all others for it, and to be protected against competition from his vendor.[178]

By paying for the restriction of the former owner's ability to practice, the buyer effectively purchases some of the personal goodwill that would otherwise take away clients.[179] The transition may also include a consulting contract, whereby the seller is compensated for remaining at the corporation to help transition the company to the buyer, thereby transferring a portion of his or her personal goodwill to the corporation.

---

[176] Fishman, "Personal Goodwill v. Enterprise Goodwill."

[177] Jay E. Fishman, Shannon P. Pratt, and Clifford Griffith, "PPC's Guide to Business Valuation," at 1205.19. Reference to Minnesota case, *Sweere v. Gilbert-Sweere*, 534 N.W.2d 294 (Minn. Ct. App. 1995).

[178] *Mcfadden v. Jenkins* , 40 N.D.422, 442, 169 N.W. 151, 155-56 (1918) (quoting *Cowan v. Fairbrother*, 118 N.C. 406, 411-12, 24 S.E. 212, 213 (1896)).

[179] John Dwight Ingram, "Covenants Not to Compete," 36 *Akron Law Review*, No. 49 (2002), at 51.

The existence of a covenant not to compete may transfer some of an individual's goodwill to the enterprise. Interestingly, the necessity of a covenant indicates two important points. The first is that the buyer perceives that eventually the goodwill can be transferred, and the second is that at the valuation date, some or all of the goodwill still belongs to the seller. Since personal goodwill, by its very nature, is inextricably tied to the individual, most states consider a covenant not to compete as separate property.

In other words, jurisdictions in which the value in exchange premise is used most often consider a covenant not to compete as proof that some goodwill is indeed personal and therefore excludable from the marital estate, and therefore any proceeds from such covenant would be separate property. In a value to the holder state, however, the issue is typically not addressed because a sale is not necessarily contemplated.

The Florida case *Williams v. Williams*[180] considers the effect of a covenant not to compete. In this case, the Court of Appeals elaborated on the decision in *Thompson v. Thompson*, where the fair market value standard was decided to be the determining factor in valuing goodwill.

WILLIAMS V. WILLIAMS

Mr. Williams sought review of the lower court's valuation of property, which determined his accounting practice had distributable goodwill. The court acknowledged that under Florida law, the goodwill of a professional practice may be distributed if indeed it exists and was developed during the marriage. However, relying on the decision of the *Thompson* court, it must exist separately from the reputation of an individual.

Mrs. Williams's expert discussed the sales of other accounting practices, but the court found little similarity between those businesses and that of Mr. Williams. Mr. Williams's expert testified that no one would buy his practice without a covenant not to compete. Essentially, without that covenant, there is reason to believe that Mr. Williams's clients would follow him to his new practice, and his old practice would have little if any value above the net assets.

The court decided that the existence of goodwill in the practice was not established, as Mr. Williams was the only accountant, performing all the work and dealing with the clients himself.

---

[180] 667 So.2d 915.

The South Carolina case *Ellerbie v. Ellerbie*[181]is an example where a court decided that the value of an actual covenant not to compete should not be included as distributable property. In this case, there was an actual transaction with a sale agreement entitled "Merger Asset Acquisition Agreement and Covenant Not to Compete." This agreement indicated that $422,000 was paid for the assets of the business and $1,200,000 was paid for a covenant not to compete. The court decided that, in this case, the value of the covenant not to compete was separate property and therefore should not be included in the value of the business. It should be mentioned that in these examples it is assumed that the covenants were to prevent sellers who were capable of competing from being able to compete and not just an alternative way of structuring a sale.

The Oregon case of *Slater v. Slater*[182] addressed the issue of whether one should assume that the business owner would execute a covenant not to compete as part of a transaction. The Court of Appeals of Oregon indicated that:

> On de novo review, we agree with the husband that the trial court erred in predicating its value of the business—and, particularly, its goodwill—on the assumption that the husband would execute a noncompetition covenant.[183]

The court reversed and remanded it to the trial court to determine a value for the chiropractic practice without the execution of a covenant by the owner/husband.

The Minnesota case *Sweere v. Gilbert Sweere*[184] specifically addressed the value of a covenant not to compete. In this case, the court had to decide whether $200,000 from a noncompete agreement should be included in the divorce settlement as marital property. The court found that the portion of the money paid that compensates the spouse for restricting post-marital personal service was separate property. However, any of the payments made to secure transfer of corporate assets was marital property. Ultimately, the court concluded that the purpose of the agreement may have been to prevent Mr. Sweere from interfering with the transfer of goodwill. To this extent, the noncompete was representative of marital goodwill, not post-marital labor and was included in the marital property.[185]

---

[181] 323 S.C. 283; 473 S.E.2d 881; 1996 S.C. App. LEXIS 113.

[182] 245 P.3d 676 (Ore. Ct. App. 2010).

[183] *Id* .

[184] 534 N.W.2d 294; 1995 Minn. App. LEXIS 912.

[185] Fishman, Pratt, and Griffith, "PPC's Guide to Business Valuation."

As we have discussed, value in exchange states assume that there will be a hypothetical sale and seek to value the asset based on what would be realizable in a such a sale between a willing buyer and a willing seller at or near a specifically delineated valuation date. These states choose to exclude personal goodwill.

Exhibit 5.6 shows the value in exchange portion of the continuum of value and case examples of the differing treatments of the covenants not to compete falling under the associated standards, premises, and treatments of intangible value.

At the leftmost end of the continuum of value are the states in which the title holder is viewed as if he or she would not sign a covenant and would compete immediately with anyone who would buy the business. Assuming that the business's goodwill was personal, typically, in this case, there will be very little value to the business above the tangible assets, if the practice has not merged the personal goodwill into enterprise goodwill. The further one moves to the right on the continuum, the longer the transition between the sale and the departure of the seller.

EXHIBIT 5.6 Continuum of Value: Intangible Assets under Value in Exchange with Case Examples

Premise of Value	Value in Exchange		
Standard of Value	Fair Market Value		Fair Value
Intangible Value Case Example	Enterprise Goodwill May Be Minimal or Nonexistent	Enterprise Goodwill Only	
	Williams v. Williams	*Thompson v. Thompson/Sweere v. Gilbert-Sweere*	
Underlying Assumption	Walk Away and Compete	Covenant Not to Compete Included	Court's
	Covenant Not to Compete Excluded from Value	Covenant Not Addressed	Discretion

As set forth in the continuum of value chart in Appendix C:

1. Four states (Delaware, Kansas, Mississippi and South Carolina) appear to hold that neither enterprise nor personal goodwill is marital.
2. Thirty-three states (Alaska, Arkansas, Connecticut, District of Columbia, Florida, Georgia, Hawaii, Idaho, Illinois, Indiana, Kentucky, Louisiana, Maine, Maryland, Massachusetts, Minnesota, Missouri, Nebraska, New Hampshire, North Dakota, Ohio, Oklahoma, Oregon, Pennsylvania, Rhode Island, Tennessee, Texas, Utah, Vermont, Virginia,

West Virginia, Wisconsin, and Wyoming) hold that only enterprise goodwill is marital.

3. Eleven states (Arizona, California, Colorado, Michigan, Montana, Nevada, New Jersey, New Mexico, New York, North Carolina, and Washington) hold that both are marital.

4. Three states (Alabama, Iowa, and South Dakota) have no clear decisions concerning this issue.

Before moving on to the treatment of intangible assets under value to the holder and the standard of investment value, we need to address shareholder-level discounts and the weight afforded buy–sell agreements as viewed under value in exchange.

Lack of Control and Marketability Discounts under Value in Exchange

Lack of control and marketability discounts are also issues that merit discussion in the context of value in exchange as compared to value to the holder. A state's treatment of these discounts can be another indicia of the premise and standard of value under which courts in that state view valuation in divorce matters. Theoretically, those standards of value that fall under the value in exchange premise typically require the explicit consideration of lack of control and marketability discounts (commonly referred to as *shareholder-level discounts*) to the value of the owner's shares in recognition of what a willing buyer would pay for the owner's shares upon a hypothetical sale. Alternatively, a standard of value falling under a value to the holder premise does not require explicit consideration of these discounts, as they would be applicable only upon sale, and a sale is not contemplated under this standard. Some states do not fit neatly into either category. Additionally, some states apply a standard more closely akin to fair value as used in dissenting shareholder matters, as buyers or sellers may not be willing, as required by fair market value. These states generally do not apply shareholder-level discounts.

In the U.S. Tax Court, discounts for lack of control and of marketability are generally considered and, when appropriate, applied in the determination of fair market value. The application of these types of shareholder-level discounts in matters of dissenting and oppressed shareholders and the divorce context can be more problematic. As we discussed in Chapter 3, in dissenting and oppressed shareholder matters, absent extraordinary circumstances, the courts and the law associations have been trending toward the elimination of shareholder-level discounts. The reasoning for this trend is that, since neither buyer nor seller are willing participants, the moving party should be compensated for what was taken—either the pro rata share of a going concern or what the owner would have reasonably expected to receive from continuing involvement with the enterprise.

In our view, the treatment of shareholder-level discounts can provide additional insight into separating states into value in exchange, value to the holder, or hybrid states. Typically, value in exchange states that use the fair market value standard require consideration of shareholder-level discounts; value to the holder states using some version of investment value do not. Hybrid states use a combination of standards and may also use fair value as a standard.

Does intention to sell matter in the application of discounts? Typically, under the fair market value standard, the intention to sell may have an impact only on the size of the discounts. Since fair market value assumes a hypothetical sale of the business or business interest, normally shareholder-level discounts such as a discount for lack of control or marketability are considered and, where appropriate, applied. However, in some instances there is a question of whether shareholder-level discounts should be applied at all, given the facts and circumstances of the case. The fair market value standard mandates *consideration* of shareholder-level discounts, not the automatic application of them.

To some courts, the intention to sell is an important factor in determining what stream of income the individual can expect to receive and whether shareholder-level discounts should be applied. The Oregon case *Tofte v. Tofte*[186] directly addresses this point.

TOFTE V. TOFTE

At the dissolution of marriage, the husband worked at and had a minority interest in his family's amusement park business. He had various responsibilities, including supervision of maintenance and designing and creating attractions for the park.

Both appraisers used the capitalization of net earnings method of valuation, agreeing on a multiple of nine times net earnings. Their valuations differed on the application of discounts. The trial court relied on the husband's expert's testimony that to arrive at fair market value, the shares should be discounted 35% for the shares being a minority interest and lacking marketability.

(continued)

---

[186] 134 Ore. App. 449; 895 P.2d 1387; 1995 Ore. App. LEXIS 772.

The wife's expert argued that the yearly bonus awarded to the husband would be attractive enough to entice a willing buyer to pay full price. However, the husband's expert testified that the bonuses bore no relation to the shares held. The bonus was not seen as a return on the shares of stock.

Additionally, the wife argued that discounts should not be included in the calculation of husband's stock value as he had no intention to sell his share of the company. The court found that intention to sell did not matter in the determination of value of a close family corporation, and discounts should therefore be applied.

The Colorado Supreme Court was confronted with similar circumstances in *In re: Marriage of Thornhill*[187] as the wife argued that no discounts should be applied and the standard of value for divorce purposes should be fair value.

IN RE: MARRIAGE OF THORNHILL

This is a 27-year marriage where the husband worked in the oil business. Husband started an oil and gas equipment sales and service business in 2001. He owned 70.5% of the business, or a controlling interest.

During most of the parties' marriage, the husband worked various jobs in the oil and natural gas industries while the wife worked part-time at miscellaneous low-wage jobs. In 2001, he started a company called NRG, which was in the oil and gas services business.

Upon separation, parties in Colorado can enter into an agreement for maintenance and the disposition of property. Husband–wife entered into an agreement, wherein the husband's interest in the value of the business was valued at $1,625,000 after a 33% discount for lack of marketability. By the time of the hearing, the wife had realized that the husband's representation as to the value was, in her opinion, too low.

Because of the Separation Agreement, the record at the trial court level suggests that the trial court never expressly ruled on

---

[187] 2010 WL-216-9086, June 1, 2010.

> the applicability of a marketability discount, but merely found the Separation Agreement, which used such a discount when determining the value of the husband's controlling interest in the Company, for the purposes of dividing the party's assets, valid and enforceable.

Thornhill is an important case relative to the standard of value. In this case, the wife attempted to argue that the holding in *Pueblo*,[188] a dissenters' shareholder case, was equally applicable in marital dissolution matters. The Supreme Court of Colorado disagreed and indicated that, because of the statutory language in the dissenters' and oppressed statutes, fair value was appropriate.

Since no such language is contained in the marital dissolution statute, the court refused to extend the holding in *Pueblo* to marital dissolution matters.

Accordingly, although there are cases in Colorado that would indicate that certain types of assets are closer to value to the holder than others, *Thornhill* indicates that the application of the marketability discount is at the court's discretion.

Using consideration and, if appropriate, the application of shareholder-level discounts as criteria to determine the applicable standard of value, these states can be categorized as fair market value states: Alaska, Arkansas, Connecticut, Florida, Hawaii, Idaho, Illinois, Indiana, Iowa, Kentucky, Louisiana, Michigan, Minnesota, Mississippi, Missouri, Nebraska, New Hampshire, New York, North Carolina, Ohio, Oregon, Rhode Island, South Carolina, South Dakota, Texas, Vermont, West Virginia, and Wisconsin.

When one uses the treatment of goodwill along with the application of shareholder-level discounts as two criteria for determining the standard of value, one may find that a state's treatment of each issue is not consistent with just one standard of value. For example, a state may not require the distinguishing of personal from enterprise goodwill, which suggests a value to the holder premise, but the state may also require consideration of shareholder-level discounts.

Fair Value

As mentioned previously, fair value is not the same as fair market value. While fair market value considers a willing buyer and a willing seller,

---

[188] *Pueblo Bancorporation v. Lindoe, Inc.* ,63 P.3d 353 (Colorado 2003).

generally when fair value is at issue, one of the parties is not willing. There-fore, in order to compensate that party fairly, special considerations are made.

In dissenters' rights and oppressed stockholder cases, in many states, these special considerations consist of disallowing discounts or applying them only in extraordinary circumstances. Upon divorce, the court may also decide that it would be unfair to apply discounts to the value of shares, re-gardless of how it treats personal goodwill. In those instances, courts have used a spouse's pro rata share of enterprise value, which is language nor-mally associated with fair value.

The outcome of the Virginia case of *Howell v. Howell*[189] represents value in exchange without discounts. This case addresses the applicability of discounts while excluding any personal goodwill present by virtue of an individual's reputation. This case is often referred to as a fair value case.

HOWELL V. HOWELL

Mr. Howell, the defendant, had a partnership interest in Hunton & Williams, a law firm he joined during the marriage. Virginia case law indicates that transferable enterprise goodwill may be marital, but personal reputation and future earning capacity are not. Virginia law also prohibits the sale of the goodwill of a law firm. Additionally, the Hunton & Williams partnership agreement provides that when a partner withdraws from the firm, he may receive the balance of his capital account with his share of the firm's net income through the date of withdrawal. The court looked at whether any goodwill should be included in distributable assets, and if so, how to calculate it.

Citing a previous Virginia case,[190] the court acknowledged that the trial court's duty is to determine the value that represents the property's intrinsic worth to the parties and that although a restric-tive agreement may exist, it should not control value. The court re-viewed various other decisions in Virginia's courts as well as others from other states, and the commissioner determined that the evi-dence demonstrated that the partnership had goodwill regardless of the provisions of the partnership agreement.

---

[189] 46 Va. Cir. 339; 1998 Va. Cir. LEXIS 256.

[190] *Bosserman v. Bosserman*, 9 Va. App. 1, 5, 384 S.E.2d 104 (1989).

> The experts disagreed on the appropriate discount to be applied to value the shares. The defendant's expert applied a 40% lack of marketability discount, and the plaintiff's expert applied a 6.9% discount. The commissioner found that the lack of control was not an issue worth discounting, as no one partner had a controlling interest in the firm. The court similarly found that a discount for lack of marketability was inappropriate, as the highest and best use for the defendant's share was to remain with the corporation. The appellate court found that the commissioner's determination of value had been appropriate.

In this case, the court used the concept of highest and best use, reasoning that the highest value that would be realized was that which would be achieved through the owner's continued presence, not upon sale, and that therefore discounts should not be applied. While Virginia requires one to distinguish personal and enterprise goodwill, thereby implying a titled spouse's departure, the court in this case considered that the highest and best use was the title holder's continued presence. This case appears to have elements of both fair market value and investment value. We have categorized it as fair value because it calculates the value as a pro rata share of the enterprise value.

The New Jersey case *Brown v. Brown*[191] addresses the valuation of a wholesale flower distributor in a marital dissolution case in terms resembling those normally found in fair value in oppression and dissenters' rights matters. In this case, no distinction was made as to personal or enterprise goodwill, and the issue at hand between the valuation experts was whether marketability and minority discounts should be applied.

BROWN V. BROWN

James Brown was an officer of and had a 47.5% interest in a florist supply company. Mr. Brown had a reported W-2 income of $75,000, 1099 income of $75,000, and interest income of $7,131. The trial court had accepted the wife's expert's valuation of Mr. Brown's interest in the company at $561,925, excluding any discount for marketability or lack of control.

(continued)

---

[191] 348 N.J. Super. 466; 792 A.2d 463.

The wife's expert valued the business as a whole as of the date of complaint and then took a percentage to establish the husband's proportionate interest. He assumed that the pro rata value of that interest should be included in equitable distribution. The husband's expert valued the same interest but applied a 25% discount for lack of marketability and a 15% discount for lack of control.

The court found no previous decisions in New Jersey addressing the applicability of discounts for the purposes of equitable distribution. After reviewing the assumptions and elements of both valuations, the court was more persuaded by the testimony of the wife's expert. As the corporation in question was a close corporation, any liquidity issues were not of consequence as there was no intention to sell the business, and therefore the fair value should be assessed. The court referred to the fair value determination made in *Balsamides v. Protameen Chemicals, Inc.*[192] (an oppression case) and *Lawson Mardon Wheaton, Inc. v. Smith*[193] (a dissenters' rights case).

The appellate court stated:

> The ALI cautions that **valuation** contexts other than dissenting shareholder appraisal rights, such as tax **valuations,** may warrant a different approach to discounting, ALI Principles § 7.22, comment at 325-26. However, we see no reason for a different approach in equitable distribution. Even James's expert, Barson, admitted that the value of a minority bloc of stock is not to be discounted for lack of control under New Jersey's "fair value" statutes. He did not offer any explanation for adopting a different rule for purposes of equitable distribution. While Barson cited a [*490] controlling shareholder's "power to change the bottom line" as one rationale for applying a discount here, no single shareholder controlled Florist or its officers' bottom line.
>
> The record before us reveals no extraordinary circumstances related to the operation or control of the Florist to warrant a [***40] discount from the fair value of the company for lack of marketability, or a discount from the value of James's interest for his minority bloc. Under these circumstances, and consistent with the reasoning of our Supreme

---

[192] 160 N.J. 352, 368, 734 A.2d 721 (1999) (*Balsamides*).
[193] 160 N.J. 383, 397, 734 A.2d 738 (1999) (*Lawson*).

> Court, we see no reason to reduce the proportionate value of James's 47 1/2 shares (47 1/2 %) for lack of liquidity (marketability discount) or lack of control (minority discount).
>
> Given the purpose of equitable distribution to fairly divide the accumulated wealth of a marital partnership, and that the purpose of valuing the shareholder spouse's interest is to determine the non-owner spouse's fair share of other marital assets; where the shareholder will retain his shares and the **divorce** will not trigger a sale of those shares, lack of liquidity does not affect the fair value of the minority interest. Neither discount is appropriate.

Brown has elements of fair value, with its rejection of discounts, and investment value, in the consideration that the business is not likely to be sold. The case states that the husband will receive the benefits of ownership by continuing to hold the asset. As mentioned previously, *Brown* was referenced in the *Grelier*[194] case in Alabama.

GRELIER V. GRELIER

This case of first impression in Alabama dealt with an ownership interest in a real estate development entity. The case went to the Alabama Court of Appeals twice and included that court at one point withdrawing its decision upon rehearing.

In this case, the husband had a 25% ownership interest in a commercial real estate development entity. A special master valued the interest, on a pro rata basis, at just over $1 million. The trial court accepted the special master's value but applied a 40% combined discount for minority interest and lack of marketability as testified by the husband's expert. The trial court concluded that "to do otherwise would ignore the reality of the financial condition of these parties." The parties had lived beyond their means and incurred significant credit card and other debt. Moreover, a number of the husband's real development projects had negative equity.

(continued)

---

[194] *Grelier* III. 2009 WL 5149267 (Ala Civ. App.) (Dec. 30, 2009).

The wife appealed the trial court's decision on a number of issues, including the application of the 40% combined discount for minority interest and lack of marketability. The wife argued that it is inappropriate to apply such discounts to a closely held business for divorce purposes as it was a going concern and was not being sold. Initially, the Court of Civil Appeals issued an opinion that affirmed the discounts as it indicated in the agreement appointing the special master that both parties agreed to have the special master determine the fair market value of the husband's 25% interest.

Upon re-hearing, that opinion was withdrawn and the Court of Appeals issued a new opinion. In that opinion, the court analogized a divorce case to a shareholder's dissent case. Coming to a conclusion that no discount for minority interest and lack of marketability should be applied and referring to *Brown* from New Jersey, the Alabama Civil Courts indicated:

> Because the Alabama Supreme Court has adopted the same reasoning that is applied in New Jersey in dissenting-shareholder cases, it seems reasonable to conclude that it would follow the same reasoning in divorce cases involving minority ownership of closely held business organization.

North Dakota also has two decisions where the court looks to determine fair value. One of these cases[195] looked at a situation where the only way the wife could recover her interest would be to file as an oppressed shareholder; therefore, in the divorce proceeding, the court awarded her the fair value of her interest without discounts for lack of marketability and lack of control. In another case,[196] the court upheld the judgment of the trial court that a small discount for lack of control status would be equitable. In these cases, it appears that the courts may have been looking for an equitable solution and not strictly applying a particular standard of value.

In the 2003 *Sommers*[197] case and the 2011 *Nuveen*[198] case, the North Dakota courts set the standard as fair market value.

---

[195] *Fisher v. Fisher*, 1997 N.D. 176; 568 N.W.2d 728; 1997 N.D. LEXIS 195.

[196] *Kaiser v. Kaiser* , 555 N.W.2d 585; 1996 N.D. LEXIS 253.

[197] *Sommers v. Sommers* , 660 N.W.2d 586 (N.D. Supr. Ct. 2003).

[198] *Nuveen v. Nuveen* , 795 N.W.2d 308 (N.D. Supr. Ct. 2011).

In summary, three states appear to follow something close to a fair value standard under a value in exchange premise: Alabama, Massachusetts, and Virginia. Exhibit 5.7 shows the continuum of value with respect to the treatment of shareholder-level discounts.

EXHIBIT 5.7   Continuum of Value: Discounts under Fair Market Value and Fair Value

Premise of Value	Value in Exchange		Value to Holder
Standard of Value	Fair Market Value	Fair Value	
Discounts	Discounts Applied	No Discounts	
Case Example	*Tofte v. Tofte*	*Howell v. Howell*	
		Brown v. Brown	

Buy–Sell Agreements under Value in Exchange

Many times, when valuing a business, especially a professional practice, there are agreements in place between shareholders or partners that provide for the treatment of a shareholder or partner upon death, retirement, or other manner of withdrawal.

The existence of a partnership or shareholder agreement may have an impact on value because many such agreements serve to delineate the amount participants would receive upon certain circumstances. In a divorce proceeding, many view such agreements as indicia of value but not necessarily as presumptive of value. Still other states view the existence of such an agreement, if timely, arm's-length, and acted upon, as the sole indicator of value.

Logically, states that more closely adhere to a fair market value standard may be inclined to rely more heavily on such an agreement if it meets the above-mentioned criteria. However, if a buy–sell agreement exists but has never actually been used, it would have far less impact than a buy–sell agreement that is regularly updated and enforced.[199] Moreover, states that more closely adhere to an investment value standard may assign little, if any, weight to these agreements, because there is no sale. It has been our

---

[199] Frank Louis, "Economic Realism: A Proposed Standard," *New Jersey Institute of Continuing Legal Education 2005 Family Law Symposium.*

experience that under any standard of value, the weight accorded a buy–sell agreement is fact sensitive.

Under the value in exchange premise, buy–sell agreements are usually viewed in two ways. First, the agreement may be considered presumptive because, upon selling his or her shares, the amount stated in the agreement is all a shareholder would likely receive. Conversely, a court looking to apply a fair market value standard might afford the value of the buy–sell agreement little weight, as it does not represent what a hypothetical willing buyer would pay a hypothetical willing seller in an open market.

Many courts have taken the value set forth in buy–sell agreements under consideration, but few have considered such agreements consistently controlling for the purposes of divorce. For example, Pennsylvania's *Buckl v. Buckl*[200] stated that a buy–sell agreement or other such agreement should be considered as a factor in valuing a business. It does not establish, however, that the value established by that agreement must be controlling.

The Connecticut case of *Dahill v. Dahill*[201] discussed this matter as well, adhering more closely to the hypothetical nature of fair market value.

DAHILL V. DAHILL

Mr. Dahill had an interest in a family business. As Mr. Dahill was ill, he entered into a shareholder's agreement with the other shareholder. The agreement offered a right of first refusal for Mr. Dahill's shares to his son and established a purchase price upon death. Upon termination, however, Mr. Dahill had the right to sell his shares on the open market.

Mrs. Dahill's expert valued the shares at 1.5 times book value, or $1,100,000—the value from the agreement that controlled upon Mr. Dahill's death. The expert conceded that this was not the fair market value of the shares but Mr. Dahill's value in hand. Mr. Dahill testified that his shares were worth $350,000 based on an expert's valuation from 1992. However, the court felt that this date was too far past to be controlling.

The court appointed an expert who assessed the fair market value of Mr. Dahill's interest in the company at $490,000, after applying discounts for illiquidity. The court decided on a $500,000 value for Mr. Dahill's interest. The court stated that because none of the

---

[200] 373 Pa. Super. 521; 542 A.2d 65; 1988 Pa. Super. LEXIS 1048.
[201] 1998 Conn. Super. LEXIS 846 (Conn. Super. Ct. 1998).

triggering events in the shareholder's agreement had occurred, it was incorrect to base the value on that set forth in the agreement. In addition, the court stated that it was its duty to find the fair market value rather than the book value or "in-hand value."

The New Jersey case of *Stern v. Stern*[202] represents a value in exchange concept in which the buy–sell agreement was relied upon as the primary indicator of value.

STERN V. STERN

Mr. Stern was a partner in a highly respected law firm, and while conceding that his partnership interest was marital property, he objected to the trial court's determination of the valuation of the partnership. The trial court also had valued his earning capacity.

Beginning with the issue of earning capacity, the appellate court agreed that even if the earning capacity has been enhanced by the other spouse, it should not be recognized as an item of marital property, but it may be considered in determining what distribution of property would be equitable as well as being relevant in the calculation of alimony.

As for the value of the partnership interest, the appellate court looked to the terms of a partnership agreement. The agreement reflected elements of the partnership worth that were in excess of the capital account. This excess value was revised on a quarterly basis. Although within the agreement there were several values contingent upon differing situations, the court recognized the value upon the death of the partner as the value that should hold in the case of divorce.

While the value set forth by the agreement constitutes the presumptive value of the partnership (and therefore may be challenged), the court established that as far as the books of the firm are well kept and the value of the partners' interests are periodically and carefully reviewed, then the presumption of value should be subject to effective attack only if there is clear and convincing proof that the value is more or less than represented by the partnership agreement figure.

---

[202] 66 N.J. 340; 331 A.2d 257; 1975.

This case continues to cause a great deal of controversy in New Jersey, with arguments being made that the agreement should control because it is all the stockholder will ever receive. Furthermore, some practitioners argue that the terms of the agreement become more important as the stockholder ages and comes closer to the time when he will receive his buyout. This follows a value in exchange premise. Other practitioners argue that the investment value principles of *Dugan* and the fair value principles of *Brown* supersede this case. Based on the facts and circumstances of the case, ultimately the court is the arbiter of which argument will prevail.

The buy–sell agreements enhance our analysis of our chart as shown in Exhibit 5.8.

EXHIBIT 5.8   Continuum of Value: Buy–Sell Agreements under Value in Exchange

Premise of Value	**Value in Exchange**		

Standard of Value	Fair Market Value		

	Accepted as economic reality—The most a seller will ever actually receive
	Stern v. Stern
Buy/Sell	Considered as a factor in the determination of value, but not presumptive of value
	In re Marriage of Brenner
	Rejected as eonomic reality—Court looks to hypothetical willing buyer and willing seller
	Dahill v. Dahill

A review of the case law in Arkansas seems to indicate little reliance on the provisions of a buy–sell agreement as it does not adhere to a strict interpretation of fair market value. As mentioned in the *Dahill* case, some Connecticut cases place little emphasis on the provisions of a buy–sell agreement, but others seem to place more weight on such agreements. In Alaska, District of Columbia, Iowa, Oklahoma, and Texas the courts have reached a value based on buy–sell agreements. Connecticut, Florida, Georgia, Illinois, Kentucky, Minnesota, Missouri, Ohio, Oregon, Pennsylvania, West Virginia, and Wisconsin have all considered the buy–sell agreement to be case sensitive and that it may be considered in the calculation of value, but not necessarily presumptive of value.

Exhibit 5.9 presents the continuum of value under the value in exchange premise, including the fair market value and fair value standards as discussed up to this point.

EXHIBIT 5.9   Continuum of Value: Value in Exchange

Premise of Value	Value in Exchange		

Standard of Value	Fair Market Value	Fair Value
	Antolik v. Harvey	*Bobrow v. Bobrow*

Intangible Value	Enterprise goodwill may be minimal or nonexistent	Enterprise Goodwill Only
	Williams v. Williams	*Thompson v. Thompson*

Underlying Assumption	Walk Away and Compete	Covenant Not to Compete Included	Court's Discretion
	Covenant Not to Compete Excluded from Value	Covenant Not Addressed	

Discounts	Discounts applied	Discounts Not Applied
	Tofte v. Tofte	*Howell v. Howell*

Buy/Sell	Accepted as economic reality—The most a seller will ever actually receive
	Stern v. Stern
	Considered as a factor in the determination of value, but not presumptive of value
	In re Marriage of Brenner
	Rejected as eonomic reality—Court looks to hypothetical willing buyer and willing seller
	Dahill v. Dahill

In summary, based on our analysis, 40 states appear to fall under a value in exchange premise:

Alabama

Alaska

Arkansas

Connecticut

Mississippi

Missouri

Nebraska

New Hampshire

Delaware	North Dakota
District of Columbia	Ohio
Florida	Oklahoma
Georgia	Oregon
Hawaii	Pennsylvania
Idaho	Rhode Island
Illinois	South Carolina
Indiana	South Dakota
Iowa	Tennessee
Kansas	Texas
Kentucky	Utah
Louisiana	Vermont
Maine	Virginia
Maryland	West Virginia
Massachusetts	Wisconsin
Minnesota	Wyoming

VALUE TO THE HOLDER

Value to the holder states are generally those that look to identify and value the asset or assets created during the marriage as the result of the joint efforts of both spouses regardless of whether a marketable asset was created. States that favor the value to the holder premise consider the cash flows received by the title-holding spouse regardless of the asset's transferability.

Goodwill

This definition describes goodwill in a manner that largely represents an investment value in that it includes certain personal attributes in the value:

> The economic benefits that a going concern may enjoy as compared to a new firm, from (1) established relations with all the markets—both output and input, (2) established relations with government departments and other noncommercial bodies, and (3) personal relationships.[203]

States that follow an investment value standard seem to apply the notion that although a business may not be immediately salable and may not have value beyond its net tangible assets without the owner/key employee in place, the business has an ongoing value to the owner and therefore to the

---

[203] Allen Parkman, "The Treatment of Professional Goodwill in Divorce Proceedings," 18 *Family Law Quarterly*, No. 213 (1984).

marital estate. In value to holder states, the view of property is broad and recognizes that the title holder will continue to function as an owner benefiting from the asset already in place.

Dugan v. Dugan,[204] one of New Jersey's early cases with respect to the treatment of goodwill, shows the court's reasoning for including elements of personal goodwill as marital property.

DUGAN V. DUGAN

After a 20-year marriage, the Dugans separated. Mr. Dugan was a member of the New Jersey Bar and continued to practice in a professional corporation.

Mr. Dugan appealed the lower court's judgment regarding property distribution, and the New Jersey Supreme Court had to determine whether the goodwill of Mr. Dugan's law practice was an asset subject of equitable distribution, and, if so, how it should be evaluated. At the time of the case (1983), New Jersey lawyers were not permitted to sell their goodwill.

The New Jersey Supreme court distinguished intangible assets from tangible ones in that intangible assets have no intrinsic value, but do have a value related to ownership and possession of tangible assets. Intangibles such as trademarks and patents are identifiable intangible assets, whereas goodwill is based on reputation that will probably generate future business.

The court then noted that goodwill is a legally protected interest, as evidenced by the ability to prevent a seller's competition with a covenant not to compete. In addition, New Jersey inheritance tax requires consideration of goodwill. It has also been recognized as an element of value in liquidation.

Goodwill can be translated into prospective earnings and, from an accounting standpoint, can be defined as the future estimated earnings that exceed the normal return on an investment. The court distinguished goodwill and earning capacity by stating that goodwill reflects not only a possibility of future earnings, but a probability based on existing circumstances, and after divorce, the law practice will continue to benefit from goodwill as it had during the marriage. For the purposes of distribution, it would be inequitable to ignore the other spouse's contribution to the development of a valuable economic resource.

(continued)

---

[204] 92 N.J. 423; 457 A.2d 1; 1983 N.J.

> The court also acknowledged that limitations exist on the ability to sell a law practice with its goodwill; however, the goodwill itself has significant value irrespective of any limitations.
>
> The court found several problems with the valuation, including the method of determining reasonable compensation. The court felt that the method used determined the firm's efficiency rather than the plaintiff's reasonable compensation. Instead, the court noted that age, experience, education, expertise, effort, and locale should be elements considered in determining reasonable compensation. In addition, the valuator added back too many expenses to the income stream used in the valuation and compared the attorney's compensation to an average from around the country rather than a specific area. The court also took issue with an unsubstantiated capitalization rate.
>
> The important concept established by this case is that goodwill has value, if only to the holder, regardless of its marketability.

Celebrity Goodwill   Currently, New Jersey is the only state that has considered celebrity goodwill as marital property, recognizing that the development of celebrity, like that of personal goodwill in a business, is created by virtue of the noncelebrity spouse's contributions to the marital partnership.[205] New York has a similar concept but characterizes it as celebrity status, not celebrity goodwill.

In the case of *Piscopo v. Piscopo*,[206] the value of comedian Joe Piscopo's celebrity status was divided by the court upon the dissolution of his marriage.

PISCOPO V. PISCOPO

The New Jersey Superior Court addressed the topic of celebrity goodwill in the case of *Piscopo v. Piscopo* in 1989. The trial court[207] held that the marital property included Joe Piscopo's celebrity goodwill.

---

[205] Robin P. Rosen, "A Critical Analysis of Celebrity Careers as Property upon Dissolution of Marriage," 61 *George Washington Law Review*, No. 522 (January 1993).

[206] 232 N.J. Super. 559; 557 A.2d 1040; 1989.

[207] *Piscopo v. Piscopo* , 231 N.J. Super. 576, 580–581 (Ch. Div. 1988).

The court's expert found that Piscopo's income flowed through Piscopo Productions, Inc., and that Piscopo's compensation was determined at the end of each year as in any corporation. The expert valued that business as he would any other professional corporation, taking into account Piscopo's goodwill.

In valuing Piscopo's celebrity, the expert took 25% of his average gross earnings over a three-year period, calculating goodwill at $158,863. Citing *Dugan v. Dugan*,[208] the trial court accepted that goodwill was a distributable asset representing the reputation that will probably generate future business.

Piscopo claimed that this situation was distinguishable from *Dugan* because a professional has a reliable future income while show business is volatile. The court did not agree, citing that *Dugan* measured goodwill by past earning capacity and the probability that it will continue.

The appellate court also agreed with the opinion of the trial court judge, who stated that it would not be acceptable if the Court of Chancery protected a celebrity's person and business from another's "unjust enrichment by the theft of [his] goodwill," *Ali v. Playgirl, Inc.*, 447 F.Supp. 723, 729 (S.D.N.Y.1978), while another branch deprived the spouse from sharing in the same protectable interest.[209]

The court also cited the New York case of *Golub v. Golub*, 139 Misc.2d 440, 527 *N.Y.S.*2d 946 (Sup.Ct.1988), where a celebrity's earning capacity was recognized as an asset because of the increase in that earning capacity due to the efforts of the other spouse.

The appellate court agreed with the trial court in that there was a value to Piscopo's celebrity and that it should be distributed upon dissolution of the marriage.

California handed down its first reported decision on celebrity goodwill in a case involving movie director John McTiernan. The trial court held that his celebrity had value in and of itself above his assets based on the fact that his earning capacity far exceeded that which a typical director was able to earn. The judge found his profession analogous to that of an attorney, physician, dentist, architect, or any other professional, and that, in that profession, the husband had developed an earning capacity that exceeded that of

---

[208] *Dugan v. Dugan*, 92 N.J. 423 (1983).

[209] *Piscopo v. Piscopo*, 231 N.J. Super., at 579 (slip opinion at 4).

a typical director. When the appellate court reviewed the decision, however, it decided that goodwill must adhere to a business, even if it is the business of a sole proprietor or professional practice.[210] The director's career in this case was not considered a business. The case was appealed; however, the California Supreme Court declined to hear it.[211]

New York has had several cases involving the goodwill of a celebrity, but these cases dealt with the enhanced earning capacity of a spouse over the course of a marriage and called this *celebrity status*. In *Golub v. Golub*,[212] for example, the court decided that a celebrity's status and concomitant enhanced earning capacity could be included because the non-celebrity spouse contributed to its formation and appreciation during the marriage. In New York, the court followed the same basic principles in *Mann v. Mann*,[213] where the performer's career had already been established before the marriage, and the court decided that goodwill was not attributable to marital efforts and was therefore not includable in the division of property.

Personal Goodwill versus Earning Capacity   In attempting to distinguish personal goodwill as an inherently separate property, some have made the argument that personal goodwill and earning capacity (not distributable) are indistinguishable. Wisconsin's *Holbrook v. Holbrook*,[214] for example, stated: "The concept of professional goodwill evanesces when one attempts to distinguish it from future earning capacity." The court conceded that a professional's business reputation has value, but claimed that that value is not a separate property interest, as it merely assured the continuation of earnings in the future. The exclusion of goodwill was based on several factors, including the difficulty in valuation, the extent employment status is determinative of goodwill's existence, the concern that goodwill is really earning capacity, the concern for double counting (which we call *double dipping*), and the need to exchange a tangible asset (cash or its equivalent) for an intangible (the goodwill of the business) upon divorce. This view has been followed by several decisions, including South Carolina's *Donahue v. Donahue*[215] and *Hickum v. Hickum*.[216]

---

[210] *McTiernan v. Dobrow* , 133 Cal. App. 4th 1090; 35 Cal. Rptr. 3d 287; 2005 Cal. App. LEXIS 1692.

[211] 2006 Cal. LEXIS 1743.

[212] 139 Misc. 2d 440, 527 N.Y.S.2d 946 (Sup. Ct. 1988).

[213] *N.Y.L.J* ., Jan. 10, 1995, at 26 (Sup. Ct. N.Y. County).

[214] 103 Wis.2d 327, 309 N.W.2d 343, 1981 Wisc. App. LEXIS 3322 (Wis. Ct. App. 1981).

[215] S.C. (1989) 299 S.C. 353, 384 S.E.2d 741.

[216] 463 S.E.2d 321 (S.C. Ct. App. 1995).

The Wisconsin court later distinguished itself from *Holbrook* in *Peerenboom v. Peerenboom*,[217] a case that involved the valuation of a dental practice. The court reviewed the concept that a lawyer's interest in a law firm (such as that in *Holbrook*) is not salable for ethical reasons. However, no such reasons exist in a medical practice, and, therefore, goodwill that is transferable may be included in value. The court did maintain, however, that goodwill must be separate from the reputation of the individual. Peerenboom was later cited for the concept that goodwill as a going concern could be marketable and distributable.[218]

There have been several criticisms of the view that goodwill in a professional practice is indistinguishable from earning capacity, and, because the two cannot be separated, goodwill should not be included as a marital asset. First, many have argued that it does not comport with the intent of equitable distribution: that the marriage should be viewed as an economic partnership recognizing contributions of each spouse to specific assets. Second, denying the non-titled spouse a share in an asset because of difficulty in valuation is not equitable. Alternatively, some have argued that goodwill not only reflects future earnings, but also should not be recognized as a product of a marital partnership.[219]

The Colorado court in the case *In re: Bookout*[220] supported the view that goodwill is property or an asset that *supplements* the earning capacity of another asset, business, or a profession, and, therefore, is not the earning capacity itself. The case cites numerous decisions in Washington, California, and New Jersey, all separating goodwill from earning capacity. As expected, all these states seem to view, to some extent, value under a value to the holder premise.

To further illuminate the difference between goodwill and earning capacity, in the Washington case of *In re: Hall*,[221] two spouses had identical educations as doctors. One owned a practice while the other worked as a salaried teacher. The court found that although both doctors may have equal earning capacities, only the practicing doctor had goodwill, as the goodwill needed an entity to adhere to in addition to the person. The concept has been affirmed in New Jersey as well.

Value of a Professional Degree or License and Enhanced Earning Capacity   As the so-called walk-away doctrine is at one extreme of the continuum, the valuation

---

[217] 433 N.W.2d 282 (Wis. Ct. App. 1998).

[218] *Sommerfeld v. Sommerfield* , 454 N.W.2d 55 (Wis. Ct. App. 1990).

[219] Kistjardt, "Professional Goodwill in Marital Dissolution," 2.04.

[220] 833 P.2d 800 (Colo. App. 1991), *cert. denied*, 846 P.2d 189 (Colo. 1993).

[221] 103 Wn.2d 236, 692 P.2d 175 (1984).

of professional degrees, licenses, and enhanced earning capacity is at the other end of the continuum. Moreover, these items of marital property are valued without the necessity of an underlying business enterprise. *Black's Law Dictionary* defines *earning capacity* as:

> A person's ability or power to earn money, given the person's talent, skills, training, and experience. Earning capacity is one element considered when measuring damages recoverable in a personal-injury lawsuit. And in family law, earning capacity is considered when awarding child support and spousal maintenance (or alimony) and in dividing property between spouses upon divorce.[222]

Enhanced earning capacity is the enhancement of an individual's ability to earn over and above what would be earned following a so-called normal career path and resulting from joint efforts over the life of the marriage. It is often measured by attempting to quantify the difference between the amounts an individual could earn without the enhancement to the amount that individual was earning at the end of the marriage with the enhancement. This can be the result of the acquisition of a degree or license or the result of some type of training, experience, or perfection of a skill that results in the generation of extraordinary earnings over and above a normal career path. To our knowledge, it is only in New York, where professional degrees, licenses, and career enhancement are considered marital property.

New Jersey has rejected the inclusion of earning capacity as an asset subject to equitable distribution. While one trial court included earning capacity as a separate "amorphous"[223] asset, the New Jersey Supreme Court rejected the notion, stating:

> Potential earning capacity is doubtless a factor to be considered by a trial judge in determining what distribution will be "equitable" and it is even more obviously relevant upon the issue of alimony. But it should not be deemed property as such within the meaning of the statute.[224]

Normally, earning capacity is a consideration for the determination of spousal support or a factor affecting the division of assets rather than in the determination of marital property. Most states recognize that individuals enter a marriage with a certain amount of intellectual or human capital.

---

[222] Garner, *Black's Law Dictionary*, at 547.

[223] 123 N.J. Super., at 568.

[224] *Stern v. Stern*, 66 N.J. 340, at 260.

They possess skills, talents, education, and experience that have resulted in a specific earning capacity. During the marriage, by the attainment of additional education or experience, there may have been an enhancement of this human capital resulting in an extraordinary increase in the degree or license holder's earning capacity to which there was a contribution made, either directly or indirectly, by the other spouse. The rationale for considering these types of assets as marital property seems to be that, by his or her contributions, the dependent spouse should share in the future benefits he or she helped to create. This inclusion is basically the recognition of joint spousal investments in the degree or license holder's career.[225]

The view that enhanced earnings capacity can appreciate during the marriage due in part to the efforts and/or sacrifices of the dependent spouse and that this creates marital property appears to result from a conscious decision to treat increased earning capacity developed during the marriage as an asset rather than as income to determine maintenance or support. Initially, the point behind distributing enhanced earning capacity seemed to be that without distribution of his or her share of this asset, the dependent spouse who contributed to the enhancement may be left without any assets at all.[226] This reasoning can be seen in the New York case *O'Brien v. O'Brien*,[227] which established the treatment of a professional license acquired during the marriage as marital property in New York.

O'BRIEN V. O'BRIEN

In this case, during the proceeding for the divorce of a doctor and his wife, the court discussed whether a license to practice medicine had a value distributable as marital property. There were no other assets of consequential value in the marriage. The husband had recently acquired a license to practice medicine. The appellate court held that the plaintiff's license was not marital property, but remitted the case to the trial court for further proceedings. The Court of Appeals of New York disagreed with the lower appellate court, and decided that the license could be considered property under New York Domestic Relations law.

(continued)

---

[225] Kelly, "Sharing a Piece of the Future Post-Divorce," at 73.

[226] David M. Wildstein and Charles F. Vuotto, "Enhanced Earning Capacity: Is It an Asset Subject to Equitable Distribution under New Jersey Law?" (www.vuotto.com/earningcapacity.htm).

[227] 66 N.Y.2d 576; 489 N.E.2d 712; 498 N.Y.S.2d 743; 1985.

When the couple married, they were both employed as teachers at a private school. The wife had a bachelor's degree and a teaching certificate, but required further education to obtain certification in New York. The court found that she relinquished the opportunity for that permanent certification to allow her husband to pursue his education. Two years into the marriage the parties moved to Mexico, where the husband became a full-time medical student. Returning to New York three years later, the husband completed the last two semesters of medical school and the wife resumed her former teaching position. The husband received his license to practice four years later and shortly thereafter commenced the action for divorce.

During the marriage, both parties had contributed to the education and living expenses, receiving additional help from their families. The court, however, found that during the marriage, the wife had contributed 76% of the marital income while the husband earned his degree. The wife's expert presented the value of the medical license as $472,000 by comparing the average income of a general surgeon and a college graduate between the time when the husband's residency would end and the time he reached age 65. Factoring for inflation, taxes, and interest, that value was capitalized and reduced to present value. The expert also opined that the wife's contribution to the husband's education was $103,390.

The trial court made a distributive award of 40% of the value of the license to be paid in 11 annual installments. The appellate court overturned this, based on a prior case where the value of the license was not deemed to be marital property.

The husband claimed that his license should be excluded because it was not property, either marital or separate, but instead was representative of a personal attainment of knowledge. The court reviewed the portion of the statute that stated "the court shall consider: . . . (6) any equitable claim to, interest in, or direct or indirect contribution made to the acquisition of such marital property by the party not having title, including joint efforts or expenditures and contributions and services as a spouse, parent, wage earner, and homemaker, and to the career or career potential of the other party [and] the impossibility or difficulty of evaluating any component asset or any interest in a business, corporation or profession" (Domestic Relations Law § 236(B)(5)(d)(6), (9).

The Court of Appeals (New York's highest court) interpreted these words to mean that an interest in a profession or professional career is marital property. The court interpreted the history of the statute as confirming this interpretation, as the traditional common law title system had caused inequity. The purpose of that statute, considering marriage as an economic partnership, was seen to be consistent with the inclusion of the value of the license.

The Court of Appeals stated that the lack of market value or alienability was irrelevant. Ultimately, the court decided that if it receives evidence of the present value of the license and the working spouse's contribution toward its acquisition, it may make an appropriate distribution of that license as marital property.

In a concurring opinion, Judge J. Titone stated that the provisions of New York's Domestic Relations Law were intended to provide flexibility so that equity could be done.

The *O'Brien* doctrine has been criticized, however, by those who point out that the statutory language on which the doctrine is based focuses on division of property rather than the *definition* thereof. The statute instructs the court to consider "direct or indirect contributions made . . . to the career or career potential of the other party" when distributing marital assets, not while identifying them. The section advises that a spouse's contributions should be accounted for in the distribution of property.[228] Essentially, the contributing spouse should be given a bigger slice of the same pie as opposed to the pie itself being made bigger.

As personal goodwill may eventually merge with practice goodwill, some have suggested that, eventually, the value of a practitioner's license becomes subsumed in his or her practice. The New York case *McSparron v. McSparron*[229] addresses this issue and asks whether eventually the value of a license is used up by the income that it has produced. The court in this case considered factors such as a change in circumstances and location of a practicing professional and decided that, no matter how far along, the license has a value outside of one's career, concluding that it did not merge.

In the most extreme application of the value to the holder premise that we have found, the New York case of *Hougie v. Hougie*[230] involved the inclusion of the enhanced earning capacity of an investment banker in the property distribution. The facts of the case ultimately revealed that the

[228] Kenneth R. Davis, "The Doctrine of *O'Brien v. O'Brien*: Critical Analysis," 13 *Pace Law Review* (1994), at 869.

[229] 87 N.Y.2d 275; 662 N.E.2d 745; 639 N.Y.S.2d 265; 1995 N.Y. LEXIS 4451.

[230] 261 A.D.2d 161; 689 N.Y.S.2d 490; 1999 N.Y. App. Div. LEXIS 4588.

husband needed and had a license that allowed him to perform his job, but the court stated that the husband's enhanced earning capacity was a distributable asset regardless of whether a license is required.

McSparron left open the possibility that, in New York, both a license acquired during the marriage and a business or business interest acquired during the marriage can be valued and distributed in a divorce. Such was the issue in *Grunfeld v. Grunfeld.*[231] Mr. Grunfeld was a customs lawyer who acquired both his law license and practice during the marriage. At the trial court level, both were valued. However, the trial judge awarded alimony to the wife, which used the same projected professional earnings to determine the value of the license. Cognizant of not double counting, the trial court judge did not distribute the value of the license as it was included in the alimony award. The wife appealed and the First Appellate Division modified the trial court's decision and ordered that one half the value of the husband's professional license be distributed to the wife.

The husband appealed to New York's highest court, the Court of Appeals. The Court of Appeals found that:

> The value of a professional license as an asset of the marital partnership is a form of human capital dependent upon the future labor of the licensee. The asset is totally indistinguishable and has no existence separate from the projected professional earnings used to value the license also form the basis of an award of maintenance, the licensed spouse is being twice charged with distribution of the same asset value, or sharing the same income with the non-licensed spouse.[232]

The Court of Appeals agreed with the trial court that distributing the license and awarding maintenance (alimony) is double counting.

While the treatment of these assets in New York is somewhat unique it is not without its critics. A New York's Matrimonial Commission report suggested changes to the statute, recommending the elimination of New York's consideration of enhanced earning capacity, professional degrees or licenses, and celebrity status as marital property.[233] However, professional degrees, licenses, and celebrity status are considered marital property in New York. Some departments also consider enhanced earnings as marital

---

[231] *Grunfeld v. Grunfeld* , 94 N.Y. N.Y.S.2d 486 (Ct. App. 2000).

[232] *Id* .

[233] Hon. Sondra Miller, "Report to the Chief Judge of the State of New York," New York Matrimonial Commission, February 2006.

property as well. However, over the past few years, the amounts generally credited to the non-titled spouse have diminished.

Double Dipping

The value of a business is the present value of expected future benefits that can be received from that business whether determined by the asset-based, market, or income approaches. When the value of a business is distributed in a divorce, the non-business-owner spouse receives some type of asset in exchange for his or her equitable or community share of the business. The share of the business credited to the non-owner spouse is based on the expected future benefits to the owner. Double dipping can arise from the use of the same income stream for both valuation and alimony. This is an increasingly relevant issue when dealing with the interrelationship between the distribution of marital property and the award of alimony.

For example, in using an income or excess earnings method to value a company, the officer's compensation in excess of reasonable compensation is added back to the income stream of the company and capitalized. Essentially, the valuation takes a portion of the owner's compensation and capitalizes it to value the business while at the same time considering it all available for alimony and thereby using it twice.[234]

Double dipping was first addressed in the treatment of pensions as marital property. As applied to business valuation, double dipping was first addressed in the 1963 Wisconsin case *Kronforst v. Kronforst*,[235] where the court stated that "such an asset cannot be included as a principal asset in making division of the estate and then also an income item to be considered in awarding alimony." However, New Jersey's decision in *Steneken v. Steneken*[236] has allowed the use of the same income stream for both alimony and equitable distribution.

Classification of Value to the Holder Typically States by Their Treatment of Goodwill
A state using investment value will typically consider all goodwill in a professional practice or business and will not attempt to differentiate between personal and enterprise goodwill. California's *Golden v. Golden*[237] is an example of an investment value case where the rationale the court used was based on the nonprofessional spouse's contribution in assisting in the creation of this value.

---

[234] Donald J. Degrazia, "Controversial Valuation Issues in Divorce," presented at the *2003 AICPA National Business Valuation Conference.*

[235] 21 Wis.2d 54, 123 N.W.2d 528 (1963).

[236] 2005 N.J. LEXIS 57.

[237] 270 Cal. App. 2d 401; 75 Cal. Rptr. 735 (1969 Cal. App.).

Interestingly, there are significant differences between the treatment of goodwill as marital property in *Golden v. Golden* and a case like Pennsylvania's *Gaydos v. Gaydos*.[238] The courts in both cases recognized that the practice would continue after the end of the marriage and that there is a value to that continuance. California saw goodwill as a product of the ongoing value of the company that was developed during the marriage and should be shared between the parties, while Pennsylvania excluded that value as being tied too closely to the practitioner and his or her future efforts.

Washington State views personal goodwill in a slightly different manner from California as illustrated by *In re: Lukens*.[239] The Washington court acknowledged that personal goodwill may not be marketable but stated that it is an asset nonetheless. The court viewed goodwill in light of the concept of a recent graduate or an existing practitioner relocating to another state and having to start over. Although the practitioner would have the skills acquired through training and practice, he or she would not have any reputation in a new place, and therefore that reputation has to be affiliated with the practice.

As discussed earlier, New York is the only state to explicitly include professional degrees, licenses, celebrity status, or enhanced earnings capacity that was acquired during the marriage as marital assets or the incremental increase in them. Alternatively, New Jersey does not consider a professional degree or license as marital property but does consider the value of celebrity goodwill. Other states have suggested that including the value of a license or degree may be warranted in certain compelling circumstances.

Exhibit 5.10 presents the continuum of value under the value to the holder premise.

EXHIBIT 5.10   Continuum of Value: Intangible Assets under Value to the Holder with Case Examples

Premise of Value	Value to the Holder		
Standard of Value	Fair Value		Investment Value
Intangible Value	Enterprise and Personal Goodwill		Personal Intangible Value
Case Example	*Dugan v. Dugan*		*O'Brien v. O'Brien*
Underlying Assumption	Going Concern Value Assuming Owner Will Continue Ownership		Enhanced Earnings Capacity

---

[238] 693 A.2d (Pa. Super. Ct. 1993).

[239] 16 Wn. App. 481, 558 P.2d 279 (1976), *review denied*, 88 Wn.2d 1011 (1977).

Next we move to a discussion of the treatment of shareholder-level discounts and the weight accorded buy–sell agreements in states that fall under the value to the holder premise.

Shareholder-Level Discounts under the Value to the Holder Premise

Under the value to the holder premise of value, the business is valued under the assumption that the entity will continue under current ownership. As we have discussed, personal goodwill is includable as a marital asset under this premise, even though it cannot be sold. Therefore, the shareholder-level lack of control and lack of marketability discounts associated with the value in exchange premise would typically not apply.

Montana is a hybrid value state that has applied discounts in certain divorce valuations, such as that in the case of *In Re: Decosse*,[240] where a 20% lack of control discount was applied. In our view, New York is a hybrid state, which adheres to a fair market value standard in the valuation of businesses while applying the most liberal definition of marital property in the valuation of a professional degree or license and enhanced earning capacity.

The following value to the holder states, absent extraordinary circumstances, do not apply discounts: Arizona, California, Nevada, New Jersey, New Mexico, and Washington.

Fair Value

Some cases appear to use assumptions more often attributed to an investment value standard while using the language of fair value, which can be either value in exchange or value to the holder. When a case mentions a pro rata share of enterprise value, rejects shareholder-level discounts, or mentions the unwillingness of a buyer or seller, the standard of value is usually fair value. Although the New Jersey case of *Brown v. Brown*[241] and Louisiana case of *Ellington v. Ellington*[242] reference investment value concepts like continuing benefits of ownership and employment, the predominant language of these cases involves fair value.

As mentioned previously, the Louisiana case *Ellington v. Ellington* may be considered a fair value case. While the wife's expert used an excess earnings method and came to a value of $668,000, the husband's expert determined that the fair market value of liabilities outweighed assets

---

[240] 282 Mont. 212; 936 P.2d 821; 1997 Mont. LEXIS 66; 54 Mont. St. Rep. 318.

[241] 348 N.J. Super. 466; 792 A.2d 463.

[242] 842 So.2d 1160; 2003 La. App. LEXIS 675.

by approximately $55,000 and therefore the company had no value. The court rejected the testimony of both experts as each used a fair market value standard, which was not appropriate because *neither party was a willing seller*. Taking this into account, the court came to a value of $293,000. The appellate court affirmed this decision, as the husband would retain ownership and current management would remain in place and the husband would continue to benefit from the asset in place. Subsequently, the Louisiana statute was amended to require adherence to a fair market value standard and specifically excludes personal goodwill.

Exhibit 5.11 shows the continuum of value based on the treatment of discounts in divorce proceedings under the investment value and fair value and under the value to the holder premises.

EXHIBIT 5.11   Continuum of Value: Discounts under Fair Value and Investment Value

Premise of Value	Value to the Holder	
Standard of Value	Fair Value	Investment Value
Discounts	No Discounts	Not Applicable
Case Example	*Brown v. Brown*	Not Applicable

Buy–Sell Agreements under Value to the Holder

As we have seen in the *Graff* case, Colorado generally favors a value to the holder premise of value. This extends to the treatment of the buy–sell agreement, which can be seen in the case *In re: Huff*.[243]

IN RE: HUFF

In this case, the husband was a partner in a large, well-established law firm with 90 partners and 66 associates. The firm had a detailed buy–sell agreement in place for various circumstances including withdrawal and death, setting forth a partner withdrawal formula based on the value of receivables plus a portion of the firm's capital.

---

[243] 834 P.2d 244 (Colo. 1992).

No goodwill is included. The books and formulas were periodically reviewed and updated. Additionally, partners were not able to freely sell their interest as a restrictive agreement was in place.

The husband's expert offered two valuations, the first involving the partnership agreement formula and arriving at a value of $42,442 and the second using the excess earnings method and arriving at a value of $113,000. The wife's expert also used excess earnings and valued the interest at $309,500. The difference came down to the capitalization rates used. The trial court elected the $113,000 valuation as proper, as the capitalization rate of the husband's expert was more realistic than that of the wife's expert.

The husband's expert testified that the partnership agreement was in place to discourage partners from leaving the firm as it awarded a withdrawing partner 50% of his or her accounts receivable. The wife's expert testified that the excess earnings method represented the value of the partnership to the husband if he remained at the practice.

The court rejected the valuation based on the partnership agreement because the husband intended to stay with the firm. The district court decided that the partnership figure ignored "all the present facts and intentions of the parties" and that the excess earnings valuation should be used. The husband appealed that this determination was in error as the partnership agreement was binding on him and the partnership.

The district court (trial court) decided that because a partnership agreement was designed to discourage partners from leaving the firm and it appeared that the husband intended to stay with the partnership, the court felt that it was not bound to the terms of that agreement upon divorce. The Colorado Supreme Court upheld the decision.[244]

The actual use of a shareholder agreement may determine whether it is relied on by the family court. In the New Jersey case *Stern v. Stern*,[245] the court found that the agreement was updated quarterly, it established an intangible value to the business above the value of a partner's capital account, and was generally used for departing partners. In this case, the court decided that that value should not be disturbed.

---

[244]*Id.*, LEXIS 607; 16 BTR 1304.

[245] 66 N.J. 340; 331 A.2d 257; 1975.

Arizona, Colorado, Montana, New York, and Washington are states that use an investment value to value certain businesses upon divorce, and all of them have applied the notion that a buy–sell agreement may be considered but should not be binding on value. Thus, we would view buy–sell agreements in the manner shown in Exhibit 5.12 under both the value in exchange and value to the holder premises.

EXHIBIT 5.12 Continuum of Value: Buy–Sell Agreements under Value in Exchange and Value to the Holder

Premise of Value	Value in Exchange		Value to the Holder	
Standard of Value	Fair Market Value		Fair Value	Investment Value
Buy/Sell	Accepted as economic reality—The most a seller will ever actually receive		Generally Rejected	
	Considered as a factor in the determination of value, but not presumptive of value			
	Rejected as economic reality—Court looks to hypothetical willing buyer and willing seller			
Case Example	*Stern v. Stern*		*In Re Huff*	
	In re Marriage of Brenner			
	Dahill v. Dahill			

In summary, based on our analysis, five states fall under some version of a value to the holder premise:[246] Arizona, New Mexico, California, Washington, and Nevada.

In addition, there are six states that have both value in exchange and value to the holder characteristics: Colorado, New Jersey, Michigan, New York, Montana, and North Carolina.

SUMMARY

We have presented the stated or implied premises and standards of value under which each state values closely held businesses or business interest in divorce. The reality is, however, that courts are generally less concerned with the theoretical underpinnings of business valuation than they are

---

[246] New Jersey also has cases with elements of value to the holder, while having others that appear more closely akin to value in exchange. This is why we consider New Jersey a hybrid state.

with what they perceive to be a fair outcome for the parties involved. One commentator in New Jersey said this regarding the 2003 New Jersey case *Brown v. Brown:*[247]

Brown emphasized not only the importance of the concept of fairness in a divorce case, but when a conflict existed between policy concerns and appraisal methodology, policy would prevail.[248]

Valuations performed for estate, gift, or income tax purposes are often perceived as different from cases involving people who are dividing an ongoing asset (as in divorce, dissent, or oppression), sometimes unwillingly. In these cases, the courts appear more willing to seek an equitable remedy in order to fairly compensate the individuals involved.

For example, the North Carolina case *Hamby v. Hamby*[249] is one in which a different standard is stated from that which is applied. In the valuation of an insurance agency, the court directed the experts to find the fair market value less any encumbrances. The expert whose opinion the court ultimately chose stated that his purpose was to find the fair market value, which he determined was the going concern value to the individual. The expert further stated that even though the business could not be sold, there was a value to the owner above what he received as salary. While setting out to determine net value—that is, fair market value less encumbrances—based on the testimony of the wife's expert, the court arrived at a value to the holder.

In this case, there appears to be an obvious intention to fairly compensate the parties without adhering strictly to the assumptions conventionally underlying a particular standard of value. Although the *Hamby v. Hamby* case may go back and forth between premises and standards of value, other cases have looked not to a standard of value but rather, it seems to us, to a fair solution. New York did this in *O'Brien v. O'Brien,*[250] and New Jersey applied equitable principles in *Brown v. Brown.*[251]

To summarize, standards of value in divorce are determined on a state-by-state basis. We have looked at each state as a means of discerning the premises and standards of value they follow. We began with two distinct premises—value in exchange and value to the holder—and three basic standards of value—fair market value, fair value, and investment value. We then

---

[247] 348 N.J. Super. 466; 792 A.2d 463.

[248] Louis, "Economic Realism."

[249] *Hamby v. Hamby,* 143 N.C. App. 635, 547 S.E.2d 110 (2001).

[250] 66 N.Y.2d 576; 489 N.E.2d 712; 498 N.Y.S.2d 743; 1985.

[251] 348 N.J. Super. 466; 792 A.2d 463.

looked at the treatment of goodwill, shareholder-level discounts, and the weight accorded buy–sell agreements as indicia of the premise and standard of value applied in each state. Our conclusion is that one could look at a continuum of value as a way to conceptualize the intersection of valuation theory and case law and use this continuum toward a standard of value classification system in divorce. Exhibit 5.13 represents the continuum of value including premises, standards, their indicia, and representative cases. Although this construct may be helpful to valuation professionals and appraisal users, we offer a word of caution. While we think that our suggested classification system may be a useful way of interpreting how the standards of value have been used by courts, it is likely that the courts will continue to identify, value, and distribute marital property in ways they deem equitable and not feel constrained by valuation theory.

EXHIBIT 5.13   Continuum of Value

Premise of Value	Value in Exchange		Value to the Holder	

| Standard of Value | Fair Market Value | Fair Value | Investment Value | |
| | *Antolik v. Harvey* | *Brown v. Brown* | *Golden v. Golden* | |

| Intangible Value | Enterprise Goodwill May Be Minimal or Nonexistent | Enterprise Goodwill Only | Enterprise and Personal Goodwill | Personal Intangible Value |
| | *Williams v. Williams* | *Thompson v. Thompson/ Sweere v. Gilbert-Sweere* | *Dugan v. Dugan* | *O'Brien v. O'Brien* |

| Underlying Assumption | Walk Away and Compete | Covenant Not to Compete Included | Court's Discretion | Going Concern Value Assuming Owner Will Continue Ownership | Enhanced Earning Capacity |
| | Covenant Not to Compete Excluded from Value | Covenant Not Addressed | | | |

| Discounts | Discount Applied | | Discounts Not applied | | Not Applicable |
| | *Tofte v. Tofte* | | *Howell v. Howell* | *Brown v. Brown* | Not Applicable |

Buy-Sell	Accepted as Economic Reality: The most a seller will ever actually receive	Generally Rejected	
	Rejected as Economic Reality: Court looks to hypotheical willing buyer and willing seller		
	Stern v. Stern	*In re: Huff*	
	Dahill v. Dahill		

CHAPTER 6

Fair Value in Financial Reporting

Neil J. Beaton

INTRODUCTION

In May 2003, the Financial Accounting Standards Board (FASB) set forth to provide guidance on fair value in its Board Meeting Minutes (BMM). The BMM was a precursor to adding a fair value measurement project to its agenda in order to address fair value measurement issues broadly, and in June 2004, the FASB issued an Exposure Draft (ED), *Fair Value Measurements*, based on the BMM and opened such for public comment by constituents. Based on such comments, the FASB issued Statement of Financial Standards (SFAS) No. 157, *Fair Value Measurements* (SFAS 157), in September 2006, based on the ED and subsequent discussions with various stakeholders including business owner, chief financial officers, accountants, and other interested parties. Further, in July 2009, the FASB issued Accounting Standards Codification (ASC) No. 820, *Fair Value Measurement* (ASC 820), as part of its codification project that brought together various levels of generally accepted accounting principles (GAAP) into a single, unifying pronouncement. This chapter updates the theory and application of the fair value standard used in the preparation of corporate financial statements since the introduction of ASC 820 (formerly SFAS 157). Although the words are identical, the term *fair value* is not the same as fair value referred to in dissenters' rights and oppression cases, which is discussed in Chapter 3. The fair value standard in accounting literature refers to the measurement of assets and liabilities in financial statements. The current definition of *fair value* is:

> The price that would be received to sell an asset or paid to transfer a liability in an orderly transaction between market participants at the measurement date.[1]

---

[1] FASB ASC Topic No. 820, *Fair Value Measurements and Disclosures* (ASC 820).

This chapter explains the fair value standard and discusses the history of fair value in accounting literature, the use of the standard as it applies to valuations for financial reporting purposes, and an interpretation of how fair value differs from other standards of value, such as fair market value. The focus of this chapter is on fair value measurement in business combinations and asset impairment tests, since valuation practitioners frequently encounter valuations for these types of assignments. The chapter also discusses audit issues related to fair value measurement.

Fair Value in Financial Reporting: What Is It?

Fair value is the standard of value used in valuations performed for financial reporting purposes on a company's financial statements. The terminology comes from accounting literature, including GAAP and Securities and Exchange Commission (SEC) regulations. In short, fair value strives to revalue assets and liabilities on a company's balance sheet to reflect their fair values, that is, the values at which these assets and liabilities would exchange hands in an orderly transaction between market participants.

The objective of a fair value measurement is to estimate the price at which an orderly transaction to sell the asset or to transfer the liability would take place between market participants at the measurement date under current market conditions. A fair value measurement requires a reporting entity to determine *all* of the following:

- The particular asset or liability that is the subject of the measurement (consistent with its unity of account)
- For a nonfinancial asset, the valuation premise that is appropriate for the measurement (consistent with its highest and best use)
- The principal (or most advantageous) market for the asset or liability
- The valuation technique(s) appropriate for the measurement, considering the availability of data with which to develop inputs that represent the assumptions that market participants would use when pricing the asset or liability and the level of fair value hierarchy within which the inputs are categorized

In the background notes to the ED on fair value measurement, the FASB indicated that prior guidance regarding fair value measurement in the accounting literature was developed piecemeal over time and was contained in a number of different accounting pronouncements, which were not necessarily consistent with one another. The FASB indicated a desire to address these inconsistencies by establishing a framework that would be built on current practice but would also clarify fair value measurements in a manner that would be consistently applied to all assets and liabilities.[2]

ASC 820 (formerly SFAS 157) covers a wide variety of assets and liabilities, including elements of shareholders' equity. Besides typical assets and liabilities that most accountants are familiar with, ASC 820 also applies to financial derivatives, investments in securities available for sale, asset retirement obligations, guarantees, contingent consideration related to business combinations, and other financial instruments. Although there are a number of other applications of fair value for financial reporting, they are beyond the scope of this chapter. The reader is encouraged to obtain other FASB pronouncements, including ASC No. 815-15, *Derivatives and Hedging— Embedded Derivatives*, ASC No. 825-10, *Financial Instruments—Overall*, and ASC 860-50, *Transfers and Servicing—Servicing Assets and Liabilities*.

APPLICATION OF FAIR VALUE

As noted in the introduction, the definition of *fair value* is "the price that would be received to sell an asset or paid to transfer a liability in an orderly transaction between market participants at the measurement date." Under ASC 820, fair value is based on the *exit price* (i.e., the price that would be received to sell an asset or paid to transfer a liability), not the transaction price or entry price (i.e., the price that was paid for the asset or that was received to assume the liability). Although entry and exit prices can be the same, most often they are not since exit prices are typically based on current expectations about the sale or transfer price from the perspective of a market participant and not on what the asset or liability was priced at in the initial exchange. It is important to understand various concepts embodied in fair value measurements. A primary consideration in fair value measurements is the unit of account.

ASC 820-10-35-2B through 35-2E points out that fair value measurements relate to a particular asset or liability. As such, in measuring an asset or liability at fair value, an analyst should incorporate specific characteristics such as restrictions on its sale or use if market participants would take those restrictions into account when pricing the asset or liability at the measurement date. In addition to specified assets or liabilities, fair value measurement can be applied to standalone assets or liabilities or a group of related assets and/or liabilities. The determination of how the fair value measurement applies to an asset or a liability depends on the unit of

---

[2] June 2004 FASB ED, *Proposed Statement of Financial Accounting Standards—Fair Value Measurements*, paragraphs C4 and C11.

account. The unit of account is determined based on the level at which the asset or liability is aggregated or disaggregated in accordance with GAAP applicable to the particular asset or liability being measured. As is implied by the foregoing statement, the unit of account can vary depending on the circumstances surrounding the asset or liability. As is discussed later, in a goodwill impairment analysis under ASC 350 (ASC 350-30-35-21 through 35-28), the unit of account can be an entire business unit versus individual intangible asset fair value measurement under ASC 805. The analyst must consider all of the facts and circumstances when deciding on the proper unit of account.

Another important concept under ASC 820, the principal market, is found in ASC 820-10-35-5. Under the concept of a principal market, the transaction takes place either in the market with the greatest volume and level of activity for the asset or liability, or, in the absence of a principal market, in the most advantageous market. The most advantageous market is the market that maximizes the amount that would be received to sell the asset or minimizes the amount that would be paid to transfer the liability, after taking into account transaction and transportation costs. It should be noted, however, that the principal market is the market with the greatest volume and level of activity for the asset or liability being measured, not necessarily the market with the greatest volume of activity for the particular reporting entity, assuming the entity has access to that market. If there is no market for a particular asset or liability, a hypothetical market will need to be developed.

As a follow-on to the principal market, the next important concept is that of market participants. Market participants are buyers and sellers in the principal market for the asset or liability. Market participants can be thought of as unrelated parties who are knowledgeable about the asset or liability, are able to enter into a transaction for the asset or liability, and are otherwise willing to enter into a transaction for the asset or liability without compulsion.

One last concept needs to be addressed before turning to the final concept of fair value in this section. Prior to 2011, ASC 820 considered two approaches for determining the highest and best use of an asset: *in-use* and *in-exchange*. *In-use* referred to a valuation premise for an asset that provided maximum value to market participants principally through its use with other assets as a group. *In-exchange*, on the other hand, referred to a valuation premise for an asset that provided maximum value to market participants on a standalone basis. The amended guidance eliminates the use of these two approaches in favor of other guidance. Under the amended guidance, the concepts of the valuation premise and highest and best use are relevant only when measuring the fair value of nonfinancial assets. Accordingly, the fair value of financial instruments must be measured individually at the level of the unit of account discussed earlier.

The final concept covered in this section is the *fair value hierarchy* (ASC 820-10-35) from which inputs to valuation techniques used to measure fair value are prioritized into three broad levels, as follows:

1. Level 1 inputs are defined as "quoted prices (unadjusted) in active markets for identical assets or liabilities that the reporting entity has the ability to access at the measurement date. An active market for the asset or liability is a market in which transactions for the asset or liability occur with sufficient frequency and volume to provide pricing information on an ongoing basis. A quoted price in an active market provides the most reliable evidence of fair value and shall be used to measure fair value whenever available."

2. Level 2 inputs are defined as "inputs other than quoted prices included within Level 1 that are observable for the asset or liability, either directly or indirectly." If the asset or liability has a specified (contractual) term, a Level 2 input must be observable for substantially the full term of the asset or liability. Level 2 inputs include the following:
   (a) Quoted prices for similar assets or liabilities in active markets.
   (b) Quoted prices for identical or similar assets or liabilities in markets that are not active, that is, markets in which there are few transactions for the asset or liability, the prices are not current, or price quotations vary substantially either over time or among market makers (for example, some brokered markets), or in which little information is released publicly (for example, a principal-to-principal market).
   (c) Inputs other than quoted prices that are observable for the asset or liability (for example, interest rates and yield curves observable at commonly quoted intervals, volatilities, prepayment speeds, loss severities, credit risks, and default rates).
   (d) Inputs that are derived principally from or corroborated by observable market data by correlation or other means (market-corroborated inputs).

3. Level 3 inputs are defined as "unobservable inputs for the asset or liability. Unobservable inputs shall be used to measure fair value to the extent that observable inputs are not available, thereby allowing for situations in which there is little, if any, market activity for the asset or liability at the measurement date. However, the fair value measurement objective remains the same, that is, an exit price from the perspective of a market participant that holds the asset or owes the liability. Therefore, unobservable inputs shall reflect the reporting entity's own

assumptions about the assumptions that market participants would use in pricing the asset or liability (including assumptions about risk). Unobservable inputs shall be developed based on the best information available in the circumstances, which might include the reporting entity's own data. In developing unobservable inputs, the reporting entity need not undertake all possible efforts to obtain information about market participant assumptions. However, the reporting entity shall not ignore information about market participant assumptions that is reasonably available without undue cost and effort. Therefore, the reporting entity's own data used to develop unobservable inputs shall be adjusted if information is reasonably available without undue cost and effort that indicates that market participants would use different assumptions."

Level 1 inputs should be used whenever such evidence is available. Inputs subject to contracts must be observable for substantially the full term to qualify as Level 2. Valuations using Level 3 inputs require significantly more disclosure, and, when material, sensitivity testing. The level designation in the fair value hierarchy is based on the lowest level input that is significant to the fair value measurement, although the term *significant* is not defined in ASC 820. In assessing the significance of a market input, the appraiser should consider the sensitivity of the asset's or liability's fair value to changes in the input used. Assessing the significance of an input will require judgment considering factors specific to the asset or liability being valued. By the design of the principles-based standard, determining the significance of a market input is a matter of judgment. As such, different practitioners assigning level designations to the same asset or liability using similar unobservable inputs may reach different fair value conclusions.

Although ASC 820 contains a plethora of other guidance, for purposes of this chapter, the focus is on the use of fair value as a standard of value in financial reporting. As such, other concepts contained in the pronouncement are beyond the scope of this chapter. The reader is again encouraged to read the entire ASC 820 and the amendments contained in Accounting Standard Updates (ASUs) to gain a fuller understanding of this comprehensive fair value statement.

History of Fair Value in U.S. Accounting Literature

Fair value is a term that has long been used in the accounting literature. However, the term was often mentioned without providing either a definition or guidance on how to measure it. Therefore, the theory and application of fair value for financial reporting purposes was developed piecemeal over time.[3] Early reference to the term *fair value* dates to 1953 with the issuance of Accounting Research Bulletin No. 43—*Restatement and Revision of Accounting Research Bulletins.* ARB 43 is itself a restatement of even earlier accounting statements. Other early accounting pronouncements that reference fair value include Accounting Principles Board Opinions APB No. 29, *Accounting for Non-monetary Transactions,* issued in 1973, and FASB No. 15, *Accounting by Debtors and Creditors for Troubled Debt Restructurings,* issued in 1977.

Accounting statements in the United States are promulgated by the FASB. Prior to a project that resulted in the 2004 issuance of an ED on fair value measurement, the FASB had formally addressed the definition and usage of the fair value standard primarily in the context of reporting for financial instruments.[4] Examples of financial instruments include cash and short- and long-term investments. In 1986, the FASB added a project to its agenda on financial instruments and off-balance-sheet financing, which ultimately led to the issuance in 1991 of SFAS No. 107, *Disclosures About Fair Value for Financial Instruments,* and the issuance in 1998 of Financial Accounting Standards No. 133, *Accounting for Derivative Instruments and Hedging Activities.* In developing these statements, the FASB adopted a long-term objective of measuring *all* financial instruments at fair value.[5]

Use of the fair value standard in business combinations dates to APB 16 and APB 17, which were issued in 1970. These rulings were in effect for over 30 years and provided no definition of the term and little guidance on how to measure it. During the 1980s, there was a significant increase in the amount of merger and acquisition activity. At the same time, the U.S. economy's shift toward service-oriented and information-oriented businesses continued. With these phenomena, the stock of some public companies began trading at increasingly higher multiples of *book value.* Interest increased in how to explain these phenomena as being the result of *intangible* value, either developed internally or purchased in a business combination. Intangible assets included intellectual property such as trademarks, trade names, patented technology, knowhow, trade secrets, formulas and recipes, and the value of research and development.

As intangible value became more important to the enterprise value of corporations, discussions on how to account for intangible value increased.

---

[3] June 2004 FASB ED, *Proposed Statement of Accounting Standards—Fair Value Measurements,* paragraph C4.

[4] *Id.,* at paragraph C6.

[5] *Id.,* at paragraph C7.

Internally developed intangible assets are not recorded on a company's balance sheet for financial reporting purposes, but intangible assets purchased in a business combination are. However, lack of sufficient guidance on how to measure the fair value of assets in business combinations led to diversity of practice and the potential for different results in the measurement of comparable assets across a broad spectrum of businesses. For example, some companies combined their intangible assets, purchased in a business combination with goodwill, whereas other companies did not.

In some cases abuses were alleged, for example, in the valuation and write-offs of large amounts of in-process research and development (IPR&D) for business combinations in the technology sector in the mid-to-late 1990s. In a 1998 letter from the SEC to the American Institute of Certified Public Accountants (AICPA), then–chief accountant of the SEC, Lynn Turner,

> challenged the AICPA to take a larger leadership role, by developing detailed, broad-based guidance on valuation models and methodologies used (a) to measure fair value, under the oversight of the FASB, and (b) in auditing fair value estimates.[6]

The AICPA responded by forming a task force of accountants and valuation professionals to study the issue. In 2001, the AICPA Practice Aid, *Assets Acquired in a Business Combination to Be Used in Research and Development Activities: A Focus on Software, Electronic Devices, and Pharmaceutical Industries* (IPR&D Practice Aid), was issued. The introduction to the IPR&D Practice Aid cites that its purpose was:

> to bring together a task force to determine best practices in the valuation of IPR&D for financial reporting in business combinations.[7]

Meanwhile, the SEC continued to voice its opinion by also offering comments on the application on the fair value of assets in financial reporting

---

[6] Jackson M. Day, Deputy Chief Accountant, Office of the Chief Accountant, U.S. Securities and Exchange Commission, "Fair Value Accounting—Let's Get Together and Get It Done!" remarks to the *28th Annual National Conference on Current SEC Developments*, December 5, 2000.

[7] AICPA Practice Aid, *Assets Acquired in a Business Combination to Be Used in Research and Development Activities: A Focus on Software, Electronic Devices and Pharmaceutical Industries*, Introduction.

to a variety of other topics, including segregation of identifiable intangible assets from goodwill, goodwill impairment charges, customer-related intangible assets, and amortization of finite-lived intangible assets. In a 2000 speech at the Annual Conference on Current SEC Developments, a member of the SEC staff suggested:

> Standard-setters must provide more detailed, how-to accounting, valuation, and auditing guidance.
>
> The profession must work together and with others outside the profession including users and valuation experts.
>
> Preparers, auditors, and users must become better educated about fair value accounting.[8]

Whereas that speech specifically referred to fair value for financial instruments, its guidance has broader application to all assets that require fair value measurement for financial reporting.

The SEC also commented on valuators' and auditors' responsibilities. In a 2001 speech at a securities conference, Mr. Turner stated:

> Whether it is in conjunction with the acquisition of a business, the performance of the impairment test, or the evaluation of recorded intangible assets at transition, in almost every instance, companies will be required to obtain the assistance of a competent and knowledgeable professional to assist in the valuation of these intangible assets. Based on the staff's past experiences . . . I have concerns about the results of this process due to the lack of any meaningful guidance on valuation models and methodologies used to measure fair value and the auditing of those measurements.[9]

Accounting organizations and rulemaking bodies have responded to these challenges in recent years. As a result, the guidance on fair value for financial reporting has increased.

In 2000, the FASB issued FASB Concepts Statement No. 7, *Using Cash Information and Present Value in Accounting Measurements*, which was

---

[8] Day, "Fair Value Accounting."

[9] Lynn E. Turner, Chief Accountant, U.S. Securities and Exchange Commission, "The Times, They Are a–Changing," remarks to the *33rd Rocky Mountain Securities Conference*, May 18, 2001.

the result of a project the FASB had added to its agenda in 1988 to consider present value issues in accounting measurements.[10] And, citing increased amounts of merger and acquisition activity as a principal reason, the FASB undertook a new project in 1996 related to accounting for business combinations. This resulted in the issuance in 2001 of SFAS No. 141, *Business Combinations*, and SFAS No. 142, *Goodwill and Other Intangible Assets*. Both of these statements provide more specific guidance on fair value than did APB 16 and 17. Of course, since that time, SFAS 141 has been replaced by ASC 805 and SFAS 142 by ASC 350.

In 2003, the FASB formed the Valuation Resource Group (VRG), made up of preparers, auditors, and valuation specialists, to provide a standing resource to the FASB on fair value measurement issues.[11] Also in 2003, the Auditing Standards Board issued Statement of Auditing Standards (SAS) No. 101, *Auditing Fair Value Measurements and Disclosures*.

In the background notes to the ED on fair value measurement that was issued in June 2004, the FASB indicated that prior guidance regarding fair value measurement in the accounting literature was developed piecemeal over time and was contained in a number of different accounting pronouncements, which were not necessarily consistent with one another. The FASB indicated a desire to address these inconsistencies by establishing a framework that would be built on current practice but would also clarify measurement of fair value measurements in a manner that can be consistently applied to all assets and liabilities.[12] After an open comment period and further deliberations by FASB, working drafts of the proposed new accounting standard were issued in October 2005 and in March 2006. The adopted version of the new accounting standard on fair value measurement was issued in September 2006. Finally, in July 2009, the FASB launched the ASC discussed in detail in the foregoing sections. The ASC didn't change GAAP, but rather provided a new structure for organizing accounting pronouncements by accounting topic. ASC 820 is now the sole source for guidance on how entities should measure and disclose fair value in their financial statements. Since July 2009, the FASB has made several updates to ASC 820 and other fair value guidance through ASU amendments.

---

[10] FASB Concepts Statement No. 7, *Using Cash Flow Information and Present Value in Accounting Measurement*, paragraph 2.

[11] June 2004 FASB ED, *Proposed Statement of Accounting Standards—Fair Value Measurements*, paragraph C13.

[12] *Id.*, at paragraphs C4 and C11.

APPLICATION OF THE FAIR VALUE STANDARD TO BUSINESS COMBINATIONS

Use of the fair value standard in business combinations dates to APB 16 and APB 17, which were issued in 1970. APB 16 defines two accounting methods permissible for use in accounting for business combinations: the pooling of interests method and the purchase method. APB 16 compares and contrasts the two methods and delineates the conditions that would trigger the requirement to use one or the other. APB 17 deals with accounting for acquired intangible assets, both identifiable and unidentifiable (i.e., goodwill), which were acquired either singly or in groups, including in business combinations.

In APB 16, fair value is relevant to the purchase method. Fair value is used in connection with the "historical cost" principle as a way to determine the "cost" of the assets acquired.[13] In particular, fair value is the standard prescribed to allocate the "cost" of the acquisition to assets that were acquired as a group. APB 16 states:

> Acquiring assets in groups requires not only ascertaining the cost of the assets as a group but also allocating the cost to the individual assets which comprise the group. . . . A portion of the total cost is then assigned to each individual asset acquired on the basis of its fair value. A difference between the sum of the assigned costs of the tangible and identifiable intangible assets acquired less liabilities assumed and the cost of the group is evidence of unspecified intangible values.[14]

Despite providing guidance on using the fair value standard, APB 16 contained no definition of the term, and made no mention of how fair value is to be measured. APB 16 does indicate that independent appraisals could be used as an aid[15] in measuring fair value.

APB 17 deals with accounting for intangible assets, both identifiable and unidentifiable (the most common unidentifiable intangible asset being goodwill), that have been acquired by a business. APB 17 describes the characteristics of intangible assets as lacking physical qualities, making evidence

---

[13] APB No. 16, *Business Combinations*, paragraph 66. The purchase method was described as "following principles normally applicable under historical-cost accounting to recording acquisitions of assets and issuances of stock and to accounting for assets and liabilities after acquisition."

[14] *Id.*, at paragraph 68.

[15] *Id.*, at paragraph 87.

of their existence elusive. Furthermore, APB 17 states that the value of an intangible asset is often difficult to estimate and its useful life may be indeterminable.[16]

The historical cost principle is invoked in APB 17,[17] as it is in APB 16. The treatment of acquired intangible assets is to record them at cost on the date they are acquired. Intangible assets acquired as groups are recorded at cost, and the cost is allocated to each identifiable intangible asset in the group based on its fair value.[18]

APB 17 treats unidentified intangible assets (i.e., goodwill) differently from identifiable intangible assets. Unidentified intangible assets are accounted for using a residual method:

> The cost of unidentifiable intangible assets is measured by the difference between the cost of the group of assets or enterprise acquired and the sum of the assigned costs of individual tangible and identifiable intangible assets acquired less liabilities assumed.[19]

APB 17, like APB 16, does not define the term *fair value*, and the opinion does not mention how fair value is to be determined. With the lack of a definition for fair value and little guidance in the accounting literature as to how it should be measured, practitioners adapted various methodologies, based on facts and circumstances applicable to particular assignments, including versions of cost, market, and income approaches, to the valuation of tangible and intangible assets for financial reporting purposes in business combinations. As a result, a diversity of practice developed among valuators in the application of fair value to business combinations for financial reporting.

SFAS 141 and SFAS 142 superseded APB 16 and APB 17 in 2001. SFAS 141 reduced the acceptable methods for accounting for business combinations from two to one. The pooling of interests method was eliminated, and effective with the adoption of SFAS 141, all business combinations were to be accounted for using the purchase method. However, SFAS 141 did not fundamentally change the guidance of APB 16 in treating the cost of an acquired entity as its fair value. Absent persuasive evidence to the contrary, the transaction price between buyer and seller was presumed to be the cost of the acquired entity, and hence its fair value. The requirement to allocate cost to the acquired assets based on their fair values remained the same and

---

[16] APB No. 17, *Intangible Assets*, paragraph 2.

[17] *Id.*, at paragraph 15.

[18] *Id.*, at paragraph 26.

[19] *Id.*, at paragraph 26.

continues to the present, although now under ASC 805 for business combinations and ASC 350 for goodwill impairment testing.

With a few exceptions, ASC 805 requires the measurement of assets acquired and liabilities assumed at their acquisition-date fair values. ASC 805 uses the same definition of fair value as that used in ASC 820. As such, ASC 820 precludes the use of entity-specific assumptions and requires measurement of fair value based on assumptions from the perspective of market participants (if entity-specific assumptions are inline with the perspective of market participants, such assumptions are allowed to be used in fair value measurement). Accordingly, an acquirer must determine the fair value of assets acquired and liabilities assumed without considering the acquirer's intended use. This often gets tricky, as many companies acquire specific assets for purposes unique to those companies themselves. As a result, the acquirer may be required to develop hypothetical markets and to consider multiple valuation techniques even though these hypothetical markets were not contemplated by the actual acquirer. This is often a complex exercise requiring the use of valuation specialists trained in fair value measurements.

The other key change in SFAS 141 from APB 16 was that it provided additional guidance on the identification of intangible assets that were to be segregated from goodwill and valued separately. These concepts were carried over into ASC 805 but the valuation techniques used to apply fair value measurements were expanded and outlined in greater detail.

ASC 820 states that the transaction price equals fair value under certain circumstances, such as when, on the transaction date, the transaction to buy an asset takes place in the market in which the asset would be sold. However, as discussed in ASC 820-10-30-3A, and noted earlier in this chapter, a transaction price may not represent the fair value of an asset or a liability at initial recognition if certain conditions exist. Some of these conditions include related-party transactions, the transaction is forced, or the transaction is consummated in other than the principal market. To assist in measuring fair value of assets acquired or liabilities assumed, ASC 820 describes three valuation approaches used to measure fair value: the market approach, the income approach, and the cost approach. Since these approaches are more than adequately covered in other texts, this chapter merely highlights their application with specific relevance to business combinations.

ASC 820 does not prescribe the use of a specific income-based methodology to measure fair value. Rather, ASC 820 suggests that a reporting entity should use the appropriate technique based on facts and circumstances specific to the asset or liability being measured and the market in which they are transacted. However, ASC 820-10-55-4 does discuss specific present value techniques, including the *discount rate adjustment technique (DRAT)* and the *expected cash flow (expected present value) technique (EPVT)*. Again, a detailed explanation of these specific techniques is beyond the scope of this chapter, but the reader is encouraged to review the full narrative of ASC 820. However, an important point to remember is that if the initial recognition of the transaction price is considered fair value and a valuation technique that uses unobservable inputs is used to measure that fair value in subsequent periods, the valuation technique should be adjusted so that, at initial recognition, the result of the valuation technique would be equal to the transaction price.

In utilizing various valuation techniques, valuation inputs are required. These inputs generally refer to the assumptions that market participants use to make pricing decisions. ASC 820 distinguishes between (1) observable inputs, which are based on market data obtained from sources independent of the reporting entity, and (2) unobservable inputs, which reflect the reporting entity's own assumptions about the assumptions market participants would use. As noted earlier, ASC 820 emphasizes that a reporting entity's valuation technique for measuring fair value should maximize observable inputs and minimize unobservable inputs, regardless of whether the reporting entity is using the market approach, income approach, or cost approach. Inputs may include price information, volatility factors, specific and broad credit data, liquidity statistics, and all other factors that have more than an insignificant effect on the fair value measurement.

APPLICATION OF THE FAIR VALUE STANDARD TO ASSET IMPAIRMENT TESTS

Business combinations deal with the "initial recognition" of assets and liabilities. The ongoing accounting treatment for assets and liabilities after their initial recognition deals with depreciation and amortization for wasting assets as well as testing for impairment of both long-lived (wasting) assets and assets with an indefinite or indeterminable life (non-wasting).

In 1995, FASB issued SFAS No. 121, *Accounting for the Impairment of Long-Lived Assets and for Long-Lived Assets to Be Disposed Of*. SFAS 121 applied to tangible assets, certain identifiable intangible assets, and goodwill related to those assets. Once it has been determined that an impairment loss should be recognized, the measurement of that loss is to be determined by reference to the fair value of the asset.

As an update to SFAS 121, in 2001 the FASB issued SFAS No. 144, *Accounting for the Impairment of Disposal of Long-Lived Assets*, which superseded SFAS 121. The discussion of fair value in SFAS 144 was similar to SFAS 121, but was updated to be consistent with guidance included in Concepts 7, issued in 2000.

In 2001, FASB also issued SFAS No. 142, *Goodwill and Other Intangible Assets.* SFAS 142 addressed intangible assets with indefinite lives.

A key change in SFAS 142 from APB 17 was in the treatment of goodwill and other indefinite-lived intangible assets; they were no longer amortized, but rather were tested at least annually for impairment. The impairment test comprised a two-step testing process. Consistent with the Codification process, the FASB replaced SFAS 142 with ASC 350 and SFAS 144 with ASC 360. Many of the same principles contained in SFAS 142 and 144 were carried over initially into ASC 350 and 360.

However, in September 2011, the FASB issued ASU No. 2011-08 (ASU 2011-08), which stemmed from concerns expressed by preparers of private company financial statements regarding the cost and complexity of complying with ASC No. 350, *Intangibles—Goodwill and Other.* These preparers suggested a more qualitative approach to impairment testing be adopted to ease the cost and complexity of compliance. Previous guidance under ASC 350 required an entity to test goodwill for impairment at least annually, employing a two-step process (described below). Based on the ASU, companies can now assess goodwill using qualitative factors to determine whether it is "more likely than not" that the fair value of a reporting unit would be less than its carrying value, implying impairment. The more-likely-than-not threshold is defined as having a likelihood of more than 50%. If the fair value of the reporting unit is less than its carrying amount, then the second step of the test must be performed. Although the original cost concerns focused on private companies, public companies also expressed concerns about cost and complexity. As such, the ASU now applies equally to both public and private companies that have goodwill on their financial statements.

Although companies now have the option to first assess qualitative factors for goodwill impairment pursuant to ASU 2011-08, they are free to bypass the qualitative assessment for any reporting unit in any period and proceed directly to performing the first step of the impairment test. Nonetheless, an entity may resume performing a qualitative assessment in any subsequent period. It should also be noted, however, that the practice under SFAS 142 where an entity was permitted to carry forward its detailed calculation of a reporting unit's fair value from a prior year is no longer allowed. These amendments are effective for annual and interim goodwill impairment tests performed for fiscal years beginning after December 15, 2011.

While ASU 2011-08 does not address the current guidance for testing other indefinite-lived intangible assets for impairment, the FASB added a separate project to explore alternative approaches for such measurement in September 2011. In January 2012, the FASB issued a proposed ASU for ED on indefinite-lived intangible asset impairment testing, with the intent to simplify complexity and reduce the cost of complying with ASC No. 350, *Intangibles—Goodwill and Other*. Similar to ASU 2011-08, preparers would be allowed the option to first assess qualitative factors to determine whether it is "more likely than not" that the fair value of an indefinite-lived intangible asset would be less than its carrying value, implying impairment. The more-likely-than-not threshold is consistent between ASU 2011-08 and the proposed ASU for ED. The amendments included in the proposed ASU for ED would be effective for annual and interim impairment tests performed for fiscal years beginning after June 15, 2012, and early adoption would be permitted. The proposed ASU for ED was open for public comment until April 2012, and is expected to be ratified later in 2012. Now, let us turn to the first and second steps in a goodwill impairment test.

The first step of a goodwill impairment test can be described as the *identification* of potential impairment, and the second step can be described as the *measurement* of the amount of the impairment loss. The first step in the test for goodwill is performed at the reporting unit level. A reporting unit is defined as a collection of assets that operate together as a going-concern business. A reporting unit can be one level below a reporting segment and is described as the lowest level at which management captures and analyzes the financial data of a business. Additionally, a reporting unit has its own management and contains unique risk relative to other businesses in the reporting segment.

The first step of the test entails fair value measurement of the reporting unit and comparison of the fair value of that reporting unit to its carrying value. Carrying value is the amount of assets net of liabilities recorded on the balance sheet of the reporting unit. If the fair value exceeds its carrying value, no further work is required. However, if the fair value of the reporting unit is below its carrying value, the second step of the test is required. The second step of the test is akin to a valuation assignment for a fair value analysis of assets acquired and liabilities assumed (often, mistakenly for a purchase price allocation). A fair value analysis of assets acquired and liabilities assumed involves identifying and valuing each of the reporting unit's tangible and intangible assets in order to calculate the implied fair value of each reporting unit's goodwill. The amount of goodwill impaired is not necessarily the difference between the fair value and carrying value of the reporting unit, since the fair value of the reporting unit's underlying assets may be more or less than their carrying values. The second step of the test is required to determine the amount of goodwill impairment.

The fair value definition in ASC 350 is identical to the fair value definition in ASC 805, both of which follow ASC 820. ASC 350 also describes the same preference, or hierarchy, of methods for fair value measurement: (1) Quoted market prices in active markets are the best evidence of fair value, if available, and (2) in the absence of quoted market prices, estimates of fair value should be based on the best information available, including prices for similar assets and/or present value techniques.

INTERPRETATION OF FAIR VALUE COMPARED TO OTHER STANDARDS OF VALUE

Fair Value in Financial Reporting versus Fair Value in Dissenters' Rights Cases

Fair value as it is used in accounting literature for valuations in financial reporting is not the same as fair value as it applies to valuations in dissenters' rights and oppression cases. Fair value in dissenters' rights and oppression cases is a judicially created concept that appears in state statutes and case law and was utilized as a factor to distinguish valuation concepts in those cases from fair market value.

Fair Value in Financial Reporting versus Investment Value

Fair value in financial reporting differs from investment value in that:

Fair value reflects value in the market and is determined based on the assumptions of marketplace participants (willing buyers and sellers). In contrast, investment value reflects value to a particular investor (buyer or seller) and is often considered from the perspective of that investor as a basis for making investment (buy and sell) decisions. Differences between fair value and investment value may be attributable to varying factors (including synergies). Synergies refer generally to the benefits of combining two or more assets or asset groups (for example, operating units) and fall into two broad categories: (a) synergies generally available to all marketplace participants (marketplace synergies) and (b) synergies specific to a particular buyer not generally available to other marketplace participants (buyer-specific synergies).[20]

---

[20] June 2004 FASB ED, *Proposed Statement of Accounting Standards—Fair Value Measurements*, paragraph B2.

Fair Value in Financial Reporting versus Fair Market Value

Fair value in financial reporting differs from fair market value in several respects. Fair market value is prevalent in valuations for tax purposes, whereas fair value is required for financial reporting purposes. Although issued years ago, the explanation of the differences between fair value in financial statement reporting and fair market value contained in the ED on fair value measurement still holds:

> The definition of fair value used for financial reporting purposes often is confused with the similar definitions of fair market value used for valuation purposes. Specifically, Internal Revenue Service Revenue Ruling 59-60 defines fair market value as "price at which property would change hands between a willing buyer and a willing seller when the former is not under any compulsion to buy and the latter is not under any compulsion to sell, both parties having reasonable knowledge of the relevant facts." That definition of fair market value represents the legal standard of value in many valuation situations. Because the definitions of fair market value and fair value are similar, both emphasizing the need to consider the actions of marketplace participants (willing buyers and sellers) in the context of a hypothetical exchange transaction, some constituents asked the Board whether, in its view, they are the same or different. The Board believes that the measurement objectives embodied in the definitions are essentially the same. However, the Board observed that the definition of fair market value has a significant body of interpretive case law, developed in the context of the tax regulation. Because such interpretive case law, in the context of financial reporting, may not be relevant, the Board chose not to simply adopt the definition of fair market value, and its interpretive case law, for financial reporting purposes.[21]

Some valuators view the practical application of fair market value as a transaction-based approach whereas fair value is used to value an asset or group of assets within the context of a larger transaction (e.g., assets valued in a post-transaction allocation of purchase price). Fair market value is based on a value-in-exchange premise whereas the fair value of assets acquired and liabilities assumed, for example, is often based on a premise of value in-use. The current guidance under ASC 820, however, utilizes a valuation premise based on the highest and best use of the asset (financial assets

---

[21] *Id.*, at paragraph C27.

are treated differently) from the perspective of a market participant, which may be different from the reporting entity's intended use.

In the context of fair value of assets in business combinations, each asset of an acquired business is valued based on its contribution to the business as a whole, regardless of whether that asset could individually be bought or sold. An example would be a non-contractual customer relationship. This asset is usually not separable by itself from the business and under the definition of fair market value would have limited value in exchange by itself. Under the definition of fair value, the customers can have considerable value in-use as these relationships could represent the primary income-earning asset of the business.

In applying ASC 805, the price paid for the business is assumed to be the fair value of the acquired business, since it is the result of an arm's-length transaction between unrelated parties (willing buyer and willing seller) akin to the fair market value definition. Absent persuasive evidence to the contrary, it is difficult to successfully argue a fair value for an acquired business other than the transaction price. In this circumstance, fair value is determined by the price paid in one transaction.

Another example of fair value is in the derivation of the fair value of a specific asset in the context of purchase accounting. It is common practice to consider the tax benefits that an asset would generate if the asset were sold on a standalone basis when an income approach is applied to deriving value. The market approach is assumed to already have the tax benefits embedded in the market-based transaction prices. Debate and diversity of practice exist as to whether the application of a cost approach should include the tax benefit consideration.

A final example of an interpretive difference between fair value and fair market value is in the area of "cheap stock." Cheap stock issues are typically related to private companies that are approaching an initial public offering (IPO). In conjunction with the IPO, financial statements are issued that reflect the historic performance of the subject company for multiple years prior to the offering. A cheap stock expense often requires valuation and is commonly determined based on the difference between the strike price of options issued by the company to its management and others and the fair value of the underlying common equity. Interestingly, the FASB explicitly excluded ASC No. 718, *Stock-Based Compensation*, from the definition of fair value under ASC 820.

The SEC in its review of the financial statements has sometimes questioned any difference between the IPO price of the shares and the deemed fair value of the shares within six months of the IPO, even though the IPO event is subsequent to the valuation date. Application of marketability and lack of control discounts due to the uncertainty of completion of the IPO are rejected at times. One reason might be the subjective nature surrounding the magnitude of these discounts. Another reason may be a preference to use the subsequent IPO price since it is verifiable (i.e., it is not subjective). Either way, fair value in the context of cheap stock issues may rely heavily on after-the-fact events and sometimes a burden of proof is placed on the company to refute the assumption that a subsequent IPO price differs from fair value.

In contrast, subsequent events (i.e., the IPO price) are not given this same importance in the application of the fair market value standard. Further, marketability and lack of control discounts, changes in risk, and changes in business issues are each expected consideration in arriving at a value conclusion.

AUDIT ISSUES

The rise in accounting pronouncements dealing with fair value has created a need for increased guidance to auditors in their auditing of fair value determinations. In the absence of specific audit guidance, different perspectives among auditors, managements, and valuation specialists created inconsistencies in the auditing of assets and liabilities recorded on the balance sheet at their fair values. In 2003, the Auditing Standards Board (ASB) issued SAS No. 101, *Auditing Fair Value Measurements and Disclosures*.

SAS 101 notes that GAAP require certain items to be measured at fair value. SAS 101 refers to the definition of fair value contained in Concepts 7. SAS 101 notes that GAAP expresses a preference for using observable market prices to make fair value measurements, but notes that other valuation techniques are also acceptable, especially when observable market prices are not available. Key concepts included in SAS 101 include:

- *Management assumptions* used in preparing fair value estimates include assumptions developed by management under direction of the board as well as assumptions developed by a valuation specialist.
- *Market information and marketplace participants.* Valuation methods must incorporate information that marketplace participants would use, whenever market information is available.
- *Reasonable basis.* The auditor must evaluate whether management's assumptions are reasonable and/or not inconsistent with market information.
- *Valuation specialist.* The auditor should evaluate the experience and expertise of those making fair value estimates; management should

assess the extent to which an entity employs valuation specialists, and auditors should determine whether to engage a valuation specialist in auditing fair value estimates.

- *Subsequent events.* Events that occur after the balance sheet date but before completion of audit fieldwork may be used to substantiate fair value estimates.

Since SAS 101 was issued, the ASB discontinued its written guidance on audit issues, deferring instead to the FASB for accounting guidance. As such, SAS 101 has not been updated even though it continues to be a source of guidance to the accounting industry.

The audit environment today is increasingly focused on fair value measurement in general and the auditor's responsibilities regarding fair value measurements. Many of the largest accounting firms have established departments of valuation specialists working with their audit groups to assist with the auditing of fair value measurements. In addition, the FASB has regularly published ASUs to address specific issues and concerns of the accounting industry. The ASCs have provided a tremendous amount of consistency to accounting pronouncements and recent ASUs reflect the FASB's sensitivity to the cost and complexity of various accounting pronouncements.

SUMMARY

In recent years, there has been consistent communication in the accounting literature and GAAP of the use of fair value measurements in financial statements. Prior to the 1990s, the fair value standard for financial reporting was used less frequently, and guidance regarding its definition and measurement was vague and/or inconsistent. From the work done by FASB on financial instruments in the 1990s, to the issuance of Statement of Concepts 7 in 2000, which contains the fair value definition in use today, to the ED on fair value measurement issued in 2004, and finally the ASC in 2009, the use of fair value measurement in financial reporting continues to grow. The FASB has indicated that clearer guidance on fair value in the accounting literature will improve the consistency of its application, thereby improving financial reporting, and the SEC has called for this effort to continue. Although it was not touched on in this chapter, the FASB's initiative for convergence with the International Financial Reporting Standards (IFRS) is ongoing, as detailed in many ASUs. There has been consistent, albeit slow, movement toward total convergence between U.S. GAAP and IFRS, but significant hurdles to full convergence still exist.

Valuation specialists have an opportunity to participate in the growing emphasis on fair value measurement in financial reporting, and the need for valuation specialists in financial reporting has increased significantly. However, it is incumbent upon valuation specialists to understand the various fair value accounting pronouncements to determine consistent and appropriate valuation methodologies for financial reporting valuations. Fortunately, the AICPA has embarked on a number of initiatives to improve the consistency of fair value reporting among valuation practitioners, including practice aids for in-process research and development, goodwill impairment testing, contingent consideration, and share-based compensation.

Trends to watch in the continual evolution of fair value measurement in financial reporting include:

- Expansion of fair value measurement guidance, both in the United States and internationally:
  - Recent ASUs have addressed such issues as measuring the fair value of liabilities and investments in certain entities that calculate net asset value per share.
  - The FASB continues to work with accounting rulemaking bodies around the world to pursue convergence of U.S. GAAP with international accounting standards. This should increase consistency of U.S. valuation practices with those of other developed nations if full convergence is actually achieved.
  - There have been serious attempts by valuation practitioners to develop consistency in the application of valuation techniques to fair value measurements.
  - The Appraisal Issues Task Force has been established as an ad-hoc committee of valuation practitioners to discuss the expanding issues related to fair value and to build consensus for the development of consistent practices in the performance of valuations for financial reporting purposes.
  - Development of new practices in the auditing of fair value measurements.
  - Increasing role of valuation specialists in auditing firms, to assist with the auditing of fair value measurements.

APPENDIX: SOURCES OF INFORMATION

Accounting Research Bulletin (ARB) No. 43, *Restatement and Revision of Accounting Research Bulletins*

Accounting Principles Board Opinions (APB) No. 16, *Business Combinations*

APB No. 17, *Intangible Assets*

American Institute of Certified Public Accountants (AICPA) Statement of Position (SOP) 90-7, *Financial Reporting by Entities in Reorganization Under the Bankruptcy Code*

AICPA Practice Aid, *Valuation of Privately-Held-Company Equity Securities Issued as Compensation*

AICPA Practice Aid, *Assets Acquired in a Business Combination to Be Used in Research and Development Activities: A Focus on Software, Electronic Devices, and Pharmaceutical Industries*

AICPA Exposure Draft, *Proposed Statement on Standards for Valuation Services (SSVS)—Valuation of a Business, Business Ownership Interest, Security or Intangible Asset*

Financial Accounting Standards Board (FASB) Concepts Statement No. 7, *Using Cash Flow Information and Present Value in Accounting Measurement*

FASB Exposure Draft, *Proposed Statement of Accounting Standards—Fair Value Measurements*

FASB Working Draft, *Proposed Statement of Accounting Standards—Fair Value Measurements*

Statement on Auditing Standards (SAS) No. 73, *Using the Work of a Specialist*

SAS No. 101, *Auditing Fair Value Measurements and Disclosures*

Statement of Financial Accounting Standards (SFAS) No. 121, *Accounting for the Impairment of Long-Lived Assets and for Long-Lived Assets to Be Disposed Of*

SFAS No. 141, *Business Combinations*

SFAS No. 142, *Goodwill and Other Intangible Assets*

SFAS No. 144, *Accounting for the Impairment or Disposal of Long-Lived Assets*

Day, Jackson M., Deputy Chief Accountant, Office of the Chief Accountant, U.S. Securities and Exchange Commission, "Fair Value Accounting— Let's Work Together and Get It Done!" remarks to the *28th Annual National Conference on Current SEC Developments*, December 5, 2000

Kokenge, Chad A., Professional Accounting Fellow, Office of the Chief Accountant, U.S. Securities and Exchange Commission, "Speech by SEC

Staff: 2003 Thirty-First AICPA National Conference on Current SEC Developments," December 11, 2003

Letter, dated September 16, 2004, from the Accounting Standards Executive Committee to the FASB, commenting on the FASB Exposure Draft on fair value measurement

Turner, Lynn E., Chief Accountant, U.S. Securities and Exchange Commission, Letter dated September 9, 1998 to Robert Herz, Chair AICPA SEC Regulations Committee.

Turner, Lynn E., Chief Accountant, U.S. Securities and Exchange Commission, "The Times, They Are-a-Changing," remarks to *33rd Rocky Mountain Securities Conference*, sponsored by Continuing Legal Education in Colorado, Inc. and the Central Regional Office of the U.S. Securities and Exchange Commission, Denver, Colorado, May 18, 2001

International Business Valuation Standards

INTRODUCTION

International business valuation standards are in a stage of evolution. Most efforts to develop international business valuation standards beyond North America are within the context of broader valuation standards, that is, standards that include not only business valuation but also valuation of other types of property, such as real estate and personal property.

INTERNATIONAL VALUATION STANDARDS COUNCIL

By far the oldest and most developed of the international valuation standards movements is the International Valuation Standards Council (IVSC), a nongovernmental organization (NGO) of the United Nations.

The IVSC has been in existence since 1981, under the name of The International Assets Valuation Standards Committee (TIAVSC). The Committee changed its name in 1994 to the International Valuation Standards Committee (IVSC). As demand increased for valuation standards in different sectors and markets, it had become clear to the IVSC that its constitution and structure no longer could provide it with the legitimacy or resources required to meet these new challenges. In January 2007, the IVSC published proposals for a radical restructuring to transform the IVSC from a committee of representatives of its member valuation organizations into an independent body. At this time, the organization's name was changed to the International Valuation Standards Council.

The organization currently has three main bodies:

1. An independent Board of Trustees responsible for the strategic direction and funding of the IVSC and for appointments to the Standards Board and Professional Board
2. A Standards Board with autonomy over its agenda and the creation and revision of valuation standards
3. A Professional Board to promote the development of the profession around the world through producing professional and educational material in support of the standards[1]

Valuation Organization

Membership traditionally has been available to one national association per country. However, the Appraisal Institute of the United States, the Appraisal Institute of Canada, the Canadian Institute of Chartered Business Valuators, as well as the American Society of Appraisers (ASAs) are full members.[2] At this writing, there are about 72 full organization members. For about five years, the ASA's representative to the IVSC was Vern Blair. Since November 2011, the ASA's representative is Anthony Aaron.

The IVSC business valuation standards are closely aligned with the Uniform Standards of Professional Appraisal Practice (USPAP), which are promulgated by the Appraisal Foundation of the United States.

In 2011, it issued the ninth edition of *International Valuation Standards*. The major updates in the latest edition include:[3]

1. Created an IVS Framework containing much of the material in IVS 100–103. Because this material was in the nature of a discussion about valuation concepts and principles, it needs to be clearly separated from those standards that provide a clear direction as to what should be done in the course of a valuation assignment.
2. Created a new "General Standard" dealing with the implementation phase of a valuation assignment.
3. Reorganized the Asset Standards so that the requirements of each standard are more clearly distinguished from the background discussion.

---

[1] International Valuation Standards Council, *About the International Valuation Standards Council (IVSC)*, April 20, 2012 (http://www.ivsc.org/about/index.html).

[2] International Valuation Standards Council, *Membership*, April 20, 2012 (http://www.ivsc.org/members/index.html).

[3] International Valuation Standards Council, *The International Valuation Standards (IVS)*, April 20, 2012 (http://www.ivsc.org/standards/index.html).

4. Restructured the Financial Reporting Standards. The majority of the text was retained, but clearly presented as guidance on various valuation requirements under International Financial Reporting Standard (IFRS), and will make it clear that IFRS, or such other accounting standard that may be relevant, are the standards that must be followed.

5. Added new Standards for Real Property Interests, Businesses and Business Interests, Valuation of Plant and Equipment and Intangible Assets, Consideration of Hazardous and Toxic Materials, and Valuation of Historic Property.

In the ninth edition, the standards are organized as follows:[4]

1. IVS Definitions
   This contains those words or phrases that have a specific meaning in the context of the standards and that appear in more than one standard. Definitions that are used only in a single standard are defined only in that standard.

2. IVS Framework
   This contains generally accepted valuation concepts and principles upon which the IVS are based and that are to be considered and applied when following the standards.

3. General Standards
   The three General Standards have general application for all valuation purposes, subject only to variations or additional requirements specified in the Assets Standards or the Valuation Applications. The General Standards are IVS 101, *Scope of Work*, IVS 102, *Implementation*, and ICS 103, *Reporting*.

4. Asset Standards
   The Asset Standards consist of a standard and commentary. The standard sets our requirements that either modify, or are additional to, those in the General Standards and examples of how the principles in the General Standards are applied to the particular asset class. The commentary provides additional background information that describes the characteristics and methods used for their valuations. The Asset Standards include IVS 200, *Businesses and Business Interests*, IVS 210, *Intangible Assets*, IVS 220, *Plant and Equipment*, IVS 230, *Real Property Interests*, IVS 233, *Investment Property Under Construction*, and IVS 250, *Financial Instrument*.

---

[4]International Valuation Standards Council, *Staff Draft—Proposed Revised International Valuation Standards*, at 3–4, April 27, 2012 (http://www.ivsc.org/standards/20110214_staff_draft.pdf).

5. Valuation Applications

Valuation Applications are produced for two of the most common purposes for which valuations are required: financial reporting and secured lending. Each application contains a standard and guidance.

Broad Definitions

The IVSC standards define *value* broadly in this way:

> Value is not a fact, but an opinion, of either: a) the most probable price to be paid for an asset in an exchange or, b) the economic benefits of owning an asset. A value in exchange is a hypothetical price and the hypothesis on which the value is estimated is determined by the purpose of the valuation. A value to the owner is an estimate of the benefits that would accrue to a particular party from ownership.
>
> The word "valuation" can be used to refer to the estimated value (the valuation conclusion) or to refer to the preparation of the estimated value (the act of valuing). In these standards, it should generally be clear from the context which meaning is intended. Where there is potential for confusion, or a need to make a clear distinction between the alternative meanings, additional words are used.[5]

The IVSC standards define *market value* as:

> The estimated amount for which an asset should exchange on the valuation date between a willing buyer and a willing seller in an arm's length transaction, after proper marketing and where the parties had each acted knowledgeably, prudently, and without compulsion.[6]

The standards define *investment value*, or *worth*, as:

> The value of an asset to the owner or prospective owner for individual investment or operational objectives. This is an entity-specific basis of value. Although the value of an asset to the owner may be the same as the amount that could be realized from its sales to another party, the basis of value reflects the benefits received by an entity from holding the assets and, therefore, does not necessarily

---

[5] International Valuation Standards Council, *IVS Framework*, April 27, 2012 (http://www.ivsc.org/standards/reg_framework.html).

[6] *Id.*, at 8.

involve a hypothetical exchange. Investment value reflects the circumstances and financial objectives of the entity for which the valuation is being produced. It is often used for measuring investment performance.[7]

Approaches to Valuation

According to the IVSC standards, the three approaches described and defined in the Framework are the main approaches used in valuation. They all are based on the economic principles of price equilibrium, anticipation of benefits, or substitution:

Market Approach. This comparative approach provides an indication of value by comparing the subject assets with identical or similar assets for which the price information is available. In general, a property being valued (a subject property) is compared with sales of similar properties that have been transacted in the open market. Listings and offerings may also be considered.

Income Approach. This comparative approach provides an indication of value by converting future cash flows to a single current capital value. The Income Approach considers the income that an asset will generate over its useful life and indicates value through a capitalization process. Capitalization involves the conversion of income into a capital sum through the application of an appropriate discount rate. The income stream may be derived under a contract or contracts, or be non-contractual, e.g. the anticipated profit generated from either the use of or holding of the assets. Methods that fall under the Income Approach include: 1) Income Capitalization Method, 2) Discount Cash Flow Method, 3) various Option Pricing Models. In general, the principle of substitution holds that the income stream which produces the highest return commensurate with a given level of risk leads to the most probable value figure.

Cost Approach. This approach provides an indication of value using the economic principle that a buyer will pay no more for an asset than the cost to obtain an asset of equal utility, whether by purchase or by construction.[8] In a real estate context, one would normally not be justified in paying more for a given property than the cost of acquiring equivalent land and constructing an alternative

---

[7]Id., at 10–11.
[8]*Id.*, at 13–14.

structure, unless undue time, inconvenience, and risk are involved. In practice, the approach also involves an estimate of *depreciation* for older and/or less functional properties where an estimate of cost new unreasonably exceeds the likely price that would be paid for the appraised property.[9]

In the latest version of *International Valuation Standard*, the discussion on non-market-based valuations was deleted.

Types of Property

The IVSC recognizes "the customary division of property into six discrete categories:"[10]

1. Businesses and Business Interests
2. Intangible Assets
3. Plant and Equipment
4. Real Property Interests
5. Investment Property Under Construction
6. Financial Instruments

IVS defines a *business* as any commercial, industrial, service, or investment activity.

The IVSC standards analyze three approaches to business valuations:

1. The market and income approaches described in the IVS Framework can be applied to the valuation of a business or business interest. The cost approach cannot normally be applied except in the case of early stage or startup businesses where profits and/or cash flow cannot be reliably determined and adequate market information is available on the entity's assets.
2. The value of certain types of businesses (e.g., an investment or holding business) can be derived from a summation of the assets and liabilities. This is sometimes called the *net asset approach* or *asset approach*. This is not a valuation approach in its own right as the values of the individual assets and liabilities are derived using one or more of the principal

---

[9] *Id.,* at 33–34. at 26.

[10] International Valuation Standards Council, *Staff Draft: Proposed Revised International Valuation Standards,* April 2012, at 79 (www.ivsc.org/standards/20110214_ staff_draft.pdf).

valuation approaches described in the IVS Framework before being aggregated.[11]

3. IVS defines a financial instrument as a contract that creates rights or obligations between specified parties to receive or pay cash or other financial consideration, or an equity instrument. The contract may require the receipt or payment to be made on or before a specific date or be triggered by a specified event. An equity instrument is any contract that creates a residual interest in the assets of an entity after deducting all of its liabilities.

There are special attentions when applying the standard of Financial Instruments:

- Many types of instruments, particularly those that are traded on exchanges, are routinely valued using computer-based automated valuation models. These models are often linked to proprietary trading platforms. It is beyond the scope of IVS to examine such models in detail.
- It is important when using a particular valuation method or model to ensure that it is calibrated with observable market information on a regular basis. This ensures that the model reflects current market conditions and identifies any potential deficiencies. As market conditions change, it might become necessary either to change the model(s) used or to make additional adjustments to the valuations.[12]

TORONTO VALUATION ACCORD

The Toronto Valuation Accord (TVA) was born in late 2003 to attempt to bring convergence between the superpowers of accounting policy—the International Accounting Standards Board (IASB) and the Financial Accounting Standards Board (FASB)—with respect to valuation for financial reporting.[13]

Signers of the TVA were:

American Society of Appraisers

Appraisal Institute

---

[11] International Valuation Standards Council, *International Valuation Standards 2011*, April 27, 2012 (www.ivsc.org/standards/reg_200.html).

[12] *Id.*

[13] The authors are grateful to Lee Hackett, FASA, executive vice president of American Appraisal Associates, Inc. and one of the Appraisal Foundations representatives to the Toronto Valuation Accord, for his input to this section.

Appraisal Institute of Canada

Royal Institution of Chartered Surveyors—United States

Royal Institution of Chartered Surveyors—Canada

Centre for Advanced Property Economics

The Appraisal Foundation[14]

The activities and concerns of the TVA should be of interest, particularly to those involved in providing services that assist financial reporting requirements.

Mission and Objectives

The TVA states its mission and objectives in this way:

> The issue of valuation for financial reporting (VFR) poses a key emerging topic for the valuation profession. Recent events in the accounting profession and in the business world have brought issues of professional independence, measurement of asset value and transparency of reporting to the forefront. Accounting standards in the United States and Canada are expected to converge to a common global standard with the international accounting community, of which a component will be methodology for the reporting of assets. Under the Basel capital accords, the banking industry must account for assets and liabilities on a market basis, which has implications for the valuation profession.
>
> Accordingly, it is important that each organization representing the valuation profession in the United States and Canada, including real property, personal property and business appraisal, participate in a coordinated fashion to ensure a unified response on behalf of valuers and valuation standards. Participation in the Toronto Valuation Accord of October 2003 was a first step in this endeavor. The following is proposed as a plan for continued progress by the organizations and the profession:
>
> 1. We recognize that the recent movement of international standards toward convergence and harmonization, and the related emphasis on market (fair) value, increases the responsibilities of valuers in Canada, the United States, and worldwide to participate in the

---

[14]International Valuation Standards Council, *Toronto Valuation Accord*, April 20, 2012 (www.ivsc.org/news/nr/2003/1022nr-toronto.pdf).

establishment of reporting standards for the benefit of the users of financial reports and the public at large;

2. We agree to work together to develop policies and establish a plan to position the valuation profession as represented by their members, as the professionals of choice in the provision of valuation for financial reporting purposes and related services;

3. We encourage each organization to establish a plan for how that organization will inform and educate its members on valuation for financial reporting issues and will identify a principal contact in each organization who will coordinate with the other organizations to exchange information regarding those issues and the organization's plan.[15]

Definitions

The IASB states current value as being fair value, which the IASB defines as "the amount for which an asset could be exchanged, or a liability settled, between knowledgeable, willing parties in an arm's length transaction." The IASB sets forth these three criteria for fair value measurement:

1. Quoted market prices in an active market
2. Recent transactions for similar assets
3. Other valuation techniques

FASB defines *fair value* as "the price that would be received to sell an asset or paid to transfer a liability in an orderly transaction between market participants at the measurement date" (e.g., other than in a forced, or liquidation, sale). It further states that valuation techniques used to estimate fair value shall emphasize market inputs, including those derived from active markets, regardless of which approach (market, income, cost) is used.

While there is unanimous concurrence on the use of current value financial reporting, within the TVA there is ongoing discussion as to the premise underlying fair value. Some members think that fair value should be abolished and current value should be defined as market value; further, they believe that market value should be premised on in-exchange, reflecting highest and best use. Other members think that fair value as set forth by the accounting superpowers is an acceptable basis (as it has been for years under Accounting Procedures Board 16/17 and currently under FASB 141) and should be based on market value concepts. Market value concepts, as defined and used within TVA, mean that the premise for market value could

---

[15] *Toronto Valuation Accord Mission Statement 2003.*

be expressed as in-exchange, in-use, or liquidation, depending on the facts and circumstances and the owner's or market participants' intent.

Fair Value Measurement

Regardless of whether current value accounting is adopted, measurement of fair value of acquired assets is under scrutiny by the IASB and FASB. IASB criteria were listed in the previous section.

FASB issued an Exposure Draft on fair value measurements on June 23, 2004. Subsequently, there have been comment period reports and two public hearings to discuss the proposals, which have led to a June 2006 post-ballot daft on fair value measurements. FASB favors a hierarchal approach to estimating fair value, which it refers to as "levels":

Level 1. Quoted prices (unadjusted) in active markets for identical assets or liabilities that the reporting entity has the ability to access at the measurement date.

Level 2. Quoted prices for similar assets or liabilities in active markets or quoted prices for identical or similar assets or liabilities in markets that are not active.

Level 3. Unobservable inputs for an asset or liability, that is, inputs that reflect the reporting entities' own assumptions about the assumptions that market participants would use in pricing the asset or liability.

Obviously, there is a priority for market inputs if available and reliable and comparable; but there is nothing to preclude valuers from their prior practice of using valuation techniques appropriate to the economic availability of data.

FASB identifies two premises of value that could be utilized in estimating fair value: in-use and in-exchange. *Value-in-use* is based on an installed machine that will be used in income-producing activities of an entity. *Value-in-exchange* is contrasted as an installed machine that will be sold to another entity. There is an implication that the intent of the buyer will drive the premise of value. However, to do so, it would be necessary to show that any likely buyer would be expected to behave in a similar manner.

FASB goes further and identifies other premises that might be employed. *Orderly liquidation* could prevail if there was a requirement to dispose of any assets because of regulatory decrees, for example. *Abandonment basis* could also be appropriate if products are to be rebranded or trademarks discontinued. FASB presented two alternative approaches regarding using present value of future cash flows in accounting measurements. Called the *traditional approach*, it is acceptable to utilize a single, best estimate of future cash flows and discount same to present value at a discount rate that reflects the risk involved. Another approach, called the *expected cash flow approach*, utilizes multiple projections of possible outcomes that can be assigned probabilities and then discounted to present value.

Discount rate treatment utilizing an expected cash flow approach may require reflection of market-based risk premiums in one of two ways. The expected cash flow can be reduced for risk and then discounted at a risk-free rate. Alternatively, the expected cash flows are discounted at a risk-adjusted discount rate.

The recent decisions of FASB and the direction FASB is promoting on the enumerated emerging issues provide us with a clear signal: FASB has recognized that worldwide financial markets are demanding a unified set of financial reporting standards. No longer will a company have to follow U.S. generally accepting accounting principles (GAAP) to list shares in New York and list the same shares in London based on U.K. GAAP or international GAAP.

Another signal of convergence is the change in treatment of in-process research and development; it is no longer allowed to be written off, but must be amortized as required under International Accounting Standards (IAS) 36 and 38. Business combination rules under IAS and FASB are likely to become identical with regard to identification of intangibles separable from goodwill.

More signs of convergence abound as IASB has adopted FASB's definition of a business combination: "a transaction or other event in which an acquirer obtains control of one or more businesses." Both groups also have converged on the definition of *goodwill*: "Goodwill is future economic benefits arising from assets that are not individually identified and separately recognized."[16]

Conclusion

The North American professional valuation groups are coming together to promote the ability of professional valuers to meet the valuation needs of the new global financial reporting standards. The accounting and regulatory community and valuers themselves must become aware of the changes to come and must study these changes in order to continue and grow in a professional valuation career.

---

[16] Lee P. Hackett, Executive Vice President of American Appraisal Associates, Inc., "Valuation for Financial Reporting," unpublished paper, Milwaukee, WI (2005).

ROYAL INSTITUTE OF CHARTERED SURVEYORS

The Royal Institute of Chartered Surveyors (RICS), based in the United Kingdom, is comprised primarily of real estate appraisers. RICS published its first set of valuation standards in 1974. The purpose of the RICS standards is to provide users of valuation services with confidence that a valuation provided by an RICS-qualified valuer has been undertaken in compliance with the highest professional standards. The standards have evolved to the RICS *Appraisal and Valuation Standards*, last revised in March 2012.[17]

RICS defines market value as:

> The estimated amount for which an asset or liability should exchange on the valuation date between a willing buyer and a willing seller in an arm's-length transaction after proper marketing and where the parties had each acted knowledgeably, prudently and without compulsion.[18]

It is the stated goal of RICS to narrow as much as possible the differences between the RICS standard and the *International Valuation Standards*.

INTERNATIONAL FINANCIAL REPORTING STANDARDS

The International Financial Reporting Standards were previously known as International Accounting Standards (IAS) and are set by the International Accounting Standards Board (IASB). This board works closely with the Financial Accounting Standards Board in the United States. To draw a parallel, the IASB is to the FASB as the International Valuation Standards Committee is to USPAP.

---

[17] *RICS Appraisal and Valuation Standards*, revised (RICS Business Services Limited, a wholly owned subsidiary of the Royal Institute of Chartered Surveyors, Coventry, UK, January 2005).

Isurv, *VS 3.2 Market Value*, July 25, 2012 (www.isurv.com/site/scripts/documents_info.aspx?categoryID=1158&documentID=4764&pageNumber).

[18] *Id.*, at glossary at 2.

Chart—Fair Value in Dissent and Oppression

STATE	ALABAMA	ALASKA	ARIZONA
Valuation Term	Fair Value	Dissent: Fair Value Dissolution: Fair Value (under Liquidation)	Fair Value
Precedent in Allowing Discounts	(Case law) Rejects discounts.		(Case law) Rejects discounts.
Cases Addressing Discounts	*Ex parte Baron Services, Inc.* 874 So.2d 545 (Ala. 2003) No discounts applied.		*Pro Finish USA v. Johnson* 63 P3d 288 (Ariz. App. 2003) No discounts applied.
Definition of Valuation Term	§ 10A-2-13.01(4): Fair value excludes any appreciation or depreciation in anticipation of the corporate action unless exclusion would be inequitable.	Appraisal: § 10.06.580(c): In fixing the fair value of the shares, the court shall consider the nature of the transaction giving rise to the right to dissent, its effects on the corporation and its shareholders, the concepts and methods customary in the relevant securities and financial markets for determining the fair value of shares of a corporation engaging in a similar transaction under comparable circumstances, and other relevant factors. Oppression: § 10.06.630(a): The fair value shall be determined on the basis of the liquidation value as of the valuation date but taking into account the possibility, if any, of sale of the entire business as a going concern in a liquidation.	§ 10-1301(4): Fair value excludes any appreciation or depreciation in anticipation of the corporate action unless exclusion would be inequitable.
Valuation Date	§ 10A-2-13.01(4): Immediately before the effectuation of the corporate action to which the dissenter objects.	§ 10.06.580(c): The close of business on the day before the date on which the vote was taken approving the proposed corporate action.	§ 10-1301: Immediately before the effectuation of the corporate action to which the dissenter objects.
Dissolution by shareholder as a remedy for oppression or oppressive behavior?	Yes—§ 10A-2-14.30(2)(ii)	Yes—§ 10.06.628(b)(4) [*Oppression* not used as term in statute.]	Yes—§ 10-1430 (B)(2)
Buyout election in lieu of dissolution?	Yes—§ 10A-2-14.34(d)	Yes—§ 10.06.630	Yes—§ 10-1434
Dissolution Valuation Date	§ 10A-2-14.34(d): The day before the date the petition was filed or as of the other date the court deems appropriate under the circumstances.		§ 10-1434(D): The day before the date the petition was filed or as of another date as the court deems appropriate under the circumstances.

This appendix can also be downloaded at www.wiley.com/go/fishmanappendices (password: fishman358).

STATE	ARKANSAS	CALIFORNIA	COLORADO
Valuation Term	Fair Value	Dissent: Fair Market Value Dissolution: Fair Value (under Liquidation)	Fair Value
Precedent in Allowing Discounts	(Case law) Rejects discounts.	(Case law) Rejects minority discounts; no precedent re marketability discounts.	(Case law) Rejects discounts.
Cases Addressing Discounts	*Winn v. Winn Enterprises, L.P.* 265 S.W.3d 125 (Ark. App. 2007) Rejected minority and marketability discounts.	*Brown v. Allied Corrugated Box Co.* 154 Cal. Rptr. 170 (Cal. App. 1979) Rejected minority discount.	*Pueblo Bancorp. v. Lindoe, Inc.* 37 P.3d 492 (Colo. App. 2001), *aff'd*, 37 P.3d 492 (Colo. 2003) No minority discount and, except under extraordinary circumstances, no marketability discount.
Definition of Valuation Term	§ 4-27-1301(3): Fair value means the value of the shares immediately before the effectuation of the corporate action to which the dissenter objects, excluding any appreciation or depreciation in anticipation of the corporate action unless exclusion would be inequitable.	Appraisal: § 1300(a): Fair market value excludes any appreciation or depreciation in consequence of the proposed action, but adjusted for any stock split, reverse stock split, or share dividend that becomes effective thereafter. Oppression: § 2000(a): The fair value shall be determined on the basis of the liquidation value as of the valuation date but taking into account the possibility, if any, of sale of the entire business as a going concern in a liquidation.	§ 7-113-101(4): Fair value means the value of the shares immediately before the effectuation of the corporate action to which the dissenter objects, excluding any appreciation or depreciation in anticipation of the corporate action unless exclusion would be inequitable.
Valuation Date	§ 4-27-1301(3): Immediately before the effectuation of the corporate action to which the dissenter objects.	§ 1300(a): The day before the first announcement of the terms of the proposed reorganization or short-form merger.	§ 7-113-101(4): Immediately before the effective date of corporate action.
Dissolution by shareholder as a remedy for oppression or oppressive behavior?	Yes—§ 4-27-1430(2)(iii)	Yes*—§ 1800(b)(4) [*Oppression* not used as term in statute.]	Yes—§ 7-114-301(2)(b)
Buyout election in lieu of dissolution?	No	Yes—§ 2000	No
Dissolution Valuation Date		*Trahan v. Trahan* (2002): Valuation date is the date the dissolution proceeding was initiated; § 2000(f): in the case of a suit for involuntary dissolution under § 1800, the date upon which that action was commenced.	

(*continued*)

This appendix can also be downloaded at www.wiley.com/go/fishmanappendices (password: fishman358).

STATE	CONNECTICUT	DELAWARE	DISTRICT OF COLUMBIA
Valuation Term	Fair Value	Fair Value	Fair Value
Precedent in Allowing Discounts	(Statute) Rejects discounts.	(Case law) Rejects discounts.	(Statute) Rejects discounts.
Cases Addressing Discounts	*Devivo v. Devivo* 2001 Conn. Super. LEXIS 1285 Due to extraordinary circumstances, discounts applied. [Predates statute]	*Cavalier Oil Corp. v. Harnett* 564 A.2d 1137 (Del. 1989) Minority and marketability discounts are improper under Delaware law.	
Definition of Valuation Term	§ 33-855(4): Fair value means the value of the shares immediately before the effectuation of the corporate action to which the shareholder objects using customary and current valuation concepts and techniques generally employed for similar businesses in the context of the transaction requiring appraisal, and without discounting for lack of marketability or minority status except, if appropriate, for amendments to the certificate of incorporation.	§ 262(h): Fair value means the value exclusive of any element of value arising from the accomplishment or expectation of the merger or consolidation. In determining such fair value, the court shall take taking into account all relevant factors.	§ 29-311.01(4): Immediately before the effectuation of the corporate action to which the shareholder objects using customary and current valuation concepts and techniques generally employed for similar businesses in the context of the transaction requiring appraisal and without discounting for lack of marketability or minority status except, if appropriate, for amendments to the articles pursuant to § 29-311.02(a)(5).
Valuation Date	§ 33-855(4): Immediately before the effectuation of corporate action.	§ 262(h): Date at the point before the effective date of the corporate action.	§ 29-311.01(4): Immediately before the effectuation of the corporate action to which the shareholder objects.
Dissolution by shareholder as a remedy for oppression or oppressive behavior?	Yes—§ 33-896(a)(1)(B)	No—§ 275: Majority of directors plus majority of shareholders, or all shareholders by written consent.	Yes—§ 29-312.20(a)(2)(B) [corporations]; § 29-807.01(a)(5)(B) [LLCs]
Buyout election in lieu of dissolution?	Yes—§ 33-900	No	Yes—§ 29-312.24
Dissolution Valuation Date	§ 33-900(d): The day before the date on which the petition was filed or as of such other date as the court deems appropriate under the circumstances.		§ 29-312.24(d): The day before the date on which the petition was filed or as of such other date as the court deems appropriate under the circumstances.

This appendix can also be downloaded at www.wiley.com/go/fishmanappendices (password: fishman358).

STATE	FLORIDA	GEORGIA	HAWAII
Valuation Term	Fair Value	Fair Value	Fair Value
Precedent in Allowing Discounts	(Statute) Rejects discounts for corporations with ≤10 shareholders.	(Case law) Rejects discounts.	
Cases Addressing Discounts	*Cox Enterprises, Inc. v. News-Journal Corp.* 510 F.3d 1350 (11th Cir. 2007) No marketability discount applied by federal court due to lack of evidence. *Munshower v. Kolbenheyer* 732 So.2d 385 (Fla. App. 1999) Marketability discount allowed.	*Blitch v. People's Bank* 540 S.E.2d 667 (Ga. App. 2000) No discounts permitted.	
Definition of Valuation Term	§ 607.1301(4) [corporations]; [§ 608.4351(4) [LLCs]; § [§ 620.2113(4) [LPs]]: Using customary and current valuation concepts and techniques generally employed for similar businesses in the context of the transaction requiring appraisal, excluding any appreciation or depreciation in anticipation of the corporate action unless exclusion would be inequitable to the corporation [LLC] [LP] and its remaining shareholders [members] [partners]. For a corporation [LLC] [LP] with 10 or fewer shareholders [members] [partners], without discounting for lack of marketability or minority status.	§ 14-2-1301(5) [corporations]; [§ 14-11-1001(3) [LLCs]: Fair value means the value of the shares immediately before the effectuation of the corporate [LLC] action to which the dissenter objects, excluding any appreciation or depreciation in anticipation of the corporate [LLC] action	§ 414-341: Fair value means the value of the shares immediately before the effectuation of the corporate action to which the dissenter objects, excluding any appreciation or depreciation in anticipation of the corporate action unless exclusion would be inequitable.
Valuation Date	§ 607.1301(4)(a) [corporations]; § 608.4351(4)(a) [LLCs]: Immediately before the effectuation of the corporate action to which the shareholder [member] objects	§ 14-2-1301(5) [corporations]; § 14-11-1001(3) [LLCs]: Immediately before the effectuation of corporate [LLC] action.	§ 414-341: Immediately before the effectuation of corporate action
Dissolution by shareholder as a remedy for oppression or oppressive behavior?	Yes—§ 607.1430(3)(b) (in corporations with 35 or fewer shareholders) [Oppression not used as term in statute.]	Yes—§ 14-2-1430 (2)(B): Must be brought by holders of at least 20% of shares. Yes—§ 14-2-940(a)(1): (for close corporations) [Oppression not used as term in statute.]	Yes—§ 414-411(2)(B)
Buyout election in lieu of dissolution?	Yes—§ 607.1436	Yes—under articles of a close corporation—§ 14-2-942(b)(1)	Yes—§ 414-415
Dissolution Valuation Date	§ 607.1436(4): The day before the date the petition was filed.		§ 414-415(d): The day before the date the petition was filed.

This appendix can also be downloaded at www.wiley.com/go/fishmanappendices (password: fishman358).

(continued)

363

STATE	IDAHO	ILLINOIS	INDIANA
Valuation Term	Fair Value	Fair Value	Fair Value
Precedent in Allowing Discounts	Statute (1997) rejects discounts but federal court (2006) allowed minority discount in oppression case.	(Statute 2007) Rejects discounts.	(Case law) Rejects discounts.
Cases Addressing Discounts	*Hall v. Glenn's Ferry Grazing Assn.* 2006 U.S. Dist. LEXIS 68051 (D. Idaho) Minority discount applied by federal court applying Idaho law in oppression case.	*Brynwood Co. v. Schweisberger* 913 N.E.2d 150 (Ill. App. 2009) Discounts should generally be disallowed because they inequitably harm minority shareholders.	*Wenzel v. Hopper & Galliher, P.C.* 779 N.E.2d 30 (Ind. App. 2002) No discounts applied because discounts would unfairly benefit the buyer of the shares.
Definition of Valuation Term	§ 30-1-1301(4): Immediately before the effectuation of the corporate action to which the shareholder objects using customary and current valuation concepts and techniques generally employed for similar businesses in the context of the transaction requiring appraisal and without discounting for lack of marketability or minority status except for amendments to articles of incorporation.	§ 805 ILCS 5/11.70(j)(1): Fair value means the proportionate interest of the shareholder in the corporation, without discount for minority status or, absent extraordinary circumstance, lack of marketability, immediately before the consummation of the corporate action to which the dissenter objects excluding any appreciation or depreciation in anticipation of the corporate action, unless exclusion would be inequitable.	§ 23-1-44-3: Fair value means the value of the shares excluding any appreciation or depreciation in anticipation of the corporate action unless exclusion would be inequitable.
Valuation Date	§ 30-1-1301(4)(a): Immediately before the effectuation of the corporate action.	§ 805 ILCS 5/11.70(j)(1): Immediately before the consummation of the corporate action.	§ 23-1-44-3: Immediately before the effectuation of the corporate action.
Dissolution by shareholder as a remedy for oppression or oppressive behavior?	Yes—§ 30-1-1430(2)(b) [corporations]; § 30-6-701(1)(e)(iii) [LLCs]	Yes—§ 805 ILCS 5/12.55(2)	No—§ 23-1-47-1: Only in deadlock.
Buyout election in lieu of dissolution?	Yes—§ 30-1-1434	Yes—§ 805 ILCS 5/12.55(3)	No
Dissolution Valuation Date	§ 30-1-1434(4): The day before the date the petition was filed.	§ 805 ILCS 5/12.55(3)(d): Such date as the court finds equitable.	

This appendix can also be downloaded at www.wiley.com/go/fishmanappendices (password: fishman358).

STATE	IOWA	KANSAS	KENTUCKY
Valuation Term	Fair Value	Fair Value	Fair Value
Precedent in Allowing Discounts	(Statute) Rejects discounts except for banks and bank holding companies. (Case law) Control premium may be accepted.	(Case law) Rejects discounts.	(Case law) Rejects shareholder-level discounts.
Cases Addressing Discounts	*Rolfe State Bank v. Gunderson* 794 N.W.2d 561 (Iowa 2011). Discounts rejected for bank's reverse stock split. *Northwest Investment Corp. v. Wallace* 741 N.W.2d 782 (Iowa 2007) Control premium accepted in valuing a bank.	*Arnaud. v. Stockgrowers State Bank of Ashland, Kansas* 992 P.2d 216 (Kan. 1999) Discounts are not appropriate when purchaser is the corporation or the majority.	*Shawnee Telecom Resources v. Brown* 354 S.W.3d 542 (Ky. 2011) Discounts rejected.
Definition of Valuation Term	For companies other than banks: § 490.1301(4): Fair value means the value of the shares using customary and current valuation concepts and techniques generally employed for similar businesses in the context of the transaction requiring appraisal and without discounting for lack of marketability or minority status except for amendments to 490.1302(1)(e). For banks: § 524.1406(3)(a): In determining the fair value of shares of a bank or a bank holding company, due consideration shall be given to valuation factors recognized for federal tax purposes, including discounts for minority interests and discounts for lack of marketability. However, any payment shall be in an amount not less than the stockholders' equity in the bank as disclosed in its last statement of condition.	§ 17-6712(h): Fair value means the value exclusive of any element of value arising from the accomplishment or expectation of the merger or consolidation. In determining such fair value, the court shall take into account all relevant factors.	§ 271B.13-010(3): Fair value means the value of the shares excluding any appreciation or depreciation in anticipation of the corporate action unless exclusion would be inequitable.
Valuation Date	§ 490.1301(4)(a): Immediately before the effectuation of the corporate action to which the shareholder objects.	§ 17-6712(h): Date at the point before the effective date of the corporate action.	§ 271B.13-010(3): Immediately before the effectuation of corporate action.
Dissolution by shareholder as a remedy for oppression or oppressive behavior?	Yes—§ 490.1430 (2)(b) [corporations]; § 489.701 (1)(e)(2) [LLCs]	No—§ 17-6804: Voluntary	Yes—§ 271B.14-300 (2)(b) [*Oppression* not used as term in statute.]
Buyout election in lieu of dissolution?	Yes—§ 490.1434	No	No
Dissolution Valuation Date	§ 490.1434: The day before the date the petition was filed.		

This appendix can also be downloaded at www.wiley.com/go/fishmanappendices (password: fishman358).

(continued)

STATE	LOUISIANA	MAINE	MARYLAND
Valuation Term	Fair Cash Value	Fair Value	Fair Value
Precedent in Allowing Discounts	(Case law) Allows discounts "sparingly."	(Statute) Rejects discounts.	
Cases Addressing Discounts	*Cannon v. Bertrand* 2 So.3d 393 (La. 2009) Rejected discounts, stating that "discounts must be used sparingly and only when the facts support their use."	*Kaplan v. First Hartford Corp.* 603 F. Supp. 2d 195 (D. Me. 2009) Federal court rejected discounts and adjusted market prices to reverse built-in discounts. *In re: Val. of Penobscot Shoe Co.* 2003 Me. Super. LEXIS 140 Rejected discounts. *In re: Val. of McLoon Oil Co.* 565 A.2d 997 (Me. 1989) Rejected discounts.	
Definition of Valuation Term	§ 12:140.2(C): Fair cash value means a value not less than the highest price paid per share by the acquiring person in the control share acquisition.	§ 1301(4): Fair value means the value of the shares using customary and current valuation concepts and techniques generally employed for similar businesses in the context of the transaction requiring appraisal and without discounting for lack of marketability or minority status.	§ 3-202(b)(3): Fair value may not include any appreciation or depreciation that directly or indirectly results from the transaction objected to or from its proposal.
Valuation Date	§ 12:134(3): If voted upon, the latter of the date prior to the date of the shareholders vote or the day 20 days prior to the consummation of the business combination, otherwise the date of the action.	§ 1301(4): Immediately before the effectuation of the corporate action.	§ 3-202(b)(1): On the day notice of a merger is given or the date of a stockholder vote for other transactions.
Dissolution by shareholder as a remedy for oppression or oppressive behavior?	No—§ 12:141-146: Voluntary, or deadlock; deadlock only if shareholders or corporation are suffering irreparable damage, or if the corporation has been guilty of *ultra vires* acts.	Yes—§ 1430 (2)B	Yes—§ 3-413(b)(2); § 4-602(a) (close corporations)
Buyout election in lieu of dissolution?	No	Yes—§ 1434	Yes—under articles of a close corporation—§ 4-603
Dissolution Valuation Date			§ 4-603(b)(2): As of the close of business on the day on which the petition for dissolution was filed.

This appendix can also be downloaded at www.wiley.com/go/fishmanappendices (password: fishman358).

STATE	MASSACHUSETTS	MICHIGAN	MINNESOTA
Valuation Term	Fair Value	Fair Value	Fair Value
Precedent in Allowing Discounts	(Case law) Rejects discounts.		(Case law) Rejects minority discounts; marketability discounts at court's discretion.
Cases Addressing Discounts	*Spenlinhauer v. Spencer Press, Inc.* 959 N.E.2d 436; Mass. App. 2011 No discounts applied. *BNE Massachusetts Corp. v. Sims* 588 N.E.2d 14 (Mass. App. 1992) No discounts applied.		*Advanced Communication Design, Inc. v. Follett* 615 N.W.2d 285 (Minn. 2000) Marketability discount accepted. *Foy v. Klapmeier* 992 F.2d 774 (8th Cir. 1993) Federal court rejected minority discount. *MT Properties, Inc. v. CMC Real Estate Corp.* 481 N.W.2d 38 (Minn. Ct. App. 1992) Prohibited minority discounts.
Definition of Valuation Term	Ch. 156D, § 13.01: Fair value means the value of the shares excluding any appreciation or depreciation in anticipation of the corporate action unless exclusion would be inequitable.	§ 450.1761(d): Fair value is the value of the shares excluding any appreciation or depreciation in anticipation of the corporate action unless exclusion would be inequitable.	§ 302A.473(c) [corporations]; § 322B.386 subd. 1(c) [LLCs]: Fair value means the value of the shares of a corporation [LLC] immediately before the effective date of the corporate [LLC] action.
Valuation Date	Ch. 156D, § 13.01: Day immediately before the effective date of the corporate action to which the shareholder demanding appraisal objects.	§ 450.1779: The latter of the day prior to the date of the vote and 20 days before the date of the vote, or the date of the business combination if there is no vote.	§ 302A.473 [corporations]; § 322B.386 subd. 1(c) [LLCs]: Value of the shares of a corporation [LLC] immediately before the effective date of the corporate [LLC] action.
Dissolution by shareholder as a remedy for oppression or oppressive behavior?	No—Ch. 156D, § 14.30—34: Deadlock	Yes—§ 450.1489(1)	Yes—§ 302A.751 subd. 1(b)(3) [*Oppression* not used as term in statute.]
Buyout election in lieu of dissolution?	No	Yes—§ 450.1489(1)(e)	Yes—§ 302A.751 subd. 2 [corporations]; § 322B.833 subd. 2 [LLCs]
Dissolution Valuation Date			§ 302A.751 subd. 2 [corporations]; § 322B.833 subd. 2 [LLCs]: The date of the commencement of the action or as of another date found equitable by the court.

(continued)

This appendix can also be downloaded at www.wiley.com/go/fishmanappendices (password: fishman358).

367

STATE	MISSISSIPPI	MISSOURI	MONTANA
Valuation Term	Fair Value	Fair Value	Fair Value
Precedent in Allowing Discounts	(Statute) Rejects discounts.	(Case law) Court's discretion.	(Case law) Rejects discounts.
Cases Addressing Discounts	*Dawkins v. Hickman Family Corp.* 2011 U.S. Dist. LEXIS 63101 (N.D. Miss.) Federal court rejected discounts based on Mississippi statute.	*Swope v. Siegel-Robert, Inc.* 243 F.3d 486, 492 (8th Cir. 2001) Federal court rejected discounts. *Hunter v. Mitek Indus.* 721 F. Supp. 1102 (E.D. Mo. 1989) Federal court rejected discounts, but noted that discounts are at court's discretion. *King v. F.T.J., Inc.* 765 S.W.2d 301 (Mo. Ct. App. 1988) Accepted discounts.	*Hansen v. 75 Ranch Co.* 957 P.2d 32 (Mont. 1998) Minority discounts inapplicable when the shares are purchased by the company or an insider.
Definition of Valuation Term	§ 79-4-13.01(4): Fair value means the value of the shares using customary and current valuation concepts and techniques generally employed for similar businesses in the context of the transaction requiring appraisal and without discounting for lack of marketability or minority status.	§ 351.870: Fair value means the value of the shares excluding any appreciation or depreciation in anticipation of the corporate action unless exclusion would be inequitable.	§ 35-1-826(4): Fair value means the value of the shares excluding any appreciation or depreciation in anticipation of the corporate action unless exclusion would be inequitable.
Valuation Date	§ 79-4-13.01(4)(i): Immediately before the effectuation of the corporate action to which the shareholder objects.	§ 351.455(1): As of the day prior to the date on which the vote was taken.	§ 35-1-826(4): Immediately before the effectuation of the corporate action to which the shareholder objects.
Dissolution by shareholder as a remedy for oppression or oppressive behavior?	Yes—§ 79-4-14.30(2)(ii)	Yes—§ 351.494(2)(b)	Yes—§ 35-1-938(2)(b) [corporations]; § 35-8-902(1)(e) [LLCs]; § 35-9-501(1)(a) and § 35-9-504 [close corporations]
Buyout election in lieu of dissolution?	Yes—§ 79-4-14.34	Yes—under articles of a close corporation—§ 351.790	Yes—§ 35-1-939(1)(d) [corporations]; § 35-9-503 [close corporations]
Dissolution Valuation Date	§ 79-4-14.34(d): The day before the the date the petition was filed or such other date the court deems appropriate under the circumstances.		

This appendix can also be downloaded at www.wiley.com/go/fishmanappendices (password: fishman358).

STATE	NEBRASKA	NEVADA	NEW HAMPSHIRE
Valuation Term	Fair Value	Fair Value	Fair Value
Precedent in Allowing Discounts	(Case law) Rejects discounts.	(Statute) Rejects discounts.	
Cases Addressing Discounts	*Camino Inc. v. Wilson* 59 F. Supp. 2d 962 (D. Neb. 1999) Federal court rejected discounts based on Nebraska case law. *Rigel Corp. v. Cutchall* 511 N.W.2d 519 (Neb. 1994) Discounts rejected.	*American Ethanol Inc. v. Cordillera Fund, L.P.* 252 P.3d 663 (Nev. 2011) No discounts applied. *McMinn v. MBF Operating Acq. Corp.* 164 P.3d 41 (N.M. 2007) Discounts rejected.	
Definition of Valuation Term	§ 21-20,137(4): Fair value means the value of the shares excluding any appreciation or depreciation in anticipation of the corporate action unless exclusion would be inequitable.	§ 92A.320: Fair value means the value of the shares excluding any appreciation or depreciation in anticipation of the corporate action unless exclusion would be inequitable, using customary and current valuation concepts and techniques generally employed for similar businesses in the context of the transaction requiring appraisal, and without discounting for lack of marketability or minority status.	Corporations: § 293-A:13.01(3): Fair value means the value of the shares excluding any appreciation or depreciation in anticipation of the corporate action unless exclusion would be inequitable. LLCs and LPs: § 304-C:22-a(II) [LLCs]; § 304-B:16-c(II) [LPs]: Fair value means the value of the dissenter's interest excluding any appreciation or depreciation in anticipation of the limited liability [partnership] action.
Valuation Date	§ 21-20,137(4): Immediately before the effectuation of the corporate action to which the shareholder objects.	§ 92A.320: Immediately before the effectuation of the corporate action to which the shareholder objects.	§ 293-A:13.01(3 [corporations]: Immediately before the effectuation of the corporate action to which the shareholder objects. § 304-C:22-a(II) [LLCs]: Immediately before the effective date of the limited liability action.
Dissolution by shareholder as a remedy for oppression or oppressive behavior?	Yes—§ 21-20,162(2)(a)(ii)[corporations]; § 21-147(5)(a) [LLCs]	No—In a close corporation, only if by provision of the articles of incorporation— § 78-A160	Yes—§ 293-A:14.30(b)(iii) [corporations]; § 304-C:51(IV) [LLCs] [*Oppression* not used as term in statute.]
Buyout election in lieu of dissolution?	Yes—§ 21-20,166 [corporations]; § 21-147(5) (b) [LLCs—the court may order a remedy other than dissolution.]	No	Yes—§ 293-A:14.34
Dissolution Valuation Date	§ 21-20,166: The day before the date on which the petition was filed or as of such other date as the court deems appropriate under the circumstances.		§ 293-A:14.34: The day before the date on which the petition was filed or as of such other date as the court deems appropriate under the circumstances.

This appendix can also be downloaded at www.wiley.com/go/fishmanappendices (password: fishman358).

(continued)

369

STATE	NEW JERSEY	NEW MEXICO	NEW YORK
Valuation Term	Dissent: Fair Value Oppression: Fair Value + Equitable Adjustments, if any	Fair Value	Fair Value
Precedent in Allowing Discounts	(Case law) Rejects discounts except in oppression: allows control premiums on a case-by-case consideration.	(Case law) Rejects discounts; permits control premiums at court's discretion.	(Case law) Allows marketability discounts; rejects minority discounts.
Cases Addressing Discounts	*Casey v. Brennan* 780 A.2d 553 (N.J. Super. 2001) Control premium permitted but cannot include future benefits of merger. *Lawson Mardon Wheaton Inc. v. Smith* 734 A.2d 738 (N.J. 1999) No discounts applied. *Balsamides v. Protameen Chemicals, Inc.* 734 A.2d 721 (N.J. 1999) Marketability discount applied to reflect potential discount if company was sold.	*Peters Corp. v. New Mexico Banquest Investors Corp.* 188 P.3d 1185 (N.M. 2008) Control premium rejected based on facts of case. *McMinn v. MBF Operating Acq. Corp.* 164 P.3d 41 (N.M. 2007) Discounts rejected.	*Application of Adelstein* 2011 N.Y. Misc. LEXIS 5956 (N.Y. Supr.) Marketability discount applied, but not minority discount. *Murphy v. United States Dredging Corp.* 74 A.D.3d 815 (N.Y. App. Div. 2010) New York law prohibits minority discounts but allows marketability discounts.
Definition of Valuation Term	§ 14A:11-3: Fair value shall exclude any appreciation or depreciation resulting from the proposed action.	§ 53-15-4(A): Fair value means the value excluding any appreciation or depreciation in anticipation of the corporate action.	§ 623(h)(4): In fixing the fair value of the shares, the court shall consider the nature of the transaction giving rise to the shareholder's right to receive payment for shares and its effects on the corporation and its shareholders, the concepts and methods then customary in the relevant securities and financial markets for determining fair value of shares of a corporation engaging in a similar transaction under comparable circumstances and all other relevant factors.
Valuation Date	§ 14A:11-3(3): The day prior to the day of the [corporate action].	§ 53-15-4(A): The date prior to the day on which the vote was taken for the corporate action.	§ 623(h)(4): The close of business on the day prior to the shareholders' authorization date.
Dissolution by shareholder as a remedy for oppression or oppressive behavior?	Yes—§ 14A:12-7(1)(c)	Yes—§ 53-16-16(A)(1)(b)	Yes—§§ 1104-a(a)(1)
Buyout election in lieu of dissolution?	Yes—§ 14A:12-7	No	Yes—§ 1118
Dissolution Valuation Date	§ 14A:12-7: The date of the commencement of the action or such earlier or later date deemed equitable by the court.		§ 1118(b): The day prior to the date on which the petition was filed.

This appendix can also be downloaded at www.wiley.com/go/fishmanappendices (password: fishman358).

STATE	NORTH CAROLINA	NORTH DAKOTA	OHIO
Valuation Term	Fair Value	Fair Value	Fair Cash Value
Precedent in Allowing Discounts	(Case law) Court's discretion but disfavors discounts.		(Statute) Fair market value standard. (Case law) Permits discounts.
Cases Addressing Discounts	*Vernon v. Cuomo* 2010 NCBC LEXIS 7 (N.C. Super.) Rejected minority discount. *Garlock v. South Eastern Gas & Power, Inc.* 2001 NCBC LEXIS 9 (N.C. Super.) Rejected minority and marketability discounts as inequitable but permitted key-man discount applied.		*English v. Artromick Intl., Inc.* 2000 Ohio App. LEXIS 3580 Discounts applied, distinguishing "fair cash value" standard from "fair value." *Armstrong v. Marathon Oil Co.* 513 N.E.2d 776 (Ohio App. 1987) Valued dissenters' shares at pre-announcement market price.
Definition of Valuation Term	55-13-01(5): Fair value means the value of the shares immediately before the effectuation of the corporate action as to which the shareholder asserts appraisal rights, excluding any appreciation or depreciation in anticipation of the corporate action unless exclusion would be inequitable, using customary and current valuation concepts and techniques generally employed for similar business in the context of the transaction requiring appraisal, and without discounting for lack of marketability or minority status except, if appropriate, for amendments to the articles.	§ 10-19.1-88(b) [corporations]; § 10-32-55(1)(a) [LLCs]: Fair value of the shares means the value of the shares the day immediately before the effective date of a corporate [LLC] action.	§ 1701.85(C) [corporations]; § 1705.42(B) [LLCs]; § 1782.437(B) [LPs]: Fair cash value is the amount that a willing seller who is under no compulsion to sell would be willing to accept and that a willing buyer who is under no compulsion to purchase would be willing to pay, but in no event shall the fair cash value exceed the amount specified in the demand of the particular shareholder [member] [partner]. Any appreciation or depreciation in market value resulting from the proposal [merger, consolidation, or conversion] shall be excluded. (Corporations only): Any control premium or any discount for lack of marketability or minority status shall be excluded. The fair cash value of a share listed on a national securities exchange shall be the closing sale price immediately before the effective time of a merger or consolidation.
Valuation Date	§ 55-13-01(3): Immediately before the effectuation of the corporate action to which the shareholder objects.	§ 10-19.1-88(b) [corporations]; § 10-32-55(1)(a) [LLCs]: Day immediately before the effective date of a corporate [LLC] action objected to.	§ 1701.85(C) [corporations]; § 1705.42(B) [LLCs]; § 1782.437(B) [LPs]: The day prior to that on which the shareholders' [members'] [partners'] vote on the transaction was taken or the day before the day on which the request for approval or other action was sent.
Dissolution by shareholder as a remedy for oppression or oppressive behavior?	Yes—§ 55-14-30(2)(ii) [corporations]; § 57C-6-02(2)(ii) [LLCs] [*Oppression* not used as term in statute.]	Yes—§ 10-19.1-115(1)(b) [corporations]; § 10-32-119(1)(b) [LLCs] [*Oppression* not used as term in statute.]	No—§ 1701.91: Attorney general if corporation has acted unlawfully, voluntary dissolution; when it is established that it is beneficial to the shareholders that the corporation be judicially dissolved.
Buyout election in lieu of dissolution?	Yes—§ 55-14-31(d) [corporations]; § 57C-6-02.1(d) [LLCs]: After dissolution has been okayed by court.	Yes—§ 10-19.1-115(3) [corporations]; § 10-32-119(2) [LLCs]: within the court's discretion.	No
Dissolution Valuation Date		§ 10-19.1-115(3)(a) [corporations]; § 10-32-119(2)(a) [LLCs]: The date of the commencement of the action or as of another date found equitable by the court.	

This appendix can also be downloaded at www.wiley.com/go/fishmanappendices (password: fishman358).

(continued)

STATE	OKLAHOMA	OREGON	PENNSYLVANIA
Valuation Term	Fair Value	Fair Value	Fair Value
Precedent in Allowing Discounts	(Case law) Rejects discounts.	(Case law) Rejects discounts.	
Cases Addressing Discounts	*Woolf v Universal Fidelity Life Ins. Co.* 849 P.2d 1093 (Okla. App. 1992) Discounts rejected.	*Marker v. Marker* 242 P.3d 638 (Ore. App. 2010) No discounts applied. *Hayes v. Olmsted & Associates, Inc.* 21 P.3d 178 (Ore. App. 2001) Discounts rejected.	
Definition of Valuation Term	§ 1091(H): Fair value means the value exclusive of any element of value arising from the accomplishment or expectation of the merger or consolidation. In determining such fair value, the court shall take into account all relevant factors.	§ 60.551(4): Fair value means the value of the shares excluding any appreciation or depreciation in anticipation of the corporate action unless exclusion would be inequitable.	§ 1572: The fair value of shares taking into account all relevant factors, but excluding any appreciation or depreciation in anticipation of the corporate action.
Valuation Date	§ 1091: Effective date of the merger or consolidation.	§ 60.551(4): Immediately before the effectuation of the corporate action to which the shareholder objects.	§ 1572: Immediately before the effectuation of the corporate action to which the shareholder objects.
Dissolution by shareholder as a remedy for oppression or oppressive behavior?	No—§ 1096: Majority of shareholders	Yes—§ 60.661(2)(b); § 60.952(1)(b)	Yes—§ 1981 (a)(1)
Buyout election in lieu of dissolution?	No	Yes—close corporation provision only—§ 60.952(1)(k)	No
Dissolution Valuation Date		§ 60.952(6)(f): The day before the date on which the proceeding was filed or such other date as the court deems appropriate under the circumstances.	

This appendix can also be downloaded at www.wiley.com/go/fishmanappendices (password: fishman358).

STATE	RHODE ISLAND	SOUTH CAROLINA	SOUTH DAKOTA
Valuation Term	Fair Value	Fair Value	Fair Value
Precedent in Allowing Discounts	(Case law) Rejects discounts.	(Case law) Rejects discounts.	(Statute) Rejects discounts.
Cases Addressing Discounts	*DiLuglio v. Providence Auto Body, Inc.* 755 A.2d 757 (R.I. 2000) Discounts rejected.	*Morrow v. Martschink* 922 F. Supp. 1093 (D. S.C.1995) Federal court found that discounts are inapplicable in intra-family transfers in closely held company or in forced sale under S.C. law.	*First Western Bank of Wall v. Olsen* 621 N.W.2d 611 (S.D. 2001) Discounts rejected. [Predates statute]
Definition of Valuation Term	§ 7-1.2-1202(a): Fair value means the value of the shares excluding any appreciation or depreciation in anticipation of the corporate action.	§ 33-13-101(3): Fair value means the value of shares excluding any appreciation or depreciation in anticipation of the corporate action to which the dissenter objects, excluding any appreciation or depreciation in anticipation of the corporate action unless exclusion would be inequitable. To be determined by generally accepted techniques in the financial community.	§ 47-1A-1301(4): Fair value means the value of the shares using customary and current valuation concepts and techniques generally employed for similar businesses in the context of the transaction requiring appraisal; and without discounting for lack of marketability or minority status except, if appropriate, for amendments to the articles pursuant to subdivision (5) of § 47-1A-1302.
Valuation Date	§ 7-1.2-1202(a): As of the day prior to the date on which the vote was taken approving the proposed corporate action.	§ 33-13-101(3): Immediately before the effectuation of the corporate action to which the dissenter objects.	§ 47-1A-1301(4): Immediately before the effectuation of the corporate action to which the dissenter objects.
Dissolution by shareholder as a remedy for oppression or oppressive behavior?	Yes—§ 7-1.2-1314(a)(1)(ii)	Yes—§ 33-14-300(2)(iii) [corporations]; § 33-18-400(a)(1) & § 33-18-430 [close corporations]; § 33-44-801(4)(e) [LLCs]	Yes—§ 47-1A-1430(b)
Buyout election in lieu of dissolution?	Yes—§ 7-1.2-1315	Yes—§ 33-14-310(d)(4) [corporations] (within the court's discretion); close corporation provision—§ 33-18-420	Yes—§ 47-1A-1434
Dissolution Valuation Date	§ 7-1.2-1315: The day on which the petition for dissolution was filed.		§ 47-1A-1434.3: The day before the date on which the petition was filed or as of such other date as the court deems appropriate under the circumstances.

(continued)

This appendix can also be downloaded at www.wiley.com/go/fishmanappendices (password: fishman358).

STATE	TENNESSEE	TEXAS	UTAH
Valuation Term	Fair Value	Fair Value	Fair Value
Precedent in Allowing Discounts		(Statute) Rejects discounts. (Case law) Permitted discounts when shareholder had intent to sell to third party.	(Case law) Rejects discounts.
Cases Addressing Discounts		*Ritchie v. Rupe* 339 S.W.3d 275 (Tex. App. 2011) Discounts are applicable when minority shareholder has expressed intent to sell.	*Hogle v. Zinetics Medical, Inc.* 63 P.3d 80 (Utah 2002) Discounts rejected.
Definition of Valuation Term	§ 48-23-101(4) [corporations]; § 48-231-101(2) [LLCs]: Fair value means the value of the shares excluding any appreciation or depreciation in anticipation of the corporate [LLC] action.	§ 10.362 (a): Any appreciation or depreciation in the value of the ownership interest occurring in anticipation of the proposed action or as a result of the action must be specifically excluded from the computation of the fair value of the ownership interest. (b) Consideration must be given to the value of the domestic entity as a going concern without including in the computation of value any control premium, any minority ownership discount, or any discount for lack of marketability.	§ 16-10a-1301(4): Fair value means the value of the shares excluding any appreciation or depreciation in anticipation of the corporate action.
Valuation Date	§ 48-23-101(4) [corporations]; § 48-231-101(2) [LLCs]: Immediately before the effectuation of the corporate [LLC] action to which the dissenter objects.	§ 10.362(a): The date preceding the date of the action that is the subject of the appraisal.	§ 16-10a-1301(4): Immediately before the effectuation of the corporate action to which the dissenter objects.
Dissolution by shareholder as a remedy for oppression or oppressive behavior?	Yes—§ 48-24-301(2)(B)	No	Yes—§ 16-10a-1430(2)(b) [corporations]; § 48-3-701(5) [LLCs]
Buyout election in lieu of dissolution?	No	No	Yes—§ 16-10a-1434 [corporations]; § 48-3-702 [LLCs]
Dissolution Valuation Date			§ 16-10a-1434 [corporations]; § 48-3-702(4) [LLCs]: The day before the date the petition was filed or as of any other date the court determines to be appropriate under the circumstances and based on the factors the court determines to be appropriate.

This appendix can also be downloaded at www.wiley.com/go/fishmanappendices (password: fishman358).

STATE	VERMONT	VIRGINIA	WASHINGTON
Valuation Term	Fair Value	Fair Value	Fair Value
Precedent in Allowing Discounts	(Case law) Rejects discounts; accepts control premiums.	(Statute) Rejects discounts.	(Case law) Rejects discounts.
Cases Addressing Discounts	*In re: Shares of Madden, Fulford and Trumbull* 2005 Vt. Super. LEXIS 112 Control premium applied. *Waller v. American Intl. Distrib. Corp.* 706 A.2d 460 (Vt. 1997) No minority discount when oppression is found. *In re: Shares of Trapp Family Lodge, Inc.* 725 A.2d 927 (Vt. 1999) Control premium applied.	*U.S. Inspect, Inc. v. McGreevy* 2000 Va. Cir. LEXIS 524 Discounts rejected.	*Matthew G. Norton Co. v. Smyth* 51 P.3d 159 (Wash. App. 2002) No discounts applied.
Definition of Valuation Term	11A V.S.A. § 13.01(3): Fair value means the value of the shares excluding any appreciation or depreciation in anticipation of the corporate action unless exclusion would be inequitable.	§ 13.1-729: Fair value means the value of the shares immediately before the effectuation of the corporate action to which the shareholder objects; using customary and current valuation concepts and techniques generally employed for similar businesses in the context of the transaction requiring appraisal; and without discounting for lack of marketability or minority status except, if appropriate, for amendments to the articles pursuant to subdivision A 5 of § 13.1-730.	§ 23B.13.010(3) [corporations]; § 25.15.425(3) [LLCs]; § 25.10.831(2) [LPs]: Fair value means the value of the shares excluding any appreciation or depreciation in anticipation of the corporate action [merger] unless exclusion would be inequitable.
Valuation Date	11A V.S.A. § 13.01(3): Immediately before the effectuation of the corporate action to which the dissenter objects.	§ 13.1-729: Immediately before the effectuation of the corporate action to which the dissenter objects.	§ 23B.13.010(3) [corporations]; 25.15.425(3) [LLCs]; § 25.10.831(2) [LPs]: Immediately before the effectuation of the corporate action [merger] to which the dissenter objects.
Dissolution by shareholder as a remedy for oppression or oppressive behavior?	Yes—11A V.S.A. § 14.30(2)(B) [corporations]; 11 V.S.A. § 3101(5)(E) [LLCs]	Yes—§ 13.1-747(A)(1)(b)	Yes—§ 23B.14.300(2)(b)
Buyout election in lieu of dissolution?	Yes—close corporation provision—11A V.S.A.§ 20.15	Yes—§ 13.1-749.1	No
Dissolution Valuation Date	11A V.S.A.§ 20.15: As of the close of the business on the day on which the petition for dissolution was filed.	§ 13.1-749.1(D): The day before the date the petition was filed or as of such other date as the court deems appropriate under the circumstances.	

This appendix can also be downloaded at www.wiley.com/go/fishmanappendices (password: fishman358).

(continued)

STATE	WEST VIRGINIA	WISCONSIN	WYOMING
Valuation Term	Fair Value	Fair Market Value (for business combinations); Fair Value (for all other transactions)	Fair Value
Precedent in Allowing Discounts	(Statute) Rejects discounts by statute.	(Case law) Fair value rejects discounts for lack of control and lack of marketability; court's discretion.	(Statute) Rejects discounts.
Cases Addressing Discounts		*Edler v. Edler* 745 N.W.2d 87 (Wisc. App. 2007) Discounts rejected. *HMO-W Inc. v. SSM Health Care System* 611 N.W.2d 250 (Wisc. 2000) Discounts rejected.	*Brown v. Arp and Hammond Hardware Co.* 141 P.3d 673 (Wyo. 2006) Minority discount rejected; marketability discount not applied by lower court.
Definition of Valuation Term	§ 31D-13-1301(4): Fair value means the value of the shares using customary and current valuation concepts and techniques generally employed for similar businesses in the context of the transaction requiring appraisal and without discounting for lack of marketability or minority status except for amendments to § 31D-13-1302(5)(a).	For business combinations: § 180.1130(9)(a): Market value means, if shares are publicly traded, the highest closing sales price per share during the valuation period; if not publicly traded, the fair market value as determined in good faith by the board of directors. For all other transactions: § 180.1301(4): Fair value means the value of the shares immediately before the effectuation of the corporate action to which the dissenter objects, excluding apprecia-tion or depreciation in anticipation of the corporate action unless exclusion would be inequitable.	§ 17-16-1301(a)(iv): Fair value means the value of the shares using customary and current valuation concepts and techniques generally employed for similar businesses in the context of the transaction requiring appraisal; and without discounting for lack of marketability or minority status except, if appropriate, for certain amendments to the articles.
Valuation Date	§31D-13-1301(4): Immediately before the ef-fectuation of the corporate action to which the shareholder objects.	§ 180.1301(4): Immediately before the effectuation of the corporate action.	§ 17-16-1301(a)(iv)(A): Immediately before the effectuation of the corporate action to which the dissenter objects.
Dissolution by shareholder as a remedy for oppression or oppressive behavior?	Yes—§ 31D-14-1430(2)(B) [corporations]; § 31B-8-801(b)(5)(iv) [LLCs]	Yes—§ 180.1430(2)(b) [corporations]; § 183.0902 [LLCs]	Yes—§ 17-16-1430 (a)(iii)(B) [corporations]; § 17-17-140(a)(i) [close corporations]; § 17-29-701(a)(iv)(B) [LLCs]
Buyout election in lieu of dissolution?	Yes—§ 31D-14-1434	Yes—close corporation provision—§ 180.1833	Yes—§ 17-16-1434 [corporations]; § 17-17-142 [close corporations]
Dissolution Valuation Date	§ 31D-14-1434(d): The day before the date the petition was filed or as of another date as the court deems appropriate under the circumstances.		§ 17-16-1434: The day before the date the petition was filed or as of such other date as the court deems appropriate under the circumstances.

This appendix can also be downloaded at www.wiley.com/go/fishmanappendices (password: fishman358).

376

Standards of Value in Divorce Classifications by State and Standard of Value

This chart is intended to be used as *guidance* on the applicable standard of value in a given state. We do *not* intend it to be used as **determinative** of the standard of value in each state, or how goodwill, discounts, and buy–sell agreements are (or should be) treated. We have listed case examples and the substance of the decisions in those cases that assisted us in developing our suggested classification of the standards of value. Before relying on any case, the full text of the decision should be reviewed to determine whether the fact pattern in the case distinguishes it from the facts and circumstances in the subject valuation. A state with an empty box means that we have been unable to identify cases applicable to our analysis. In each state, where possible, we have gathered a selection of representative cases for the applicable categories. This is not a full list of the cases on each topic in each state.

	VALUE IN EXCHANGE		VALUE TO THE HOLDER	
	Fair Market Value	Fair Value	Investment Value	
		ALABAMA		
Goodwill				
Discounts		***Grelier v. Grelier***, 63 So.3d 668 (Alab. Civ. App 2010): The Alabama civil appeals court concluded that no discount for minority interest and lack of marketability should be applied; citing *Brown* of New Jersey. The court indicated: "Because the Alabama Supreme court has adopted the same reasoning that is applied in New Jersey in dissenting-shareholder cases, it seems reasonable to conclude that it would follow the same reasoning in divorce cases involving minority ownership of closely held business organizations."		
Buy-Sell				
SOV in Statute or Case Law		***In Hartley v. Hartley***, 50 So.3d 1102 (Alab. Civ. App. 2010): Court of civil appeals of Alabama made the "determination that valuation in divorce actions is to be based upon a 'fair value' concept and not necessarily a 'fair market value' principle."		

Based on *Grelier* (2009), we characterize Alabama as a fair value state in that it rejects minority and marketability discounts except in extraordinary circumstances as applied in dissenting-shareholder cases and as set forth in New Jersey's *Brown* case.

This appendix can also be downloaded at www.wiley.com/go/fishmanappendices (password: fishman358).

	VALUE IN EXCHANGE		VALUE TO THE HOLDER	
	Fair Market Value	Fair Value	Investment Value	
	ALASKA			
Goodwill	*Walker v. Walker*, 151 P.3d 444 (Alas. Supr. Ct. 2007): If the trial court determines either that no goodwill exists or that goodwill is unmarketable, then no value for goodwill should be considered in dividing the marital assets. *Fortson v. Fortson*, 131 P. 3d 451 (Alas. Supr. Ct. 2006): Lack of marketable goodwill in a dermatology clinic renders goodwill valuation moot. *Richmond v. Richmond*, 779 P.2d 1211 (Alas. Supr. Ct. 1989): Professional goodwill must be marketable in order for it to be included in a marital estate. *Moffit v. Moffit*, 749 P.2d 343 (Alas. Supr. Ct 1988): If the trial court determines either that no goodwill exists or that goodwill is unmarketable, then no value for goodwill should be considered in dividing the marital assets.			
Discounts	*Hanson v. Hanson*, 125 P.3d 299 (Alas. Supr. Ct. 2005): "Nowhere in *Money v. Money* did the Supreme Court of Alaska require application of minority discounts in all instances. Instead the court simply acknowledged that such discounts could be utilized and resolved a dispute about the size of a particular discount (marketability)." *Money v. Money*, 852 P.2d 1158 (Alas. Supr. Ct. 1993): The Superior Court concluded that such a minority discount was inappropriate in this case because the minority interest was being acquired by the party that also controlled the rest of the shares. The Supreme Court found that the Superior Court's valuation was not unreasonable using a marketability discount higher than 15%.			
Buy–Sell	*Money v. Money*, 852 P.2d 1158 (Alas. Supr Ct.1993): Accepts buy–sell as means of valuing business.			

(continued)

	VALUE IN EXCHANGE		VALUE TO THE HOLDER
	Fair Market Value	Fair Value	Investment Value
SOV in Statute or Case Law	*Fortson v. Fortson*, 131 P.3d 451 (Alas. Supr. Ct. 2006): "Regarding marital assets, the Supreme Court of Alaska has defined fair market value as the amount at which property would change hands, between a willing buyer and a willing seller, neither being under compulsion to buy or sell and both having reasonable knowledge of the relevant facts."		
	We characterize Alaska as a fair market value state. The Supreme Court of Alaska defined fair market value in *Fortson* (2006) as "the amount at which property would change hands, between a willing buyer and a willing seller, neither being under compulsion to buy or sell and both having reasonable knowledge of relevant facts." Both *Moffitt* (1988) and *Richmond* (1989) require that goodwill must exist and be marketable in order to be considered as marital property. In addition, minority and marketability discounts have been applied in Alaska cases, notably the *Money* case.		
	ARIZONA		
Goodwill			*Walsh v. Walsh* Arizona 2012 Ct. App. (1-CA-CV-110269): This case involves an interest in a large national law firm. The trial court departed from state precedent and found that goodwill was limited to the amount stated on the firm's stock purchase agreement. The trial court decision indicated that value emanated from what was "realizable" (which we understand to be what is saleable). Following Arizona case law precedent, the Appellate Court reversed and held that goodwill does not have to be realizable in order to have value, and distinguished between professional goodwill, which should be included as a marital asset, and future earning capacity which should not be included. *Mitchell v. Mitchell*, 732 P.2d 208 (Ariz. Supr. Ct. 1987): Valuation of intangible component of a professional practice attributable to goodwill was proper despite partnership agreement that specified goodwill had no value. *Wisner v. Wisner*, 631 P.2d 115 (Ariz. App. 1981): A sole proprietor corporation may have a goodwill value.

	VALUE IN EXCHANGE		VALUE TO THE HOLDER
	Fair Market Value	Fair Value	Investment Value
Discounts			
Buy–Sell			*In re: Marriage of Kells*, 897 P.2d 1366 (Ariz. Ct. App. 1995): A buy–sell agreement or other such agreement should be considered as a factor in valuing a business but it is not determinative of the value of marital stock.
SOV in Statute or Case Law			

Investment value appears to be the predominant standard of value in Arizona. The Arizona decisions generally view that goodwill exists in a sole proprietorship and a professional practice, and considers the practitioner's age, health, past earning power, reputation in the community for judgment, skill and knowledge, and comparative professional success as elements of goodwill. *Wisner* (1981) specifically rejects the contention that goodwill must be marketable to have value, and *Mitchell* (1987) follows *Wisner* (1981) on that principle. *Kells* suggests that a buy–sell agreement should be considered, but not necessarily relied upon in determining value.

ARKANSAS

	VALUE IN EXCHANGE		VALUE TO THE HOLDER
	Fair Market Value	Fair Value	Investment Value
Goodwill	*Cole v. Cole*, 201 S.W.3d 21 (Ark. App. 2005): Expert report for a surgery center was accepted based upon fair market value. Personal goodwill was determined to be 50% of fair market value. *Tortorich v. Tortorich*, 902 S.W.2d 247 (Ark. App. 1995): Business goodwill must be independent of individual goodwill in a sole proprietorship. *Wilson v. Wilson*, 741 S.W.2d 640 (Ark. 1987): For goodwill to be marital property, it has to be a business asset with value independent of the presence or reputation of a particular individual.		
Discounts	*Farrell v. Farrell*, 231 S.W.3d 619; Ark. (Supr. Ct. Ark. 2006) : "A minority discount was appropriate, even though Ms. Farrell presently has control of a majority of the voting stock of ARC, because the value of the shares can best be established by the past actual sales of the stock." *Crisman v. Crisman*, 34 S.W.3d 763 (Ark. App. 2000): Allows marketability discount of 12% because that reflects expenses that would be incurred in marketing and selling a partnership interest.		

(continued)

	VALUE IN EXCHANGE		VALUE TO THE HOLDER
	Fair Market Value	Fair Value	Investment Value
Buy–Sell	*Cole v. Cole*, 201 S.W.3d 21; (Ark. App. 2005): Trial court erred by valuing the former husband's 50% interest in a surgery center based on his buy–sell agreement with another shareholder instead of by determining the fair market value as required by statute.		
SOV in Statute or Case Law	**Arkansas Statute § 9-12-315(4):** "When stocks, bonds, or other securities issued by a corporation, association, or government entity make up part of the marital property, the court shall designate in its final order or judgment the specific property in securities to which each party is entitled, or after determining the fair market value of securities, may order and adjudge that the securities be distributed to one (1) party on condition that one-half (1/2) the fair market value of the securities in money or other property be set aside and distributed to the other party in lieu of division and distribution of the securities." **Arkansas Statute § 9:2801.2:** "In a proceeding to partition the community, the court may include in the valuation of any community-owned corporate, commercial, or professional business, the goodwill of the business. However, that portion of the goodwill attributable to any personal quality of the spouse awarded the business shall not be included in the valuation of a business."		

We categorize Arkansas as a fair market value state, primarily because of the statutory requirement that securities be valued at their fair market value. Arkansas case law follows this principle. Additionally, these cases require that goodwill be a business asset, independent of the presence or reputation of a particular individual.

	VALUE IN EXCHANGE		VALUE TO THE HOLDER	
	Fair Market Value	Fair Value	Investment Value	
		CALIFORNIA		
Goodwill			*In re: Marriage of Fenton,* 184 Cal. Rptr. 597 (Cal. Ct. App. 1982): Personal goodwill is included in marital estate; proper valuation of community goodwill (business or personal) is not necessarily its fair market value. *In re: Foster,* 117 Cal. Rptr. 49 (1974): The value of community goodwill is not necessarily the specified amount of money that a willing buyer would pay for such goodwill. In view of exigencies that are ordinarily attendant to a marriage dissolution, the amount obtainable in the marketplace might well be less than the true value of the goodwill. *Golden v. Golden,* 75 Cal. Rptr. 735 (Cal. App. 1969): In a matrimonial matter, the practice of a sole practitioner husband will continue with the same intangible value as it had during the marriage. Under the principles of community property law, the wife, by virtue of her position of wife, made to that value the same contribution as does a wife to any of the husband's earnings and accumulations during the marriage. She is as much entitled to the recompense for that contribution as if it were represented by the increased value of a stock in a family business.	
Discounts				
Buy–Sell	*In re: Marriage of Micalizio,* 199 Cal. App. 3d 662; 245 Cal. Rptr. 673 (Cal. App. 1988); citing *In re: Marriage of Rosan* (1972) 24 Cal. App. 3d 885: " . . . an agreement between the husband and the majority shareholder provided that the husband's shares could not be sold or transferred to anyone other than the corporation or the other shareholder without prior written consent." The other		

(continued)

	VALUE IN EXCHANGE		VALUE TO THE HOLDER
	Fair Market Value	Fair Value	Investment Value
Buy–Sell (*continued*)	shareholder could purchase such shares for the lower of their "computed value" or the price offered by a third party. "Computed value" was to be determined by a formula based primarily on the book asset value of the stock. Moreover, if the husband quit or was terminated for cause, the other shareholder could purchase the husband's stock for 70% of its "computed value." The trial court was justified in assessing the value of the stock at 70% of its "computed value." Although that was its lowest value except in the event of a sale to a third person for less, it was the only value that was relatively certain.		
SOV in Statute or Case Law	*In re: Marriage of Olga L. and Howard J. Cream,* 13 Cal. App. 4th 81; 16 Cal. Rptr. 2d 575 (Cal. App. 1993): "Pursuant to Cal. Civ. Code § 4800, the trial court must divide the community property equally and cannot delegate the responsibility to fix the fair market value of the community estate where assets were not divided in kind. The appellate court remanded the case to the trial court to determine the fair market value of the property on the date of the bid. The fair market value of a marketable asset in marital dissolution cases is the highest price on the date of valuation that would be agreed to by a seller, being willing to sell but under no obligation or urgent necessity to do so, and a buyer being ready, willing and able to buy but under no particular necessity for so doing."		

We categorize California as predominantly an investment value state. California cases have considered goodwill as a community asset, whether adhering to an individual or a business. *Golden* (1969), the earliest case on this issue in California, argued that the spouse makes an equal contribution to the other spouse's goodwill by his or her contributions as spouse. Further, both *Foster* (1974) and *Fenton* (1982) establish that the proper valuation of goodwill is not necessarily its fair market value. However, some argue that in California, community assets considered marketable should be valued using the fair market value standard of value. They cite *In Marriage of Cream* as the basis for the view that marketable assets should be valued at their fair market value. What constitutes a "marketable asset" is undefined and, in our view, the issue is unsettled.

VALUE IN EXCHANGE		VALUE TO THE HOLDER	
Fair Market Value	Fair Value	Investment Value	
COLORADO			

Hybrid—Review case law

	VALUE IN EXCHANGE		VALUE TO THE HOLDER
Goodwill			*In re: Marriage of Graff*, 902 P.2d 402 (Colo. App. 1994): Goodwill was included in valuation of a one-man insurance agency. The judge stated "The value of goodwill is not necessarily what a willing buyer would pay for such goodwill, rather, the important consideration is whether the business has a value to the spouse over and above tangible assets." *In re: Huff*, 834 P.2d 244 (Colo. Supr. Ct. 1992): In determining the intangible value of the husband's business, the important consideration is whether the business has a value to him above and beyond the tangible assets. Valuation does not necessarily depend on what a willing buyer would pay.
Discounts	*In re: Marriage of Thornhill*, 232 P.3d 782 (Colo. Supr. Ct. 2010): The Colorado Supr. court confirmed its Appellate division rejecting *Pueblo*, 63 P.3d at 369, which rejected marketability discounts in the context of dissenting shareholder. The court found that "trial courts may, in their discretion, apply marketability discounts when valuing an ownership interest in a closely held corporation in marital dissolution proceedings."		
Buy–Sell			*In re: Huff*, 834 P.2d 244 (Colo. Supr. Ct. 1992): Trial court is not bound by partnership agreement in determining value of law practice. Where partnership agreement was designed to discourage partners from leaving the firm and it appeared the husband intended to stay with firm, court was free to use an alternate valuation method, such as the excess earnings method.

(continued)

	VALUE IN EXCHANGE		VALUE TO THE HOLDER
	Fair Market Value	Fair Value	Investment Value
SOV in Statute or Case Law			
	Colorado's case, *In re: Huff* (1992), suggests that Colorado is predominantly an investment value state, endorsing the principles of the value to the holder premise, that an asset may have a value to the owner of that asset above and beyond what a willing buyer would pay for it. However, *In re: Marriage of Thornhill* (2010) allows the court to apply marketability discounts to an ownership interest in a closely held corporation, a fair market value concept. The court made it clear that the holding in *Pueblo* is not necessarily applicable in divorce cases. Therefore, we classify Colorado as a hybrid state.		
	CONNECTICUT		
Goodwill	***Eslami v. Eslami***, 591 A.2d 411 (Conn. Supr. Ct. 1991): Goodwill of a radiology medical practice must be marketable in order to be included in the marital assets. "To the extent that the goodwill of the practice cannot be detached from the personal reputation and ability of the practitioner through a sale, it cannot be said to have any significant market value, even though it may enhance the earning power of the same practitioner so long as he continues to work in the same community. If goodwill depends on the continued presence of a particular individual, such goodwill, by definition, is not a marketable asset distinct from the individual."		
Discounts	***Ferguson v. Ferguson***, No. FA 960713118, 1998 WL 851426 (Conn. Super. Ct. 1998): Applied marketability discount.		
Buy–Sell	***Dahill v. Dahill***, 1998 Conn. Super. LEXIS 846 (Conn. Super. Ct. 1998): In a divorce proceeding, the court did not accept the valuation of stock in a closely held corporation offered by the husband's expert, where it was based on the shareholder agreement and none of the triggering events in the shareholder agreement had occurred. ***Stearns v. Stearns***, 494 A.2d 595 (Conn. App. Ct. 1985): A buy–sell agreement or other such agreement should be considered as a factor in valuing a business, but it is not necessarily determinative of the value of marital stock.		

	VALUE IN EXCHANGE		VALUE TO THE HOLDER
	Fair Market Value	Fair Value	Investment Value
SOV in Statute or Case Law	***Dahill v. Dahill***, 1998 Conn. Super. LEXIS 846 (Conn. Super. Ct. Mar. 30 1998): "It was the court's duty to find the *fair market value*, not the book value or the 'in-hand value' to the husband."		
	Connecticut's decisions suggest that it generally follows a fair market value standard. *Eslami* (1991) establishes the principle that goodwill must be marketable in order to be included in the marital assets and *Dahill* (1998) suggests that although a buy–sell agreement may be in place, the court is looking to find the fair market value, which is not necessarily the value established by that agreement. Connecticut courts have also applied marketability discounts, as in *Ferguson* (1998).		
DELAWARE			
Goodwill	***S.S. v. C.S.***, LEXIS 213 (Del. Fam. Ct. 2003): Goodwill should be dealt with in the context of alimony rather than property distribution, so that the risks and rewards may both be shared, instead of ascribing a current value on a speculative future income stream. ***E.E.C. v. E.J.C.***, 457 A.2d 688 (Del. Supr. Ct. 1983): Rejected capitalization of husband's earnings to determine value of business for marital assets. The parties agreed that there were no excess earnings and therefore no goodwill in a sole proprietorship.		
Discounts			
Buy–Sell			
SOV in Statute or Case Law			
	Delaware cases have established that a business should be valued as the market value company's tangible assets, in excess of its liabilities, its accounts receivable, and work-in-progress. They have also suggested that although goodwill may exist, it should be handled in the form of alimony, where risks and rewards are shared. Because of this treatment of goodwill in the valuation of stock, we believe that Delaware may be predominantly categorized as a walk-away fair market value state.		

(continued)

387

	VALUE IN EXCHANGE		VALUE TO THE HOLDER	
	Fair Market Value	Fair Value	Investment Value	

DISTRICT OF COLUMBIA

Goodwill	***McDiarmid v. McDiarmid***, 649 A.2d 810 (D.C. App. 1994): Goodwill may exist in a professional practice and if acquired during the marriage is marital property. However, a partner's ability to realize that goodwill upon exiting affects whether that goodwill has any value.	
Discounts		
Buy–Sell	***McDiarmid v. McDiarmid***, 649 A.2d 810 (D.C. App. 1994): Trial judge erred in valuing goodwill of husband's partnership interest in law firm, given express terms of partnership agreement that made goodwill nonsalable and the absence of any other factors that could make the goodwill valuable.	
SOV in Statute or Case Law	The court in *McDiarmid* (1994) recognized that goodwill exists in a professional practice, but suggested that the value of the goodwill was dependent on the ability of the professional to realize that value upon exit, and the partnership agreement limited the partner's ability to sell the goodwill. Because of this, we classify the District of Columbia as being fair market value. The case did not consider the value of the goodwill as if the owner remained, but instead, it valued the goodwill based on the owner's ability to realize it upon exit.	

FLORIDA

Goodwill	***Held v. Held***, 912 So.2d 637 (Fla. App 2005): The adjusted book value was used in determining the fair market value of the business. The court rejected the inclusion of a non-solicitation agreement in enterprise goodwill. ***Williams v. Williams***, 667 So.2d 915 (Fla. Dist. Ct App. 1996): Business goodwill of a professional practice is a marital asset subject to division if it exists and was developed during the marriage. However, if a noncompete agreement would be required pursuant to a sale, there is no reason to believe that the goodwill adheres to the enterprise.	

	VALUE IN EXCHANGE		VALUE TO THE HOLDER	
	Fair Market Value	Fair Value	Investment Value	

Goodwill (*continued*)	*Thompson v. Thompson*, 576 So.2d 267 (Fla. Supr. Ct.1991): Fair market value approach should be the exclusive method of measuring business goodwill.
Discounts	*Erp v. Erp*, 976 So.2d 1234 (Fla. App. 2007): "A trial court should be accorded the discretion to determine whether a marketability discount should apply to the valuation of a closely held corporation in a dissolution of marriage case where the court is traditionally charged with achieving equity through the use of various remedies." The appeals court found "no abuse of discretion in the trial court's decision to apply a ten-percent marketability discount in this case."
Buy–Sell	*Garcia v. Garcia*, 25 So.3d 687 (Fla. App. 2010): "The sale price set by restrictive provisions on transfer of closely held stock is not conclusive as to the value. However, restrictive transfer covenants affect value through impaired marketability and must be considered when a trial court determines the value of stock for purposes of equitable distribution. When stock is subject to a restrictive transfer agreement the price fixed by such provisions will not control its value, but the restriction on transfer is a factor which affects the value of the stock for purposes of equitable distribution."
SOV in Statute or Case Law	*Christians v. Christians*, 732 So. 2d 47; (Fla. App.1999): "The valuation of a business is calculated by determining the fair market value of the business which is the amount a willing buyer and willing seller would exchange assets absent duress." citing Makowski v. Makowski 613 So. 2d 924, 926 (Fla. 3d DCA 1993).

Because of the treatment of goodwill in the valuation of businesses in Florida, we consider Florida a walk-away fair market value state. Although business goodwill may be included in a valuation, Florida cases have recognized business goodwill in a professional practice. However, Florida indicated that the business is to be valued absent the efforts of the owner and assumes the owner is free to compete. We have categorized these assumptions as a "walk-away" doctrine.

(*continued*)

	VALUE IN EXCHANGE		VALUE TO THE HOLDER	
	Fair Market Value	Fair Value	Investment Value	
		GEORGIA		
Goodwill	***Miller v. Miller***, 288 Ga. 274 (Ga. Supr.Ct. 2010): In this case involving a medical practice, the court found that enterprise goodwill is marital and personal goodwill is not. "Enterprise or commercial goodwill is transferred whenever the enterprise to which it attaches is bought and sold as an ongoing concern. Individual or personal goodwill is not transferable when the enterprise is bought and sold, and instead resides primarily in the personal reputation of the owner. The strong general rule is that enterprise goodwill must be included when valuing a business entity as marital property."			
Discounts				
Buy-Sell	***Barton v. Barton***, 639 S.E.2d 481 (Ga. Supr. Ct. 2007): The Georgia Supreme Court answers the question: "Whether in placing a value on the stock of a closely-held corporation for purposes of dividing marital property, was the court bound by the value set forth in a buy-sell provision of the stockholder agreement? The short answer was 'no'. A clear majority of courts held that the value established in the buy-sell agreement of a closely-held corporation, not signed by the non-shareholder spouse, was not binding on the non-shareholder spouse, but was considered along with other factors, in valuing the interest of the shareholder spouse. The rationale for this rule was simply because the buy-sell price in a closely-held corporation could be manipulated and did not necessarily reflect true value."			
SOV in Statute or Case Law				

	VALUE IN EXCHANGE		VALUE TO THE HOLDER
	Fair Market Value	Fair Value	Investment Value
	Miller (2010) follows the line of thinking that enterprise goodwill is marital, but personal goodwill is not. Accordingly, we categorize Georgia as a fair market value state.		

HAWAII

	VALUE IN EXCHANGE		VALUE TO THE HOLDER
	Fair Market Value	Fair Value	Investment Value
Goodwill	*Weinberg v. Weinberg*, 220 P.3d 264; 2009 (Haw. Interm. App. 2009): "Where goodwill is a marketable business asset distinct from the personal reputation of a particular individual, as is usually the case with many commercial enterprises, that goodwill has immediately discernible value as an asset of the business and may be identified as an amount reflected in a sale or transfer of such business. On the other hand, if goodwill depends on the continued presence of a particular individual, such goodwill, by definition, is not a marketable asset distinct from the individual. Any value which attaches to the entity solely as a result of personal goodwill represents nothing more than probable future earning capacity, which although relevant in determining alimony, is not a proper consideration in dividing marital property in a dissolution proceeding."		
Discounts	*Doe v. Roe*, LEXIS 310 (Haw. Interm. App. 2010): Husband owned 20% interest of his family's residential property in Honolulu. Each of his four siblings owned 20% as well. The family court considered testimony from experts on both sides and found testimony by the husband's expert credible that "lack of control" and "lack of marketability" adjustments should be utilized.		
Buy–Sell			
SOV in Statute or Case Law	*Antolik v. Harvey*, 761 P.2d 305 (Haw. Interm. App. 1988): When dividing and distributing the value of the property of the parties in a divorce case, the relevant value is, as a general rule, the fair market value on the relevant date.		

(continued)

VALUE IN EXCHANGE

Fair Market Value	

VALUE TO THE HOLDER

Fair Value	Investment Value

Antolik v. Harvey (1988) indicates that the relevant value is the fair market value on the relevant date. It has acknowledged that goodwill has value, but it must be distinguished from an individual's reputation. In its treatment of goodwill in this case, Hawaii considered that the goodwill in the business in the form of patient charts would not be able to be sold, because the current owner would become a competitor and maintain those patients for himself. Because of this, we classify Hawaii as a walk-away fair market value state.

IDAHO

Goodwill

Stewart v. Stewart, 152 P.3d 544 (Ida. Supr. Ct. 2007): In this case involving a dermatology practice, the court did not distinguish between enterprise goodwill and personal goodwill. The Supreme Court of Idaho states that the plaintiff "would have the court enter the morass of trying to draw a distinction between the value attributable to a professional practice by virtue of the individual attributes of the professional and the value of goodwill not attributable to those personal assets, valuing each separately and then dividing the latter but not the former. Quite frankly such an approach does not make a good deal of sense." However, the court noted that the Idaho law "treats personal skill and reputation as separate assets rather than community property." This case cites *Wolford v. Wolford*, 117 Idaho 61, [**549] [*678] 67,785 P.2d 625, 631 (1990), "holding that personal attributes, including knowledge, skill, and reputation, were not property, either separate or community." *Stewart* also cites *Olsen*, 125 Idaho at 606, 873 P.2d at 860. This case concludes that knowledge, skill, and background are personal attributes, not community property. To the extent that a professional services corporation has goodwill above these personal assets, however, that goodwill is community property. The issue in *Stewart* was whether the valuation methodology that the appellate court found was properly applied. However, clearly the intent in Idaho is to value only enterprise, not personal goodwill.

Chandler v. Chandler, 32 P.3d 140 (Ida. Supr. Ct. 2001): Trial court found that community business had intangible value independent of personal goodwill.

	VALUE IN EXCHANGE		VALUE TO THE HOLDER
	Fair Market Value	Fair Value	Investment Value
Discounts	*Olsen v. Olsen*, 873 P.2d 857 (Ida. Supr. Ct. 1994): The Supreme Court of Idaho decided that "The trial court should not have employed a capitalization rate and a discount for marketability that reduced the value of the corporation based on the concept that lower rates would force Mr. Olsen to share his future earnings with Mrs. Olsen."		
Buy–Sell			
SOV in Statute or Case Law			

Chandler (2001) distinguished the intangible value of the community business from the personal goodwill of the owner, indicating fair market value. *Stewart* (2007) does not distinguish between enterprise and personal goodwill because of the difficulty of doing so. However, *Stewart* notes that personal skill and reputation are not community property. *Stewart* cites *Wolford* and *Olsen*, two cases that conclude personal goodwill is not community property. Therefore, we believe that Idaho is a fair market value state.

ILLINOIS

Goodwill	*James Alexander v. Valery Alexander*, 857 N.E.2d 766 (Ill. App. Ct. 2006): "Enterprise goodwill is considered a marital asset for the purposes of the just division of marital property. Personal goodwill is not considered a marital asset for the purposes of the just division of marital property. The supreme court observed that because other factors under section 503(d) of the [*196] Act (750 ILCS 5/503(d) (West 2004)) (the section of the Act that sets forth factors that the circuit court is to consider when making a just division of marital property) already reflect elements that constitute personal goodwill, to consider personal goodwill in addition to these other factors would result in impermissible double-counting." *In re: Marriage of Head*, 652 N.E.2d 1246 (Ill. App. 1995): Business goodwill may be valued, but not in this case. *In re: Marriage of Zells*, 572 N.E.2d 944 (Ill. 1991): Personal goodwill should not be considered in the valuation of a business.		

(continued)

	VALUE IN EXCHANGE		VALUE TO THE HOLDER
	Fair Market Value	Fair Value	Investment Value
Discounts	*In re: Marriage of Heroy*, 895 N.E.2d 1025 (Ill. App. 2008): Trial court applied combined minority and marketability discounts of 30% and the appellate court confirmed.		
Buy–Sell	*In re: Marriage of Brenner*, 601 N.E.2d 1270 (Ill App. Ct 1992): A buy–sell agreement or other such agreement should be considered as a factor in valuing a business but it is not determinative of the value of marital stock.		
SOV in Statute or Case Law	We believe that Illinois should be categorized as predominantly following a fair market value standard. Personal goodwill is excluded from the valuation of a business, but business goodwill may be considered a marital asset where appropriate. In *Heroy* (2008), the courts have allowed minority and marketability discounts.		
	INDIANA		
Goodwill	*Balicki v. Balicki*, 837 N.E.2d 532 (Ind. App. 2005): Stated that personal goodwill was not marital, but the party wishing to remove personal goodwill must present evidence of its existence. "We conclude that if a party wishes to exclude personal goodwill from a business's valuation in a dissolution proceeding, they must submit evidence of its existence and value to the trial court by ensuring that their chosen expert provides proof of such existence and value." *Yoon v. Yoon*, 711 N.E.2d 1265 (Ind. Supreme Ct.1999): Personal goodwill is future earnings capacity and should not be included in valuation. Business goodwill is future patronage and should be considered.	*Bobrow v. Bobrow*, No. 29D01-0003-DR-166 (Hamilton County Ind. 2002): Goodwill in professional corporation adhered to the corporation itself. Value was calculated as the pro rata proportion of the value of the business as a whole.	
Discounts	*Jerry Alexander v. Susan Alexander*, 927 N.E.2d 926 (Ind. App. 2010): "We conclude that marketability discounts and minority interest discounts can be utilized by a trial court in dissolution proceedings when determining the value of ownership interest such as the interest which Susan holds in Bush and Bush farms."		

	VALUE IN EXCHANGE		VALUE TO THE HOLDER
	Fair Market Value	Fair Value	Investment Value
Discounts *(continued)*	*In re: Marriage of Conner*, 713 N.E.2d 883 (Ind. App. 1999): Trial court applied 20% discount; appellate court deemed evidence insufficient to declare discount.		
Buy–Sell		*Bobrow v. Bobrow*, No. 29D01-0003-DR-166 (Hamilton County Ind. 2002): Case used pro rata proportion of value as a going concern rather than partnership agreement value.	
SOV in Statute or Case Law	*Nowels v. Nowels*, 836 N.E.2d 481; 2005 Ind. App. LEXIS 2039: The appellate court appeared to agree with the trial court's opinion, which states, "It is the fair market value of Mr. Nowels' 50% interest in Wible Lumber which is at issue in this case, not the value of Wible Lumber as an entity, or the value of Wible Lumber to the owners as a going concern."		

Indiana follows a value in exchange premise in that personal goodwill is not subject to equitable distribution. *Conner* (1999) rejects discounts, but *Alexander* (2010) allows them. *Bobrow* (1999) valued the interest in the accounting firm, Ernst & Young, at the pro rata share of the enterprise value. *Nowels* (2005) defines the value as the fair market value, not the value as an entity or the value as a going concern. Therefore, Indiana has followed fair value concepts under *Bobrow*, but now defines value as fair market value and allows discounts under *Alexander*, leading us to identify Indiana as a predominantly fair market value state.

	IOWA		
Goodwill	*Hageland II v. Hageland*, 448 N.W.2d 678; (Iowa App. 1989): "The future or goodwill of a professional's practice is a factor that needs to be considered in assessing the economic issues in a dissolution. Where the professional will continue the practice, it is a factor that should be considered in assessing future earning capacity of the professional. This has been done here, as the substantial alimony award, guaranteed by life insurance requiring payment of premiums by John, is based at least in a large part on John's future earnings as a dentist. We therefore disagree with the trial court's decision to also treat goodwill as an asset in valuating the stock in a professional corporation."		

(continued)

	VALUE IN EXCHANGE		VALUE TO THE HOLDER	
	Fair Market Value	Fair Value	Investment Value	
Discounts	*In re: Marriage of Steele*, 502 N.W.2d 18 (Iowa Ct. App. 1993): Accepts minority discount. The court discounted the husband's stock 20% because it was a minority interest. *In re: Marriage of Hoak*, 364 N.W.2d 185 (Iowa Supr. Ct. 1985): This was a publicly owned corporation. The appellate court proposed a 20% to 30% discount because of the legal restrictions on sale. *Frett v. Frett*, LEXIS 694 (Iowa App. 2004): The appellate court found the husband's expert's marketability discount of 15% and an additional 20% key-person discount excessive. A party's interest in a corporation may be discounted for lack of marketability. They allowed a 10% discount.	*Becker v. Becker*, LEXIS 1223 (Iowa App. 2007): The appellate court did not allow a discount because they were not persuaded that the husband's expert's marketability discount was supported by evidence since there was no basis for an assumption that the business will be sold.		
Buy–Sell	*In re: Marriage of Baker*, 810 N.W.2d 25 (Iowa App. 2011): Iowa accepts value based upon the buyout provision of owner's agreement. Husband's ownership interest cannot be sold or transferred. *Hogeland II v. Hogeland*, 448 N.W.2d 678 (Iowa App. 1989): "Restrictions on marketability and legal restrictions on sale can justify a discount on stock. The Iowa court has recognized the value of stock in a dissolution is not necessarily decided by a value fixed in a stock redemption agreement where there is a finding that as a practical matter, the spouse owning the stock is not limited to the option price. In such a case the stock option price is one factor to be considered in determining the value of the interest." *In re: Marriage of Moffatt*, 279 N.W.2d 15 (Iowa Supr. Ct. 1979): A buy–sell agreement or other such agreement should be considered as a factor in valuing a business but it is not determinative of the value of marital stock.			

	VALUE IN EXCHANGE		VALUE TO THE HOLDER	
	Fair Market Value	Fair Value	Investment Value	

SOV in Statute or Case Law	*Frett v. Frett*, LEXIS 694 (Iowa App. 2004): Assets should be valued at fair market value, if this can be reasonably ascertained, citing In re: Marriage of Dennis, 467 N.W.2d 806, 808 (Iowa Ct. App. 1991).	

In *Hogeland* the Iowa Court of Appeals decided not to value goodwill in a dental practice. *Steele* and *Hoak* apply discounts. *Hogeland* (1989) and *Moffatt* (1979) considered the restrictions in the stockholder agreement. This led us to classify Iowa as a predominantly fair market value state.

KANSAS

Goodwill	*Powell v. Powell*, 648 P.2d 218 (Kan. Supr. Ct 1982): Business goodwill in a professional practice may be an asset, but because in a professional practice it adheres to the individual rather than the practice, it should not be an asset subject to distribution in a divorce.	
Discounts		
Buy–Sell		
SOV in Statute or Case Law	*Bohl v. Bohl*, 657 P.2d 1106 (Kan. Supr. Ct. 1983): "It is clear the method utilized by the trial court in arriving at the fair market value for M.W. Watson, Inc. was entirely proper."	

We classify Kansas as a fair market value state. *Powell* (1982) establishes that goodwill in Dr. Powell's practice was not an asset subject to distribution, because it was personal to the practitioner. The court established that goodwill in a professional practice is not an asset, because it is too heavily reliant on an individual. In such a business, the practitioner only serves the clients, and if he or she died, there would be no value to the business. This suggests a walk-away fair market value standard.

(*continued*)

	VALUE IN EXCHANGE		VALUE TO THE HOLDER
	Fair Market Value	Fair Value	Investment Value
		KENTUCKY	
Goodwill		*Gaskill v. Robbins*, 282 S.W.3d 306 (Ky. Supr. Ct. 2009): In this case, the Kentucky Supreme Court determined that enterprise goodwill is marital; personal goodwill is not marital. "Skill, personality, work ethic, reputation, and relationships developed by Gaskill are (wife's) alone and cannot be sold to a subsequent practitioner. In this manner, these attributes constitute nonmarital property that will continue with her regardless of the presence of any spouse. To consider this highly personal value as marital would effectively attach her future earnings, to which Robbins has no claim. Further, if he or someone similarly situated were then awarded maintenance this would amount to 'double dipping,' and cause a dual inequity to Gaskill." The court further stated that "in order to evaluate the fair market value of the practice, everything of value, including transferable goodwill, must be counted."	
Discounts		*Cornett v. Cornett*, LEXIS 843 (Ky. App. 2005): "The court took an average of the figures presented by both experts, which was within its discretion," for one of the contract mining subsidiaries and applied a combined minority and marketability discount of 17.90%. *Tatum v. Tatum*, LEXIS 139 (Ky. App. 2004): The court applied a marketability discount because a discount for marketability is used to determine fair market value. *Zambos v. Zambos*, LEXIS 182 (Ky. App. 2004): "The court reasoned that a 30% discount for lack of marketability would be more reasonable (than the husband's expert's 60% DLOM) based upon a lack of evidence that the contract with the hospital would not be renewed. The court reasoned that although a 50% ownership interest is a minority interest, a gridlock is highly unlikely in a lucrative corporation such as this. The court applied a 30% marketability discount and a minority discount of 10%.	

	VALUE IN EXCHANGE		VALUE TO THE HOLDER	
	Fair Market Value	Fair Value	Fair Value	Investment Value
Buy–Sell	***Drake v. Drake***, 809 S.W.2d 710 (Ky. App. 1991): "A buy–sell agreement for a closely held corporation which sets or provides a method for setting value on its shares for purposes of distribution is not binding on a spouse in a dissolution proceeding, rather it is to be weighed with other factors in determining value. The majority position is sound because that approach would produce a value closer to what one could receive in a free and fair market." ***Clark v. Clark***, 782 S.W.2d 56 (Ky. App. 1990): Cites *Weaver v. Weaver*, 72 N.C. App. 409, 324 S.E.2d 915 (1985), and *Stern v. Stern*, 66 N.J. 340, 331 A.2d 257 (1975): "When the terms of a partnership agreement are used, however, the value of the interest calculated is only a presumptive value, which can be attacked by either plaintiff or defendant as not reflective of the true value." Also, utilizing a buy–sell agreement in this case would be unfair as it would not recognize goodwill.			
SOV in Statute or Case Law				
We classify Kentucky as a fair market value state, because in *Gaskill* (2009) the Supreme Court established that marketable enterprise goodwill is subject to equitable distribution but personal goodwill represents the future earnings of the business owner not subject to equitable distribution. *Gaskill* also set the standard of value as fair market value.				

(continued)

399

	VALUE IN EXCHANGE		VALUE TO THE HOLDER
	Fair Market Value	Fair Value	Investment Value
		LOUISIANA	
Hybrid—Review case law			
Goodwill	*Clemons v. Clemons*, 960 So.2d 1068 (La. App. 2007): "If the underlying business is community, the goodwill will be considered as community property for purposes of partition. Goodwill that represents future earnings of a spouse may be considered a personal attribute not subject to distribution as community property. In addition, where one spouse holds a professional degree or license and the goodwill results solely from that professional's personal relationship with clients, that goodwill is not included in the community." Further, "a professional degree or license is not community property and is not subject to community property distribution." *Godwin v. Godwin*, 533 So.2d 1009 (La. App. 1988): Business goodwill in a commercial enterprise is marital property and should be considered in the valuation. *Pearce v. Pearce*, 482 So.2d 108 (La. App. 1986): Goodwill in a medical practice does not exist separately from the practitioner and thus is not part of the marital estate.	*Ellington v. Ellington*, 842 So.2d 1160 (La. App. 2003): While the experts came to a fair market value for the assets in question, the trial court rejected the expert's opinion, using the fair value language that the wife was not a willing seller and that it would be unfair not to include the value of the client base, the intangible asset.	
Discounts	*Trahan v. Trahan*, 43 So.3d 218 (La. App. 2010): The fact that this company is small, closely held, and not traded on the open market limits the available buyers and thereby reduces the price. The marketability discount was appropriate in this case—the court allowed a 20% marketability discount.	*Head v. Head*, 714 So.2d 231 (La. App. 1998): Rejected marketability discount on the basis that a third-party sale was not contemplated.	
Buy–Sell			

	VALUE IN EXCHANGE		VALUE TO THE HOLDER
	Fair Market Value	Fair Value	Investment Value
SOV in Statute or Case Law	La. statute § 9:2801-(1)(a): "Within forty-five days of service of a motion by either party, each party shall file a sworn detailed descriptive list of all community property, the *fair market value* and location of each asset, and all community liabilities" (emphasis added). La. Revised Statute 9:2801.2 prohibits the valuation of personal goodwill. La. RS. 9:2801.2, added by Acts 2003, No. 837 § 1 and amended by Acts 2004, No. 177 §1, provides that "the court may include goodwill in valuing any community-owned corporate, commercial or professional business. However that portion of goodwill attributable to any personal quality of the spouse awarded the business shall not be included in the value of the business."		

Although the Louisiana statute prescribes fair market value, we have categorized Louisiana as a hybrid value state because *Ellington* (2003) and *Head* (1998) rejected discounts and used "unwilling seller" language, which indicates fair value. This is fair value under value in exchange, because Louisiana statute bars valuation and inclusion of personal goodwill in the marital assets. However, *Trahan* (2010) allowed discounts.

		MAINE	
Goodwill		*Ahern v. Ahern*, 938 A.2d 35 (Me. Supr. Ct. 2008): "The Maine Supreme Court stated: "We now adopt the enterprise/personal framework for the purpose of evaluating the goodwill of a professional practice in the context of an equitable distribution of property. As a general principle, the personal goodwill of a professional practice, such as the dental practice at issue in this case is not a species of property. It is however, relevant to establishing a professional's earning capacity for purposes of determining support issues."	
Discounts			

(continued)

	VALUE IN EXCHANGE		VALUE TO THE HOLDER
	Fair Market Value	Fair Value	Investment Value
Buy–Sell			
SOV in Statute or Case Law			

We categorized Maine as a fair market value state under *Ahern*, in which the court found that enterprise goodwill is marital and personal goodwill is not, thereby establishing a value in exchange premise.

MARYLAND

	VALUE IN EXCHANGE		VALUE TO THE HOLDER
Goodwill	*Strauss v. Strauss, 647 A.2d 818 (Md. Ct. Spec. App. 1994):* Personal goodwill attached to a business is not marital property. *Hollander v. Hollander,* 597 A.2d 1012 (Md. App. 1991): "In order for goodwill to be marital property, it must be an asset having a separate value from the reputation of the practitioner. Goodwill cannot be based solely on the skill, experience or reputation of the practitioner if it is to be considered marital property. We hold that a dental practice can in fact have goodwill that is separate from the reputation of the dentist and therefore properly characterized as marital property." *Prahinski v. Prahinski,* 582 A.2d 784 (Md. App.1990): Goodwill of a solo law practice is personal to the individual and thus is not marketable.		
Discounts			
Buy–Sell			
SOV in Statute or Case Law			

We classify Maryland as a fair market value state due to the treatment of goodwill in both the *Strauss, Hollander* (1991), and *Prahinski* (1990) decisions. While allowing business goodwill, personal goodwill attached to a business or a sole proprietorship is not marital property.

	VALUE IN EXCHANGE		VALUE TO THE HOLDER
	Fair Market Value	Fair Value	Investment Value
	MASSACHUSETTS		
Goodwill	*Goldman v. Goldman*, 554 N.E.2d 860 (Mass. App. 1990): There was no goodwill found in a one-man professional corporation.		
Discounts		*Caveney v. Caveney*, 960 N.E.2d 331 (Mass. App. 2012): "When valuing a party's interest in a business in divorce, a minority discount should not be applied absent extraordinary circumstances." Although a minority discount was not specifically at issue in *Bernier*, the court, through dictum, made clear that such a discount "should not be applied absent extraordinary circumstances." *Bernier v. Bernier*, 873 N.E.2d 216 (Mass. Supr. Ct. 2007): The Massachusetts supreme court found that "neither marketability nor a minority discount should be applied absent extraordinary circumstances. Close corporations by their nature have less value to outsiders, but at the same time their value may be even greater to other shareholders who want to keep the business in the form of a close corporation."	
Buy–Sell			
SOV in Statute or Case Law	*Adams v. Adams*, 945 N.E.2d 844 (Mass. Supr. Judicial Ct. 2011): The special master appeared to accept the wife's expert's $9.09 billion computation of the fair market value of Wellington as a whole. However, the value was based on the discounted cash flow method with no carve out for personal goodwill. The Supreme Judicial Court "did not discern clear error in the judge's adoption of the special master's seemingly conservative projections of the husband's future income stream."	*Bernier v. Bernier*, 873 N.E.2d 216 (Mass. Supr. Ct. 2007): "Where valuation of assets occurs in the context of divorce, and where one of the parties will maintain, and the other entirely divested of, ownership of a marital assets after divorce, the judge must take particular care to treat the parties not as arm's-length hypothetical buyers and sellers in a theoretical open market but as fiduciaries entitled to equitable distribution of their marital assets."	

(*continued*)

VALUE IN EXCHANGE		VALUE TO THE HOLDER
Fair Market Value	Fair Value	Investment Value

The decision in *Goldman* (1990) establishes that Massachusetts is a value in exchange state in that only enterprise goodwill is included as a marital asset. *Bernier* (2007) and *Caveney* (2012) follow the line of thinking established in the dissenters' and oppression cases in which minority and marketability discounts are taken only in extraordinary circumstances. *Bernier* treats the parties as fiduciaries, not arm's-length hypothetical buyers and sellers. Therefore, we classify Massachusetts as being closer to a fair value state; however, in light of *Adams*, practitioners need to check whether fair market value can be applied in a particular case.

MICHIGAN

Hybrid—Review case law

	Fair Market Value	Fair Value	Investment Value
Goodwill			*Kowalesky v. Kowalesky*, 384 N.W.2d 112 (Mich. App. 1986): Goodwill was valued in a one-man professional dental practice. The doctor's expert, a business broker, valued the dental practice at value of a distressed sale. The appellate court concluded that there was no evidence the dentist was prepared to leave or that the staff would not remain. The valuation of the practice should be the value to the plaintiff as a going concern.
Discounts	*Lemmen v. Lemmen*, 809 N.W. 2d 208 (Mich. App. 2010): The court applied a 25% minority discount and a 30% discount for DLOM, which the wife's expert had applied in an earlier valuation while he did not apply discounts in his valuation for the marital dissolution. The dissenting judge criticized the court for failing to follow the *Owens*, 2003 Va. App. Lexis 639 (2003), which declined to discount the value of a family owned company in a divorce.		
Buy–Sell			
SOV in Statute or Case Law			

Michigan follows an investment value in *Kowalesky* (1986). The court valued the practice as "the value to the plaintiff as a going concern," an investment value concept. In *Lemmen* (2010), the court allowed both minority and marketability discounts, which is a fair market value concept. Thus, we classify Michigan as a hybrid state.

	VALUE IN EXCHANGE		VALUE TO THE HOLDER
	Fair Market Value	Fair Value	Investment Value
	MINNESOTA		
Goodwill	*Baker v. Baker*, LEXIS 94 (Minn. App. 2007): The court, following *Roth*, separated enterprise goodwill from personal goodwill. The issue of the non-competition agreement was addressed by the court and the court found that the non-competition agreement does not "by itself establish that a spouse will be restricted in his or her future employment." *Roth v. Roth*, 406 N.W.2d 77 (Minn. App. 1987): In this valuation of a chiropractic practice, the court determined that enterprise goodwill is marital and personal goodwill is not.		
Discounts	*Gottsacker v. Gottsacker*, 664 N.W.2d 848 (Minn. Supr. Ct. 2003): The trial court's decision to apply a marketability discount was affirmed by the court of appeals, as "nothing in the record indicates that there is a readily available market for [wife] to sell her Edcoat shares." The court applied a 28.93% marketability discount. *Berenberg v. Berenberg*, 474 N.W.2d 843 (Minn. Ct. App. 1991): Despite the existence of a buy–sell agreement, a family member redeemed shares in excess of what was set forth in the buy–sell agreement. As per *Lyons* 439 N.W.2d at 20, "a trial court acts within its discretion when it chooses not to apply a buy-sell price, but also discounts the fair market value. The current fair market value was discounted by 35% for nonmarketability and lack of control."		
Buy–Sell	*Berenberg v. Berenberg*, 474 N.W.2d 843 (Minn. Ct. App. 1991): A buy-sell agreement or other such agreement should be considered as a factor, but is not determinative of the value of marital stock (rejected here).		

(continued)

	VALUE IN EXCHANGE		VALUE TO THE HOLDER
	Fair Market Value	Fair Value	Investment Value
SOV in Statute or Case Law	**Berenberg v. Berenberg**, 474 N.W.2d 843 (Minn. Ct. App. 1991): "The establishment of a fair market value contemplates nothing more than the assignment of a fair and reasonable value to a family business as a whole to allow equitable apportionment of the marital property."		
	Because Minnesota's representative cases have looked to the market value of a company's assets in determining their value for equitable distribution, we believe that Minnesota may be classified as a fair market value state. Discounts have also been accepted in *Berenberg* (1991).		
	MISSISSIPPI		
Goodwill	**Lewis v. Lewis**, 54 So.3d 216 (Miss. Supr. Ct. 2011): Lewis involved a residential real estate development company, owned equally by the husband and wife. In citing *Singley*, *Watson*, and *Yelverton*, the court confirmed the rule that in Mississippi, the goodwill value of any business is not marital property. Two justices on the Lewis panel dissented, stating "*Watson* therefore should be read to limit the blanket rule promulgated in Singley to those cases either involving a solo professional practice or those cases that are closely analogous". **Rhodes v. Rhodes**, 52 So.3d 430; (Miss. App. 2011): The Supreme court confirmed the rule in both *Singley* and *Watson* that goodwill is simply not property; "thus it cannot be deemed a divisible marital asset." However, three of the ten justices strongly dissented from the view stating that the husband's flooring business was not a professional service firm and the Supreme Court needs to carefully examine precedent. **Yelverton v. Yelverton**, 961 So.2d.19 (Miss. 2007): The court addressed goodwill in a car dealership and found that goodwill, whether personal, business, or enterprise goodwill, should not be included in the value of the dealership.		

	VALUE IN EXCHANGE	VALUE TO THE HOLDER	
	Fair Market Value	Fair Value	Investment Value
Goodwill (*continued*)	***Goodson v. Goodson***, 910 So.2d 19 (Miss. App. 2005): "The Mississippi Supreme Court has ruled that goodwill cannot be used as a factor in valuing a business for the purpose of dividing marital property. The court decided that the jurisdictions that have excluded goodwill in determining the fair market value of a business have adopted the better rule."		
Goodwill (**cont.**)	***Watson v. Watson***, 882 So.2d.95 (Miss. Supr. 2004): The court ruled: "Although there is a distinction between 'personal goodwill' and 'business enterprise goodwill' neither should be included in the valuation of a solo professional practice for purposes of a division of marital assets. In such cases, the two are simply too interwoven and not divisible." Upon remand, the parties may address this issue by providing evidence of the valuation of the clinic, absent goodwill. In the event an asset-based approach is used, the valuation should not exceed the fair market value of the tangible assets, assuming they were sold in their current configuration. ***Singley v. Singley***, LEXIS 283 (Miss. Supr. Ct. 2003): Goodwill may not be included in the determination of a business's fair market value (walk-away value) for a dental practice sole proprietorship. "Goodwill is simply not property; thus it cannot be deemed a divisible marital asset in a divorce action."		

(*continued*)

	VALUE IN EXCHANGE		VALUE TO THE HOLDER
	Fair Market Value	Fair Value	Investment Value
Discounts	***Cox v. Cox***, 61 So.3d 927 (Miss. App. 2011): This is a case involving depreciation of a business during a marriage. No discounts were applied at the start of the marriage. At the end of the marriage, the joint expert applied a 50% discount, which he labeled a marketability discount. However, he based the discount on "a variety of changed circumstances" since the time of the company's pre-marital value. In addition to its reduced profitability, these "lack of marketability factors included the company's inability to attract new investors and secure bank financing; its inability to obtain bonding for future projects and its increased industry cost, including environmental contamination of its property." The court allowed this unconventional marketability discount.		
Buy–Sell			
SOV in Statute or Case Law	***Singley v. Singley***, LEXIS 283 (Miss. Supr. Ct. 2003): "Regardless of what method an expert might choose to arrive at the value of a business, the bottom line is one must arrive at the 'Fair market value' or that price at which property would change hands between a willing buyer and willing seller when the former is not under any compulsion to buy and the latter is not under any compulsion to sell, both parties having reasonable knowledge of the relevant facts."		

Singley defines fair market value. *Singley* (2003) and *Watson* (2004) involve solo professional practices. The court found that neither personal nor enterprise goodwill are marital. Thus, we classify Mississippi as a walk-away fair market value state. *Yelverton* (2007) extends this concept to a car dealership (i.e., no goodwill). In 2011, *Rhodes* confirmed *Singley* and *Watson*, saying there was no marital goodwill in a flooring business. *Lewis* (2011) found the same for a real estate development business. Both *Rhodes* and *Lewis* have strong dissents on the appellate panel, indicating that Mississippi may be attempting to clarify the nature of goodwill in a business enterprise as compared to a small professional practice.

	VALUE IN EXCHANGE		VALUE TO THE HOLDER
	Fair Market Value	Fair Value	Investment Value
Goodwill	*Hanson v. Hanson*, 738 S.W.2d 429 (Mo. Supr. Ct. 1987): Business goodwill may exist in both commercial and professional entities. Accepts the fair market value approach to valuing goodwill. *Taylor v. Taylor*, 736 S.W.2d 388 (Mo. Supr. Ct. 1987): Without fair market value evidence, it is proper to find no business goodwill for valuation purposes.		
Discounts	*L.R.M. v. R.K.M.*, 46 S.W.3d 24 (Mo. App. 2001): This pertains to the valuation of a partnership interest in a law firm. The court found that "there was substantial evidence to support the trial court's findings that the reasonable fair market value of husband's interest in the partnership was $99,221 based on the fair market value of the firm's assets minus liabilities, adjusted for the value of collectible accounts receivable and work in progress, and discounted for minority interest and lack of marketability."		
Buy–Sell	*Hanson v. Hanson*, 738 S.W.2d 429 (Mo. Supr. Ct. 1987): Prefers fair market value but may accept a buy–sell agreement as determinative of value.		
SOV in Statute or Case Law	*Wood v. Wood*, 361 S.W.3d 36 (Mo. App. 2011): The trial court valued the business in accordance with a formula in the buy–sell agreement. The appellate court remanded the case to the trial court to determine the fair market value and stated: "In a dissolution proceeding, the object of a business valuation is to determine fair market value."		

(continued)

409

VALUE IN EXCHANGE		VALUE TO THE HOLDER
Fair Market Value	Fair Value	Investment Value

The appellate court in *Wood* remanded the case for the determination of fair market value. *Hanson* (1987) accepts a fair market value approach to the value of goodwill. *L.R.M.* accepts a marketability discount; therefore, we consider Missouri to be a fair market value state.

MONTANA

Hybrid—Review case law

	VALUE IN EXCHANGE		VALUE TO THE HOLDER
	Fair Market Value	Fair Value	Investment Value
Goodwill			*In re: Marriage of Stufft*, 950 P.2d 1373 (Mont. Supr. Ct. 1997): Supreme Court: The court found no distinction between personal and business goodwill following Washington's *Hull* and *Fleege* that, although goodwill may not be readily marketable, it is an asset with value. According to *Stufft*, "The goodwill of a professional practice may be a marital asset subject to property division in a marriage dissolution. The determination of goodwill value can be reached with the aid of expert testimony and by consideration of such factors as the practitioner's age, health, past earning power, reputation in the community for judgment, and his comparative professional success."
Discounts	*DeCosse v. DeCosse*, 936 P.2d 821 (Supr. Ct. 1997): The trial court valued the business at $1,060,000 accepting a 20% minority and marketability discount. The Supreme Court reversed the trial court's decision, which disregarded a buy–sell agreement. Supreme Court accepted the application of a minority/marketability discount and applied it to the amount obtained as a result of the buy–sell agreement.	*In re: Marriage of Taylor*, 848 P.2d 478 (Mont. Supr. Ct. 1993): It is inappropriate to apply a discount to the stock when the value is arrived at by determining the market value of underlying assets.	

410

| | VALUE IN EXCHANGE | | VALUE TO THE HOLDER |
	Fair Market Value	Fair Value	Investment Value
Buy–Sell	**DeCosse v. DeCosse**, 936 P.2d 821 (Mont. Supr. Ct. 1997): "A majority of jurisdictions hold that a restrictive agreement while not conclusive evidence of the value of an interest in a closely held corporation, is a factor that must be considered by a trial court in the stock valuation process. There is no uniform rule for valuing stock in closely held corporations. Whatever method is used, however, must take into consideration inhibitions on the transfer of the corporate interest resulting from a limited market or contractual provisions."		
SOV in Statute or Case Law			
	Stuff holds that goodwill need not be marketable to have value, which indicates investment value. However, *DeCosse* (1997) limits the value subject to equitable distribution to the amount that the husband would receive pursuant to the buy–sell agreement if he sold his stock. This indicates fair market value. Thus we classify Montana as a hybrid state.		

NEBRASKA

| | VALUE IN EXCHANGE | | VALUE TO THE HOLDER |
	Fair Market Value	Fair Value	Investment Value
Goodwill	**Kricsfeld v. Kricsfeld**, 588 N.W.2d 210 (Neb. App. 1999): Cites Taylor v. Taylor, "If goodwill depends on the continued presence of a particular individual, such goodwill, by definition, is not a marketable asset distinct from the individual." **Taylor v. Taylor**, 386 N.W.2d 851 (Neb. Supr. Ct. 1986): *Nebraska Supreme Court*: "To be properly within the purview of this section as property divisible and distributable in a dissolution proceeding, we conclude that goodwill must be a business asset with value independent of the presence or reputation of a particular individual, an asset which may be sold, transferred, conveyed, or pledged."		

(continued)

	VALUE IN EXCHANGE		VALUE TO THE HOLDER
	Fair Market Value	Fair Value	Investment Value
Discounts	**Shuck v. Shuck**, 806 N.W.2d 580 (Neb. App. 2011): "Reduction for lack of control was acceptable in determining the fair market value of (Mr.) and (Mrs.) ownership interests in the entities, because it is undisputed that neither is a majority shareholder in any of the Shuck family businesses. With regard to the lack of marketability adjustment, such was also appropriate in calculating fair market value, because the stock in each of the entities is not publicly traded and the other stock is held by other Shuck family members—making the stock less appealing to an outside purchaser."		
Buy–Sell			
SOV in Statute or Case Law	**Shuck v. Shuck**, 806 N.W.2d 580 (Neb. App. 2011): "Reduction for lack of control was acceptable in determining the fair market value of (Mr.) and (Mrs.) ownership interests in the entities."		

We believe Nebraska predominantly follows a fair market value standard because of its requirement, expressed by *Taylor* (1986), that goodwill must be a marketable business asset independent of the reputation or presence of a particular individual. *Shuck* (2011) allowed for minority and marketability discounts in calculating fair market value.

NEVADA			
Goodwill			**Ford v. Ford**, 782 P.2d 1304 (Nev. Supr. Ct. 1989): Business goodwill based in a solo medical practice is a marital asset subject to division.
Discounts			
Buy–Sell			
SOV in Statute or Case Law			

	VALUE IN EXCHANGE		VALUE TO THE HOLDER
	Fair Market Value	Fair Value	Investment Value

We believe Nevada predominantly follows an investment value standard. The rationale in *Ford* (1989) relies on cases such as *Dugan v. Dugan* from New Jersey, *Marriage of Foster* from California, and *Marriage of Fleege* from Washington in supporting the notion that even though goodwill may not be readily marketable, it does have a value in a going business.

NEW HAMPSHIRE

	Fair Market Value	Fair Value	Investment Value
Goodwill	*In re: Watterworth*, 821 A.2d 1107 (N.H. Supr. Ct. 2003): The court upheld the lower court's decision that there was no goodwill in a medical practice because of a binding shareholder agreement setting a fair market value, as well as the fact that no one would pay for the intangible value of the practice because the owner would compete.		
Discounts	*Rattee v. Rattee*, 767 A.2d 415 (N.H. Supr. Ct. 2001): The court applied a combined 28.5% minority and marketability discount.		
Buy–Sell			
SOV in Statute or Case Law	*Martin v. Martin*, LEXIS 275 (N.H. Supr. Ct. 2006): "To determine an appropriate division of marital property, courts generally look to the fair market value of the assets." Citing Rattee v. Rattee, 146 N.H. 44, 50, 767 A.3d 415 (2001).		

We categorize New Hampshire as a fair market value state. In the *Watterworth (2003)* case, a restrictive agreement was in place limiting the marketability of the practice. Additionally, the court reasoned that no one would purchase the goodwill of the practice without a noncompete provision from the shareholder. The court focused on the ability and proceeds from the sale of the asset. Additionally, in the *Rattee* case, the court applied discounts in calculating the fair market value of the assets regardless of whether there was an intent to sell those assets.

(continued)

VALUE IN EXCHANGE		VALUE TO THE HOLDER	
Fair Market Value	Fair Value	Investment Value	
	NEW JERSEY		

Hybrid—Review case law

Goodwill			*Dugan v. Dugan*, 457 A.2d 1 (N.J. Supreme Ct. 1983): The court stated that undoubtedly goodwill exists, and the individual practitioner's inability to sell it should not affect consideration as an asset. *Piscopo v. Piscopo*, 557 A.2d 1040 (N.J. Superior Ct. App. Div. 1989): Goodwill attributable to celebrity status is asset subject to equitable distribution.
Discounts		*Brown v. Brown*, 792 A.2d 463 (N.J. Super. Ct. App. Div. 2002): Discounts rejected in valuation of a commercial flower shop based on standards of dissent and oppression statutes and case law (*Balsamides* and *Lawson*).	
Buy–Sell		*In re: Marriage of Bowen*, 473 A.2d 73 (N.J. Supr. Ct. 1984): A buy–sell agreement or other such agreement should be considered as a factor in valuing a business, but it is not determinative of the value of marital stock (rejected in this case). *Stern v. Stern*, 331 A.2d 257 (N.J. Supr. Ct. 1975): The partnership agreement allowed for the value of the capital account plus a frequently revised number indicating a certain intangible value of the individual's contribution to the firm (to be paid upon death). The court stated that if it is established that the books are well kept and the value of the partner's interests are periodically reviewed, the value should not be subject to effective attack.	

	VALUE IN EXCHANGE		VALUE TO THE HOLDER
	Fair Market Value	Fair Value	Investment Value
SOV in Statute or Case Law			
	We believe New Jersey is a hybrid state. The *Brown* case used concepts of fair value in rejecting the application of discounts in a valuation, and the court based that decision upon cases dealing with fair value in shareholder oppression and dissent. Interestingly, the language in *Brown* (2002) allows for interpretation under either a value in exchange or a value to the holder premise. *Dugan* (1983) and *Piscopo* (1989) can be considered to adhere to an investment value standard with regard to personal goodwill. Moreover, an area of controversy in New Jersey is the weight to be afforded a buy-sell agreement, especially in a professional practice, in light of the New Jersey Supreme Court case *Stern* (1975).		

NEW MEXICO

	Fair Market Value	Fair Value	Investment Value
Goodwill			*Mitchell v. Mitchell*, 719 P.2d 432 (N.M. App. Ct 1986): Both personal and enterprise goodwill constitute marital property upon divorce. In *Hurley v. Hurley*, 615 P.2d 256 (N.M. Supr. Ct. 1980: The dispositive question is not whether a doctor can sell his goodwill. As long as he maintains his practice, the physician will continue to benefit from goodwill associated with his name.
Discounts			
Buy–Sell	*Hertz v. Hertz*, 657 P.2d 1169 (N.M. Supr. Ct.1983): Where a professional spouse's stock in a corporation was subject to restrictive agreements and the value of the goodwill of the corporation was fixed by the agreements, the trial court had to use that value to determine the wife's share in a dissolution action.		*Cox v. Cox*, 775 P.2d 1315 (N.M. App. Ct. 1989): "We view Hertz as a decision based on its own facts and circumstance. It was those facts and circumstances that relegated the parties to the value assigned in the shareholders' agreement. Such is not the case here. We do not believe the supreme court intended to adopt a rule that would allow married couples to invest in a professional association without protecting the right of the non-shareholder spouse in the event of dissolution of that marriage."
SOV in Statute or Case Law			

(*continued*)

VALUE IN EXCHANGE		VALUE TO THE HOLDER
Fair Market Value	Fair Value	Investment Value

Because of the treatment of goodwill in the valuation of businesses in New Mexico, we classify New Mexico to be an investment value state. In *Mitchell* (1986), the court did not distinguish personal and enterprise goodwill. Further, the court in *Hurley* (1980) stated that there was no marketability requirement for the goodwill of a business to be valued upon divorce. However, the decision in *Hertz* (1983) required that the court in this case adhere to a binding buy–sell agreement, suggesting that the value upon exit must be considered, a concept more closely akin to fair market value. However, *Cox* (1989) holds that the special circumstances of *Hertz* relegated the parties to the value in the buy–sell agreement.

NEW YORK

Hybrid—Review case law

	Fair Market Value	Fair Value	Investment Value
Goodwill			*Moll v. Moll*, 187 Misc. 2d 770 (N.Y. Supr. Ct. 2001): This case involved the book of business of a stockbroker at Dean Witter. The court found that personal goodwill of a stockbroker's book of business is included as marital property. *McSparron v. McSparron*, 662 N.E.2d 745 (N.Y. Ct. App. 1995): In *O'Brien*, the court included the value of a professional license of a newly licensed doctor. Subsequent cases held that the value of a license merged with the career or practice of the professional. In this case, the New York Court of Appeals stated that "the merger doctrine should be discarded in favor of a commonsense approach that recognizes the ongoing independent vitality that a professional license may have and focuses solely on the problem of valuing that asset in a way that avoids duplicative awards." *O'Brien v. O'Brien*, 489 N.E.2d 712 (N.Y. Ct. App. 1985): The value of a license is includable in the marital assets.
Discounts	*Ellis v. Ellis*, 235 A.D.2d 1002, (N.Y. Supr. Ct. App. Div. 1997): Applied marketability discount in the case of a closely held furniture business of which plaintiff owned "34% acquired either prior to the parties' marriage or by gift or bequest thereafter." Marketability discount applies since "his shares in this closely held corporation could not readily be sold on a public market."		

	VALUE IN EXCHANGE		VALUE TO THE HOLDER
	Fair Market Value	Fair Value	Investment Value
Buy–Sell	*Amodio v. Amodio*, 509 N.E.2d 936 (N.Y. Ct. App. 1987): "Whatever method is used, however, must take into consideration inhibitions on the transfer of the corporate interest resulting from a limited market or contractual provisions. If transfer of the stock of a closely held corporation is restricted by a bona fide buy-sell agreement which predates the marital discord, the price fixed by the agreement, although not conclusive, is a factor which should be considered."		*Harmon v. Harmon*, 173 A.D.2d 98 (N.Y. App. Div. 1992): The court found the death benefit provision in a partnership a more compelling estimate of value than the withdrawal provision. The withdrawing partner forgoes interest in work in progress, receivables, and goodwill. The death benefit included an amount in excess of the capital account value to reflect these assets. Therefore, the death benefit reflected the economic reality of the value of a partnership interest upon divorce.
SOV in Statute or Case Law	*Beckerman v. Beckerman*, 126 A.D.2d 591 (N.Y. Supr. Ct. App. 1987), "Experts testified for both parties as to the fair market value of the business."		

New York considers professional degrees, licenses, enhanced earning capacity, and celebrity status as marital assets; however, as applied to commercial businesses, New York generally considers fair market value. Additionally, in both divorces and shareholder disputes, New York may apply marketability discounts. Because of this divergent treatment of the various elements that allow us to categorize the states, we are calling New York a hybrid state.

NORTH CAROLINA

	VALUE IN EXCHANGE		VALUE TO THE HOLDER
	Fair Market Value	Fair Value	Investment Value
Goodwill			*Hamby v. Hamby*, 547 S.E.2d 110 (N.C. App. 2001): While the court looked to determine fair market value, it used an expert's testimony of value that looked at the going-concern value of the business to the owner, an investment value standard. *Sonek v. Sonek*, 412 S.E.2d 917 (N.C. App. 1992): This involved a salaried employee on an OBGYN practice. The court found no goodwill because he had no ownership interest. The court said that North Carolina follows Washington's *Hall* and cites *Poore*, which allows for personal goodwill in a business. *Poore v. Poore*, 331 S.E.2d 266, *cert. denied*, 335 S.E.2d 316 (N.C. App. 1985): There may be goodwill in a professional practice, and if so, it should be included in the value. The court considered personal intangibles such as age, health, and reputation of the practitioner in valuing goodwill.

(continued)

	VALUE IN EXCHANGE		VALUE TO THE HOLDER
	Fair Market Value	Fair Value	Investment Value
Discounts	*Crowder v. Crowder,* 556 S.E.2d 639 (N.C. App. 2001): This is the valuation of a 50% interest in a logging company. The appellate court accepted a 25% marketability discount.		
Buy–Sell			
SOV in Statute or Case Law	*Walter v. Walter,* 561 S.E.2d 571 (N.C. App. 2002): According to *Walter,* an oral and maxillofacial surgery sole practitioner, it stated: "In an equitable distribution proceeding, the trial court is to determine the net fair market value of the property based on the evidence offered by the parties."		

While North Carolina has used the term *fair market value,* and *Crowder* allows discounts, the state has not attempted in its case law to differentiate personal and enterprise goodwill in a professional practice. *In Poore* (1985), the court considered the age, health, and professional reputation of the practitioner himself in determining goodwill. Additionally, the court agreed with the expert's assessment in *Hamby* (2001), where the going-concern value to the business owner, a value to the holder premise, was sought. These cases suggest that North Carolina is predominantly a fair market value; however, *Hamby, Sonek,* and *Poore* may provide some exceptions.

NORTH DAKOTA

	VALUE IN EXCHANGE		VALUE TO THE HOLDER
	Fair Market Value	Fair Value	Investment Value
Goodwill	*Wold v. Wold,* 744 N.W.2d 541 (N.D. Supr. Ct. 2008): This business involved pressure testing oil field equipment. The trial court valued the business at the asset value because the goodwill arose from the long hours and contacts of the owner-husband and this was not transferrable. *Sommers v. Sommers,* 660 N.W. 2d 586 (N.D. Supr. Ct. 2003): The trial court valued the business at liquidation value. The appellate court found that Dr. Sommers, an orthodontist, had no intention to sell and remanded the case to determine the value of the practice at fair market value. The appellate court defined fair market value as the price a buyer is willing to pay and the seller is willing to accept under circumstances that do not amount to coercion.		

	VALUE IN EXCHANGE		VALUE TO THE HOLDER
	Fair Market Value	Fair Value	Investment Value
Discounts		***Fisher v. Fisher,*** 568 N.W.2d 728 (N.D. Supr. Ct. 1997): Rejected application of discounts for minority shares. However, this was a unique circumstance in which the wife received the minority shares and argued for the discount. The court chose to treat her as a minority owner under the distribution statutes with all rights afforded a minority owner and did not allow a discount. ***Kaiser v. Kaiser,*** 555 N.W.2d 585 (N.D. Supr. Ct. 1996): Applied minority discounts of 11.3% of the wife's family business because the business was controlled by the family and there was no intent to sell. The Supreme Court concluded that the "trial court had discounted the applicable interest too severely after the first trial, because the business was controlled by the family there was no intent to sell."	
Buy–Sell			
SOV in Statute or Case Law	***Nuveen v. Nuveen,*** 795 N.W.2d 308 (N.D. Supr. Ct. 2011): "The fair market value of a business is ordinarily the proper method for valuing property in a divorce." ***Sommers v. Sommers,*** 660 N.W.2d 586 (N.D. Supr. Ct. 2003): "Ordinarily, fair market value, not 'liquidation value' is the proper method of valuing property in divorce. Fair market value is the price a buyer is willing to pay and the seller is willing to accept under circumstances that do not amount to coercion." Trial court should have used the fair market value of a husband's orthodontic practice during equitable distribution instead of the liquidation value because there was no evidence that a liquidation was imminent or necessary under the circumstances.	

North Dakota prescribes fair market value in its valuations of property upon divorce *(Nuveen, 2011)*. Rather than valuing the business at the net value of its assets in liquidation, the court in *Sommers* sought a going-concern fair market value. Discounts are applied on a case-by-case basis. In *Fisher* (1997), because of special circumstances, the court chose to treat the owner (wife) as a minority owner in an oppression matter. *Sommers* (2003) and *Wold* (2008) include only transferrable goodwill in the business value. Therefore, we classify North Dakota as a fair market value state.

(continued)

	VALUE IN EXCHANGE		VALUE TO THE HOLDER	
	Fair Market Value	Fair Value	Investment Value	
		OHIO		
Goodwill	*Banchefsky v. Banchefsky*, 2010 Ohio 4267; LEXIS 3611 (Ohio App. 2010): In this case involving an actual sale of a dental practice in which "a covenant-not-to-compete is considered a nonmarital asset." *Pearlstein v. Pearlstein*, 2009 Ohio 2191; LEXIS 1856 (Ohio App, 2009): "The magistrate found that goodwill should be included in the valuation of the business (medical practice) because it has been in existence for fifty years and has offices in three locations." *Bunkers v. Bunkers*, 2007 Ohio 561; LEXIS 523 (Ohio App. 2007): Appellant contended that the trial court improperly included the value of appellant's personal goodwill. The appellate court cited *Spayd v. Turner, Granzow & Hollenkamp* (1985), 19 Ohio St. 3d 55, 19 Ohio B.54, 482 N.E.2d 1232, which in turn quoted the Supreme Court of New Jersey, Dugan v. Dugan NJ 1983: "Though other elements may contribute to goodwill in the context of a professional service, such as locality and specialization, reputation is at the core. It does not exist at the time professional qualifications and a license to practice are obtained. A good reputation is earned after accomplishment and performance. Field testing is an essential ingredient before goodwill comes into being. Future earning capacity per se is not goodwill. However, when that future earning capacity has been enhanced because reputation leads to probable future patronage from existing and potential clients, goodwill may exist and have value. When that occurs the resulting goodwill is property subject to equitable distribution." The appellate court in its decision stated that the court did not abuse its discretion in valuing the appellant's orthodontic practice. *Goswami v. Goswami*, 787 N.E.2d 26 (Ohio App. 7th Dist. 2003): Personal goodwill is not marital property.			

VALUE IN EXCHANGE		VALUE TO THE HOLDER	
Fair Market Value	Fair Value	Fair Value	Investment Value
Goodwill (continued)	*Barone v. Barone,* 2000 Ohio App. LEXIS 3911 "Where the evidence established that a professional partnership has generated measurable goodwill, it is not against public policy to include that amount of goodwill as an asset upon the dissolution of the business. Future earning capacity per se is not goodwill. However, when that future earning capacity has been enhanced because reputation leads to probable future patronage from existing and potential clients, goodwill may exist and have value. When that occurs the resulting is properly subject to equitable distribution."		
	Flexman v. Flexman, No. 8834, 1985 WL 8075 (Ohio App. 1985): Business goodwill in a sole-proprietorship corporation does not exist separate of the owner and thus is not marital property.		
	Kahn v. Kahn, 536 N.E.2d 678 (Ohio App.) 1987: "Future earnings capacity per se is not goodwill. However, when that future earning capacity has been enhanced because reputation leads to probable future patronage from existing and potential clients, goodwill may exist and have value." Citing *Spayd* (19 Ohio St. 3d) at 63 19 OBR at 61, 482 N.E.2d at 1239. Therefore, according to Kahn, "a court may consider both future earnings capacity and professional goodwill without being accused of considering exactly the same assets twice."		

(continued)

	VALUE IN EXCHANGE		VALUE TO THE HOLDER
	Fair Market Value	Fair Value	Investment Value
Discounts	***Entingh v. Entingh***, 2008 Ohio 756; LEXIS 659 (Ohio App. 2008): Wife's expert "was of the opinion that the discounts were unnecessary due to the family nature of the business, with Daniel having significant input in the business decisions, and because (wife's expert) did not add in any value for the goodwill of the business." ***Bunkers v. Bunkers***, 2007 Ohio 561; LEXIS 523 (Ohio App. 2007): "Because we determined that the trial court did not err when it included goodwill in valuing appellant's practice, we further find that the court did not abuse its discretion when it limited the (marketability) discount to ten percent, or potential transaction costs, and rejected the proposed marketability discount which is, under the facts of this case, essentially a discount for goodwill." ***Oatey v. Oatey***, No. 67809, 67973, 1996 WL 200273 (Ohio App. 1996): Rejects minority discount because the husband effectively controlled the business through family ownership.	***Kapp v. Kapp***, 2005 Ohio 6830; LEXIS 6144 (Ohio App. 2005): "We conclude that the trial court abused its discretion in applying a 7.5% discount for transaction costs, because there is no indication that Mr. Kapp plans to sell KCI in the foreseeable future."	
Buy–Sell	***Herron v. Herron***, 2004 Ohio 5765; LEXIS 5209 (Ohio App. 2004): "We can not say that the trial court erred in considering the buy/sell agreement and the book value of the stock in establishing the fair market value of the Robinson Fin stock. Any willing buyer would certainly take into account the buy/sell agreement before making any offer on the stock. In fact, it would have been an abuse of discretion for the trial court to determine Robinson Fin's fair market value without considering the buy/sell agreement and the book value."		
SOV in Statute or Case Law	***Bunkers v. Bunkers***, 2007 Ohio 561; LEXIS 523 (Ohio App. 2007): "The trial court adopted use of (expert's) fair market standard of value."		

	VALUE IN EXCHANGE		VALUE TO THE HOLDER
	Fair Market Value	Fair Value	Investment Value

We consider Ohio to be a predominantly fair market value state. Ohio cases appear to use a fair market value treatment for goodwill; however, in *Kapp*, the court considered intent to sell in rejecting discounts, and in *Etingh* and *Oatey*, the court rejected discounts because "the family" controlled the business.

OKLAHOMA

Goodwill

McQuay v. McQuay, 217 P.3d 162 (Okla. Civ. App. 2009): Cites *Favell v. Favell* 1998 OK Civ App. 22 957 P.2d 556,561: The Appellate Court ruled against including goodwill in the value of a sole proprietor in the concrete business. The goodwill was dependent on the personal reputation of the husband; therefore, "there was no evidence of goodwill as a marketable business asset distinct from the husband's reputation."

Traczyk v. Traczyk, 891 P2d 1277 (Ok. Supr. Ct. 1995) : "Where goodwill is a marketable business asset distinct from the personal reputation of a particular individual, as is usually the case with many commercial enterprises, that goodwill has an immediately discernible value as an asset of the business and may be identified as an amount reflected in a sale or transfer of a business. If the goodwill depends on the continued presence of an individual, such goodwill, by definition is not a marketable asset distinct from the individual."

Ford v. Ford, 840 P.2d 36 (Okla. Ct. App. 1992): Law practitioner's personal goodwill has no value for the purpose of marital property.

Mocnik v. Mocnik, 838 P.2d 500 (Okla. Supr. Ct.1992): If business goodwill is to be divided as an asset, it should be valued using a buy–sell agreement or its fair market value.

Travis v. Travis, 795 P.2d 96 (Okla.Supr.Ct. 1990): Personal goodwill in a law practice is not subject to distribution.

Discounts

(continued)

	VALUE IN EXCHANGE		VALUE TO THE HOLDER
	Fair Market Value	Fair Value	Investment Value
Buy–Sell	*Ford v. Ford*, 840 P.2d 36 (Okla. Ct. App. 1992): Oklahoma follows jurisdictions that view a buy–sell agreement as controlling in marital dissolutions. This case involved a stockholder in a large law firm. The court held that the stockholder agreement, which paid a departing shareholder book value without goodwill, controlled because the goodwill stayed at the firm the stockholder left.		
SOV in Statute or Case Law	*Traczyk v. Traczyk*, 891 P.2d 1277 (Okla. Supr. Ct. 1995) : "If goodwill is to be divided as an asset, its value should be determined by an agreement or by its fair market value."		
	We believe that Oklahoma may be classified as a fair market value state. According to *McQuay* (2009), *Traczyk* (1995), *Ford* (1992), and *Travis* (1990), personal goodwill is not to be valued in marital dissolution. *Mocnik* goes further to prescribe either a fair market value valuation or adherence to a buy–sell agreement. *Ford* states that a buy–sell agreement is controlling as for the valuation of a large law firm.		

OREGON

	VALUE IN EXCHANGE		VALUE TO THE HOLDER
	Fair Market Value	Fair Value	Investment Value
Goodwill	*Slater v. Slater*, 245 P.3d 676 (Ore. Ct. App. 2010): "Personal goodwill is not goodwill" for purposes of valuation in the marital dissolution context. "To the extent that a noncompetition covenant corresponds to a business's future earning capacity attributable to an individual's skills, qualities, reputation, or continued presence, the value of that covenant is not cognizable in a marital property division." *In re: Marriage of Tofte*, 895 P.2d 1387 (Ore. Ct. App. 1995): To value the fair market value of a closely held corporation, one must focus on the price that a hypothetical willing buyer would pay a hypothetical willing seller.		

	VALUE IN EXCHANGE		VALUE TO THE HOLDER	
	Fair Market Value	Fair Value	Fair Value	Investment Value
Goodwill *(continued)*	*In the Matter of the Marriage of Maxwell and Maxwell*, 876 P.2d 811 (Ore. App. 1994): "A business ordinarily has value over and above the value of its assets, known as 'goodwill' value. However, when a business consists of the work of a sole practitioner, the court shall decline to assign a value for goodwill.... There is generally no goodwill in a personal services business unless the owner personally promises his services to accompany the sale of his business."			
Discounts	*In re: Marriage of Tofte*, 895 P.2d 1387 (Ore. Ct. App. 1995): After calculating the value of husband's stock to be $834 per share, the trial court, relying on husband's expert's testimony, applied a 35% discount to the fair market value of the minority shareholder interest to reflect the lack of marketability." *Matter of Marriage of Belt*, 672 P.2d 1205 (Ore. App. 1983): The court accepted a 50% discount for a 9% interest in a family-owned dairy farm with restricted by-laws.			
Buy–Sell	*In the Matter of the Marriage of Belt*, 672 P.2d 1205 (Ore. App. 1983): A buy–sell agreement or other such agreement should be considered as a factor in valuing a business but it is not determinative of the value of marital stock.			
SOV in Statute or Case Law	*In the Matter of the Marriage of Belt*, 672 P.2d 1205 (Ore. App. 1983): "Given this state of the record, we think that the most reasonable solution is to accept wife's expert witness' opinion as to the net asset value of the stock and to apply husband's expert witness opinion as to the extent of the discount to arrive at its fair market value."			

Maxwell (1994) and *Slater* (2010) do not value personal goodwill. *Tofte* (1995) defines fair market value as willing buyer/willing seller. Discounts are applied without an intent to sell. Therefore, we characterize Oregon as a fair market value state.

(continued)

	VALUE IN EXCHANGE		VALUE TO THE HOLDER
	Fair Market Value	Fair Value	Investment Value
	PENNSYLVANIA		
Goodwill	*Smith v. Smith*, 904 A.2d 15 (Pa. Superior. 2006): "That goodwill which is intrinsically tied to the attributes and/or skills or certain individuals is not subject to equitable distribution because the value thereof does not survive the disassociation of those individuals from the business . . . On the other hand, goodwill which is wholly attributable to the business itself is subject to distribution." *Butler v. Butler*, 663 A.2d 148 (Pa. Supreme. Ct. 1995): Personal goodwill is not marital property. *Beasley v. Beasley, 518 A.2d 545* (Pa. Super. Ct. 1986): One's personal reputation is not separate property, as it cannot be sold or even given away and, accordingly, courts should not become embroiled in the impossible task of evaluating professional reputation and distributing it as an asset of the marriage.		
Discounts		*Verholek v. Verholek*, 741 A.2d 792 (Pa. Super. Ct. 1999): Rejects minority discount.	
Buy–Sell	*Buckl v. Buckl*, 542 A.2d 65 (1988 Pa. Super. 1988): A buy–sell agreement or other such agreement should be considered as a factor in valuing a business, but it is not determinative of the value of marital stock.		
SOV in Statute or Case Law			

Because Pennsylvania attempts to distinguish and exclude value based on reputation or personal skill, we believe Pennsylvania may be considered a fair market value state. While the *Verholek* (1999) case rejected a minority discount, the predominant trend in the treatment of goodwill suggests a fair market value standard.

	VALUE IN EXCHANGE		VALUE TO THE HOLDER
	Fair Market Value	Fair Value	Investment Value

RHODE ISLAND

Goodwill

Moretti v. Moretti, 766 A.2d 925 (R.I. Supr. Ct. 2001): Personal goodwill is not a marital asset subject to distribution. "Enterprise goodwill is an asset of the business and accordingly is property that is divisible in a dissolution to the extent that it inheres in the business, independent of any single individual's personal efforts and will outlast any person's involvement in the business."

Discounts

Vicario v. Vicario, 901 A.2d 603 (R.I. Supr. Ct. 2006): In the valuation of a 50% interest in an actuarial consulting business, the Supreme Court accepted a 25% marketability and a 10% minority discount.

Buy–Sell

SOV in Statute or Case Law

While the case law in Rhode Island is limited, *Moretti* (2001) specifically excluded the consideration of personal goodwill in equitable distribution; we believe that Rhode Island may be classified as a fair market value state.

SOUTH CAROLINA

Goodwill

Dickert v. Dickert, 691 S.E.2d 448 (S.C. Supr. Ct. 2010): This case follows *Donahue* that enterprise goodwill is not subject to equitable distribution because it is dependent on the professional.
Donahue v. Donahue, 384 S.E.2d 741 (S.C. Supr. Ct. 1989): "The court disallows the inclusion of goodwill in a dental practice. However, the court clearly describes goodwill as personal goodwill attached to the practitioner."
Hickum v. Hickum, 463 S.E.2d 321 (S.C. App. 1995): The court declined to include goodwill in a cosmetology business because it was too speculative.

(continued)

	VALUE IN EXCHANGE		VALUE TO THE HOLDER
	Fair Market Value	Fair Value	Investment Value
Discounts	*Fields v. Fields*, 536 S.E.2d 684 (S.C. App. 2000): In this case, the appellate court upheld the valuation of an 18% interest in a family owned corporation without regard to a minority or marketability discount because the wife's father owned the other 82% of the stock.		
Buy–Sell			
SOV in Statute or Case Law	*Hickum v. Hickum*, 463 S.E.2d 321 (S.C. Ct. App. 1995): "Marital businesses are to be valued at fair market value as ongoing businesses," citing *RGM v. DEM*, 306 S.C. 145, 410 S.E.2d 564 (1991).		
South Carolina is predominantly a fair market value state with an asset dependent on the professional, not considered marital, property. A careful reading of these cases indicates some walk-away attributes.			
SOUTH DAKOTA			
Goodwill	*Endres v. Endres*, 532 N.W.2d 65 (S.D. Supr. Ct. 1995): The court valued the goodwill of a commercial business (concrete). As such the court saw no need to address the issue of personal goodwill.		
Discounts	*Priebe v. Priebe*, 556 N.W.2d 78 (S.D. Supr. Ct. 1996): South Dakota applies discounts on a case-by-case basis. The court accepted a 40% minority discount in the husband's 25% interest in a family business. The trial court stated that "a minority discount is appropriate because Steve does not own a controlling interest in any of these business interests and because any attempted sale of the properties would result in the value being discounted by a would-be purchaser."		
Buy–Sell			

	VALUE IN EXCHANGE		VALUE TO THE HOLDER
	Fair Market Value	Fair Value	Investment Value
SOV in Statute or Case Law	*Fausch v. Fausch*, 697 N.W.2d 748 (S.D. Supr. Ct. 2005): Fair market value is "the price a willing buyer would pay a willing seller, both under or no obligation to act."		
	While including goodwill in the calculation of value of a commercial concrete business, the court in *Endres* (1995) did not need to address whether goodwill adhering to an individual was includable in the marital assets, as the goodwill in this case adhered to the business. South Dakota has accepted minority discounts, but without further evidence, we believe that the state's case law appears to be fair market value.		

TENNESSEE

	VALUE IN EXCHANGE		VALUE TO THE HOLDER
Goodwill	*McKee v. McKee*, LEXIS 524 (Tenn. App. 2010): Under Tennessee law, personal goodwill is not considered a marital asset. The court disallowed the intangible value of patient records as personal goodwill because the court found they included a covenant not to compete in order to have value.		
	Nicholson v. Nicholson, LEXIS 651 (Tenn. App. 2010): "Rather than measuring its value by goodwill or potential future earnings, the correct method for valuing a sole practitioner dental practice is the value of its tangible assets such as cash on hand, accounts receivable, and equipment, less any encumbrances on these assets."		
	Roberts v. Roberts, LEXIS 738 (Tenn. App. 2010): "In valuing a professional practice it has long been held that goodwill of the business dependent as it is on the person and personality of the spouse practicing the profession, is no part of the marital estate." The court accounted for this fact by discounting the value of the practice should the husband leave.		
	Alsup v. Alsup, No. 01A01-9509-CH-00404; LEXIS 425 (Tenn. Ct. App. 1996): Business goodwill in a professional practice or sole proprietorship is not a marital asset for equitable distribution purposes.		

(continued)

VALUE IN EXCHANGE

VALUE TO THE HOLDER

	Fair Market Value	Fair Value	Investment Value
Discounts		*Fickle v. Fickle*, 287 S.W.3d 723 (Tenn. App. 2008): The husband's company held farmland as its only asset. The court disallowed a 15% marketability discount proposed by the husband's expert and valued the land at net asset value because the value of the company equaled the value of the land. *Bertuca v. Bertuca*, LEXIS 690 (Tenn. App. 2007): The court rejected the 20% marketability discount for a 90% ownership in a company that held McDonald's franchises because he had no plan to sell, concluding, "Lack of marketability . . . only affects the value if he plans to sell his interest in the partnership and the record is devoid of any suggestion that he intends to do so."	
Buy–Sell	*Inzer v. Inzer*, LEXIS 498 (Tenn. App. 2009): cites *Harmon v. Harmon* LEXIS 137 (Tenn. App. 2000) "The court summarized the view held by a majority of jurisdictions as one where "the value established in the buy-sell agreement of a closely held corporation, not signed by the non-shareholder spouse, is not binding on the non-shareholder spouse but is considered, along with other factors, in valuing the interest of the shareholder spouse."	*Bertuca v. Bertuca*, LEXIS 690 (Tenn. App. 2007): "A buy-sell provision only affects the husband's value if he plans to sell his interest in the partnership and the record is devoid on any suggestion that he intends to do so. The buy-sell provision therefore, does not affect the value of his interest in the partnership determined on a value of earnings basis."	
SOV in Statute or Case Law			

Tennessee does not value personal goodwill. *Fickle* (2008) and *Bertuca* (2007) did not apply marketability discounts where there is no intent to sell. *Bertuca* (2007) holds that the buy–sell does not control where there is no intent to sell. *Inzer* (2009) holds that the buy–sell is a consideration. On balance, Tennessee appears to be a predominantly fair market value state.

	VALUE IN EXCHANGE		VALUE TO THE HOLDER
	Fair Market Value	Fair Value	Investment Value
	TEXAS		
Goodwill	***Von Hohn v. Von Hohn,*** 260 S.W.3d 631 (Tex. App. 2008): "In order to determine whether goodwill attaches to a professional practice that is subject to division upon divorce, we apply a two prong test: (1) goodwill must be determined to exist independently of the professional spouse; and (2) if such goodwill is found to exist, then it must be determined whether that goodwill has a commercial value in which the community estate is entitled to share." ***Nowzaradan v. Nowzaradan,*** LEXIS 1021 (Tex. App. 2007): "Texas law distinguishes the personal goodwill of a professional practice from its commercial goodwill. Professional goodwill attaches to the person of the professional as a result of confidence in his skill and ability; it does not possess or constitute an asset separate and apart from the professional's person, or from his individual ability to practice his profession; and therefore would be extinguished in the event of the professional's death, retirement or disablement. In valuating a business interest for purposes of dividing community property on divorce, the personal goodwill of an individual must be excluded. The value to the community estate is limited to the commercial goodwill of the business—its value as a recognized business, separate and apart from the individual--and is properly considered an asset when dividing a community estate." ***Guzman v. Guzman,*** 827 S.W.2d 445 (Tex. App. 1992): "Goodwill in a professional business is not considered part of the marital estate unless it exists independently of the professional's skills, and the estate is otherwise entitled to share in the asset. Goodwill in a professional corporation which exists independently of a professional's personal skills may be subject to division as marital property."		

(continued)

	VALUE IN EXCHANGE	VALUE TO THE HOLDER	
	Fair Market Value	Fair Value	Investment Value
Discounts	*R.V.K. v. L.L.K.*, LEXIS 7700 (Tex. App. 2002): The appellate court remanded the valuation to the trial court because, "A company's 'enterprise value' is the highest level at which the company's worth may be assessed. But enterprise value by its nature does not include a discount based on the shares' minority status or lack of marketability. Enterprise value may thus be an appropriate means of valuing the stock of an ongoing business to determine 'fair value' in the context of a stockholder who dissents to a merger or acquisition since the purchase contemplated gives the buyer total control over the corporation. But, enterprise value is entirely inappropriate in the context of valuing a minority position in stock subject to a buy/sell agreement for purposes of divorce."		
Buy–Sell	*Mandell v. Mandell*, 310 S.W.3d 531 (Tex. App. 2010): "Because the evidence establishes the "comparable sales value" for Lance's 22,000 shares of the Association's stock was $11,000 based on prior sales by former physician-shareholders and because $11,000 is the only price Lance's stock may be sold at, the trial court did not abuse its discretion by valuing the stock at $11,000 under a comparable sales valuation and as mandated by the Shareholders Agreement even though Susan (wife) did not sign it."		
SOV in Statute or Case Law	*Mandell v. Mandell*, 310 S.W.3d 531 (Tex. App. 2010): As a general rule, the value to be accorded community property that is to be divided in a divorce proceeding is "market value." See *R.V.K. v. L.L.K*, 103 S.W.3d 612, 618. "Fair market value has been consistently defined as the amount that a willing buyer who desires to buy, but is under no obligation to buy would pay to a willing seller, who desires to sell, but is under no obligation to sell. (Quoting *Wendlandt v. Wendlandt*, 596 S.W.2d 323, 325 Tex. Civ. App.-Houston [1st Dist] 1980.)		

VALUE IN EXCHANGE			VALUE TO THE HOLDER	
Fair Market Value		Fair Value		Investment Value

Texas clearly excludes personal goodwill in *Von Hohn* (2008), *Nowzaradan* (2007), and *Guzman* (1992). *R.V.K. v. L.L.K.* mandates a fair market value valuation, not fair value. *Mandell* (2010) values the stock at the amount in the buy–sell agreement because that is all the owner will receive upon sale. Therefore, Texas may be classified as a fair market value state.

UTAH

	Fair Market Value	Fair Value	Investment Value
Goodwill	*Stonehocker v. Stonehocker,* 176 P.3d 476 (Utah App. 2008): "There can be no goodwill in a business that is dependent for its existence upon the individual who conducts the enterprise and would vanish were the individual to die, retire, or quit work. . . . The reputation of a solo practitioner is personal as is a professional degree. Unless the professional retires and his practice is sold, his reputation should not be treated differently from a professional degree or an advanced degree: both simply enhance the earning ability of the holder." *Sorenson v. Sorenson,* 839 P.2d 774, 775-776 (Utah Supr. Ct. 1992); 1992 Utah LEXIS 24: Goodwill was not included in the valuation of a solo dental practice, and would not be unless that practice was sold and the goodwill realized by the seller.		
Discounts			
Buy–Sell			
SOV in Statute or Case Law			

The court in *Sorensen (1992)* suggests Utah's classification as a fair market value state, including the value of goodwill in a marital business only if it was clear that the practice would be sold and the goodwill value would be realized by the practitioner.

(continued)

	VALUE IN EXCHANGE		VALUE TO THE HOLDER	
	Fair Market Value	Fair Value	Investment Value	
		VERMONT		
Goodwill	*Mills v. Mills*, 702 A.2d 79 (Vt. Supr. Ct. 1997): "There was no abuse of discretion in finding that plaintiff's future legal services had no market value subject to distribution. . . . Goodwill is subject to distribution only if business has value independent of particular individual. . . . Sole proprietorship law practice has no goodwill because it cannot be sold." *Goodrich v. Goodrich*, 613 A.2d 203 (Vt. Supr. Ct. 1992): Supreme court would not mandate single methodology for determining value of interest in closely held company in divorce action. The court accepted the view that for the purposes of a divorce valuation, as long as the value determined by the trial court was that which a willing buyer would pay a willing seller and that value was supported by credible evidence in record, it was not clearly erroneous.			
Discounts	*Drumheller v. Drumheller*, 972 A.2d 176 (Vt. Supr. Ct. 2009): "In a divorce case, the trial court properly refused a minority discount to the husband, who owned a one-third interest in a partnership. While the husband did not have a controlling interest in the partnership, he was certainly the most important of the three equal partners because he had effective control of the corporate tenant from which the income was derived; reducing the value of the partnership interest, while the husband received full income from the partnership based on full valuation, would be unfair to wife." *Kasser v. Kasser*, 895 A.2d 134 (Vt. Supr. Ct 2006): "The (trial) court acted within its discretion in reducing the value of husband's interests by 25% to 33% to account for his 50% ownership (in hotel interests)." *Goodrich v. Goodrich*, 613 A.2d 203 (Vt. Supr. Ct. 1992): The court applied a minority discount because "the shares are not readily marketable and could not convey a controlling interest in the company."			

	VALUE IN EXCHANGE		VALUE TO THE HOLDER
	Fair Market Value	Fair Value	Investment Value
Buy–Sell			
SOV in Statute or Case Law	**Drumheller v. Drumheller,** 972 A.2d 176 (Vt. Supr. Ct. 2009): "Thus, for property taxation purposes, fair market value is: the price which the property will bring in the market when offered for sale and purchased by another, taking into consideration all the elements of the availability of the property, its use both potential and prospective, any functional deficiencies, and all other elements such as age and condition which combine to give property a market value."		

We believe that Vermont may be classified as a fair market value state. It has allowed discounts in the valuation of businesses upon divorce and has allowed valuations to reflect what a willing buyer would pay a willing seller for shares of a business.

VIRGINIA

Goodwill		***Newman v. Newman,*** LEXIS 142 (Va. Cir. 2010): "Individual goodwill categorized as Wife's separate property." ***Carrington v. Carrington,*** LEXIS 250 (Va. App. 2008): "Goodwill does not exist in every business, nor is goodwill easy to value without expert testimony." ***Howell v. Howell,*** 523 S.E.2d 514 (Va. App. 2000): The value of goodwill can have two components: (1) professional goodwill, also designated as individual, personal, or separate goodwill, which is attributable to the individual and is categorized as separate property in a divorce action, and (2) practice goodwill, also designated as business or commercial goodwill, which is attributable to the business entity, the professional firm, and may be marital property. ***Howell v. Howell,*** 46 Va. Cir. 339 (Va. Cir. 1998): "Goodwill is defined as the increased value of the business, over and above the value of its assets, that results from the expectation of continued public patronage. The reputation of an individual, as well as his or her future earning capacity, are not considered to be components of goodwill."	

(continued)

	VALUE IN EXCHANGE		VALUE TO THE HOLDER
	Fair Market Value	Fair Value	Investment Value
Discounts		*Hoebelheinrich v. Hoebelheinrich*, 600 S.E.2d 152 (Va. App. 2004): "A discount for lack of marketability that is applied to a business that is being valued presupposes a probable sale. If a sale is improbable the discount need not be applied." *Owens v. Owens*, 589 S.E.2d 488 (Va. App. 2003): "When the controlling interests in a family company oppress a minority shareholder or use a substantial amount of the corporation's assets for their own personal benefit, the trial court may take that fact into consideration in determining the value, if any, of the minority interest. But when no evidence suggests that the stock should be discounted because it represented a minority holding, the trial court should give the stock its proportionate value." In *Owens*, "Given the absence of any suggestion of actual oppression relating to husband's alleged minority status coupled with the availability of judicial remedies for the most egregious forms of potential oppression, we reject husband's assertion that his position as an equal co-owner should entitle him as a matter of law to a minority discount for equitable distribution purposes." *Howell v. Howell*, 523 S.E.2d 514 (Va. App. 2000): Rejects minority and marketability discount. "The large discount for lack of marketability was inappropriate, as the highest and best use for the defendant's share is to remain with Hunton & Williams; an interest in a Virginia legal services corporation may not be bought or sold."	

	VALUE IN EXCHANGE		VALUE TO THE HOLDER	
	Fair Market Value	Fair Value	Investment Value	
Buy-Sell		*Scott v. Scott*, LEXIS 454 (Va. App. 2007): "For equitable distribution purposes courts reject the value set by buyout provisions, as they do not necessarily represent the intrinsic worth of the stock to the parties." *Howell v. Howell*, 523 S.E.2d 514 (Va. App. 2000): "The reason for rejecting the value set by the buyout provision is that they do not necessarily represent the intrinsic work of the stock to the parties." (Citing Bosserman 9 Va. App. at 6, 384 S.E.2d at 107.) *Bosserman v. Bosserman*, 9 Va. App. 1, 384 S.E.2d 104 (1989): A buy–sell agreement should be considered as a factor in valuing a business, but it is not determinative of the value of marital stock.		
SOV in Statute or Case Law		*Bolton v. Bolton*, LEXIS 34 (Va. Cir. 2011) cites *Bosserman v. Bosserman* 9 Va App. 1,6, 384 S.E. 2d 104, 6 Va. Law Rep. 196 (1989): "Trial courts valuing marital property for the purpose of making a monetary award must determine from the evidence that value which represents the property's intrinsic worth to the parties upon dissolution of marriage." *Owens v. Owens*, 589 S. E. 2d 488: (Va. App. 2003): "Virginia's equitable distribution law employs the concept of 'intrinsic value' when determining the worth of certain types of marital assets." *Howell v Howell*, 523 S.E.2d 514 (Va. App. 2000): "Intrinsic value for equitable distribution in a dissolution of marriage proceeding is a very subjective concept that looks to the worth of the property to the parties. The methods of valuation must take into consideration the parties themselves and the different situations in which they exist. The item may have no established market value, and neither party may contemplate selling the item; indeed, sale may be restricted or forbidden. Commonly, one party will continue to enjoy the benefits of the property while the other must relinquish all future benefits. Still, its intrinsic value must be translated into a monetary amount."		

(continued)

437

	VALUE IN EXCHANGE		VALUE TO THE HOLDER	
	Fair Market Value	Fair Value	Investment Value	
	We believe Virginia predominantly follows a fair value standard. Virginia views goodwill under the value in exchange premise; that is, only enterprise goodwill may be included in the valuation of a business for the purposes of divorce. However, the state also rejects minority and marketability discounts in favor of a pro rata share of the enterprise value, suggesting a fair value standard.			
	WASHINGTON			
Goodwill			*In re: Marriage of Hall*, 692 P.2d 175 (Wash. Supr. Ct.1984): Both personal and enterprise goodwill may be included in the value of a professional practice as community property. *Matter of Marriage of Fleege*, 588 P.2d 1136 (Wash. Supr. Ct. 1979): Business goodwill is the expectation of continued public patronage, and value of business goodwill to a professional spouse, enabling him to continue to enjoy the patronage engendered by that goodwill is a community asset subject to division.	
Discounts	*Baltrusis v. Baltrusis*, LEXIS 2241 (Wash. App. 2002): The court rejected the use of marketability discounts, using fair value language that the husband was more like a dissenting shareholder: an unwilling seller of the interest.			
Buy–Sell	*Overbey v. Overbey*, LEXIS 1651 (Wash. App. 2007): Washington courts have consistently found that valuation provisions contained in buy–sell agreements, "while relevant to a determination of value, constitute 'one factor to be considered, but [are] not determinative.'" *In re: Luckey*, 868 P.2d 189 (Wash. App. 1994): Accepts buy–sell agreement as means of valuing business. *In re: Marriage of Brooks*, 756 P.2d 161 (Wash. Ct. App. 1988): A buy–sell agreement or other such agreement should be considered as a factor in valuing a business, but it is not determinative of the value of marital stock (rejected in this case).			
SOV in Statute or Case Law				

	VALUE IN EXCHANGE		VALUE TO THE HOLDER	
	Fair Market Value	Fair Value	Investment Value	

Washington appears to follow a value to the holder treatment of goodwill. Both the *Fleege* (1979) and *Hall* (1984) cases include goodwill in the valuation of a professional practice without distinguishing and excluding goodwill adhering to the professional. *Baltrusis* (2002), however, uses fair value language in the rejection of discounts to account for the fact that the husband was an unwilling seller of the interest. Overall, however, the state's treatment of goodwill and the established principles in *Hall* and *Fleege* suggest that Washington may be classified as an investment value state.

WEST VIRGINIA

Goodwill	*Wilson v. Wilson*, 706 S.E.2d 354 (W. Va. Supr. Ct. 2010): "Goodwill of a service business, such as a professional practice, consists largely of personal goodwill." Further, "Personal goodwill, which is intrinsically tied to the attributes and/or skills of an individual, is not subject to equitable distribution. On the other hand enterprise goodwill, which is wholly attributable to the business itself is subject to equitable distribution." *Helfer v. Helfer*, 686 S.E.2d 64 (W. Va. Supr. Ct. 2009) : "Enterprise goodwill which is wholly attributable to the business itself is subject to equitable distribution." *May v. May*, 589 S.E.2d 536 (W.Va. Supr. Ct. 2003): Distinguished between the business's enterprise goodwill, which was marital property, and the husband's personal goodwill, which was not subject to equitable distribution. *Tankersley v. Tankersley*, 390 S.E.2d 826 (W. Va. Supr. Ct. 1990): Net value will be the amount realized should the corporation be sold for fair market value.
Discounts	*Arneault v. Arneault*, 639 S.E.2d 720 (W. Va. Supr. Ct. 2006) : "We reverse the circuit court's order that permitted Mr. Arneault to pay Mrs. Arneault a discounted value for her portion of MTR stock over a period of time and award Mrs. Arneault one-half of the parties' MTR stock in kind. Additionally Mrs. Arneault is charged with one-half of the debt attributable to the acquisition of the parties' MTR stock." *Michael v. Michael*, 469 S.E.2d 14 (W. Va. Supr. Ct. 1996): Accepts marketability discount.

(continued)

VALUE IN EXCHANGE

VALUE TO THE HOLDER

	Fair Market Value	Fair Value	Investment Value
Buy–Sell	*Bettinger v. Bettinger*, 396 S.E.2d 709 (W. Va. Supr. Ct. 1990): Buy–sell in closely held corporation setting stock value for equitable distribution should not be considered binding but should be considered as a factor.		
SOV in Statute or Case Law	*May v. May*, 589 S.E.2d 536 (W.Va. Supr. Ct. App. 2003): "Again the pertinent inquiry is what is the net sum that will be realized by the owner of the business if it is sold for its fair market value."		

We believe West Virginia may be classified as a fair market value state. The case *May v. May* (2003) reviews case law from varying jurisdictions and decides to follow those states that exclude goodwill adhering to an individual from the marital property. Further, *Tankersley* (1990) specifically refers to fair market value in its valuation, and *Michael* (1996) applies discounts.

WISCONSIN

Goodwill	*McReath v McReath*, 800 N.W.2d 399 (Wisc. Supr. Ct 2011): "Pursuant to Wis. Stat. §767.61, Wisconsin case law and the policy supporting the presumption of equality in the division of the marital estate, we hold that a circuit court shall include salable professional goodwill in the divisible marital estate when the business interest to which the goodwill is attendant is an asset subject to §767.61. . . . Where the salable professional goodwill is developed during the marriage it defies the presumption of equality to exclude it from the divisible marital estate because the wife, by virtue of position of wife made to that goodwill value the same contribution as does a wife to any of the husband's earnings and accumulations during the marriage." *Sommerfeld v. Sommerfeld*, 454 N.W.2d 55 (Wis. App. 1990): Property to be divided at divorce is to be valued at its fair market value. *Peerenboom v. Peerenboom*, 433 N.W.2d 282 (Wis. App. 1988): If business goodwill exists in a professional practice, it should be included in the distributable assets.		

	VALUE IN EXCHANGE		VALUE TO THE HOLDER
	Fair Market Value	Fair Value	Investment Value
Discounts	*Franzen v. Franzen*, 658 N.W.2d 87 (Wisc. App. 2003): The husband owned 50% of a Piggly Wiggly franchise. The court allowed a 20% minority discount and a 20% marketability discount. *Arneson v. Arneson*, 355 N.W.2d 16 (Wis. App. 1984): "The application of the 25% discount for minority status and nonmarketability is supported by certain of the expert testimony in this case."		
Buy–Sell	*Herlitzke v. Herlitzke*, 724 N.W.2d 702 (Wisc. App. 2006): "A buy-sell agreement may provide a method to determine the fair market value of a partnership interest, but such agreement does not establish the value as a matter of law." *Lewis v. Lewis*, 336 N.W.2d 171 (Wis. App. 1983): The trial court may consider a cross-purchase formula in a partnership agreement in determining the value of the partnership interest, including professional goodwill.		
SOV in Statute or Case Law	*Herlitzke v. Herlitzke*, 724 N.W.2d 702 (Wisc. App. 2006): "When valuing marital assets, courts are not required to accept one valuation method over another, but must ensure that a fair market value is placed on the property. Fair market value is the price that property will bring when offered for sale by one who desires but is not obligated to sell and bought by one who is willing but not obligated to buy."		

Wisconsin case law suggests that it may be classified as a fair market value state. *Sommerfeld* (1990) establishes that property to be divided upon divorce should be valued at its fair market value. Further, Wisconsin has included business goodwill, accepted discounts, and considered buy–sell agreements where applicable.

(continued)

441

VALUE IN EXCHANGE

VALUE TO THE HOLDER

WYOMING

	Fair Market Value	Fair Value	Investment Value
Goodwill	*Root v. Root,* 65 P.3d 41 (Wyo.Supr. Ct. 2003): Personal goodwill should not be included in marital assets.		
Discounts			
Buy–Sell			
SOV in Statute or Case Law	**Neuman v. Neuman,** 842 P.2d 575 (Wyo. Supr. Ct. 1992): Supreme Ct. Wyo. stated that "a Trial Court is free to assess expert opinion and determine fair market value in light of testimony regarding the nature of the business, the corporation's fixed and liquid assets at the actual or book value, the corporation's net worth, the marketability of the shares, past earnings or losses and future earning potential."		

Because of the court's decision in *Root* (2003) to exclude personal goodwill from the distributable assets, we believe that Wyoming may be classified as a fair market value state.

Index